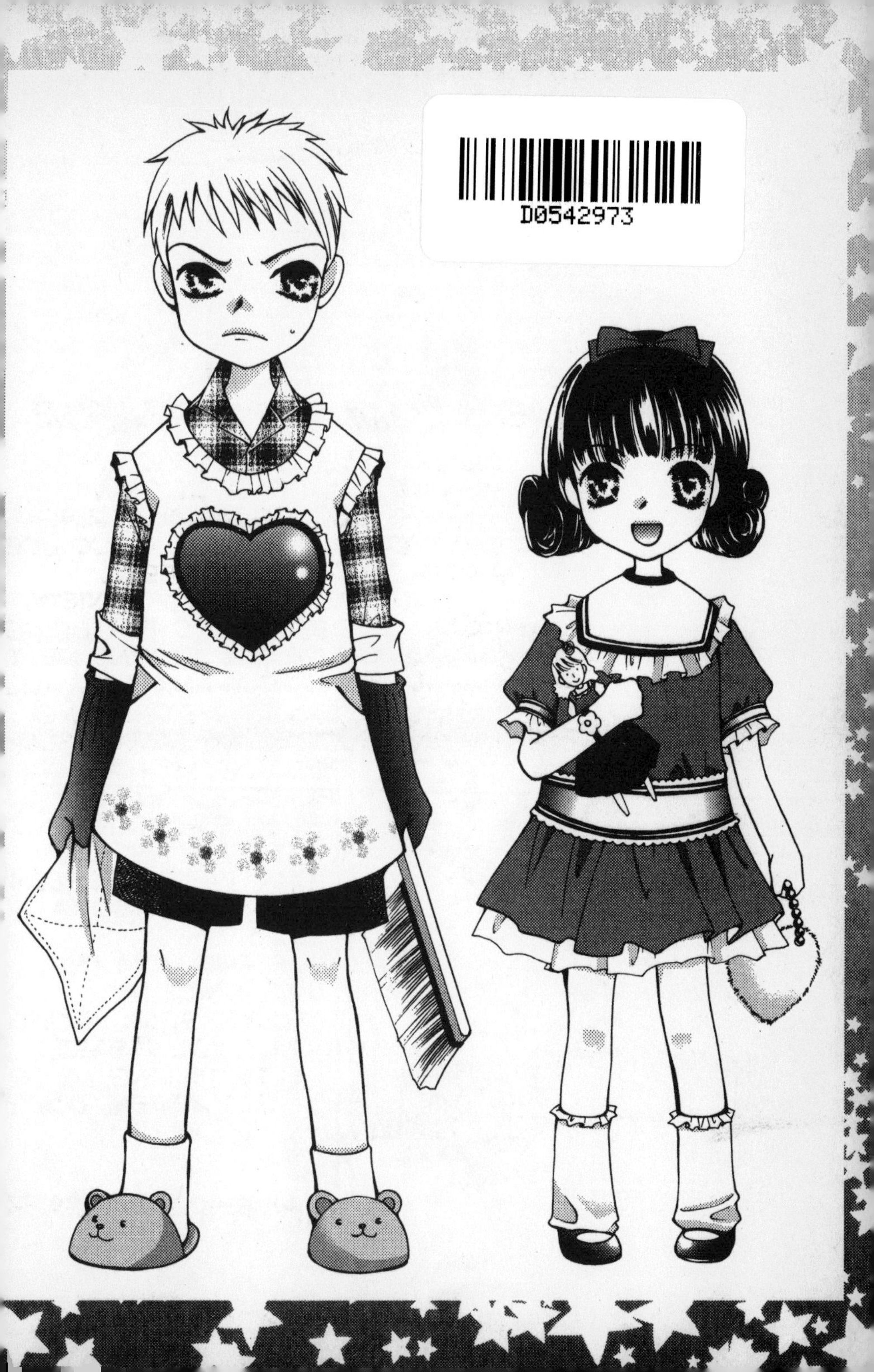

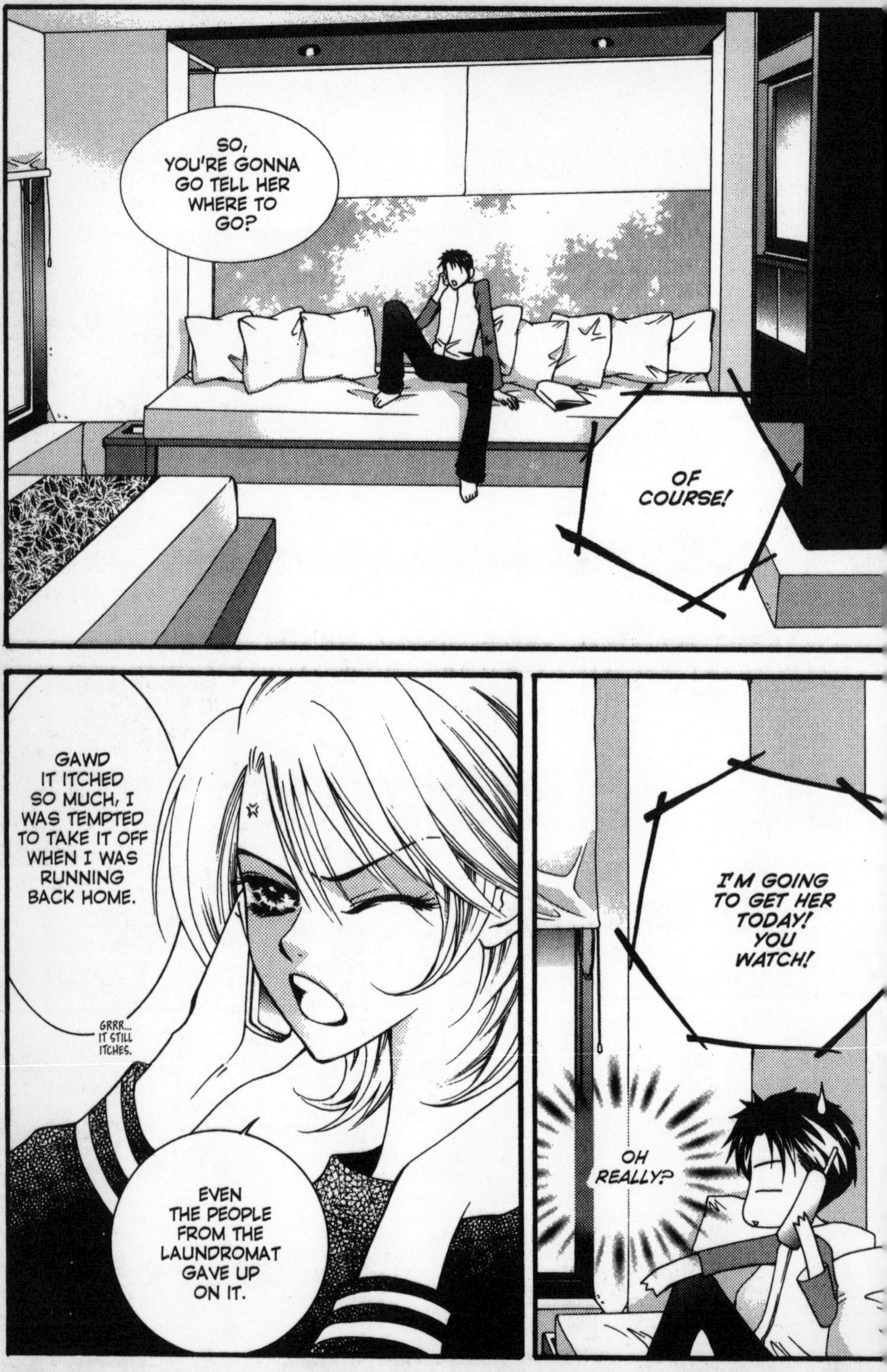
SO, YOU'RE GONNA GO TELL HER WHERE TO GO?
OF COURSE!
GAWD IT ITCHED SO MUCH, I WAS TEMPTED TO TAKE IT OFF WHEN I WAS RUNNING BACK HOME.
GRRR... IT STILL ITCHES.
EVEN THE PEOPLE FROM THE LAUNDROMAT GAVE UP ON IT.
I'M GOING TO GET HER TODAY! YOU WATCH!
OH REALLY?

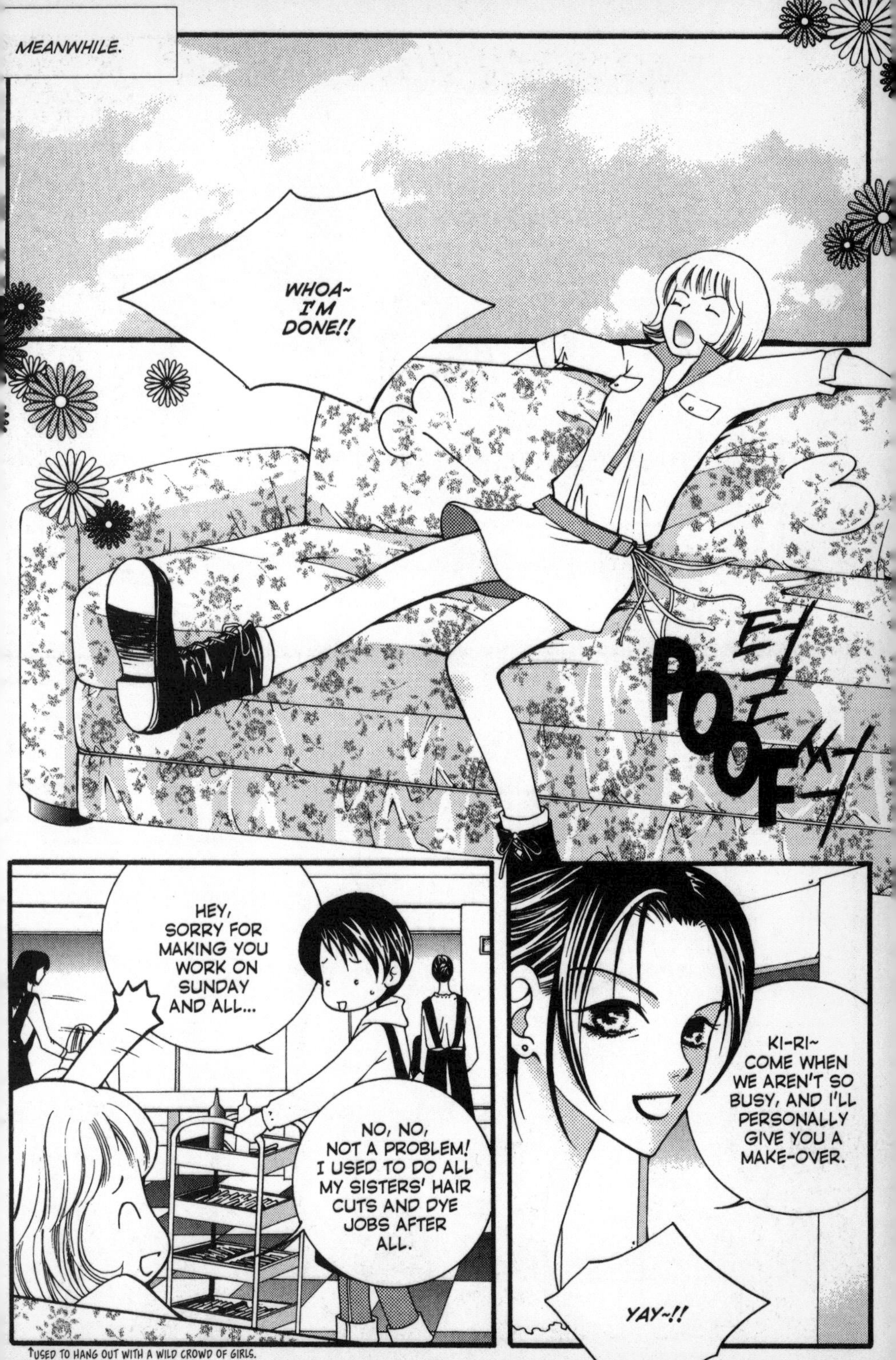
MEANWHILE.
WHOA~ I'M DONE!!
POOF
HEY, SORRY FOR MAKING YOU WORK ON SUNDAY AND ALL...
NO, NO, NOT A PROBLEM! I USED TO DO ALL MY SISTERS' HAIR CUTS AND DYE JOBS AFTER ALL.
KI-RI~ COME WHEN WE AREN'T SO BUSY, AND I'LL PERSONALLY GIVE YOU A MAKE-OVER.
YAY~!!

↑USED TO HANG OUT WITH A WILD CROWD OF GIRLS.

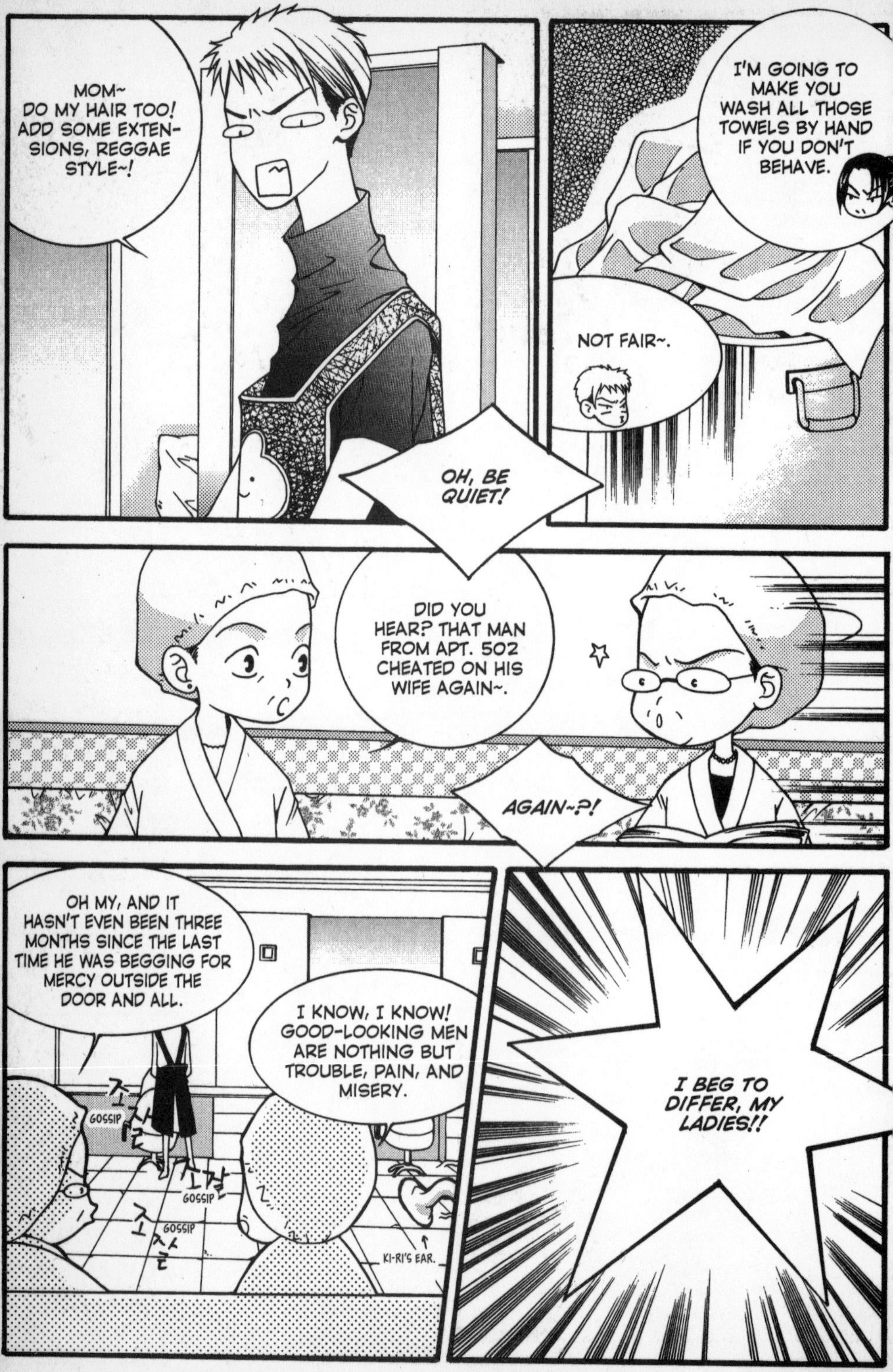
MOM~ DO MY HAIR TOO! ADD SOME EXTEN-SIONS, REGGAE STYLE~!
I'M GOING TO MAKE YOU WASH ALL THOSE TOWELS BY HAND IF YOU DON'T BEHAVE.
NOT FAIR~.
OH, BE QUIET!
DID YOU HEAR? THAT MAN FROM APT. 502 CHEATED ON HIS WIFE AGAIN~.
AGAIN~?!
OH MY, AND IT HASN'T EVEN BEEN THREE MONTHS SINCE THE LAST TIME HE WAS BEGGING FOR MERCY OUTSIDE THE DOOR AND ALL.
I KNOW, I KNOW! GOOD-LOOKING MEN ARE NOTHING BUT TROUBLE, PAIN, AND MISERY.
GOSSIP
GOSSIP
GOSSIP
KI-RI'S EAR.
I BEG TO DIFFER, MY LADIES!!

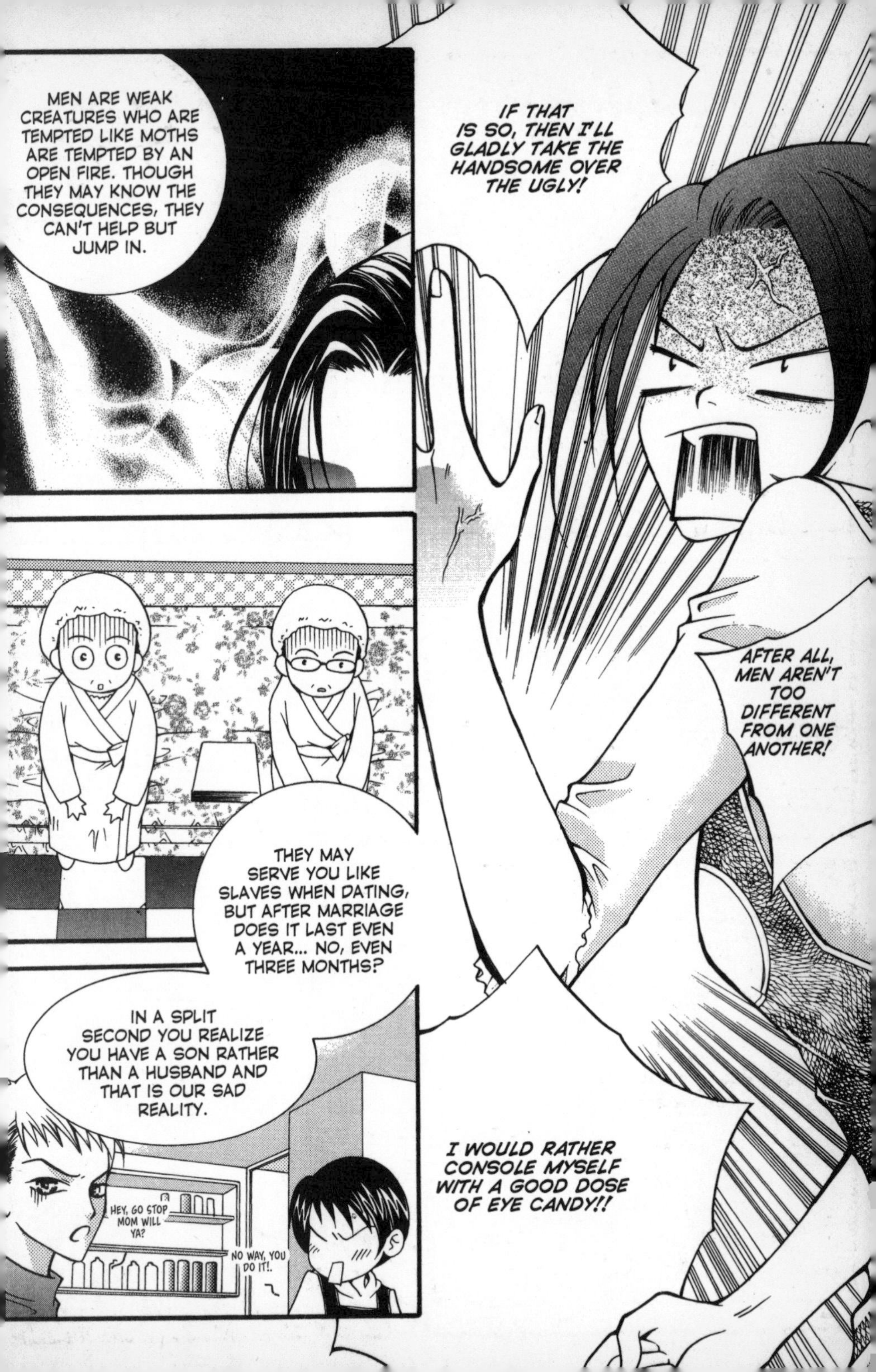
MEN ARE WEAK CREATURES WHO ARE TEMPTED LIKE MOTHS ARE TEMPTED BY AN OPEN FIRE. THOUGH THEY MAY KNOW THE CONSEQUENCES, THEY CAN'T HELP BUT JUMP IN.
THEY MAY SERVE YOU LIKE SLAVES WHEN DATING, BUT AFTER MARRIAGE DOES IT LAST EVEN A YEAR... NO, EVEN THREE MONTHS?
IN A SPLIT SECOND YOU REALIZE YOU HAVE A SON RATHER THAN A HUSBAND AND THAT IS OUR SAD REALITY.
HEY, GO STOP MOM WILL YA?
NO WAY, YOU DO IT!.
IF THAT IS SO, THEN I'LL GLADLY TAKE THE HANDSOME OVER THE UGLY!
AFTER ALL, MEN AREN'T TOO DIFFERENT FROM ONE ANOTHER!
I WOULD RATHER CONSOLE MYSELF WITH A GOOD DOSE OF EYE CANDY!!

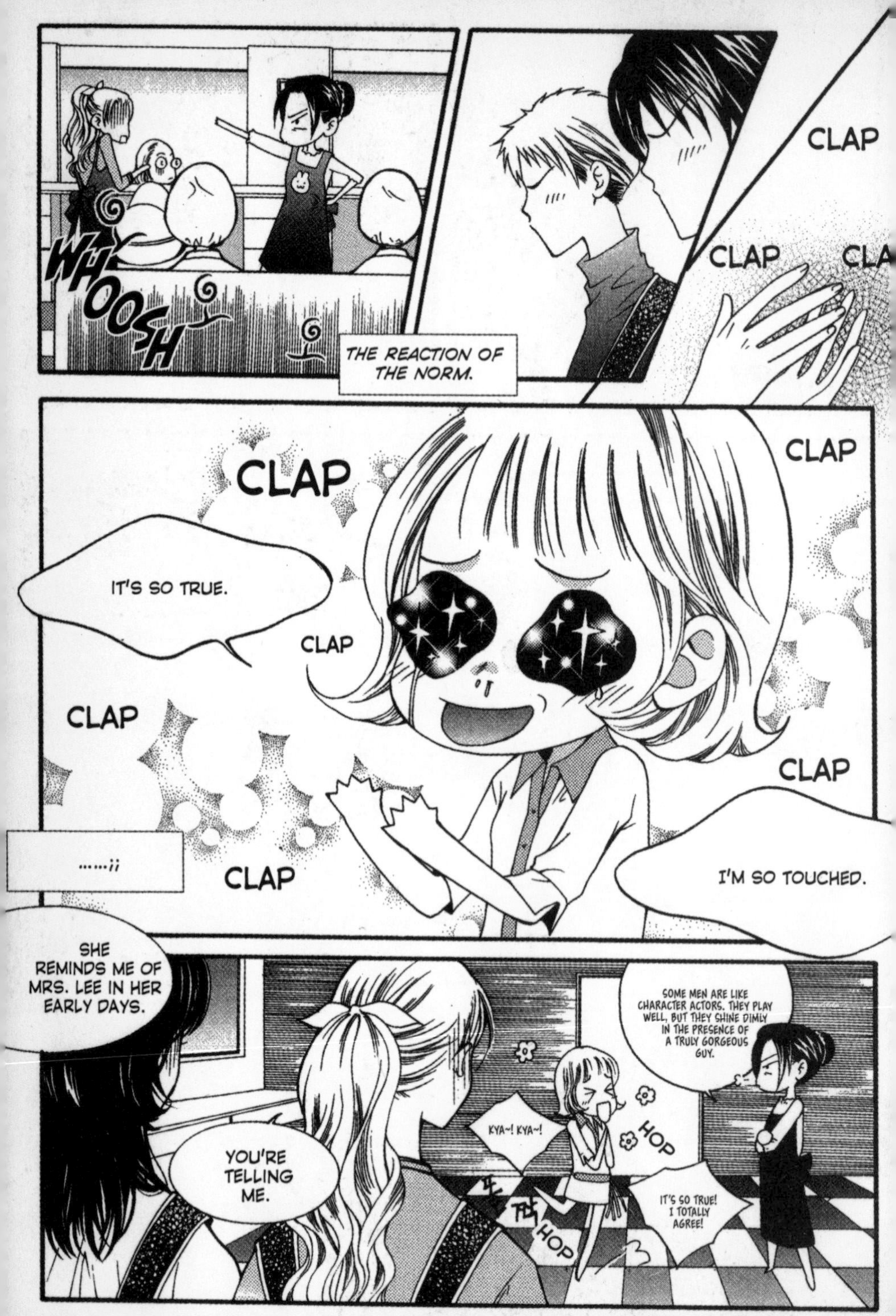
WHOOSH
THE REACTION OF THE NORM.
CLAP
CLAP
CLAP
IT'S SO TRUE.
CLAP
CLAP
……¡¡
CLAP
CLAP
CLAP
I'M SO TOUCHED.
SHE REMINDS ME OF MRS. LEE IN HER EARLY DAYS.
YOU'RE TELLING ME.
KYA~! KYA~!
SOME MEN ARE LIKE CHARACTER ACTORS. THEY PLAY WELL, BUT THEY SHINE DIMLY IN THE PRESENCE OF A TRULY GORGEOUS GUY.
HOP
IT'S SO TRUE! I TOTALLY AGREE!
HOP

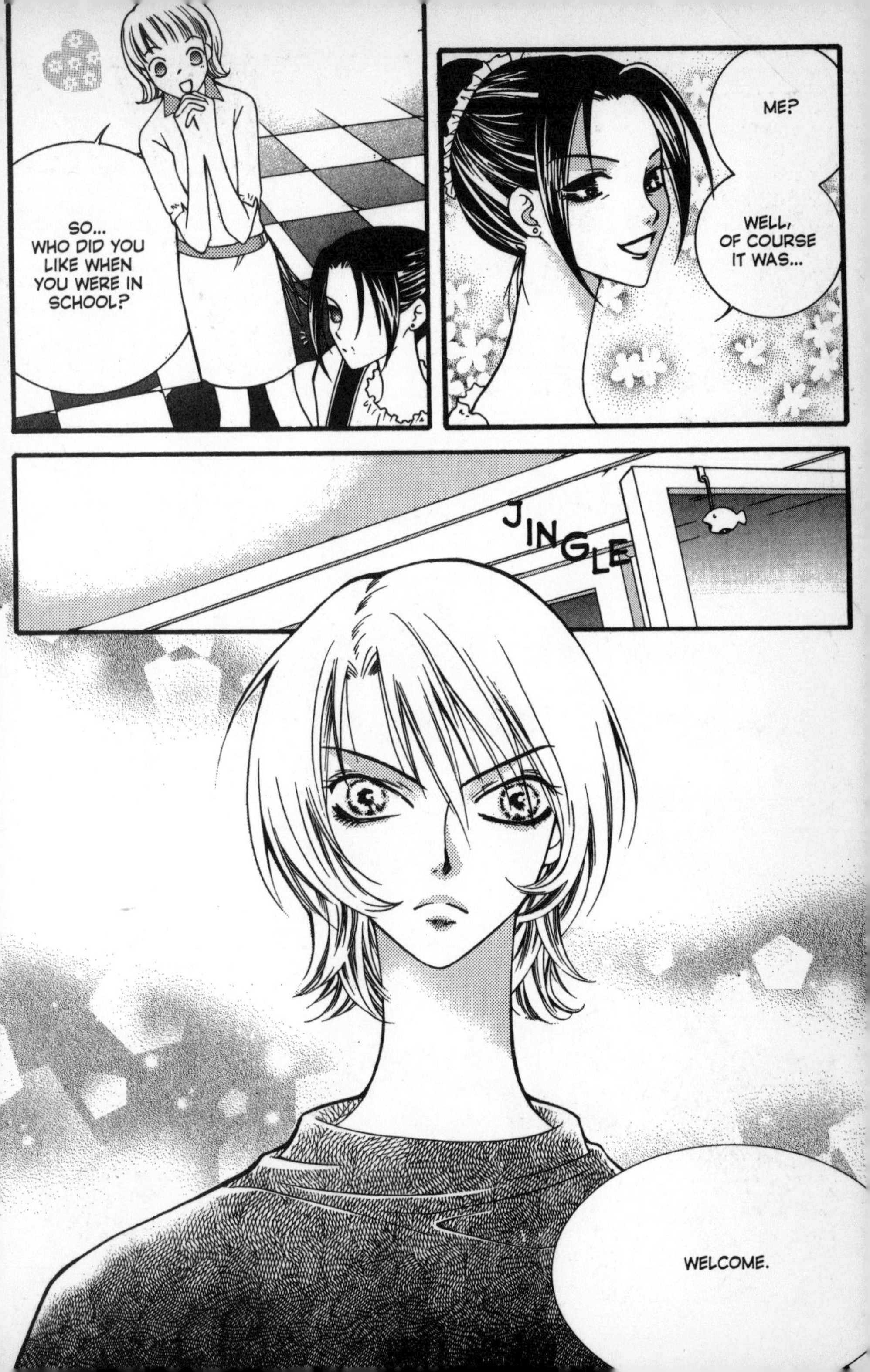
SO... WHO DID YOU LIKE WHEN YOU WERE IN SCHOOL?
ME?
WELL, OF COURSE IT WAS...
JINGLE
WELCOME.

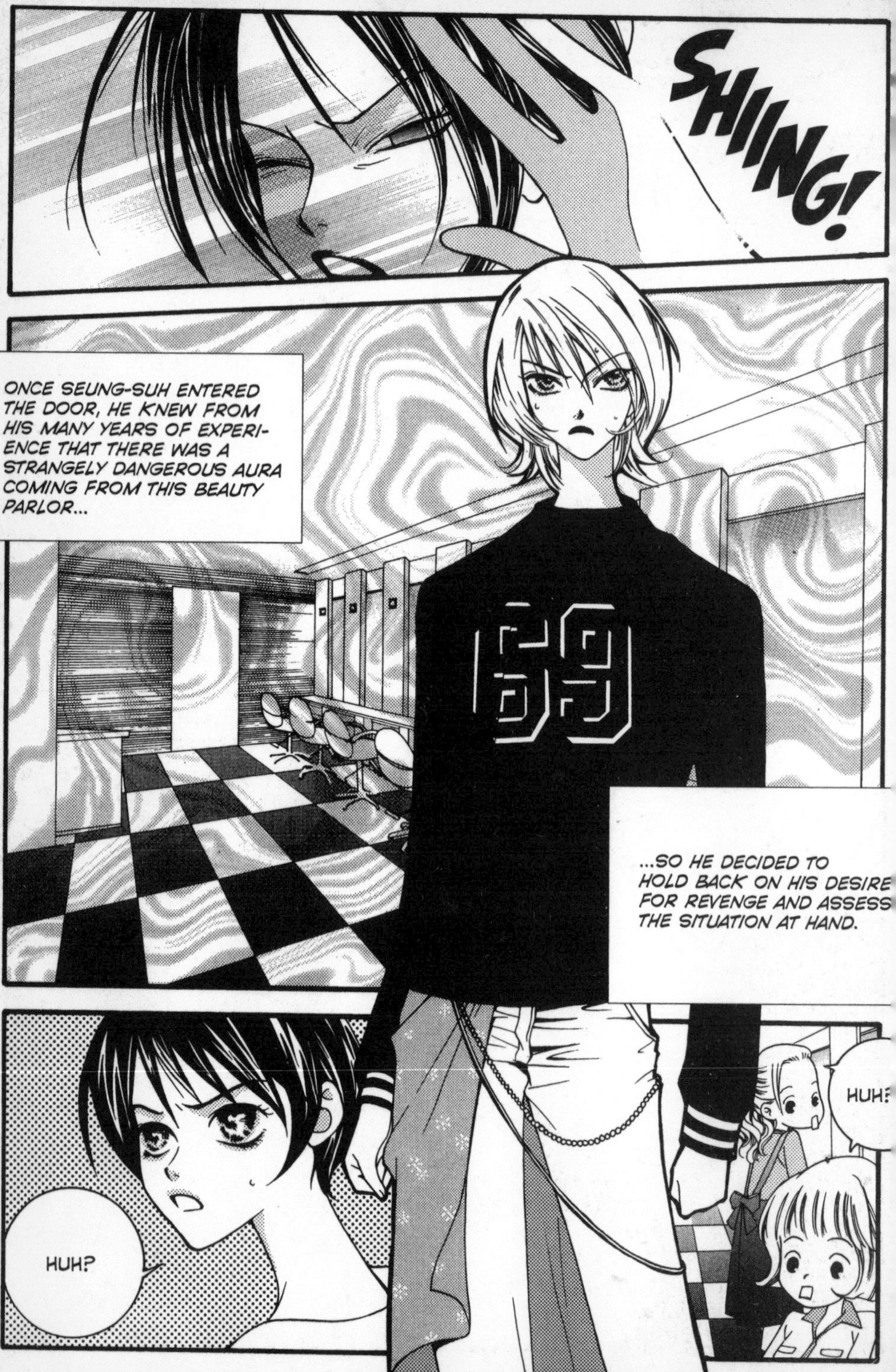
SHING!
ONCE SEUNG-SUH ENTERED THE DOOR, HE KNEW FROM HIS MANY YEARS OF EXPERIENCE THAT THERE WAS A STRANGELY DANGEROUS AURA COMING FROM THIS BEAUTY PARLOR...
...SO HE DECIDED TO HOLD BACK ON HIS DESIRE FOR REVENGE AND ASSESS THE SITUATION AT HAND.
HUH?
HUH?

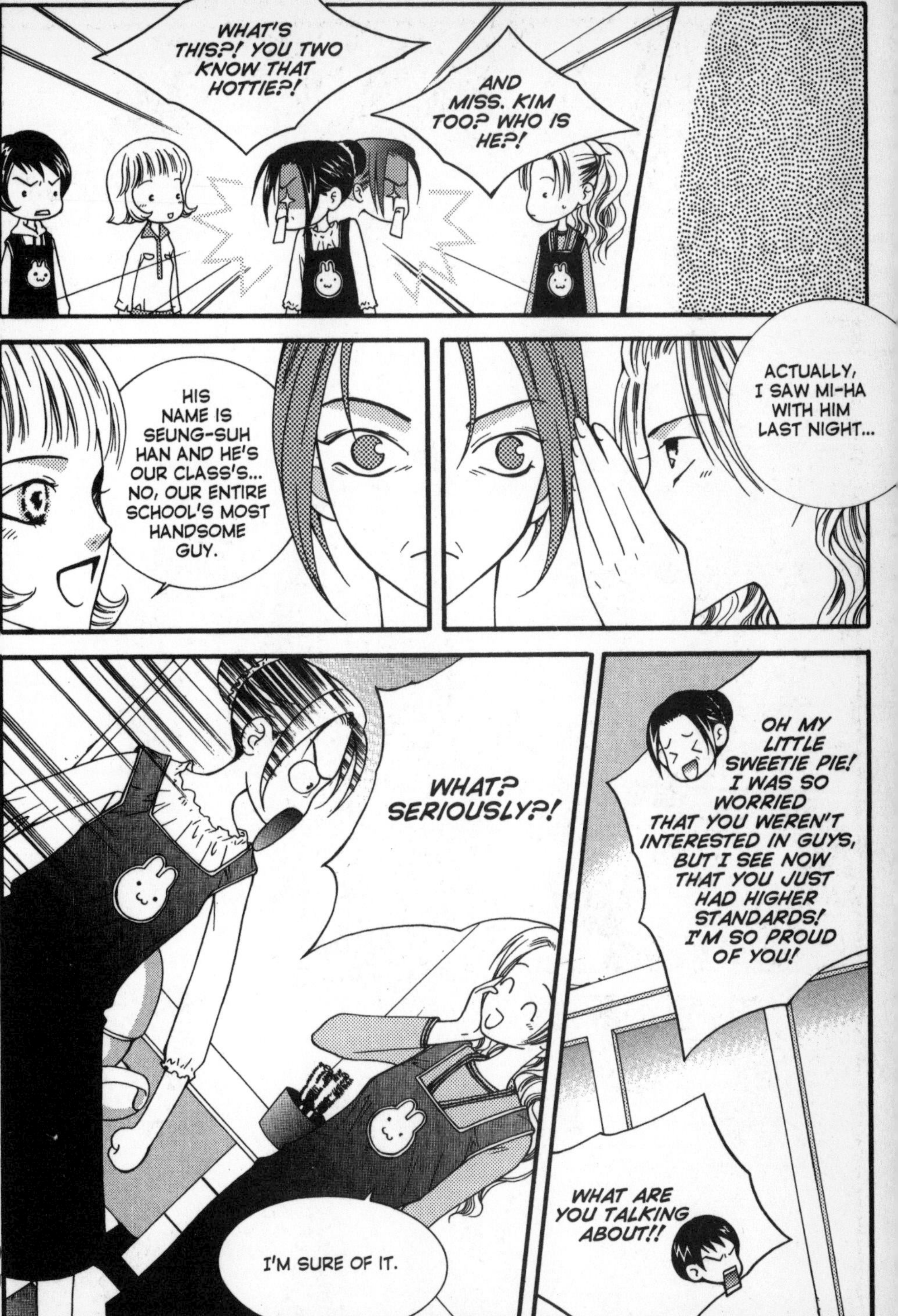
WHAT'S THIS?! YOU TWO KNOW THAT HOTTIE?!
AND MISS. KIM TOO? WHO IS HE?!
HIS NAME IS SEUNG-SUH HAN AND HE'S OUR CLASS'S... NO, OUR ENTIRE SCHOOL'S MOST HANDSOME GUY.
ACTUALLY, I SAW MI-HA WITH HIM LAST NIGHT...
WHAT? SERIOUSLY?!
I'M SURE OF IT.
OH MY LITTLE SWEETIE PIE! I WAS SO WORRIED THAT YOU WEREN'T INTERESTED IN GUYS, BUT I SEE NOW THAT YOU JUST HAD HIGHER STANDARDS! I'M SO PROUD OF YOU!
WHAT ARE YOU TALKING ABOUT!!

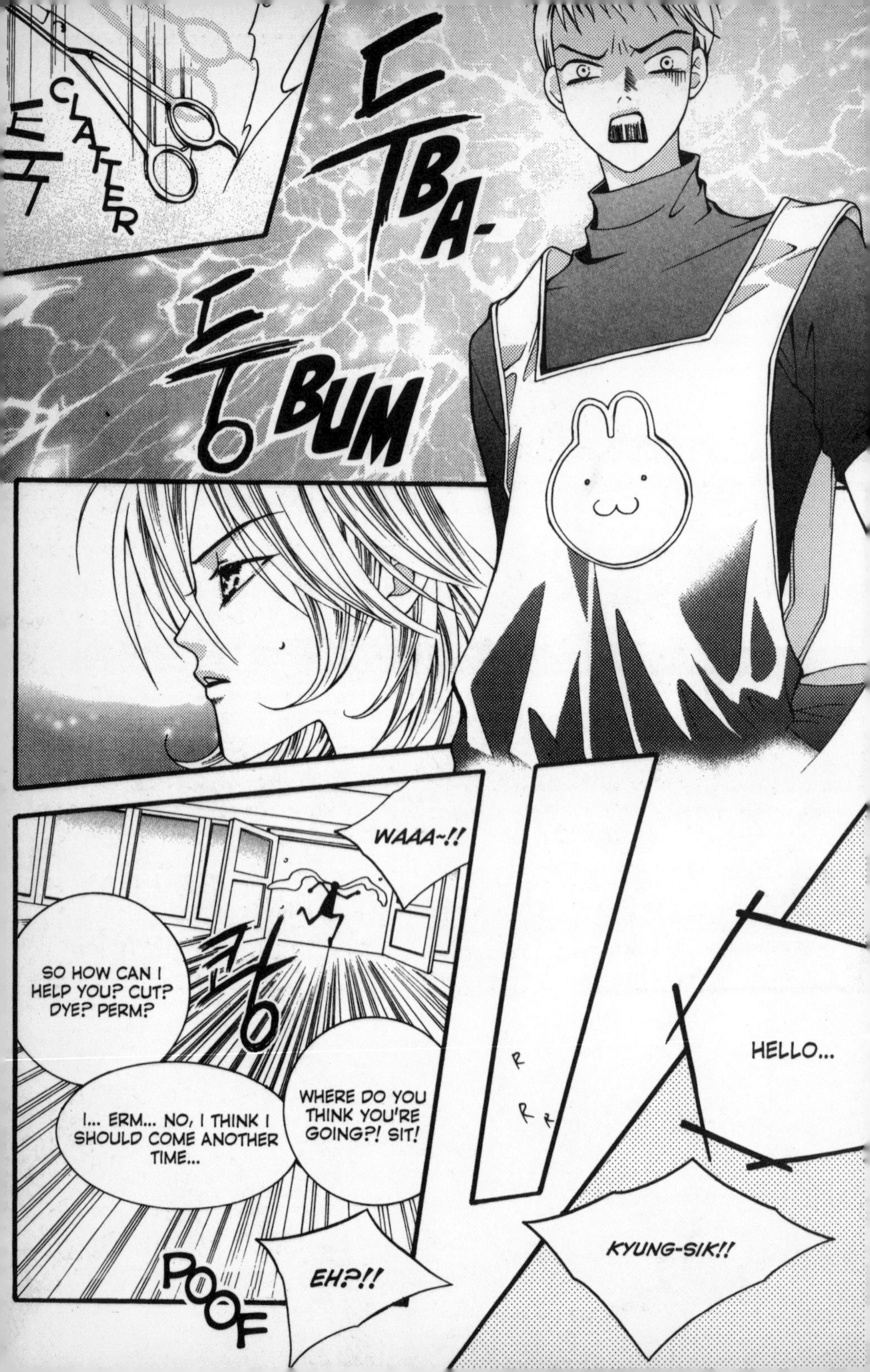
CLATTER
BA-
BUM
WAAA~!!
SO HOW CAN I HELP YOU? CUT? DYE? PERM?
I... ERM... NO, I THINK I SHOULD COME ANOTHER TIME...
WHERE DO YOU THINK YOU'RE GOING?! SIT!
POOF
EH?!!
HELLO...
KYUNG-SIK!!

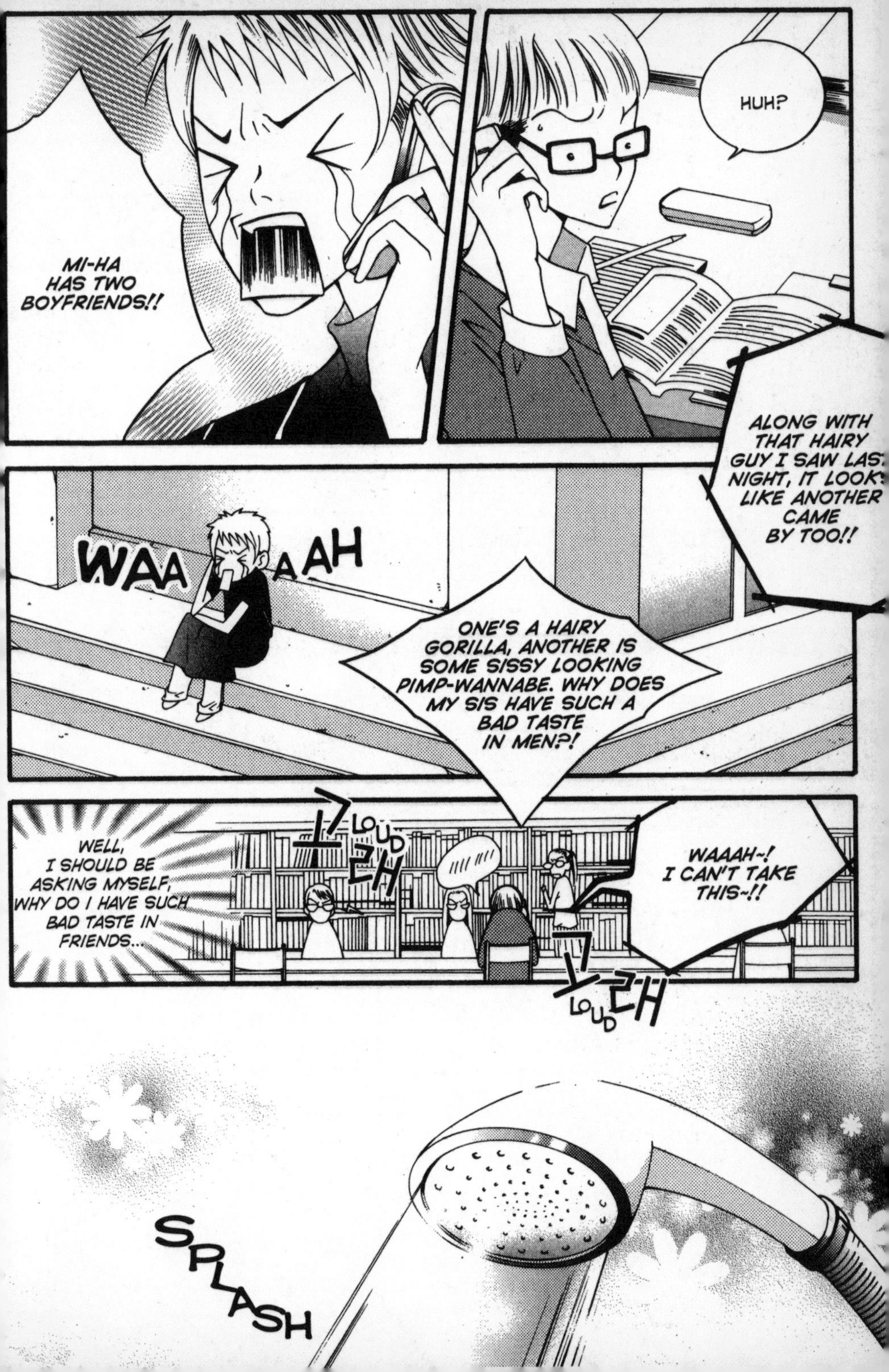
MI-HA HAS TWO BOYFRIENDS!!
HUH?
ALONG WITH THAT HAIRY GUY I SAW LAS NIGHT, IT LOOK LIKE ANOTHER CAME BY TOO!!
WAA AAH
ONE'S A HAIRY GORILLA, ANOTHER IS SOME SISSY LOOKING PIMP-WANNABE. WHY DOES MY SIS HAVE SUCH A BAD TASTE IN MEN?!
WELL, I SHOULD BE ASKING MYSELF, WHY DO I HAVE SUCH BAD TASTE IN FRIENDS...
LOUD
WAAAH~! I CAN'T TAKE THIS~!!
LOUD
SPLASH

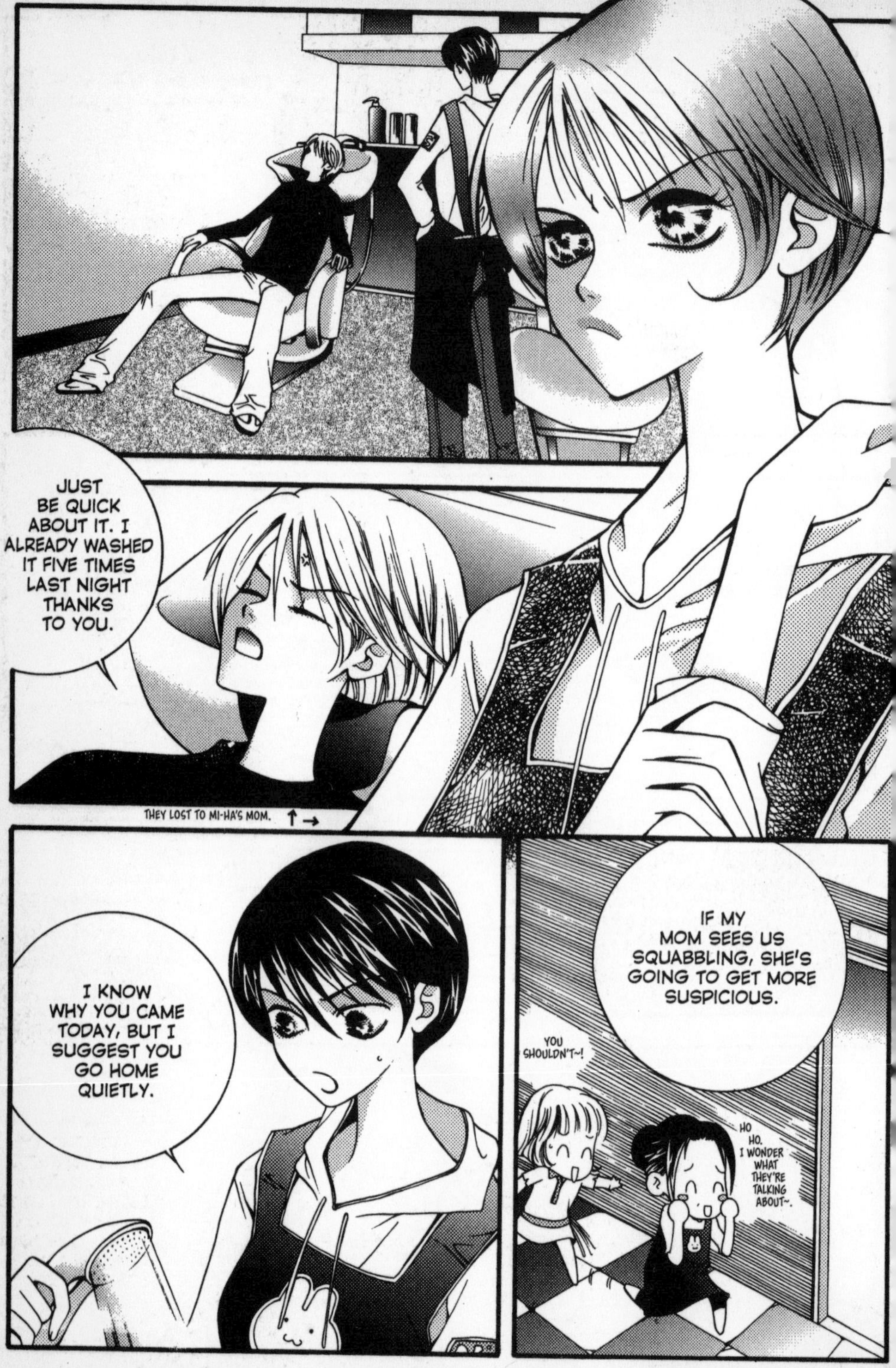
JUST BE QUICK ABOUT IT. I ALREADY WASHED IT FIVE TIMES LAST NIGHT THANKS TO YOU.
THEY LOST TO MI-HA'S MOM. ↑ →
I KNOW WHY YOU CAME TODAY, BUT I SUGGEST YOU GO HOME QUIETLY.
IF MY MOM SEES US SQUABBLING, SHE'S GOING TO GET MORE SUSPICIOUS.
YOU SHOULDN'T~!
HO HO. I WONDER WHAT THEY'RE TALKING ABOUT~.

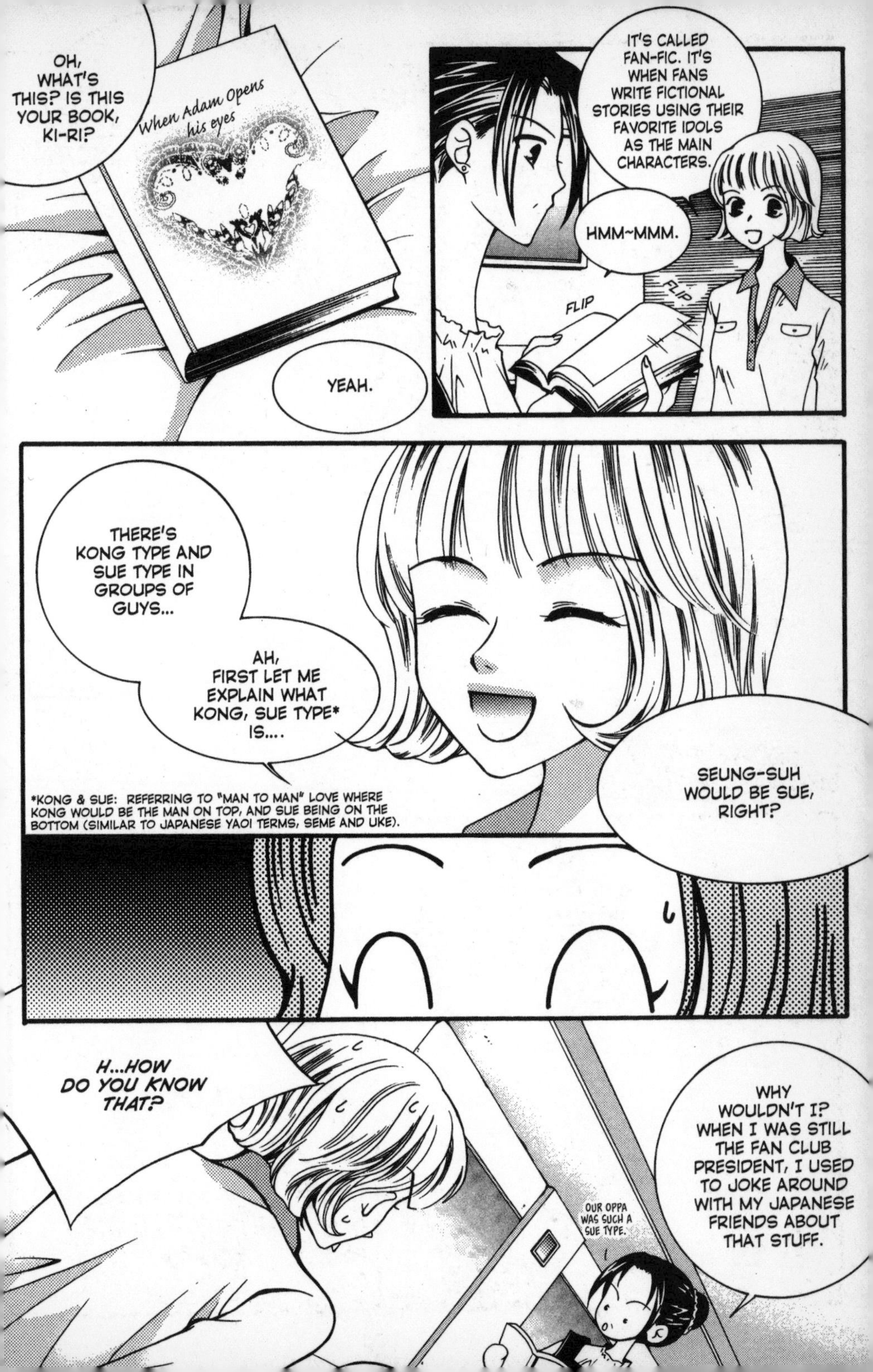
OH, WHAT'S THIS? IS THIS YOUR BOOK, KI-RI?
When Adam Opens his eyes
YEAH.
IT'S CALLED FAN-FIC. IT'S WHEN FANS WRITE FICTIONAL STORIES USING THEIR FAVORITE IDOLS AS THE MAIN CHARACTERS.
HMM~MMM.
FLIP
FLIP
THERE'S KONG TYPE AND SUE TYPE IN GROUPS OF GUYS...
AH, FIRST LET ME EXPLAIN WHAT KONG, SUE TYPE* IS....
*KONG & SUE: REFERRING TO "MAN TO MAN" LOVE WHERE KONG WOULD BE THE MAN ON TOP, AND SUE BEING ON THE BOTTOM (SIMILAR TO JAPANESE YAOI TERMS, SEME AND UKE).
SEUNG-SUH WOULD BE SUE, RIGHT?
H...HOW DO YOU KNOW THAT?
WHY WOULDN'T I? WHEN I WAS STILL THE FAN CLUB PRESIDENT, I USED TO JOKE AROUND WITH MY JAPANESE FRIENDS ABOUT THAT STUFF.
OUR OPPA WAS SUCH A SUE TYPE.

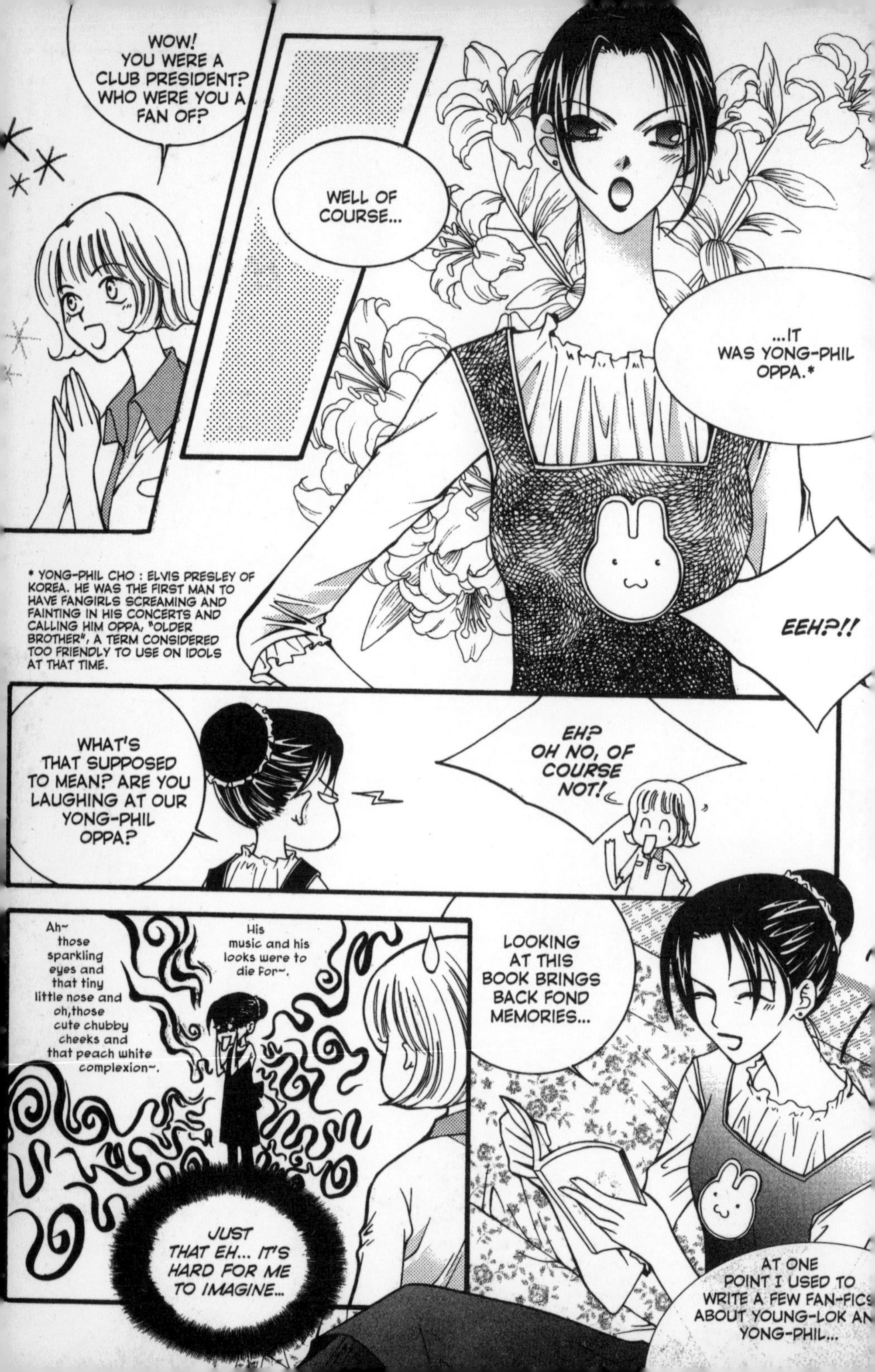
WOW! YOU WERE A CLUB PRESIDENT? WHO WERE YOU A FAN OF?
WELL OF COURSE...
...IT WAS YONG-PHIL OPPA.*
* YONG-PHIL CHO : ELVIS PRESLEY OF KOREA. HE WAS THE FIRST MAN TO HAVE FANGIRLS SCREAMING AND FAINTING IN HIS CONCERTS AND CALLING HIM OPPA, "OLDER BROTHER", A TERM CONSIDERED TOO FRIENDLY TO USE ON IDOLS AT THAT TIME.
EEH?!!
WHAT'S THAT SUPPOSED TO MEAN? ARE YOU LAUGHING AT OUR YONG-PHIL OPPA?
EH? OH NO, OF COURSE NOT!
Ah~ those sparkling eyes and that tiny little nose and oh,those cute chubby cheeks and that peach white complexion~.
His music and his looks were to die for~.
JUST THAT EH... IT'S HARD FOR ME TO IMAGINE...
LOOKING AT THIS BOOK BRINGS BACK FOND MEMORIES...
AT ONE POINT I USED TO WRITE A FEW FAN-FICS ABOUT YOUNG-LOK AN YONG-PHIL...

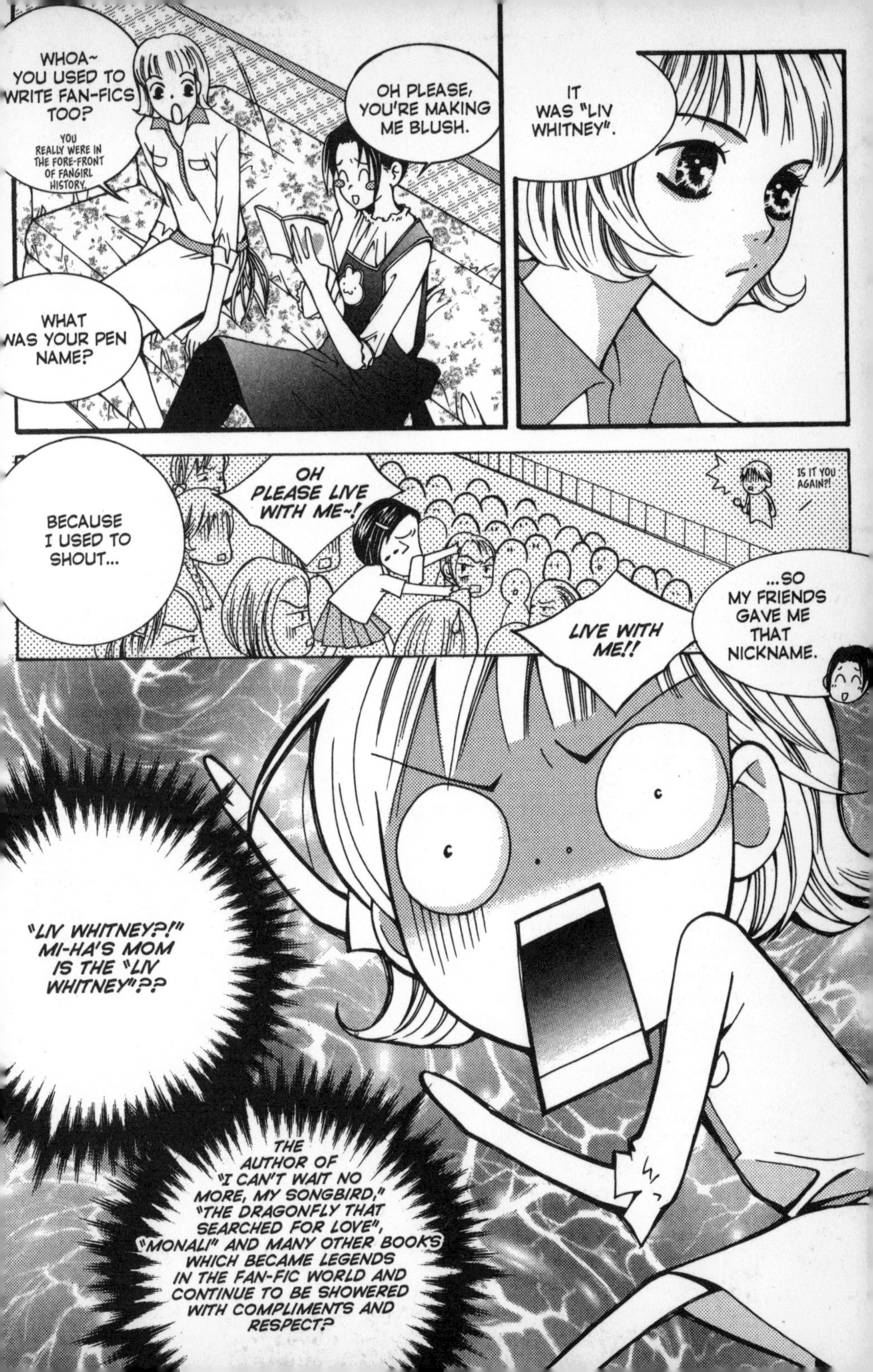
WHOA~ YOU USED TO WRITE FAN-FICS TOO?
YOU REALLY WERE IN THE FORE-FRONT OF FANGIRL HISTORY.
OH PLEASE, YOU'RE MAKING ME BLUSH.
WHAT WAS YOUR PEN NAME?
IT WAS "LIV WHITNEY".
BECAUSE I USED TO SHOUT...
OH PLEASE LIVE WITH ME~!
IS IT YOU AGAIN?!
LIVE WITH ME!!
...SO MY FRIENDS GAVE ME THAT NICKNAME.
"LIV WHITNEY?!" MI-HA'S MOM IS THE "LIV WHITNEY"??
THE AUTHOR OF "I CAN'T WAIT NO MORE, MY SONGBIRD," "THE DRAGONFLY THAT SEARCHED FOR LOVE", "MONALI" AND MANY OTHER BOOKS WHICH BECAME LEGENDS IN THE FAN-FIC WORLD AND CONTINUE TO BE SHOWERED WITH COMPLIMENTS AND RESPECT?

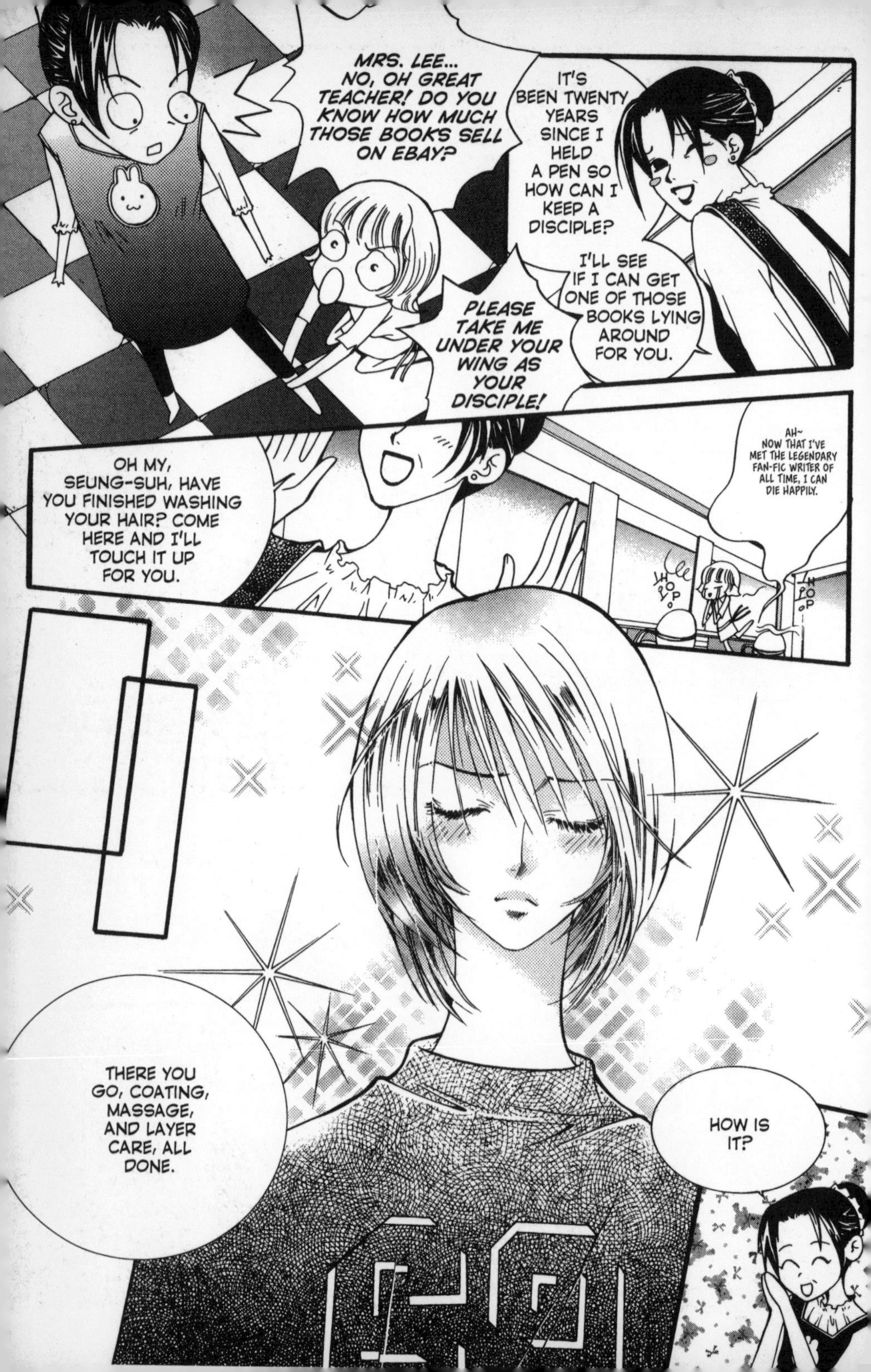
MRS. LEE... NO, OH GREAT TEACHER! DO YOU KNOW HOW MUCH THOSE BOOKS SELL ON EBAY?
IT'S BEEN TWENTY YEARS SINCE I HELD A PEN SO HOW CAN I KEEP A DISCIPLE?
PLEASE TAKE ME UNDER YOUR WING AS YOUR DISCIPLE!
I'LL SEE IF I CAN GET ONE OF THOSE BOOKS LYING AROUND FOR YOU.
OH MY, SEUNG-SUH, HAVE YOU FINISHED WASHING YOUR HAIR? COME HERE AND I'LL TOUCH IT UP FOR YOU.
AH~ NOW THAT I'VE MET THE LEGENDARY FAN-FIC WRITER OF ALL TIME, I CAN DIE HAPPILY.
THERE YOU GO, COATING, MASSAGE, AND LAYER CARE, ALL DONE.
HOW IS IT?

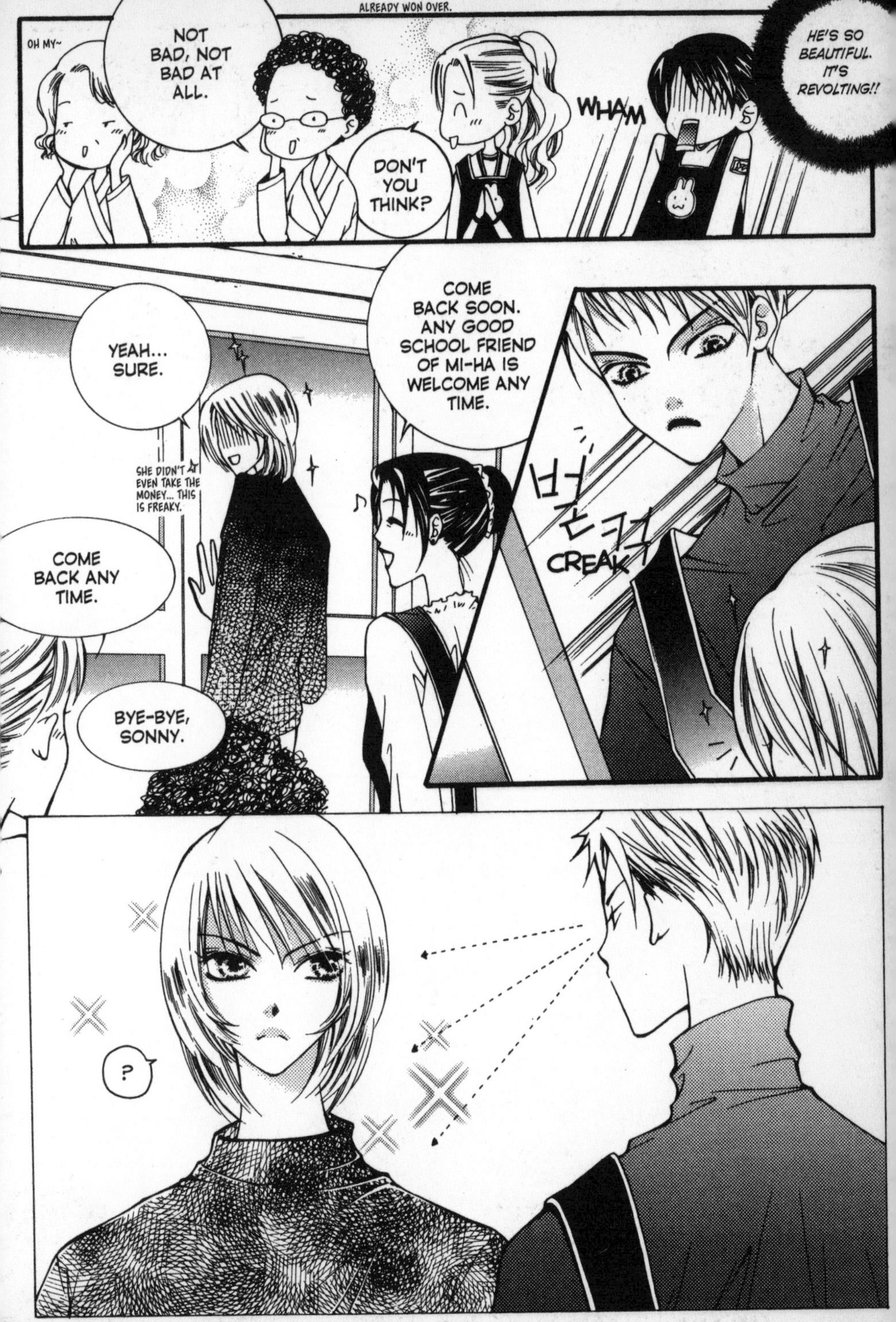
ALREADY WON OVER.
OH MY~
NOT BAD, NOT BAD AT ALL.
DON'T YOU THINK?
WHAM
HE'S SO BEAUTIFUL. IT'S REVOLTING!!
YEAH... SURE.
COME BACK SOON. ANY GOOD SCHOOL FRIEND OF MI-HA IS WELCOME ANY TIME.
SHE DIDN'T EVEN TAKE THE MONEY... THIS IS FREAKY.
COME BACK ANY TIME.
BYE-BYE, SONNY.
CREAK
?

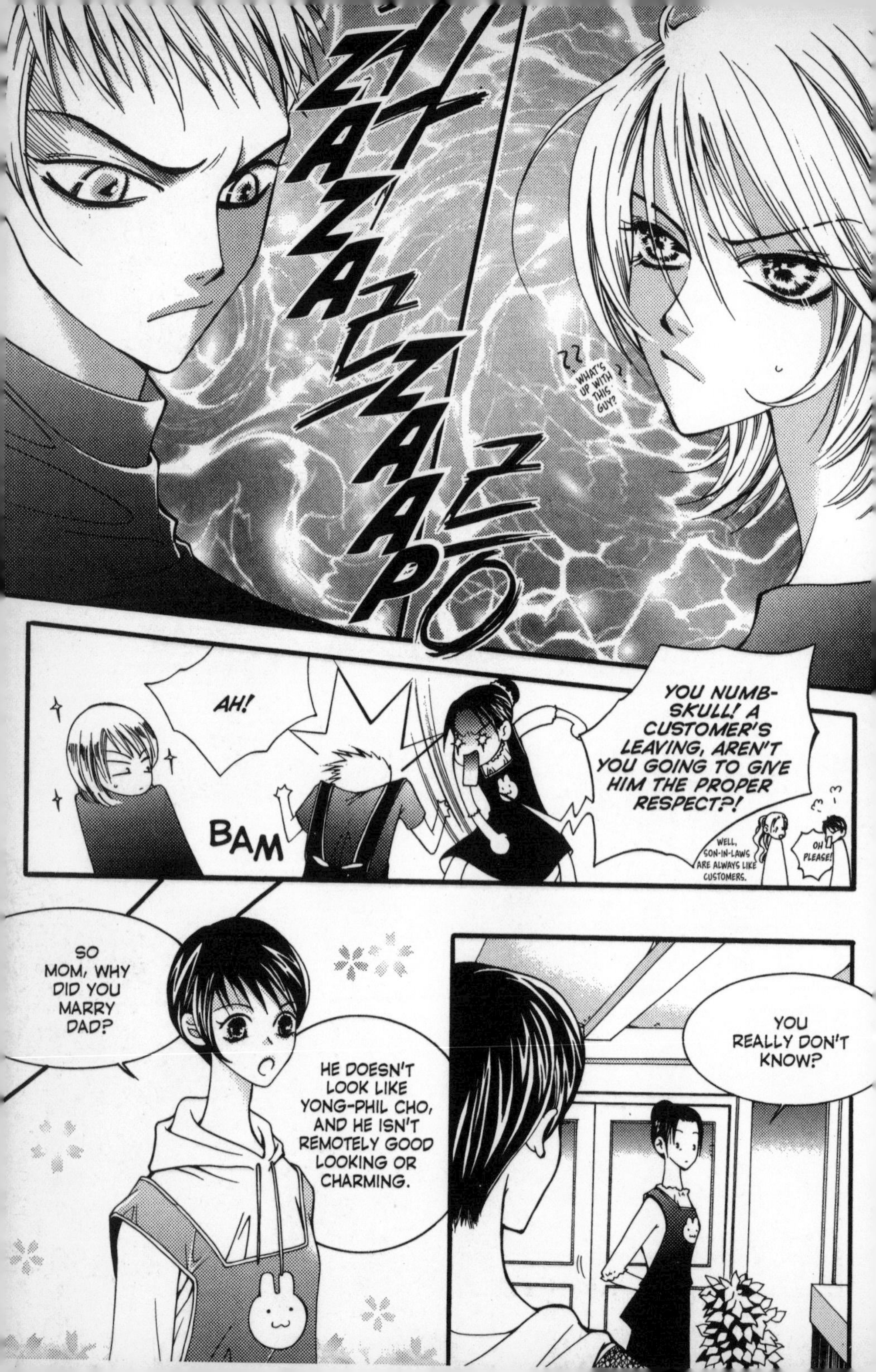
WHAT'S UP WITH THIS GUY?
AH!
BAM
YOU NUMB-SKULL! A CUSTOMER'S LEAVING, AREN'T YOU GOING TO GIVE HIM THE PROPER RESPECT?!
WELL, SON-IN-LAWS ARE ALWAYS LIKE CUSTOMERS.
OH PLEASE!
SO MOM, WHY DID YOU MARRY DAD?
HE DOESN'T LOOK LIKE YONG-PHIL CHO, AND HE ISN'T REMOTELY GOOD LOOKING OR CHARMING.
YOU REALLY DON'T KNOW?

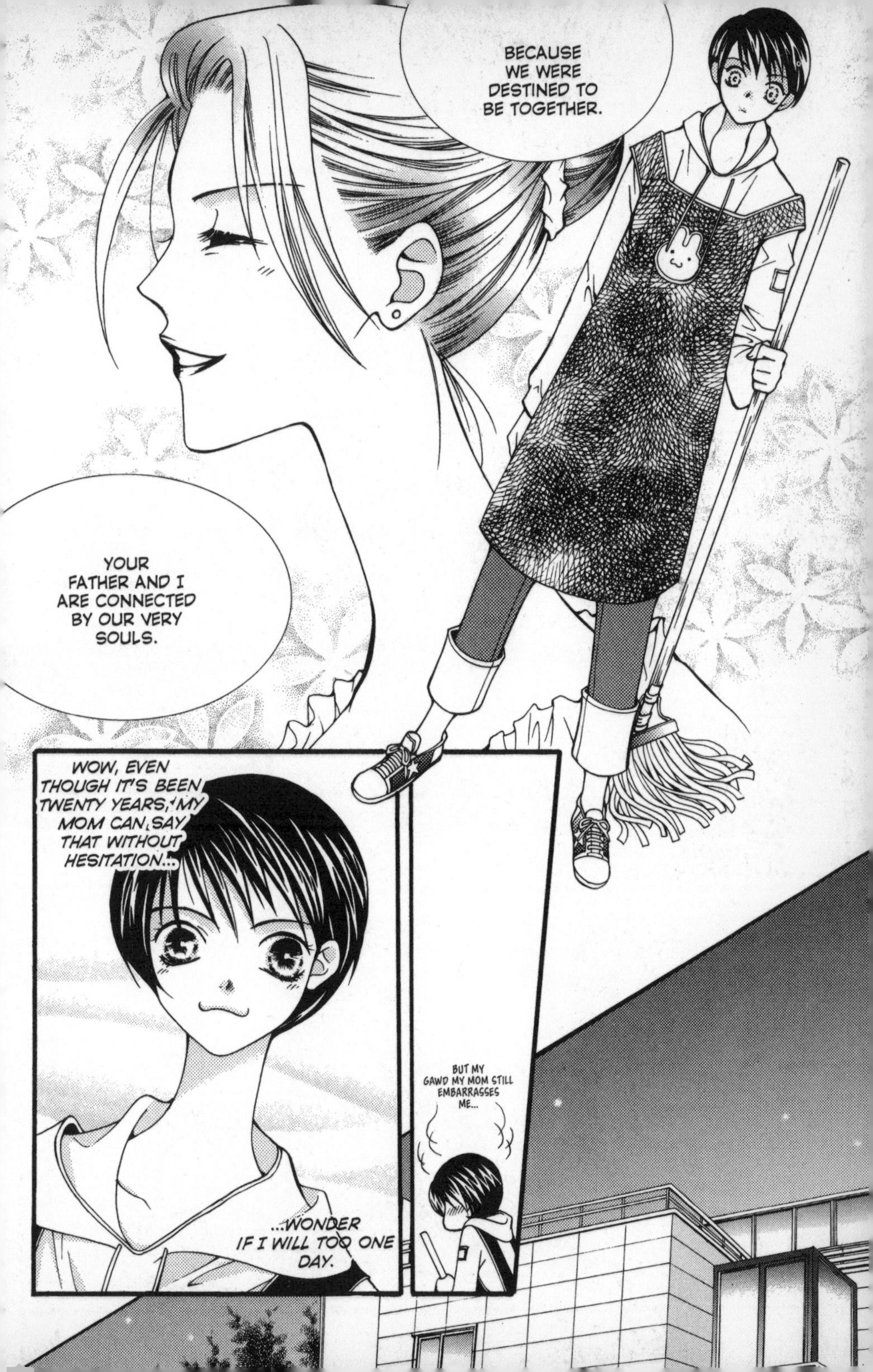
BECAUSE WE WERE DESTINED TO BE TOGETHER.
YOUR FATHER AND I ARE CONNECTED BY OUR VERY SOULS.
WOW, EVEN THOUGH IT'S BEEN TWENTY YEARS, MY MOM CAN SAY THAT WITHOUT HESITATION...
...WONDER IF I WILL TOO ONE DAY.
BUT MY GAWD MY MOM STILL EMBARRASSES ME...

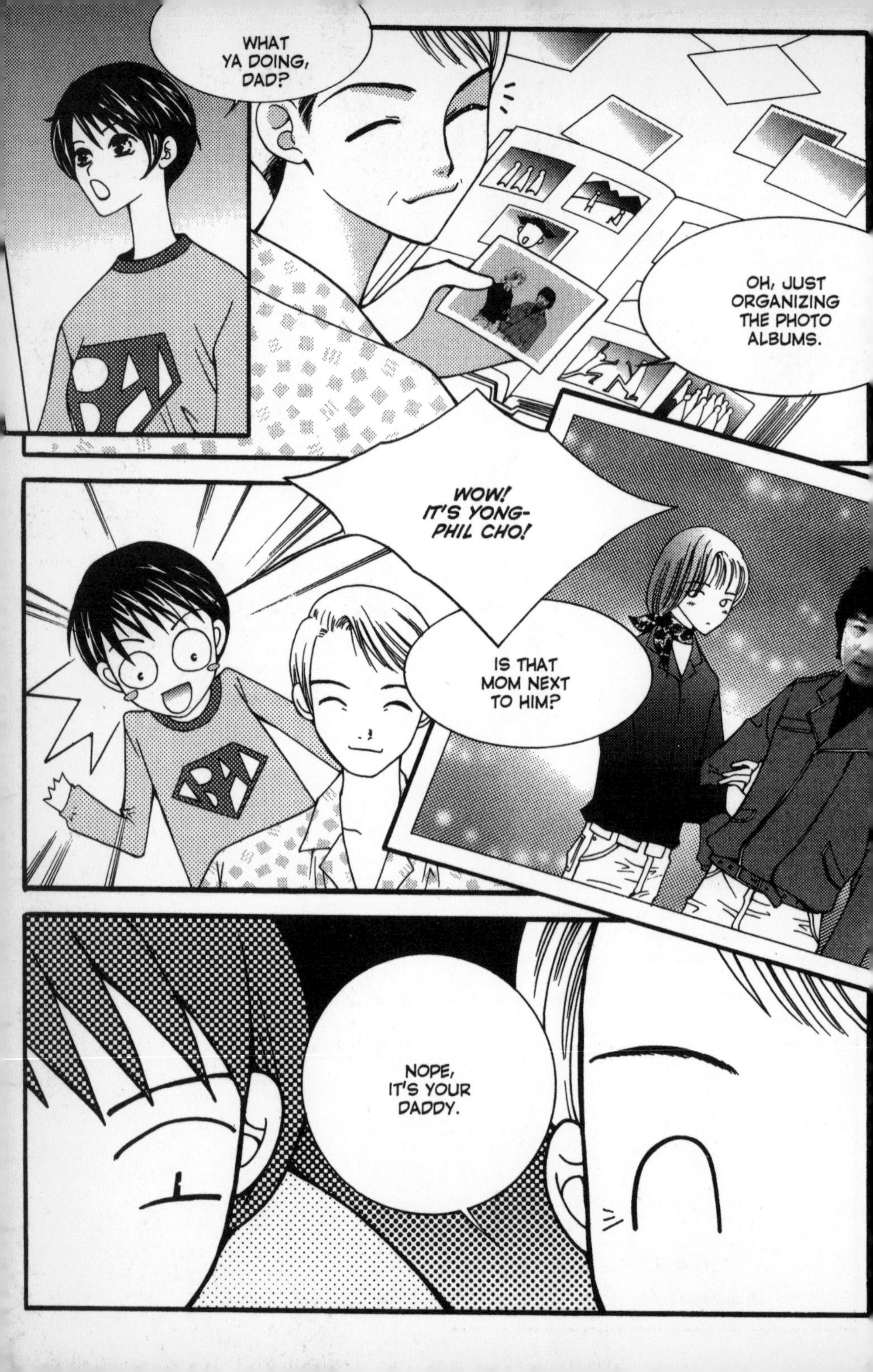
WHAT YA DOING, DAD?
OH, JUST ORGANIZING THE PHOTO ALBUMS.
WOW! IT'S YONG-PHIL CHO!
IS THAT MOM NEXT TO HIM?
NOPE, IT'S YOUR DADDY.

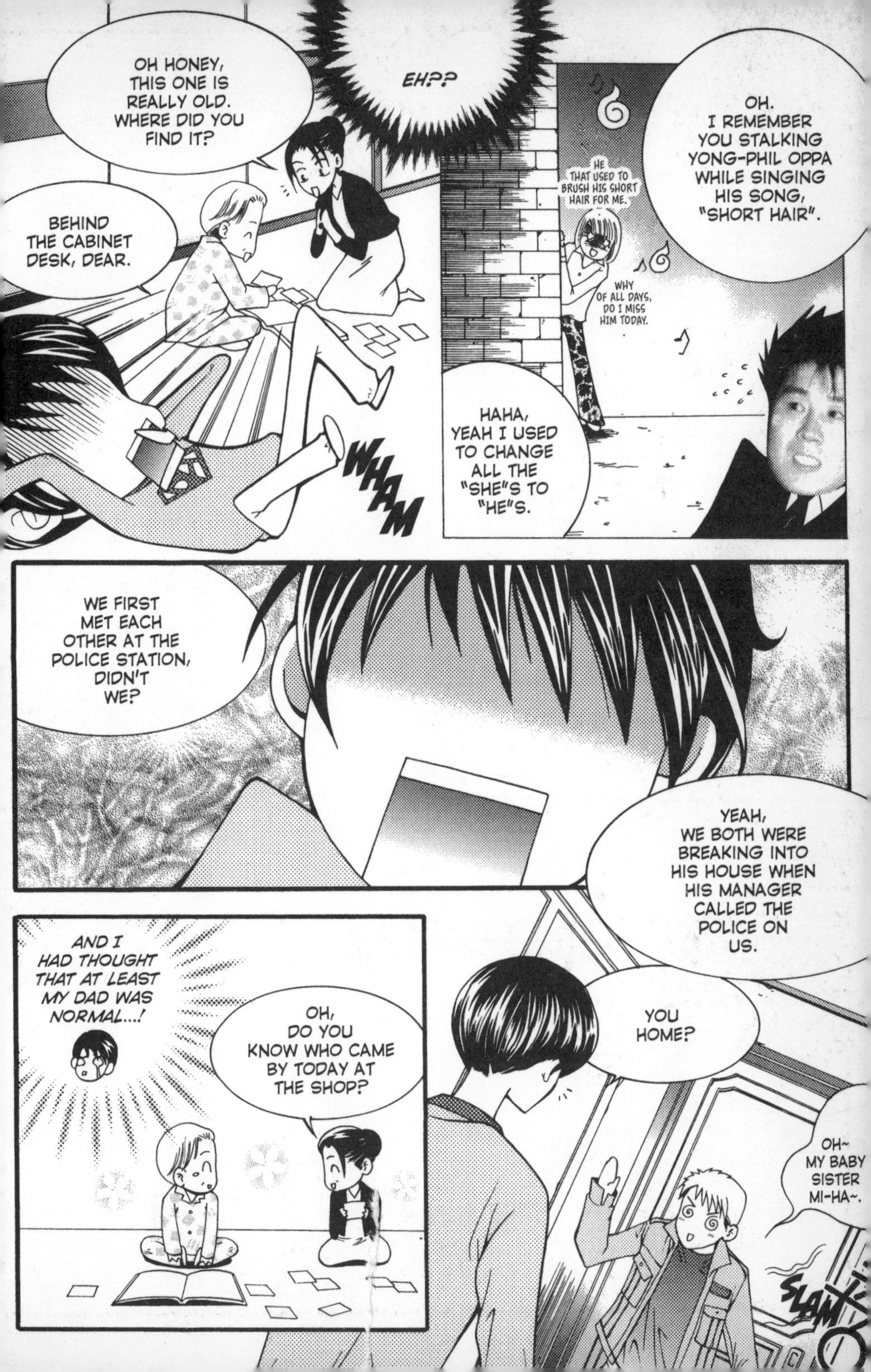
EH??
OH HONEY, THIS ONE IS REALLY OLD. WHERE DID YOU FIND IT?
BEHIND THE CABINET DESK, DEAR.
WHAM
OH. I REMEMBER YOU STALKING YONG-PHIL OPPA WHILE SINGING HIS SONG, "SHORT HAIR".
HE THAT USED TO BRUSH HIS SHORT HAIR FOR ME.
WHY OF ALL DAYS, DO I MISS HIM TODAY.
HAHA, YEAH I USED TO CHANGE ALL THE "SHE"S TO "HE"S.
WE FIRST MET EACH OTHER AT THE POLICE STATION, DIDN'T WE?
YEAH, WE BOTH WERE BREAKING INTO HIS HOUSE WHEN HIS MANAGER CALLED THE POLICE ON US.
AND I HAD THOUGHT THAT AT LEAST MY DAD WAS NORMAL...!
OH, DO YOU KNOW WHO CAME BY TODAY AT THE SHOP?
YOU HOME?
OH~ MY BABY SISTER MI-HA~.
SLAM

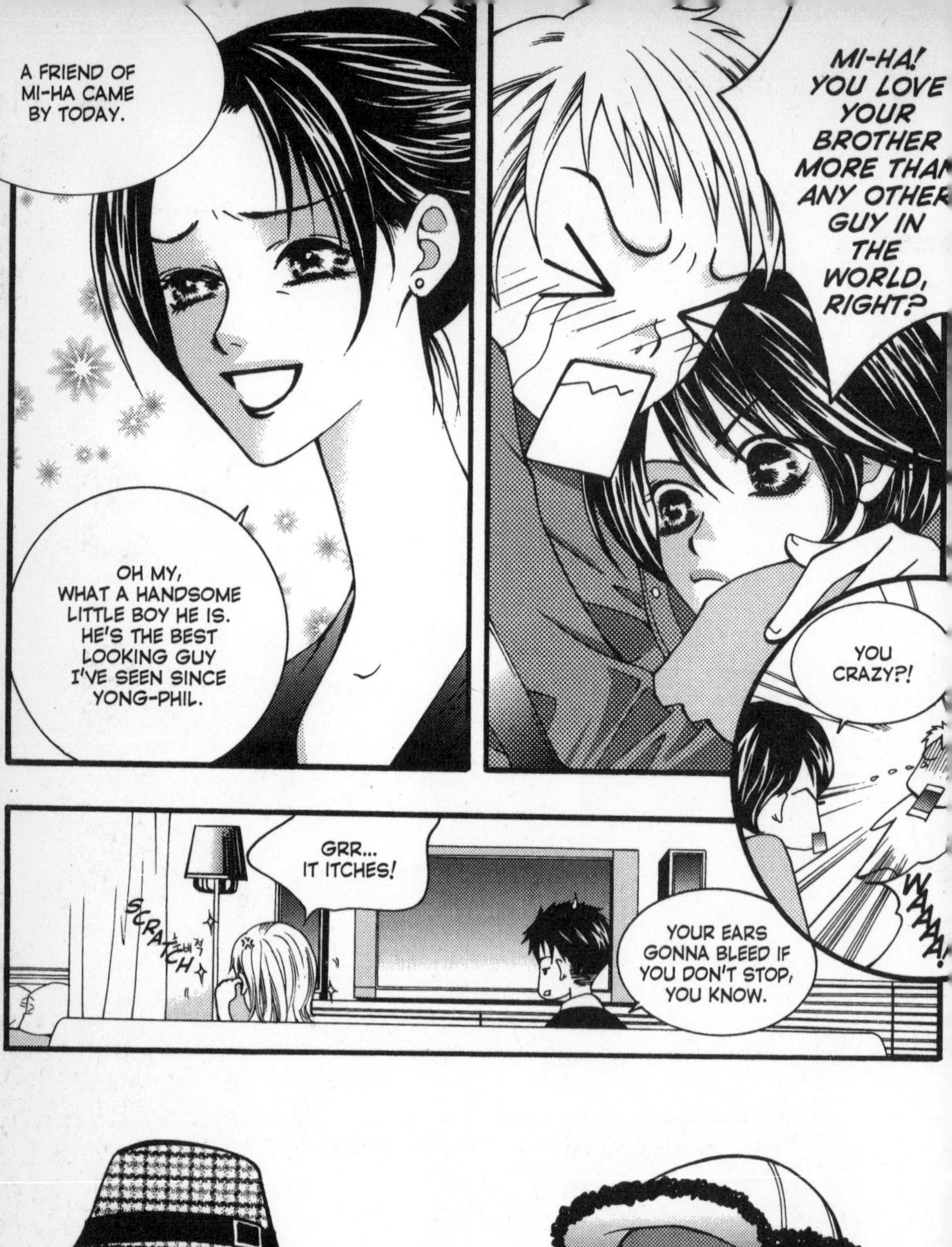
A FRIEND OF MI-HA CAME BY TODAY.
OH MY, WHAT A HANDSOME LITTLE BOY HE IS. HE'S THE BEST LOOKING GUY I'VE SEEN SINCE YONG-PHIL.
MI-HA! YOU LOVE YOUR BROTHER MORE THAN ANY OTHER GUY IN THE WORLD, RIGHT?
YOU CRAZY?!
WAAAA!
GRR... IT ITCHES!
SCRATCH
YOUR EARS GONNA BLEED IF YOU DON'T STOP, YOU KNOW.

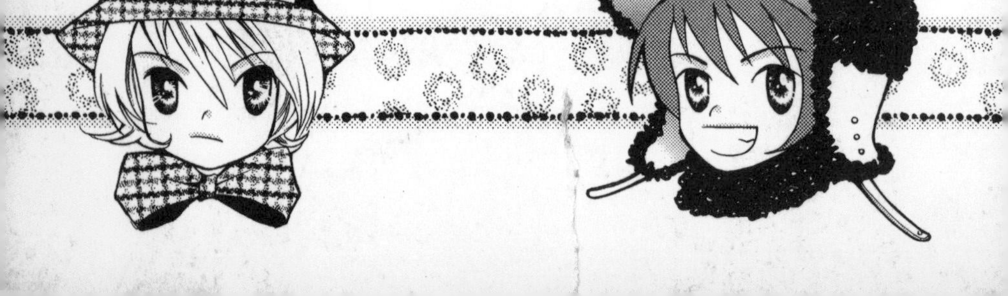

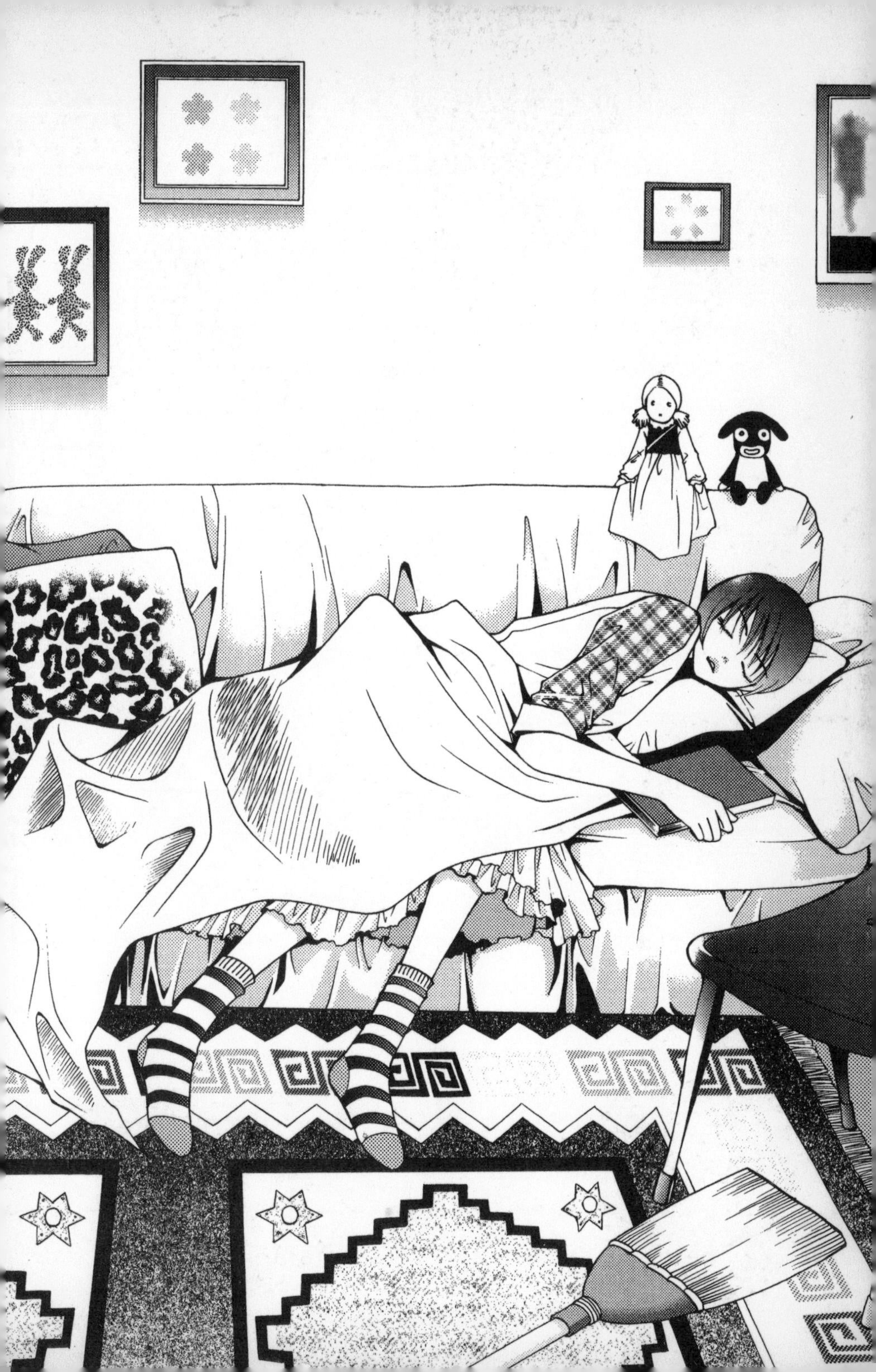

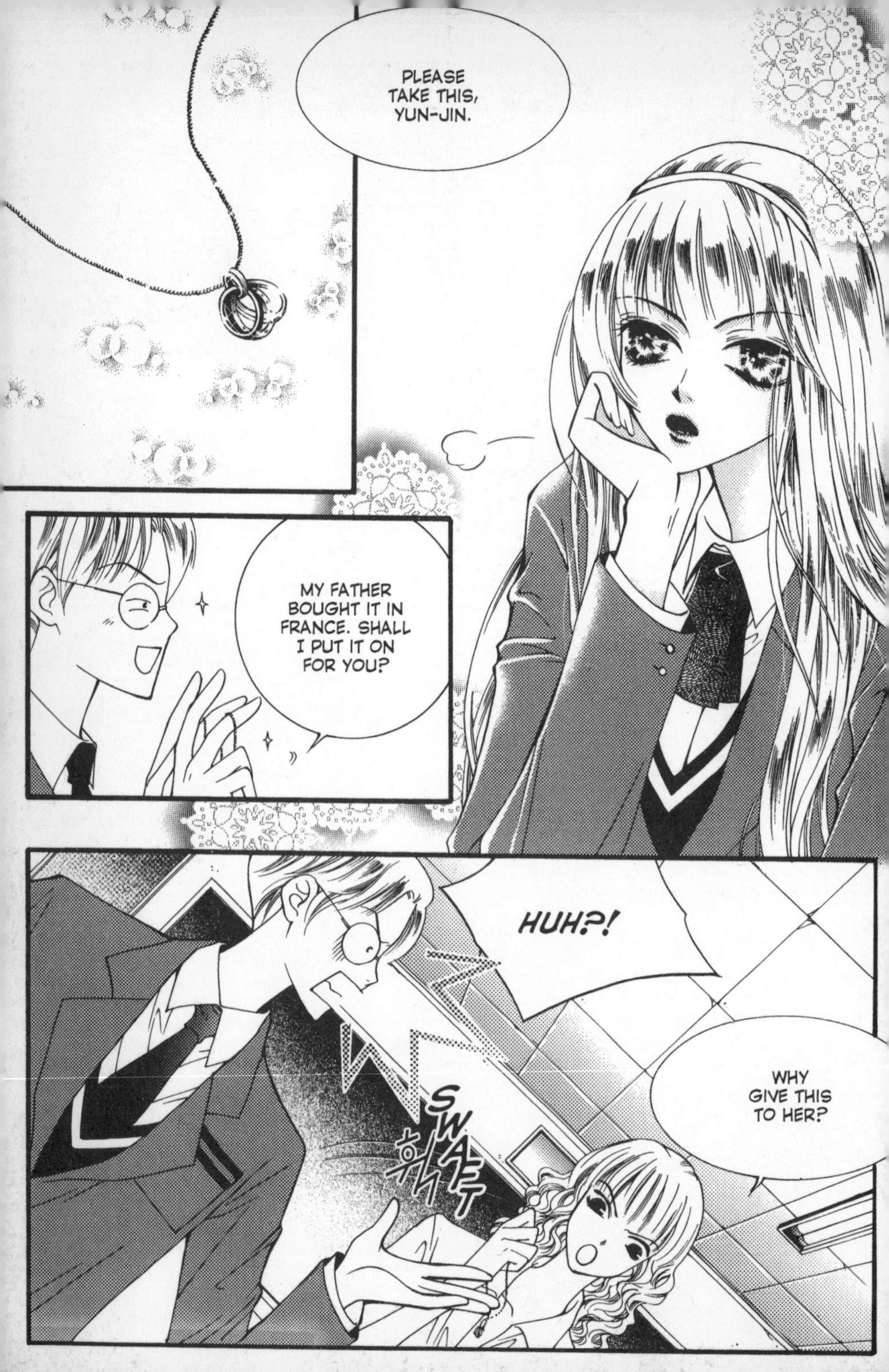
PLEASE TAKE THIS, YUN-JIN.
MY FATHER BOUGHT IT IN FRANCE. SHALL I PUT IT ON FOR YOU?
HUH?!
SWAT
WHY GIVE THIS TO HER?

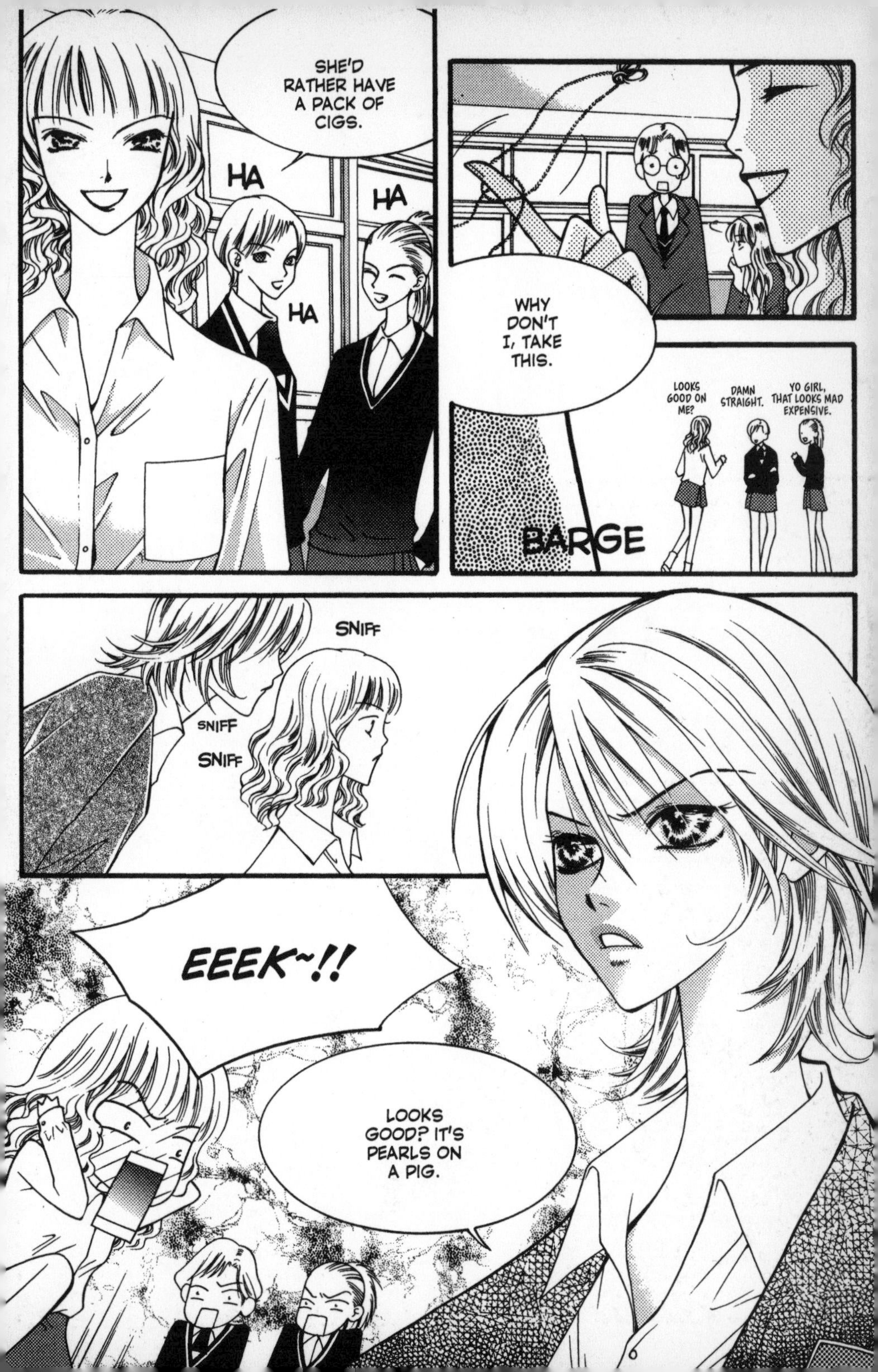
SHE'D RATHER HAVE A PACK OF CIGS.
HA
HA
HA
WHY DON'T I, TAKE THIS.
BARGE
LOOKS GOOD ON ME?
DAMN STRAIGHT.
YO GIRL, THAT LOOKS MAD EXPENSIVE.
SNIFF
SNIFF
SNIFF
EEEK~!!
LOOKS GOOD? IT'S PEARLS ON A PIG.

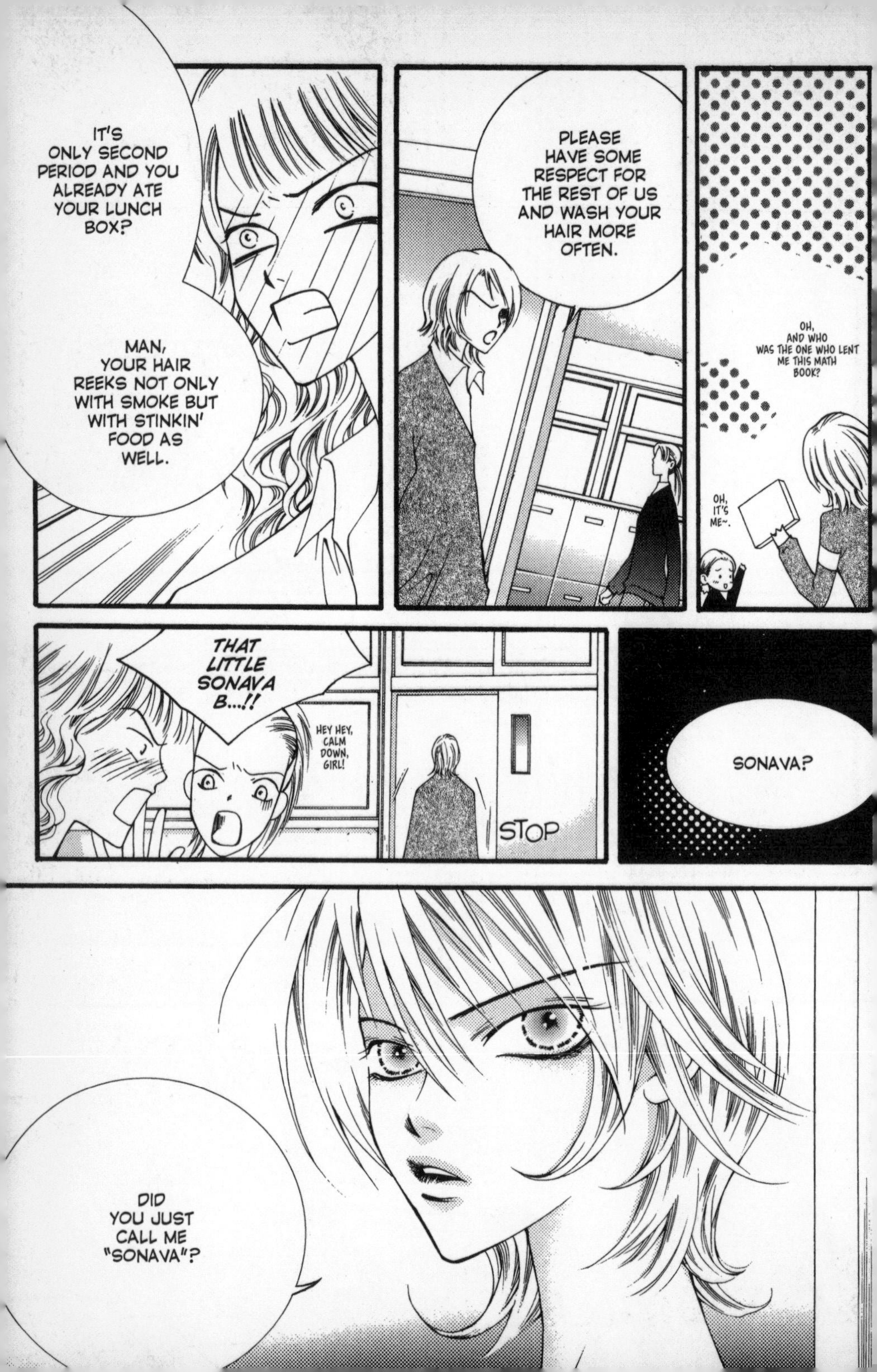
IT'S ONLY SECOND PERIOD AND YOU ALREADY ATE YOUR LUNCH BOX?
MAN, YOUR HAIR REEKS NOT ONLY WITH SMOKE BUT WITH STINKIN' FOOD AS WELL.
PLEASE HAVE SOME RESPECT FOR THE REST OF US AND WASH YOUR HAIR MORE OFTEN.
OH, AND WHO WAS THE ONE WHO LENT ME THIS MATH BOOK?
OH, IT'S ME~.
THAT LITTLE SONAVA B...!!
HEY HEY, CALM DOWN, GIRL!
STOP
SONAVA?
DID YOU JUST CALL ME "SONAVA"?

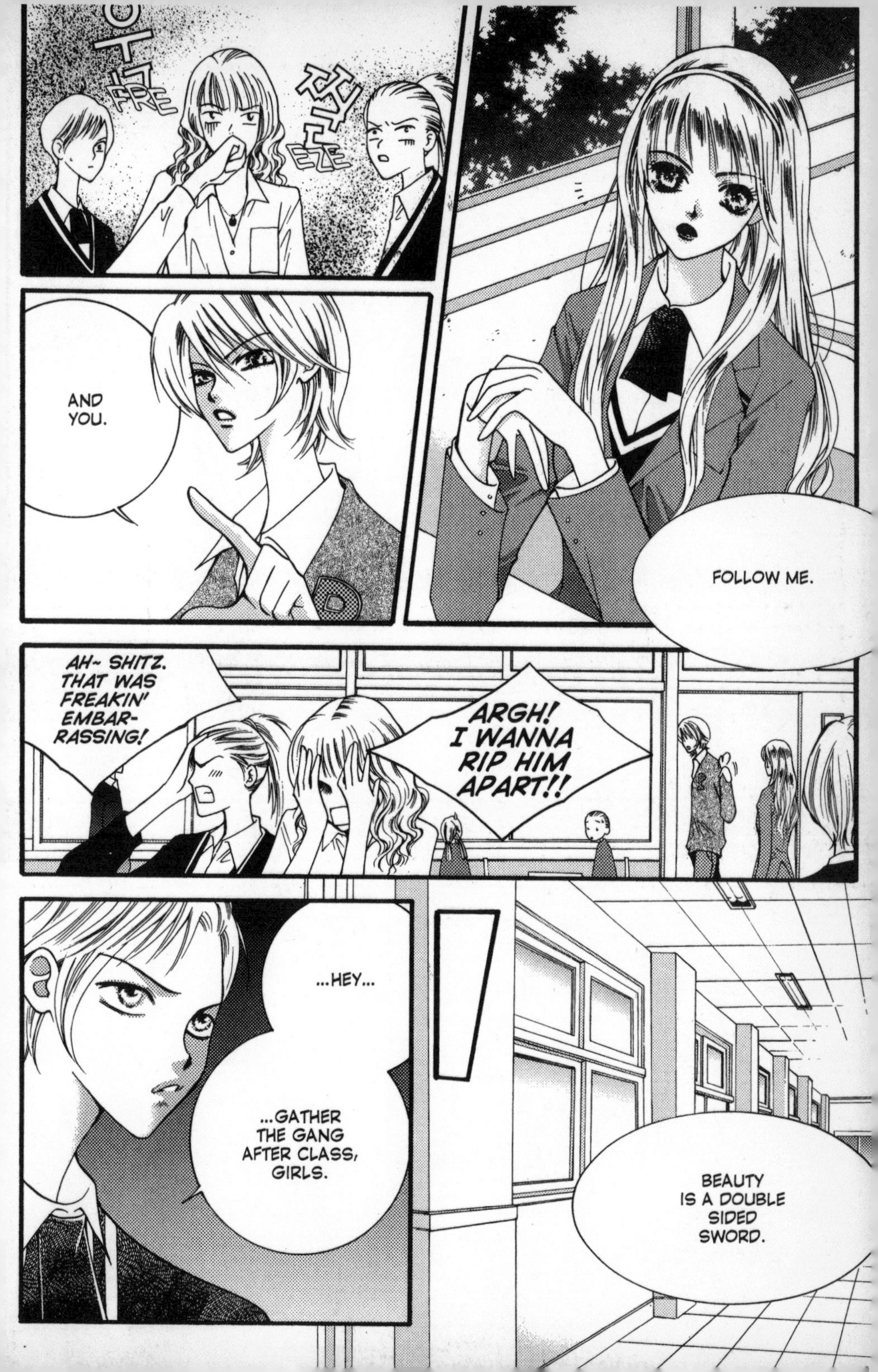
FRE
EZE
AND YOU.
FOLLOW ME.
AH~ SHITZ. THAT WAS FREAKIN' EMBARRASSING!
ARGH! I WANNA RIP HIM APART!!
...HEY...
...GATHER THE GANG AFTER CLASS, GIRLS.
BEAUTY IS A DOUBLE SIDED SWORD.

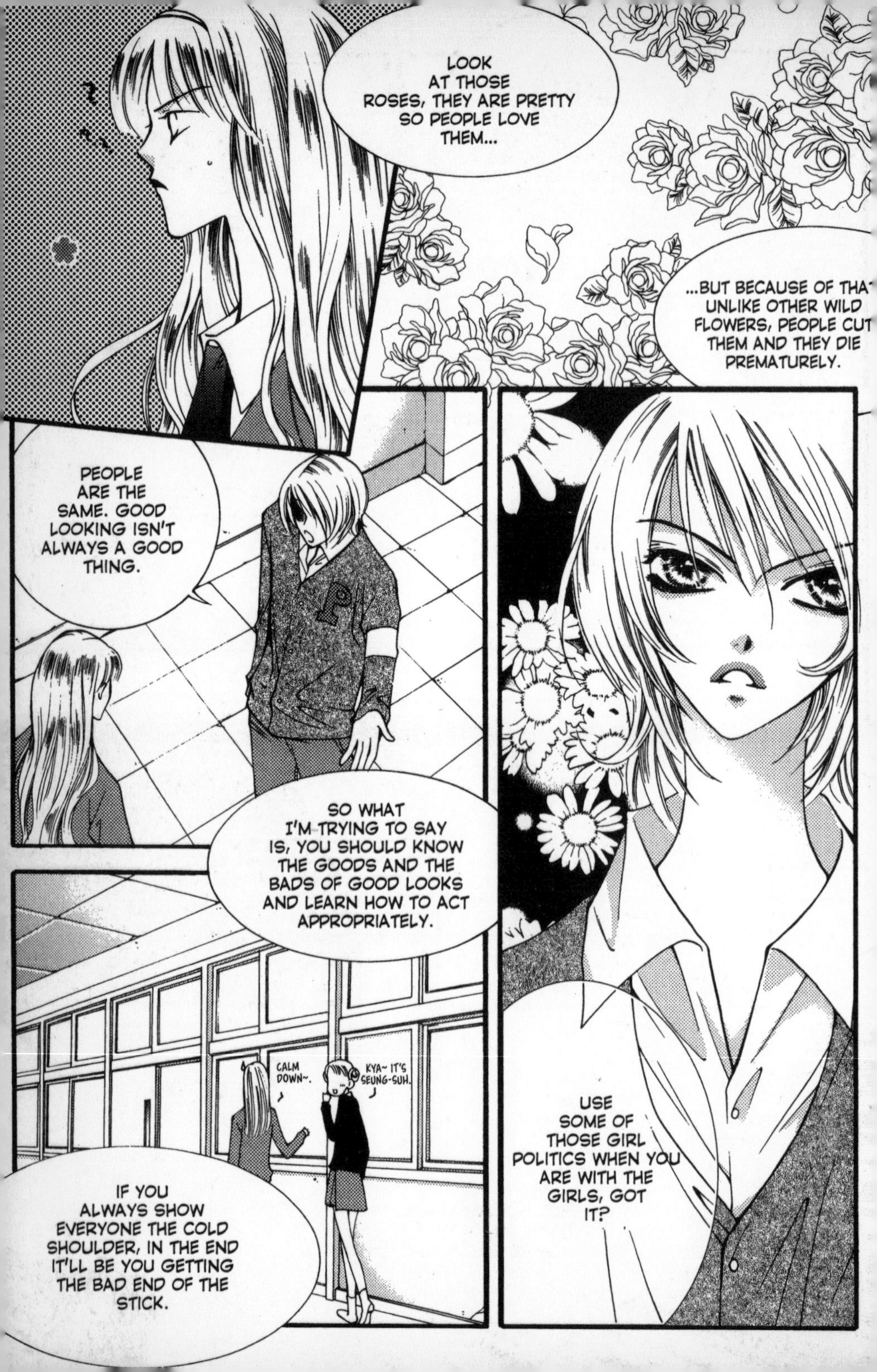

LOOK AT THOSE ROSES, THEY ARE PRETTY SO PEOPLE LOVE THEM...
...BUT BECAUSE OF THAT UNLIKE OTHER WILD FLOWERS, PEOPLE CUT THEM AND THEY DIE PREMATURELY.
PEOPLE ARE THE SAME. GOOD LOOKING ISN'T ALWAYS A GOOD THING.
SO WHAT I'M TRYING TO SAY IS, YOU SHOULD KNOW THE GOODS AND THE BADS OF GOOD LOOKS AND LEARN HOW TO ACT APPROPRIATELY.
CALM DOWN~.
KYA~ IT'S SEUNG-SUH.
IF YOU ALWAYS SHOW EVERYONE THE COLD SHOULDER, IN THE END IT'LL BE YOU GETTING THE BAD END OF THE STICK.
USE SOME OF THOSE GIRL POLITICS WHEN YOU ARE WITH THE GIRLS, GOT IT?

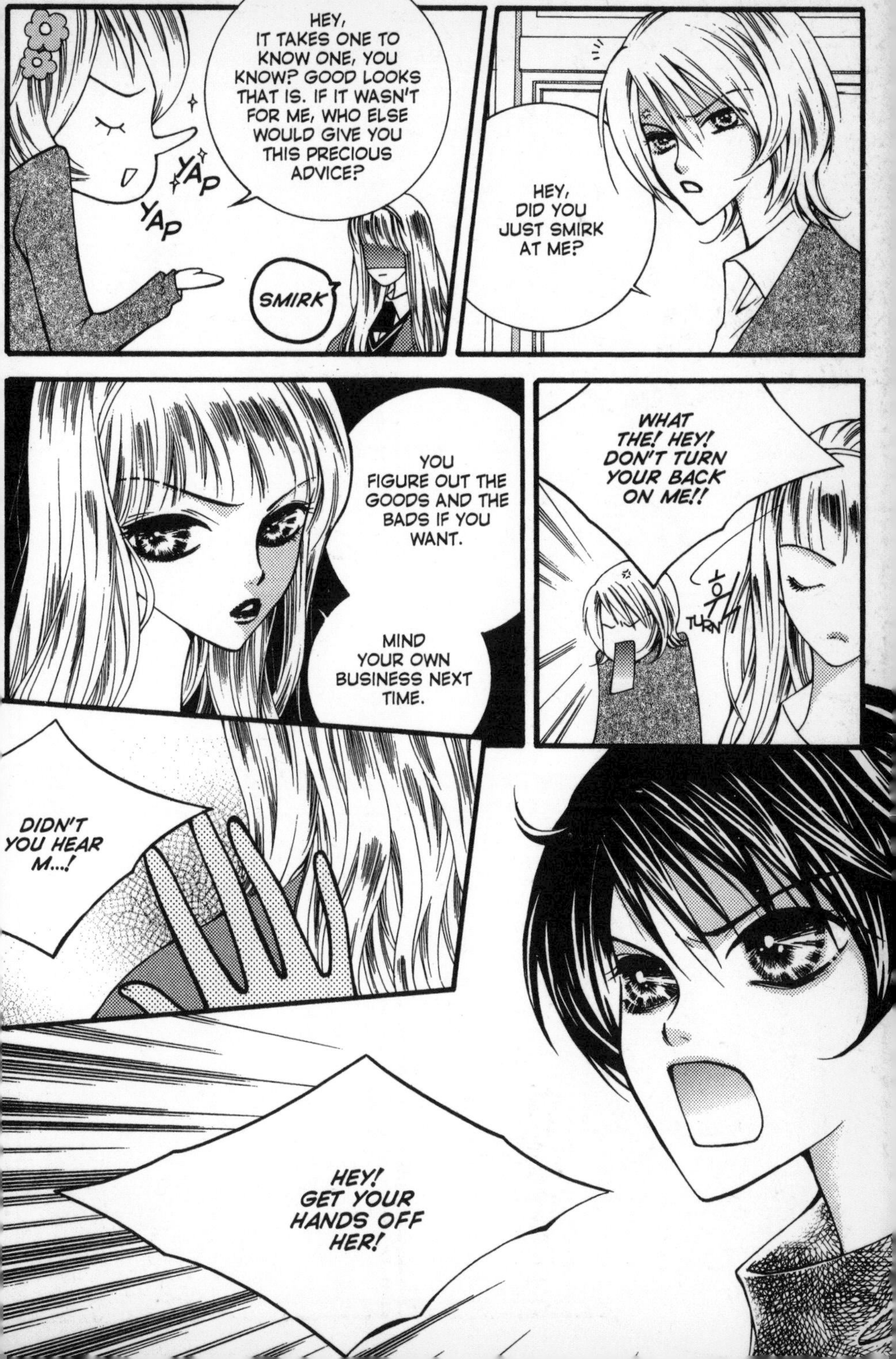
HEY, IT TAKES ONE TO KNOW ONE, YOU KNOW? GOOD LOOKS THAT IS. IF IT WASN'T FOR ME, WHO ELSE WOULD GIVE YOU THIS PRECIOUS ADVICE?
YAP YAP
SMIRK
HEY, DID YOU JUST SMIRK AT ME?
YOU FIGURE OUT THE GOODS AND THE BADS IF YOU WANT.
MIND YOUR OWN BUSINESS NEXT TIME.
WHAT THE! HEY! DON'T TURN YOUR BACK ON ME!!
TURN
DIDN'T YOU HEAR M...!
HEY! GET YOUR HANDS OFF HER!

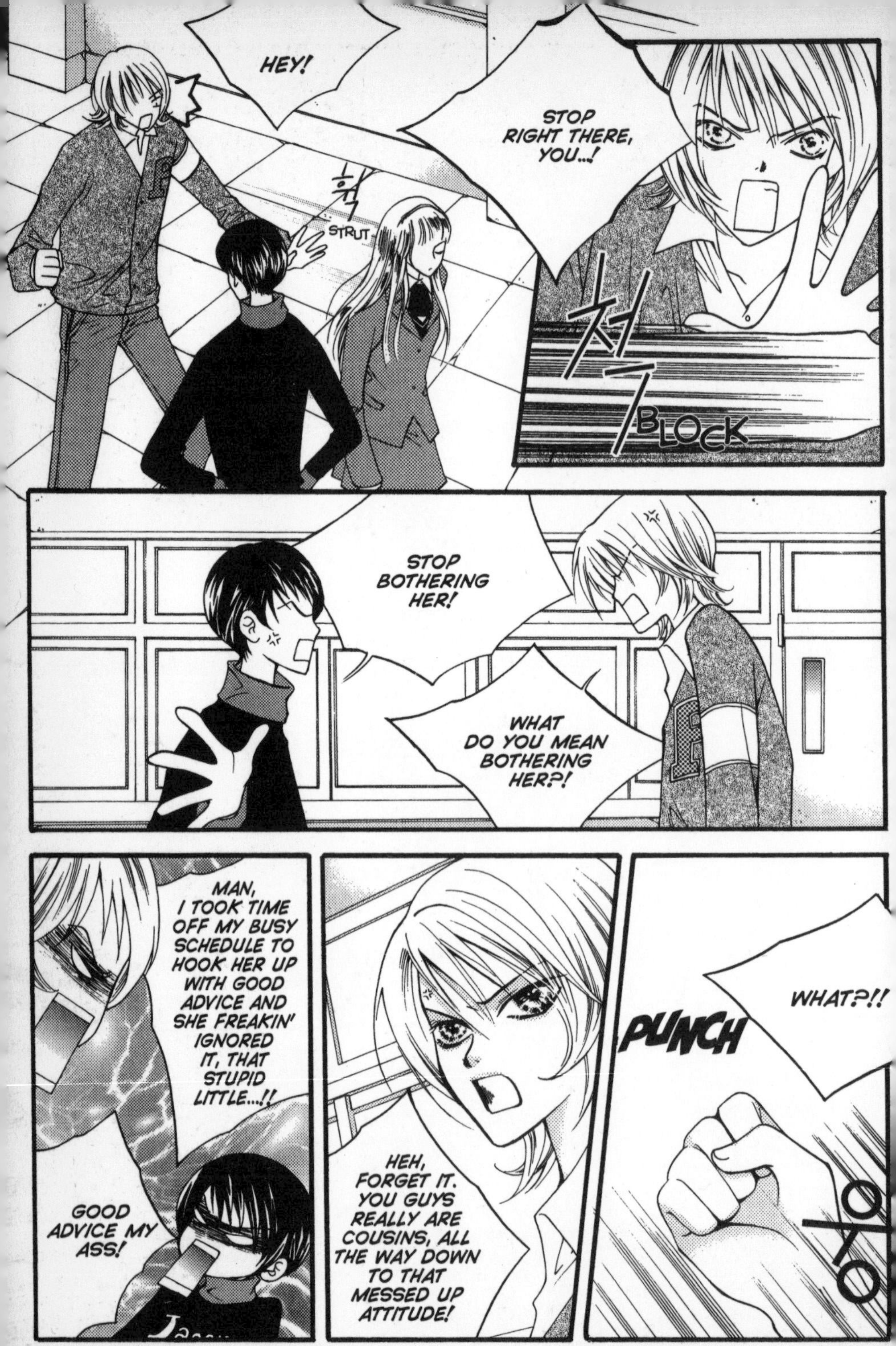
HEY!
STRUT
STOP RIGHT THERE, YOU...!
BLOCK
STOP BOTHERING HER!
WHAT DO YOU MEAN BOTHERING HER?!
MAN, I TOOK TIME OFF MY BUSY SCHEDULE TO HOOK HER UP WITH GOOD ADVICE AND SHE FREAKIN' IGNORED IT, THAT STUPID LITTLE...!!
GOOD ADVICE MY ASS!
HEH, FORGET IT. YOU GUYS REALLY ARE COUSINS, ALL THE WAY DOWN TO THAT MESSED UP ATTITUDE!
PUNCH
WHAT?!!

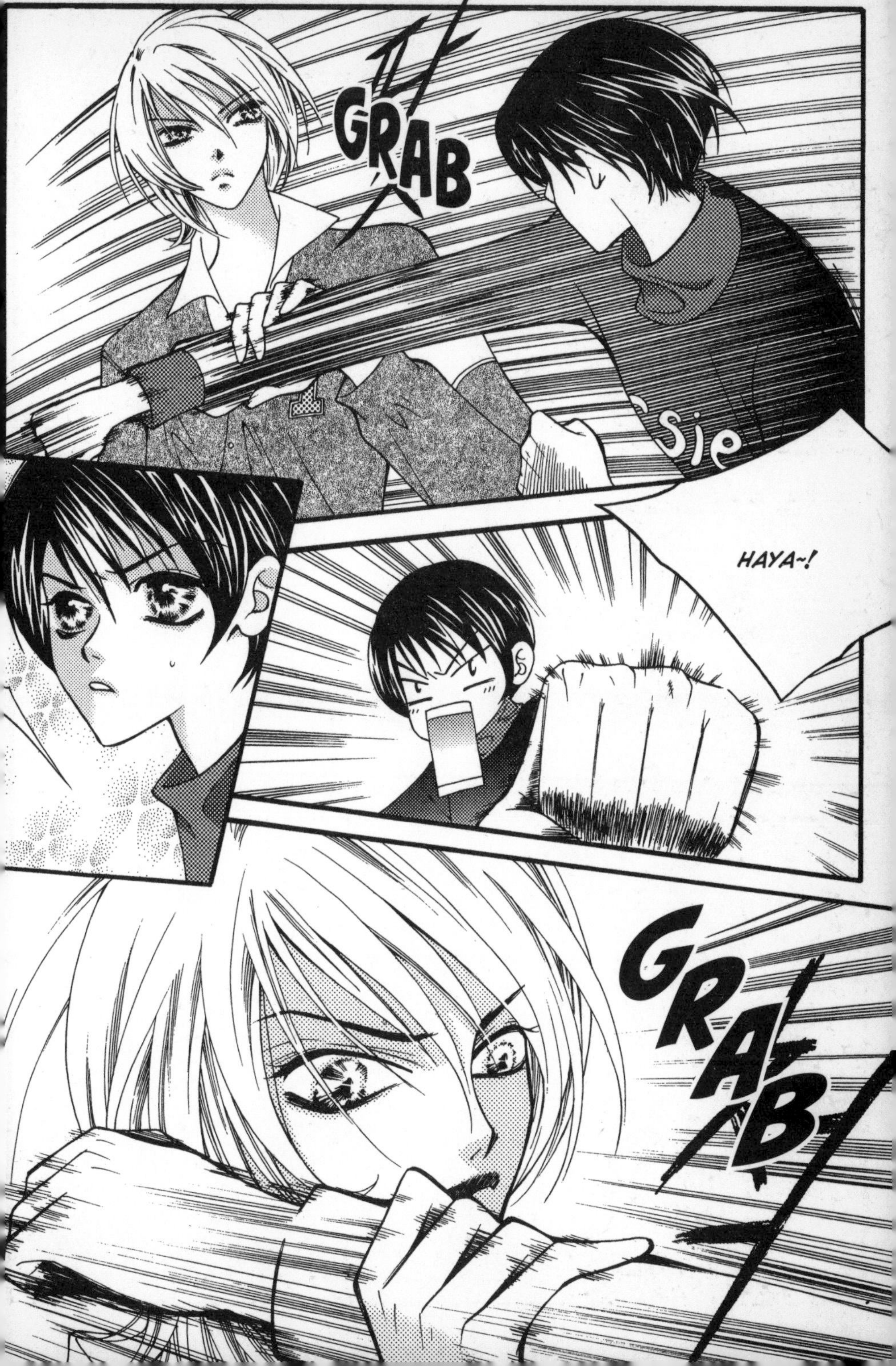
GRAB
HAYA~!
GRAB

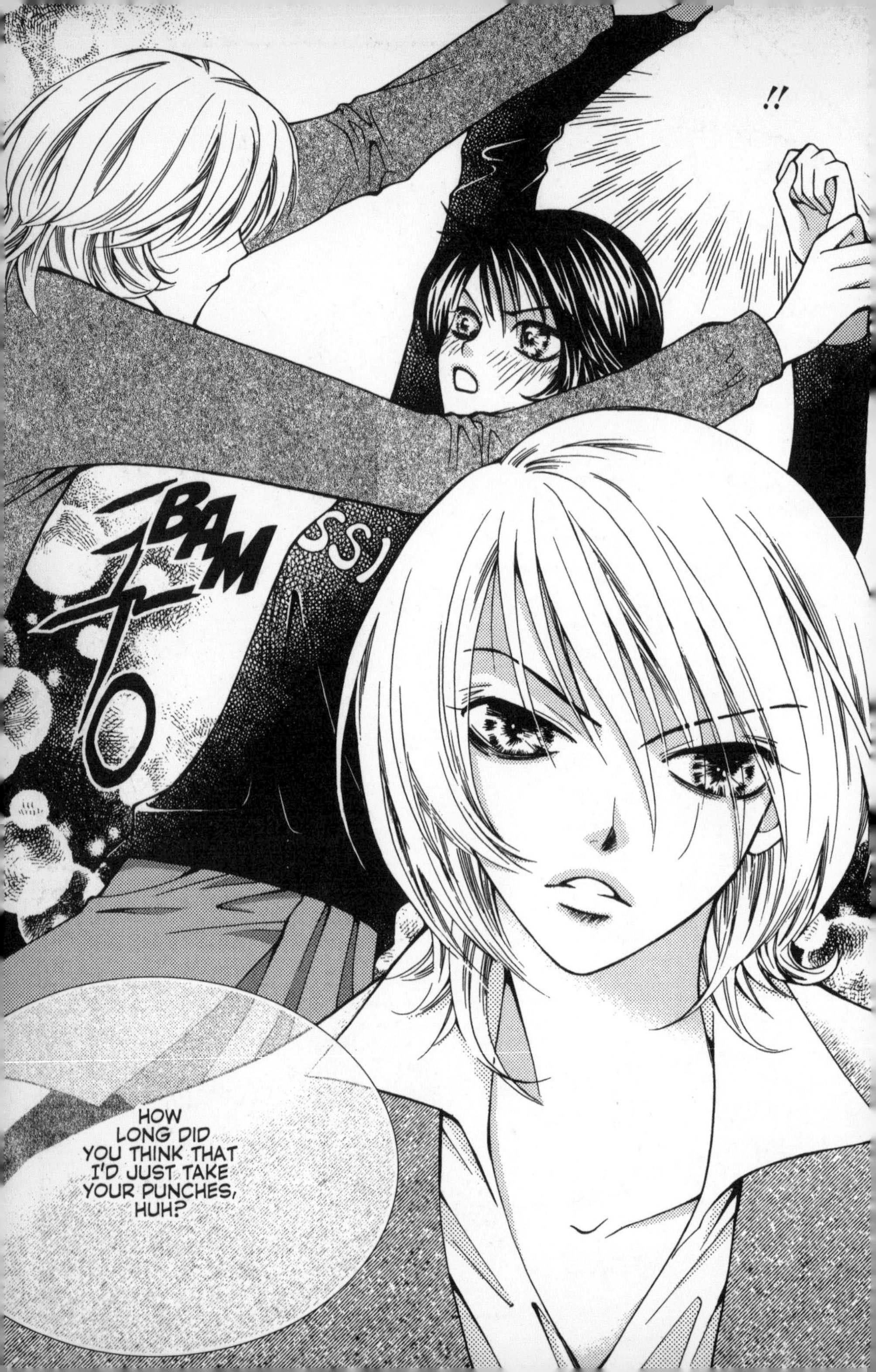
!!
BAM
HOW LONG DID YOU THINK THAT I'D JUST TAKE YOUR PUNCHES, HUH?

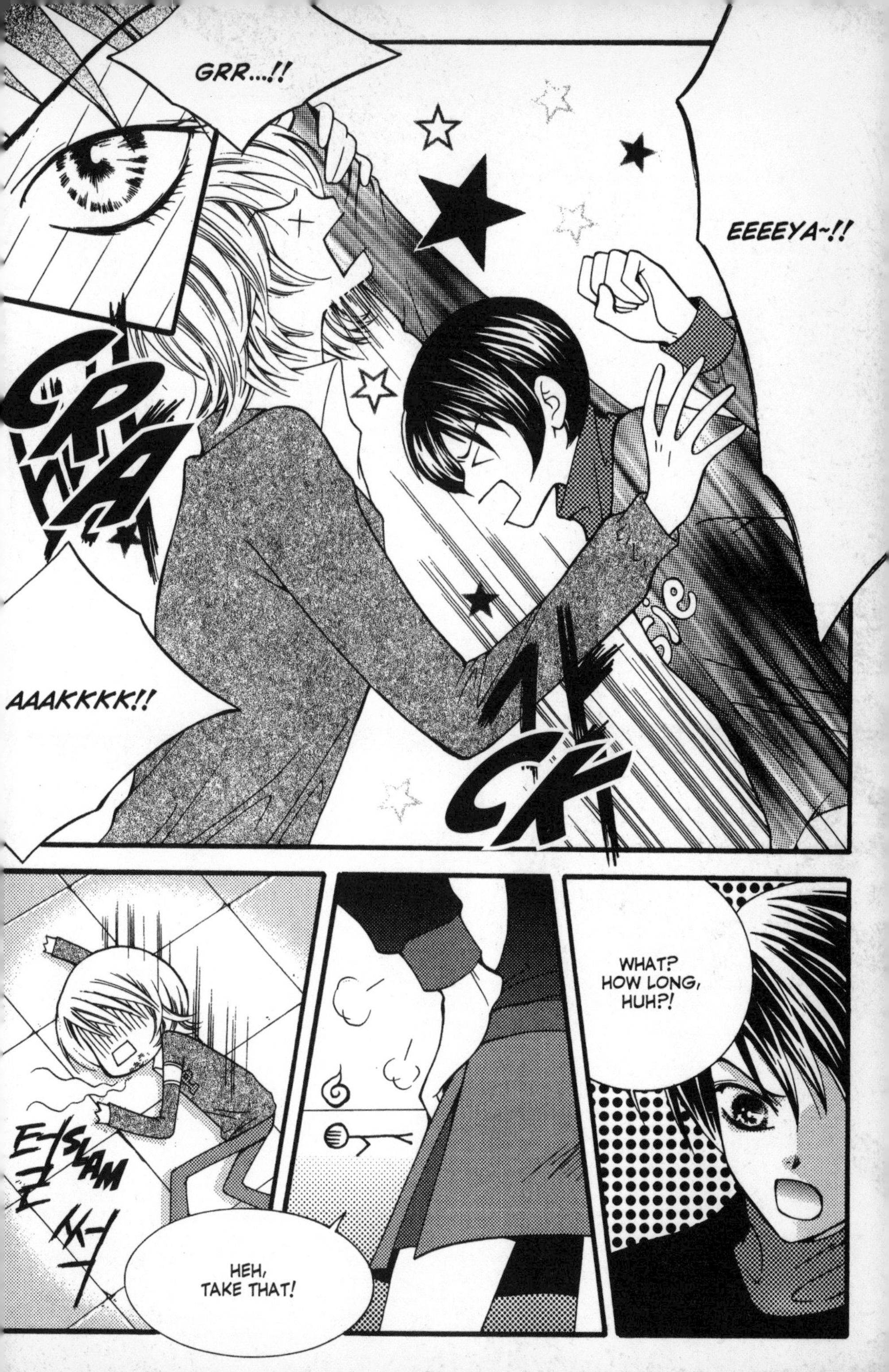
GRR...!!
EEEEYA~!!
AAAKKKK!!
SLAM
HEH, TAKE THAT!
WHAT? HOW LONG, HUH?!

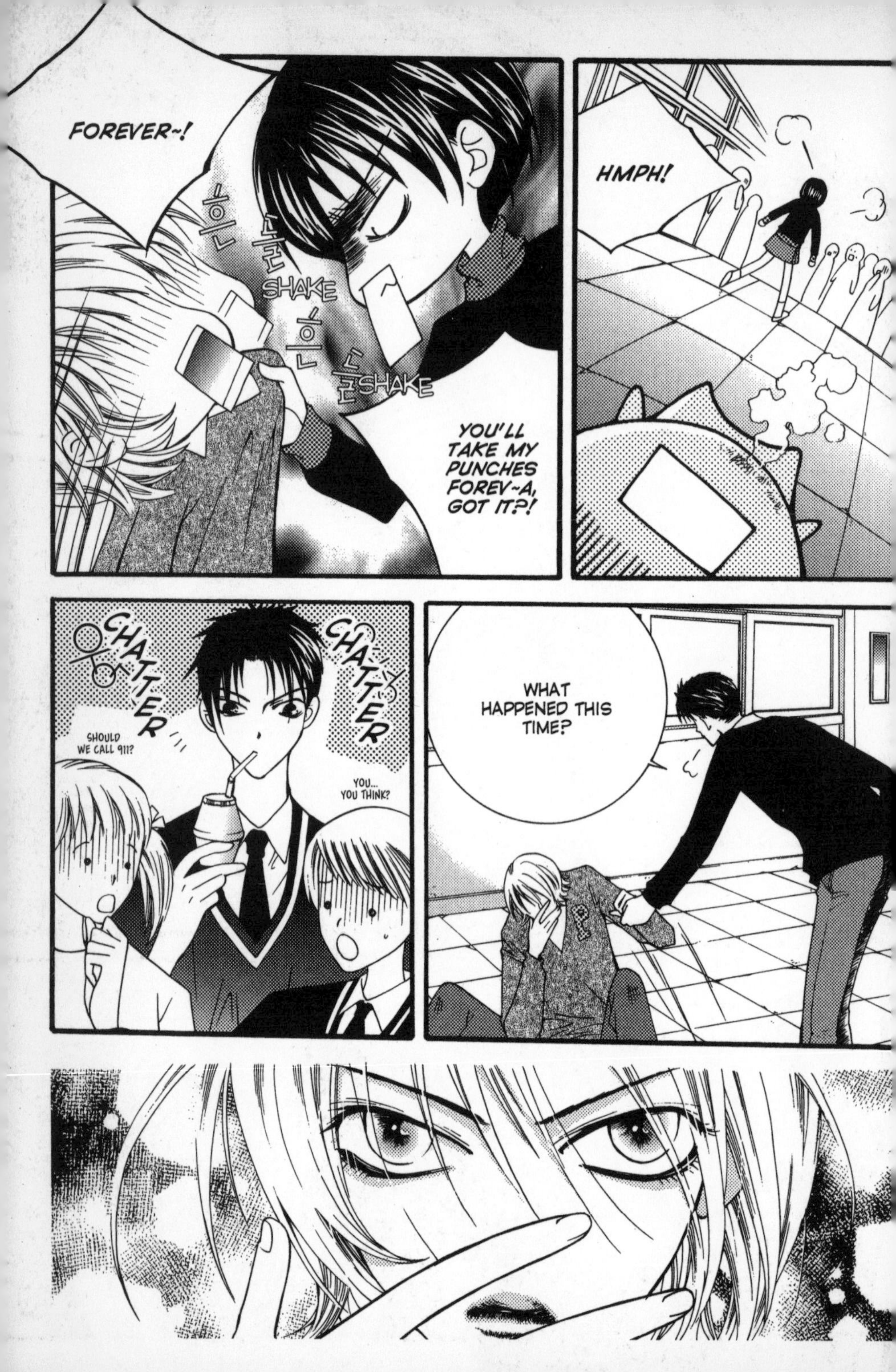
FOREVER~!
흔들 SHAKE
흔들 SHAKE
YOU'LL TAKE MY PUNCHES FOREV~A, GOT IT?!
HMPH!
CHATTER
SHOULD WE CALL 911?
YOU... YOU THINK?
CHATTER
WHAT HAPPENED THIS TIME?

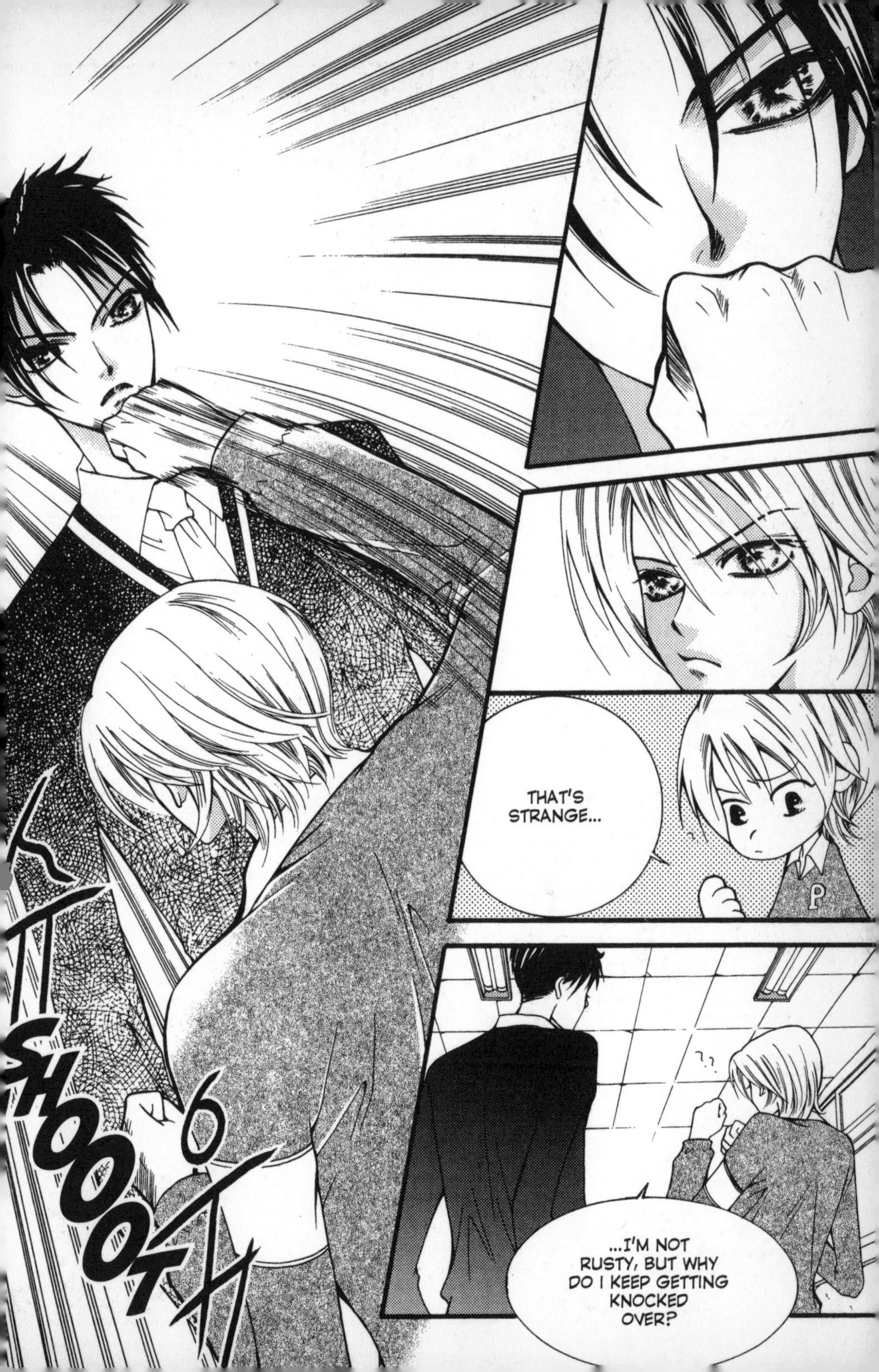
SHOOOT
THAT'S STRANGE...
...I'M NOT RUSTY, BUT WHY DO I KEEP GETTING KNOCKED OVER?

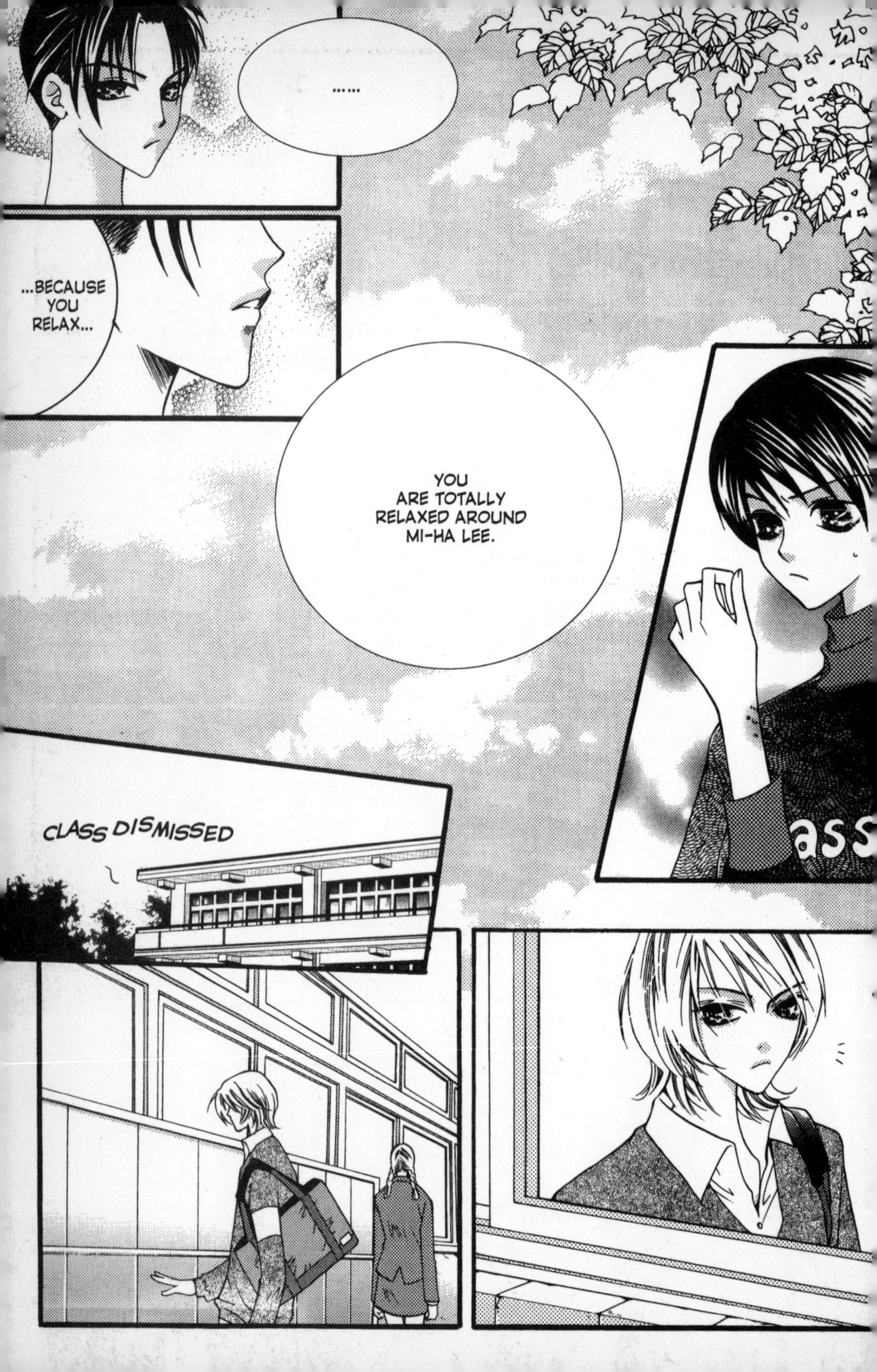
......
...BECAUSE YOU RELAX...
YOU ARE TOTALLY RELAXED AROUND MI-HA LEE.
CLASS DISMISSED

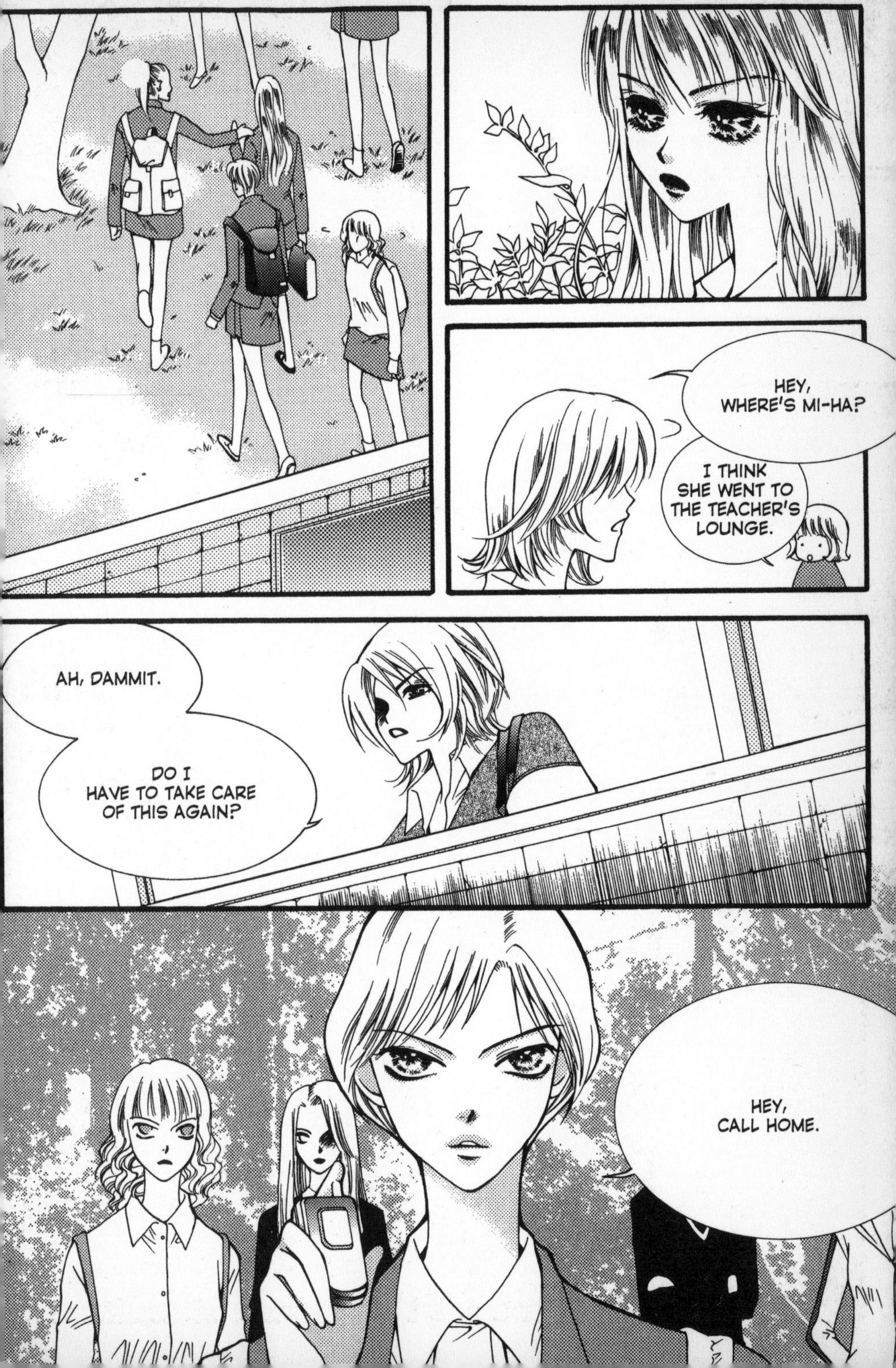
HEY, WHERE'S MI-HA?
I THINK SHE WENT TO THE TEACHER'S LOUNGE.
AH, DAMMIT.
DO I HAVE TO TAKE CARE OF THIS AGAIN?
HEY, CALL HOME.

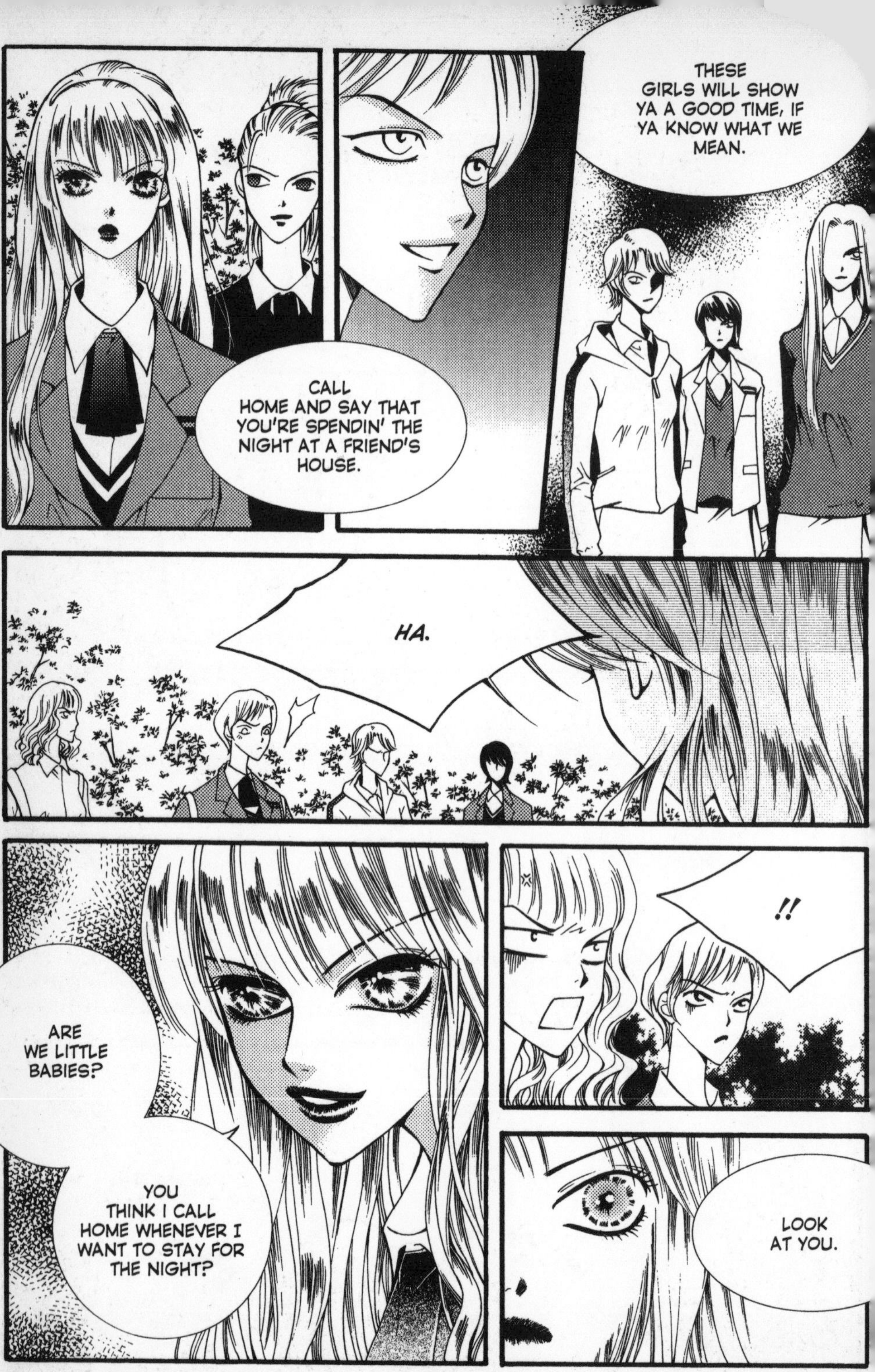
CALL HOME AND SAY THAT YOU'RE SPENDIN' THE NIGHT AT A FRIEND'S HOUSE.
THESE GIRLS WILL SHOW YA A GOOD TIME, IF YA KNOW WHAT WE MEAN.
HA.
ARE WE LITTLE BABIES?
YOU THINK I CALL HOME WHENEVER I WANT TO STAY FOR THE NIGHT?
!!
LOOK AT YOU.

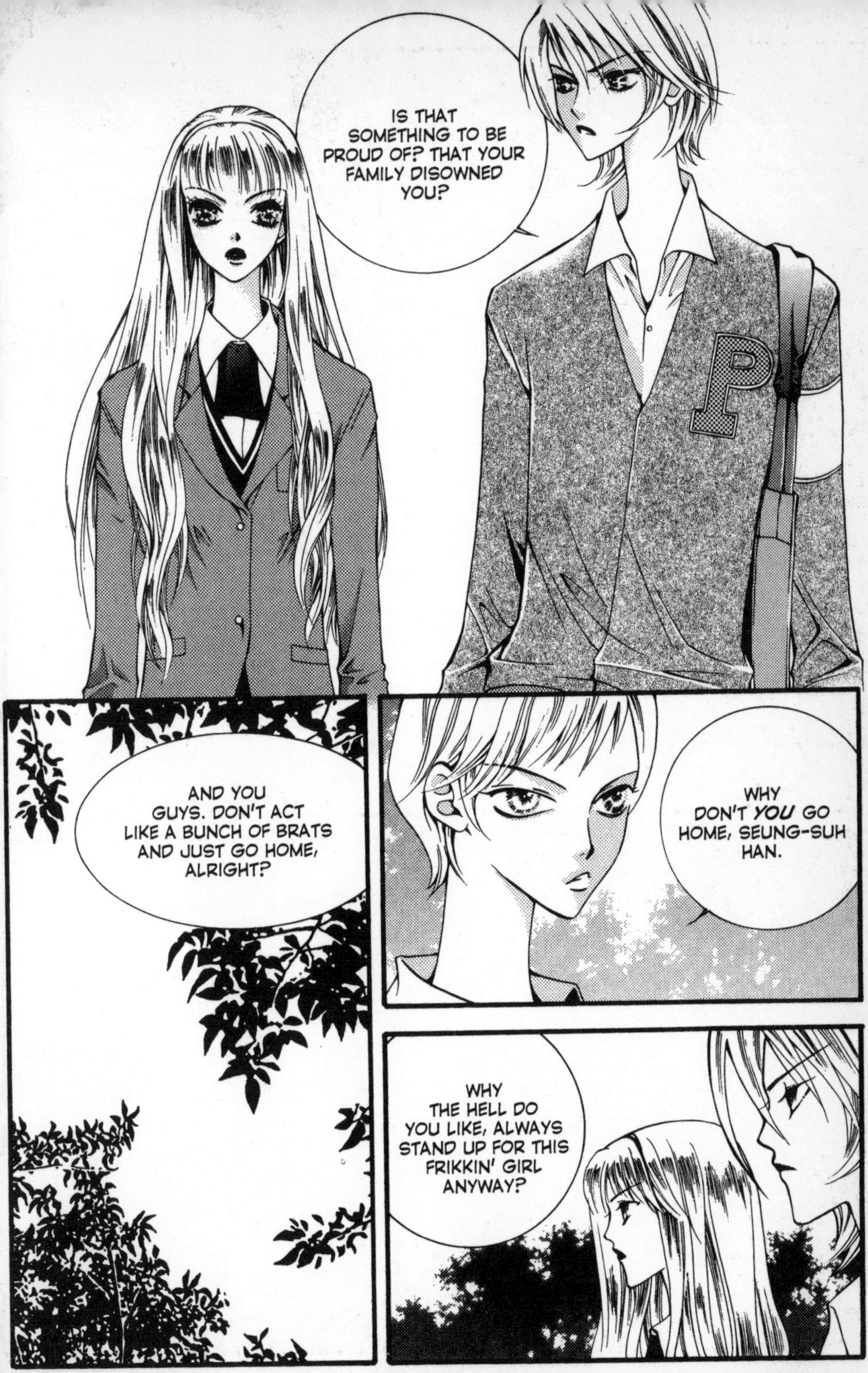
IS THAT SOMETHING TO BE PROUD OF? THAT YOUR FAMILY DISOWNED YOU?
AND YOU GUYS. DON'T ACT LIKE A BUNCH OF BRATS AND JUST GO HOME, ALRIGHT?
WHY DON'T *YOU* GO HOME, SEUNG-SUH HAN.
WHY THE HELL DO YOU LIKE, ALWAYS STAND UP FOR THIS FRIKKIN' GIRL ANYWAY?

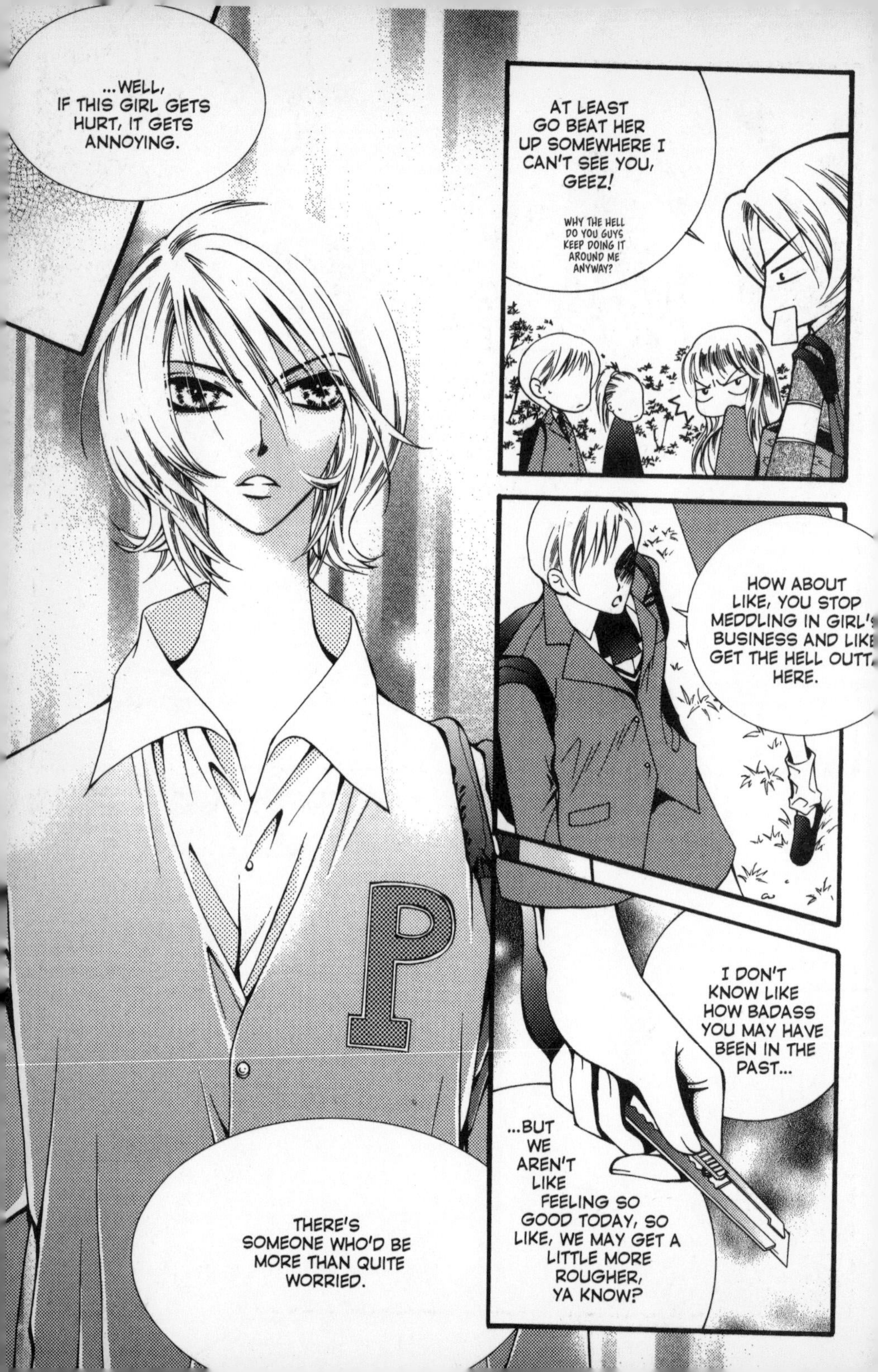
...WELL, IF THIS GIRL GETS HURT, IT GETS ANNOYING.
THERE'S SOMEONE WHO'D BE MORE THAN QUITE WORRIED.
AT LEAST GO BEAT HER UP SOMEWHERE I CAN'T SEE YOU, GEEZ!
WHY THE HELL DO YOU GUYS KEEP DOING IT AROUND ME ANYWAY?
HOW ABOUT LIKE, YOU STOP MEDDLING IN GIRL'S BUSINESS AND LIKE GET THE HELL OUTT HERE.
I DON'T KNOW LIKE HOW BADASS YOU MAY HAVE BEEN IN THE PAST...
...BUT WE AREN'T LIKE FEELING SO GOOD TODAY, SO LIKE, WE MAY GET A LITTLE MORE ROUGHER, YA KNOW?

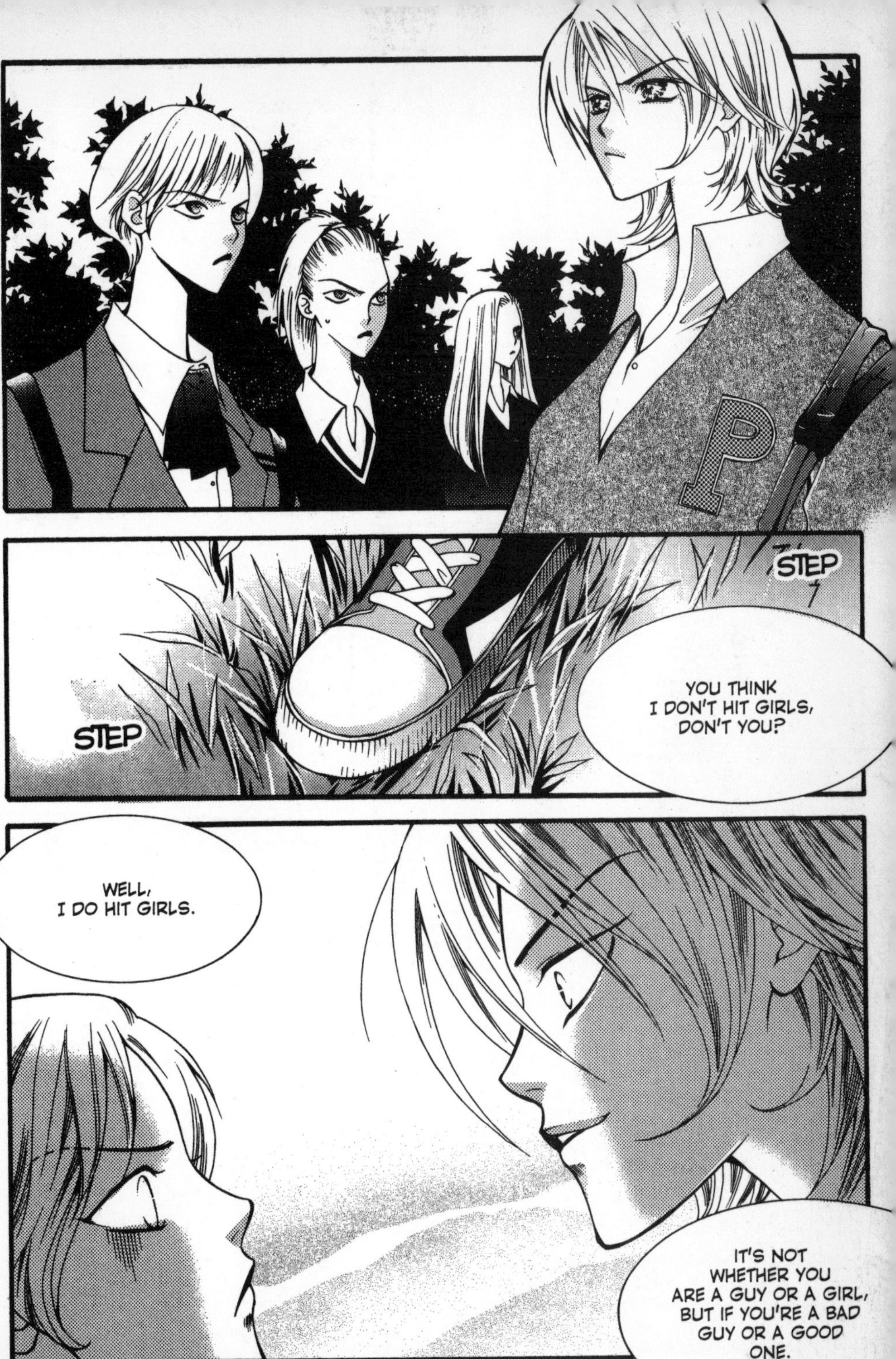
STEP
STEP
YOU THINK I DON'T HIT GIRLS, DON'T YOU?
WELL, I DO HIT GIRLS.
IT'S NOT WHETHER YOU ARE A GUY OR A GIRL, BUT IF YOU'RE A BAD GUY OR A GOOD ONE.

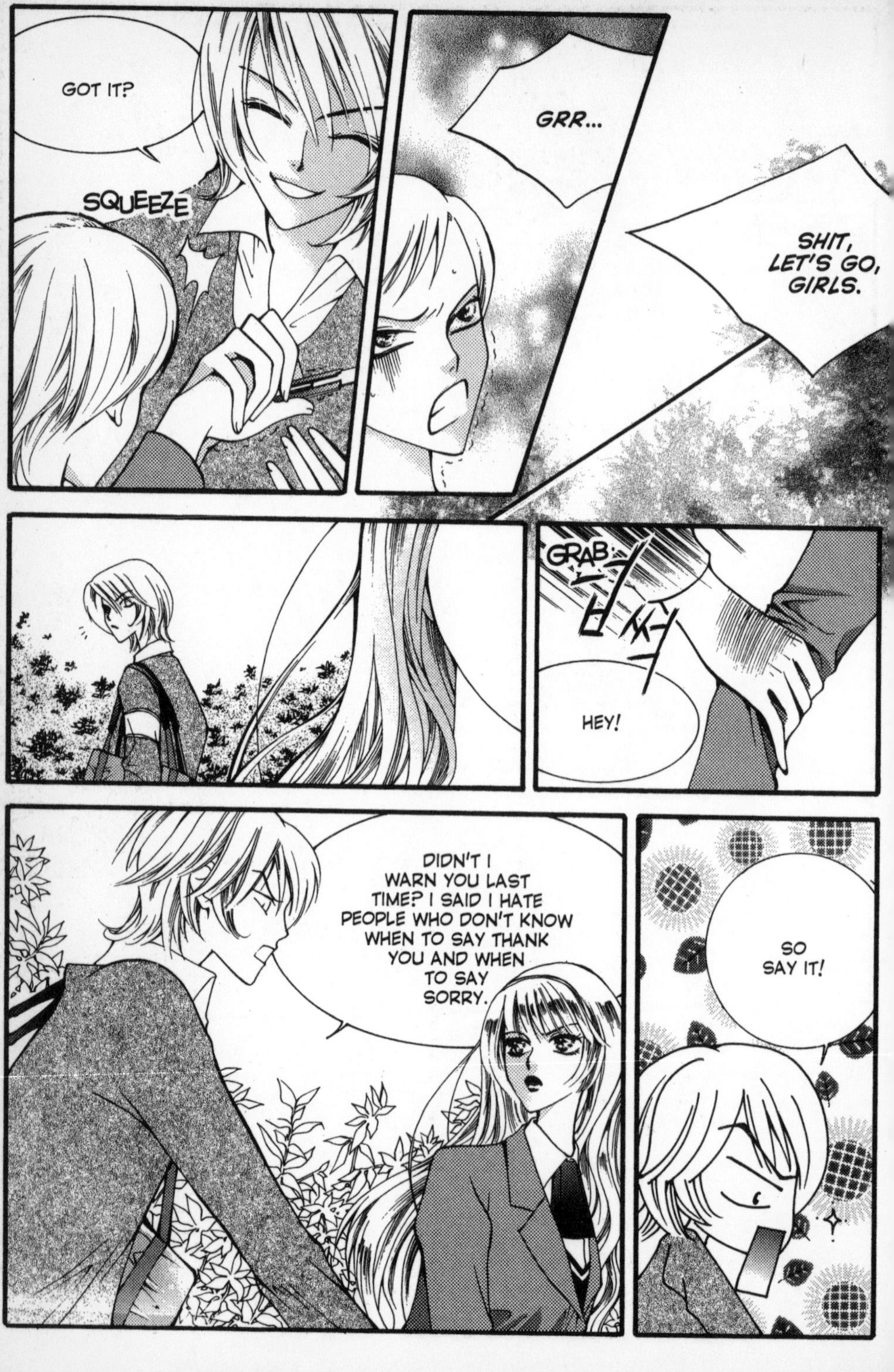
GOT IT?
SQUEEZE
GRR...
SHIT, LET'S GO, GIRLS.
GRAB
HEY!
DIDN'T I WARN YOU LAST TIME? I SAID I HATE PEOPLE WHO DON'T KNOW WHEN TO SAY THANK YOU AND WHEN TO SAY SORRY.
SO SAY IT!

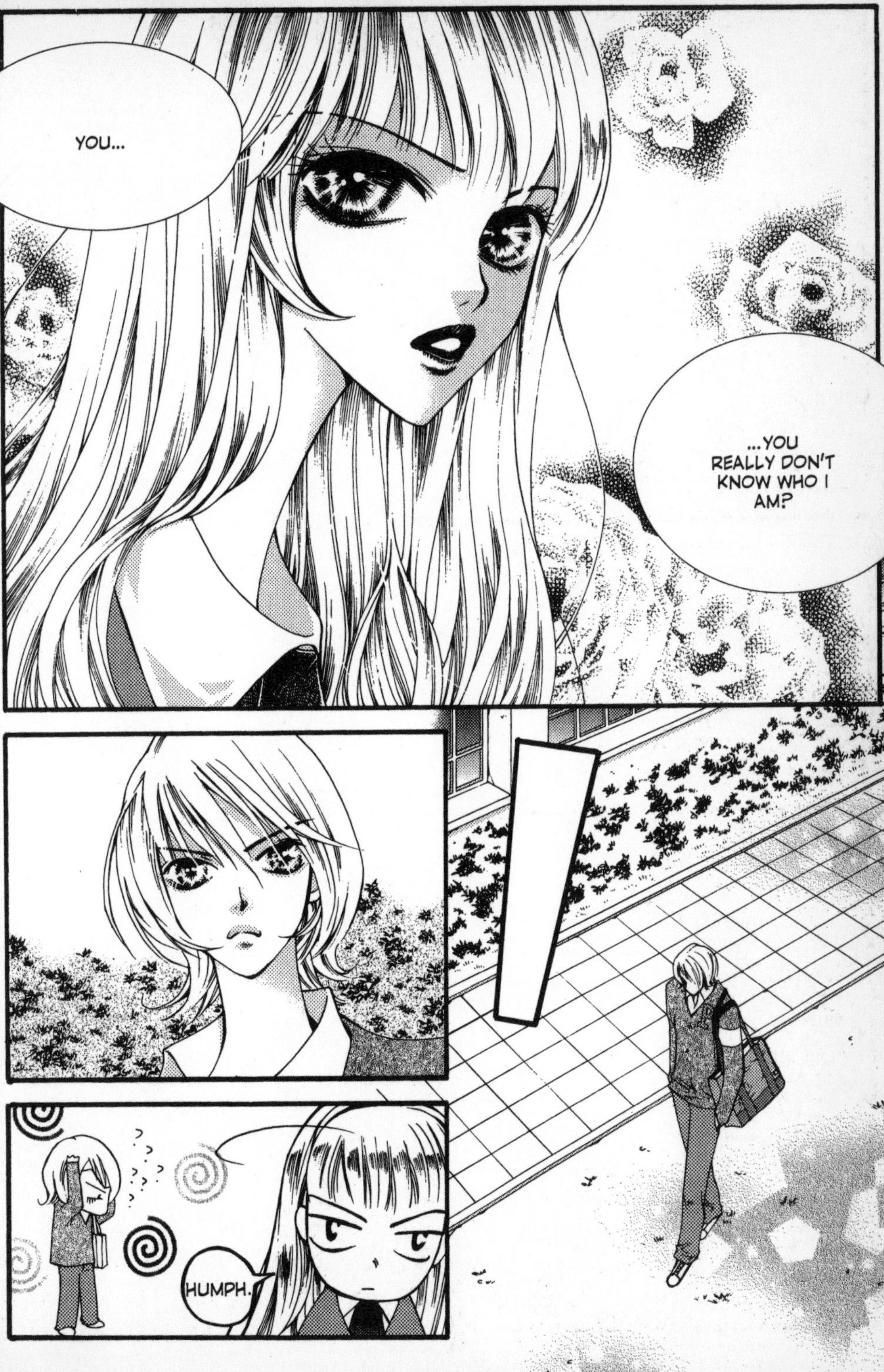
YOU...
...YOU REALLY DON'T KNOW WHO I AM?
!
HUMPH.

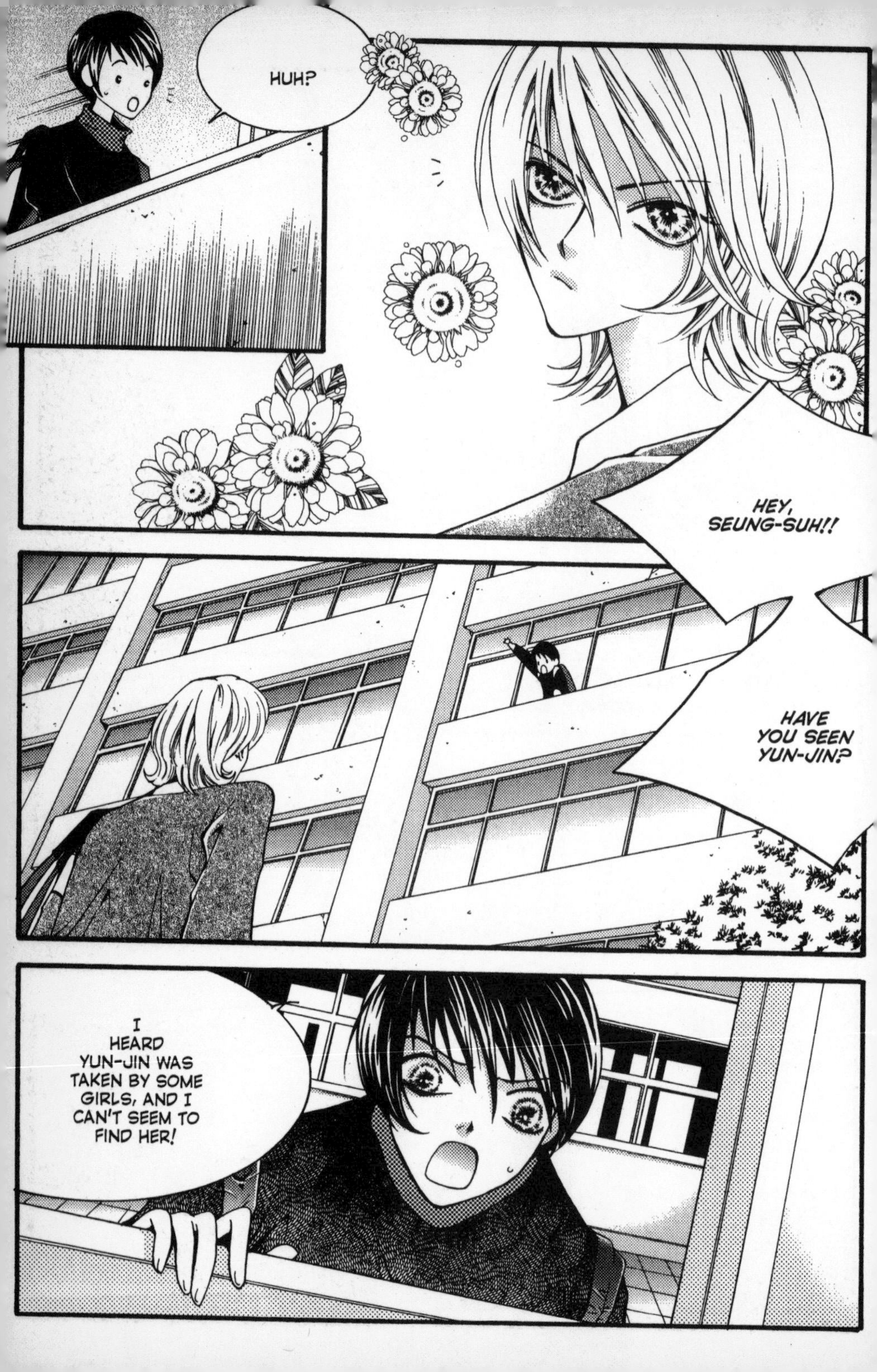
HUH?
HEY, SEUNG-SUH!!
HAVE YOU SEEN YUN-JIN?
I HEARD YUN-JIN WAS TAKEN BY SOME GIRLS, AND I CAN'T SEEM TO FIND HER!

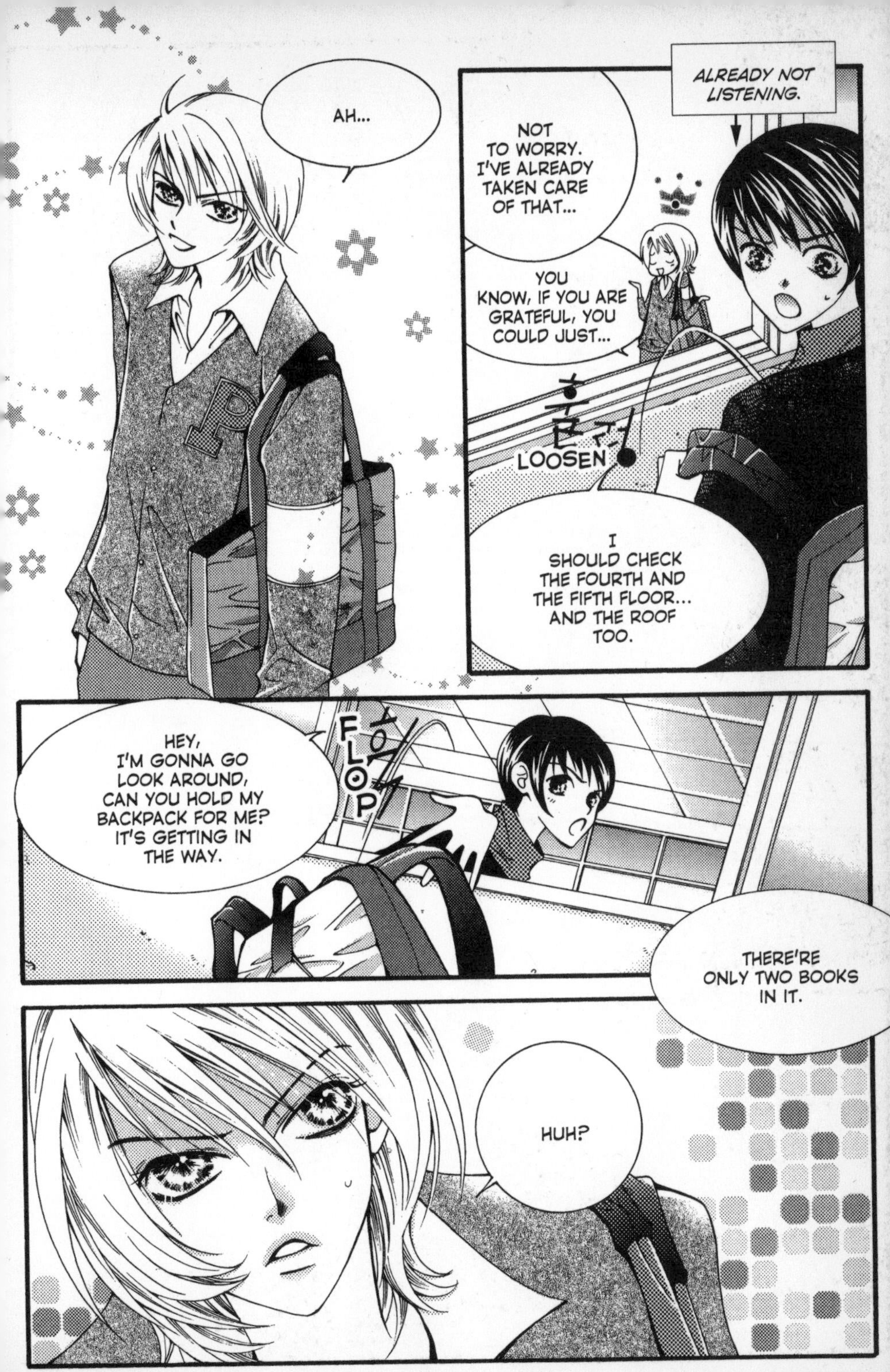
AH...
ALREADY NOT LISTENING.
NOT TO WORRY. I'VE ALREADY TAKEN CARE OF THAT...
YOU KNOW, IF YOU ARE GRATEFUL, YOU COULD JUST...
LOOSEN
I SHOULD CHECK THE FOURTH AND THE FIFTH FLOOR... AND THE ROOF TOO.
HEY, I'M GONNA GO LOOK AROUND, CAN YOU HOLD MY BACKPACK FOR ME? IT'S GETTING IN THE WAY.
FLOP
THERE'RE ONLY TWO BOOKS IN IT.
HUH?

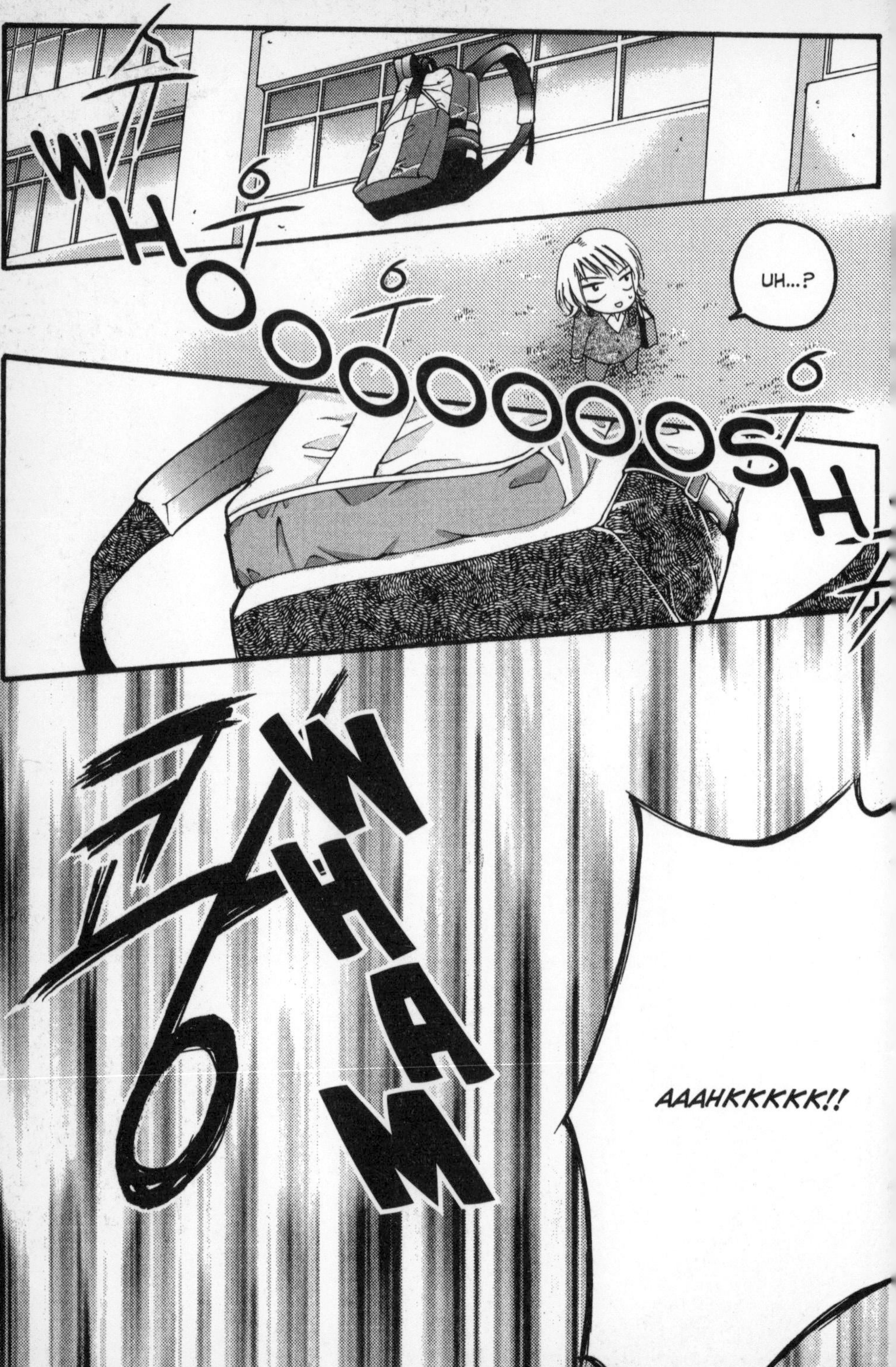
WHOOOOOOOSH
UH...?
WHAM
AAAHKKKKK!!

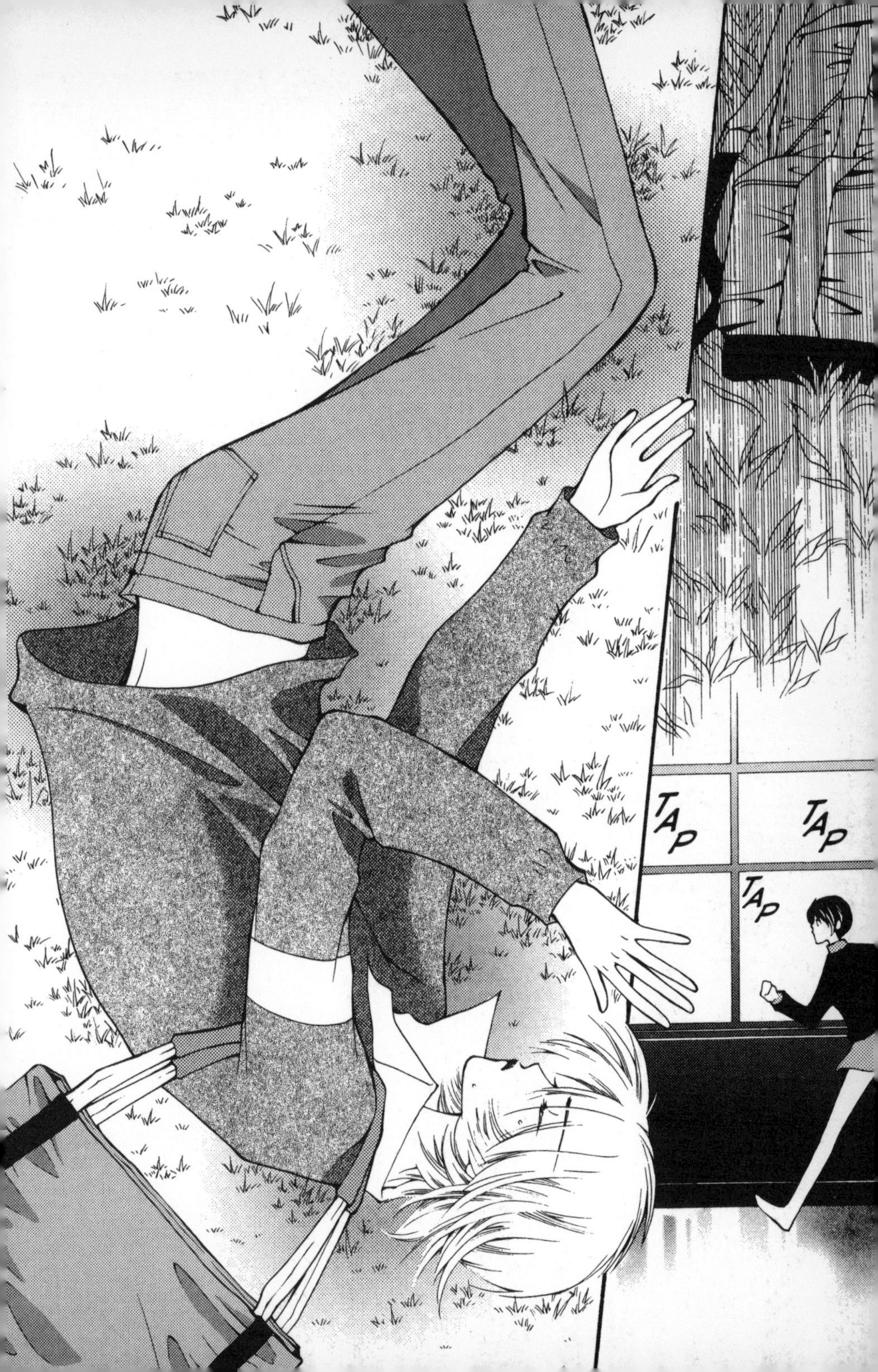
TAP
TAP
TAP

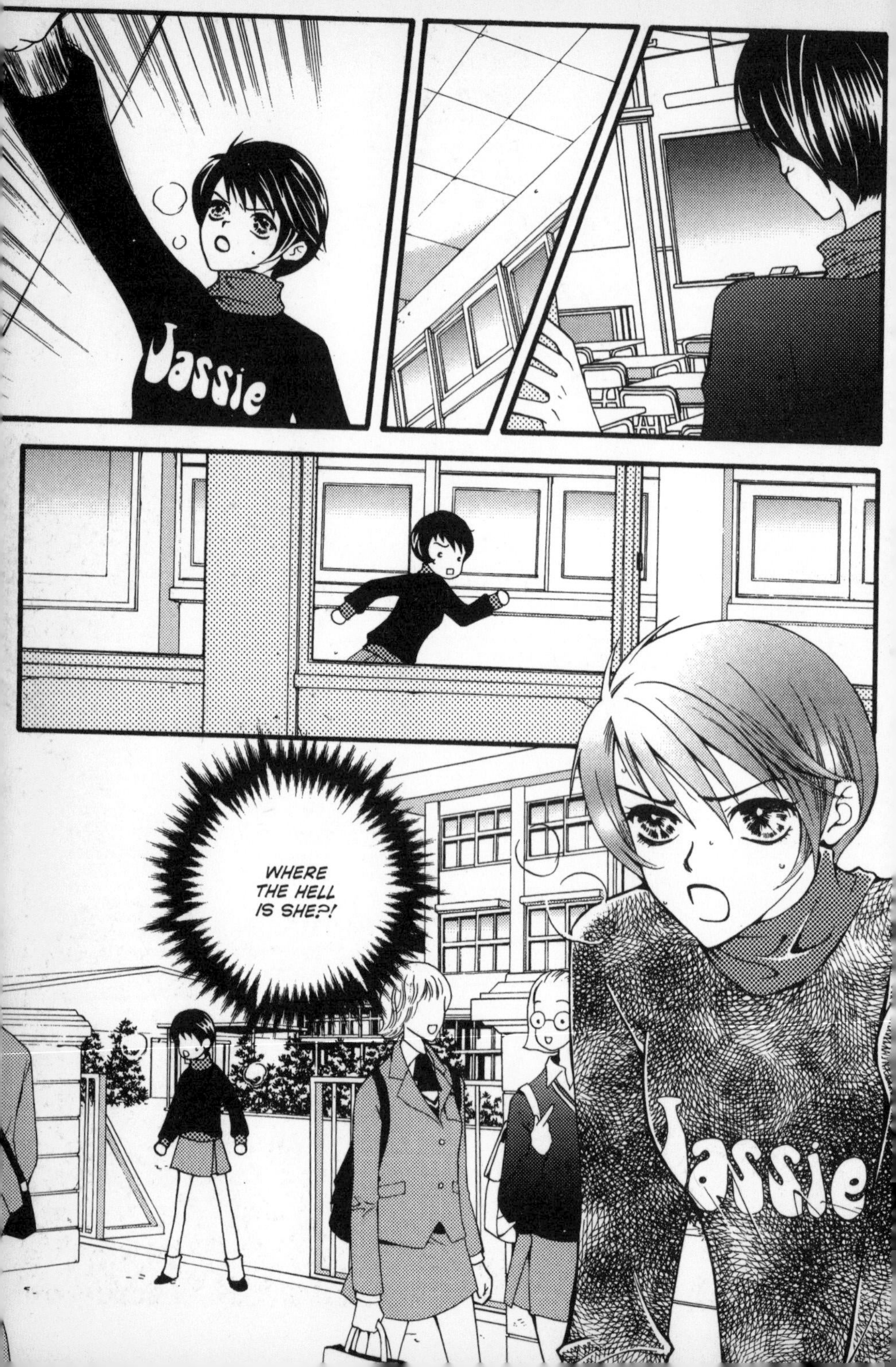
Jassie
WHERE THE HELL IS SHE?!
Jassie

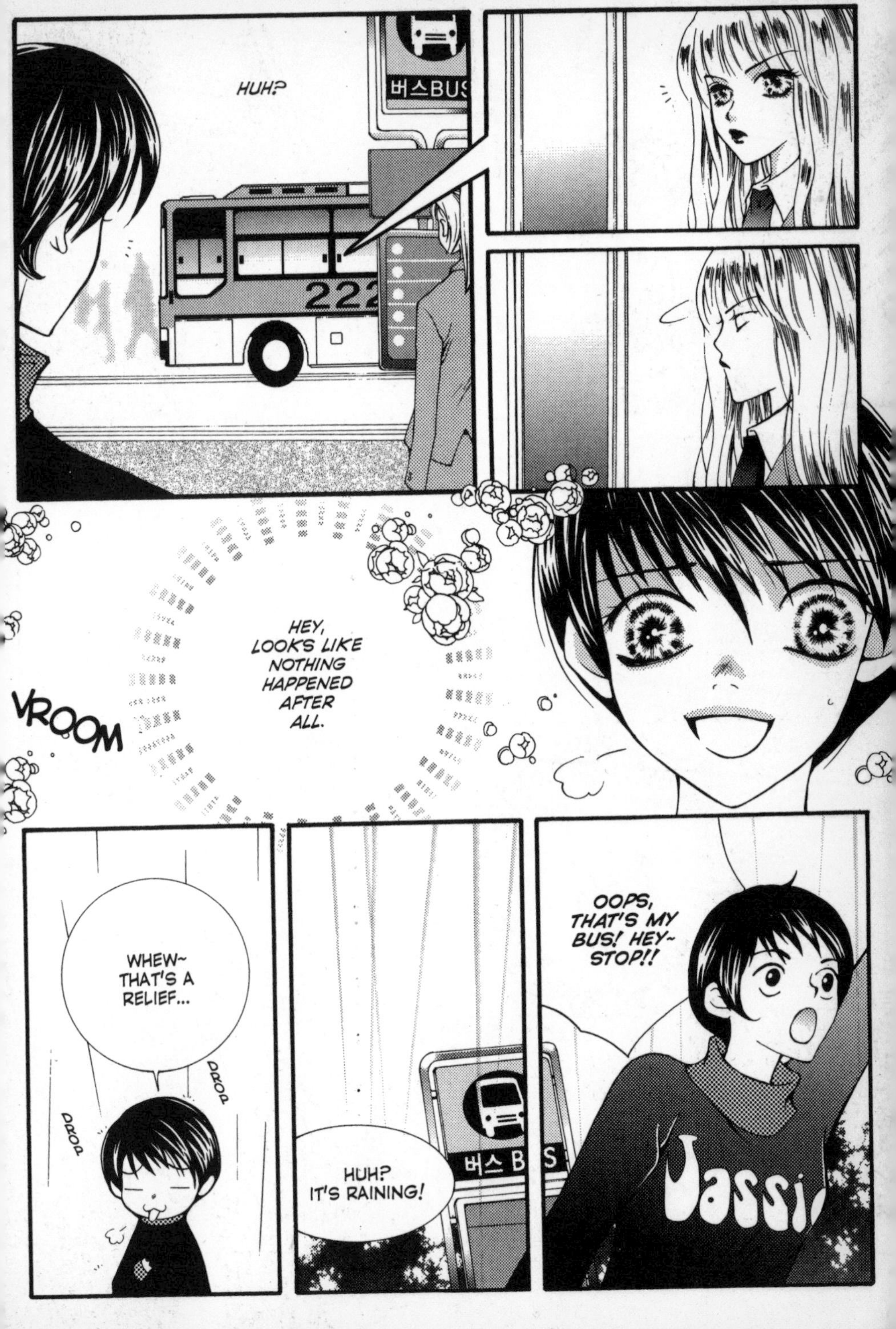
버스BUS
HUH?
VROOM
HEY, LOOKS LIKE NOTHING HAPPENED AFTER ALL.
WHEW~ THAT'S A RELIEF...
DROP
DROP
HUH? IT'S RAINING!
OOPS, THAT'S MY BUS! HEY~ STOP!!

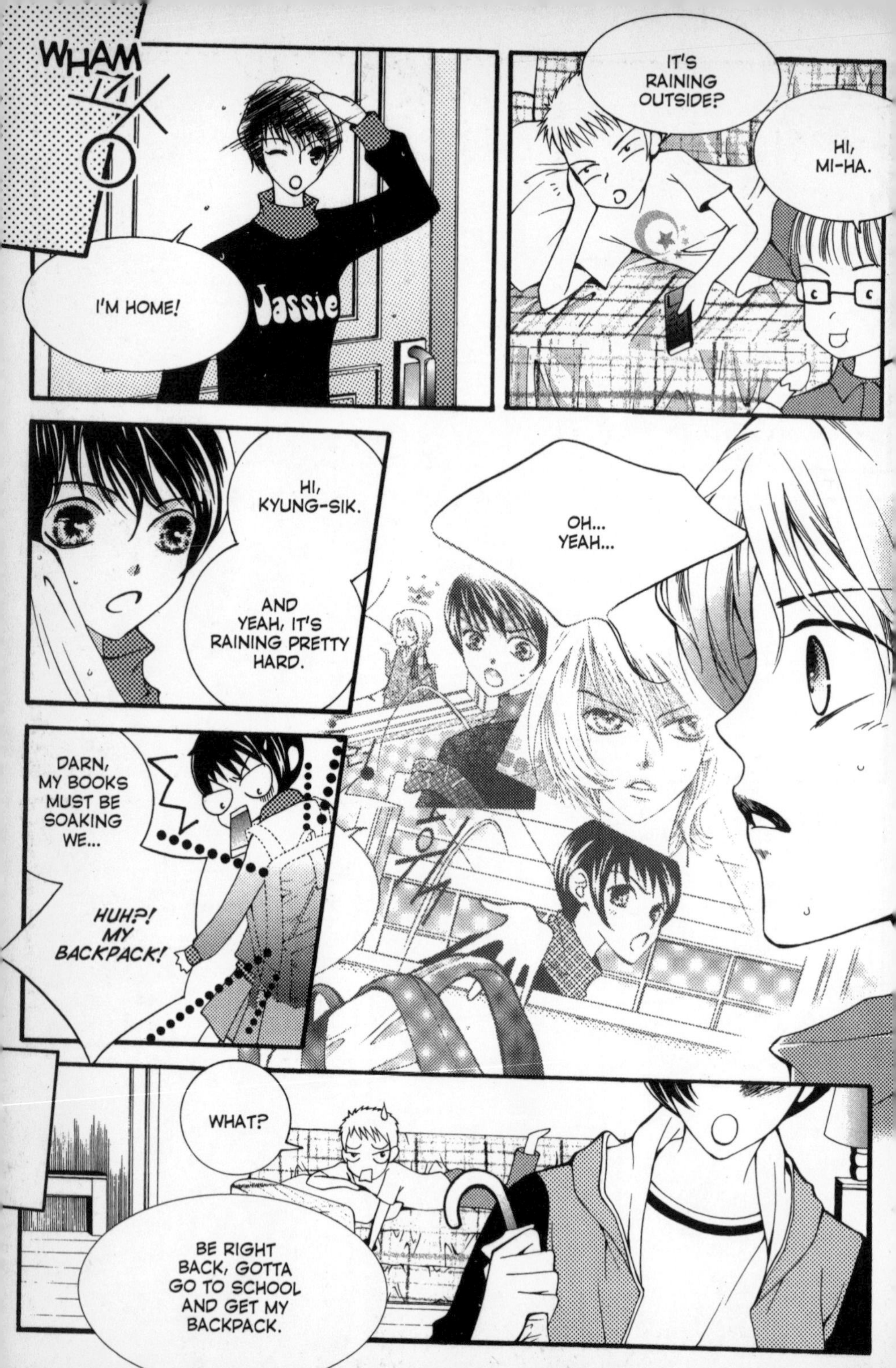
WHAM
I'M HOME!
IT'S RAINING OUTSIDE?
HI, MI-HA.
HI, KYUNG-SIK.
AND YEAH, IT'S RAINING PRETTY HARD.
DARN, MY BOOKS MUST BE SOAKING WE...
HUH?! MY BACKPACK!
OH... YEAH...
WHAT?
BE RIGHT BACK, GOTTA GO TO SCHOOL AND GET MY BACKPACK.

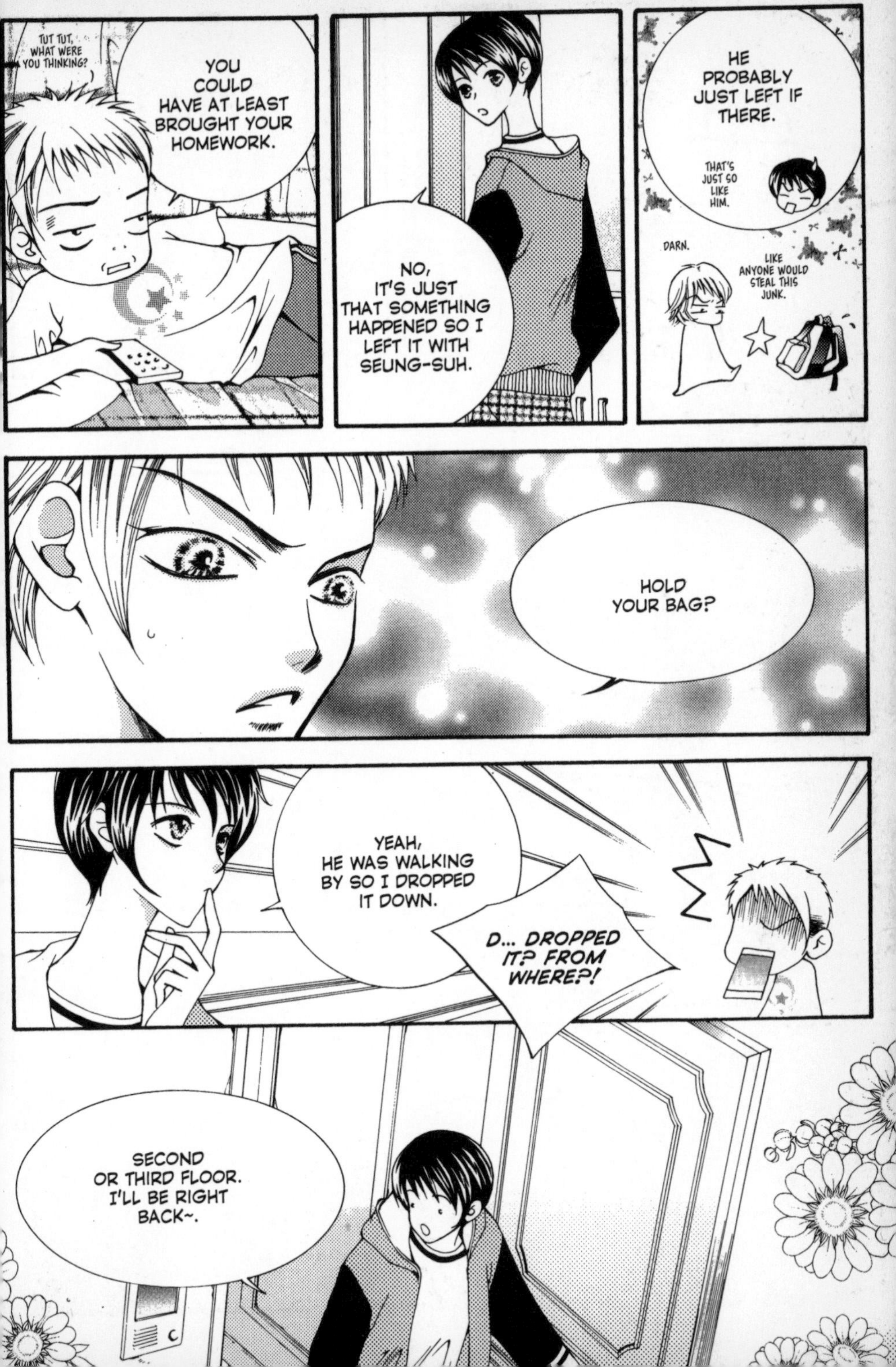
TUT TUT, WHAT WERE YOU THINKING?
YOU COULD HAVE AT LEAST BROUGHT YOUR HOMEWORK.
NO, IT'S JUST THAT SOMETHING HAPPENED SO I LEFT IT WITH SEUNG-SUH.
HE PROBABLY JUST LEFT IF THERE.
THAT'S JUST SO LIKE HIM.
DARN.
LIKE ANYONE WOULD STEAL THIS JUNK.
HOLD YOUR BAG?
YEAH, HE WAS WALKING BY SO I DROPPED IT DOWN.
D... DROPPED IT? FROM WHERE?!
SECOND OR THIRD FLOOR. I'LL BE RIGHT BACK~.

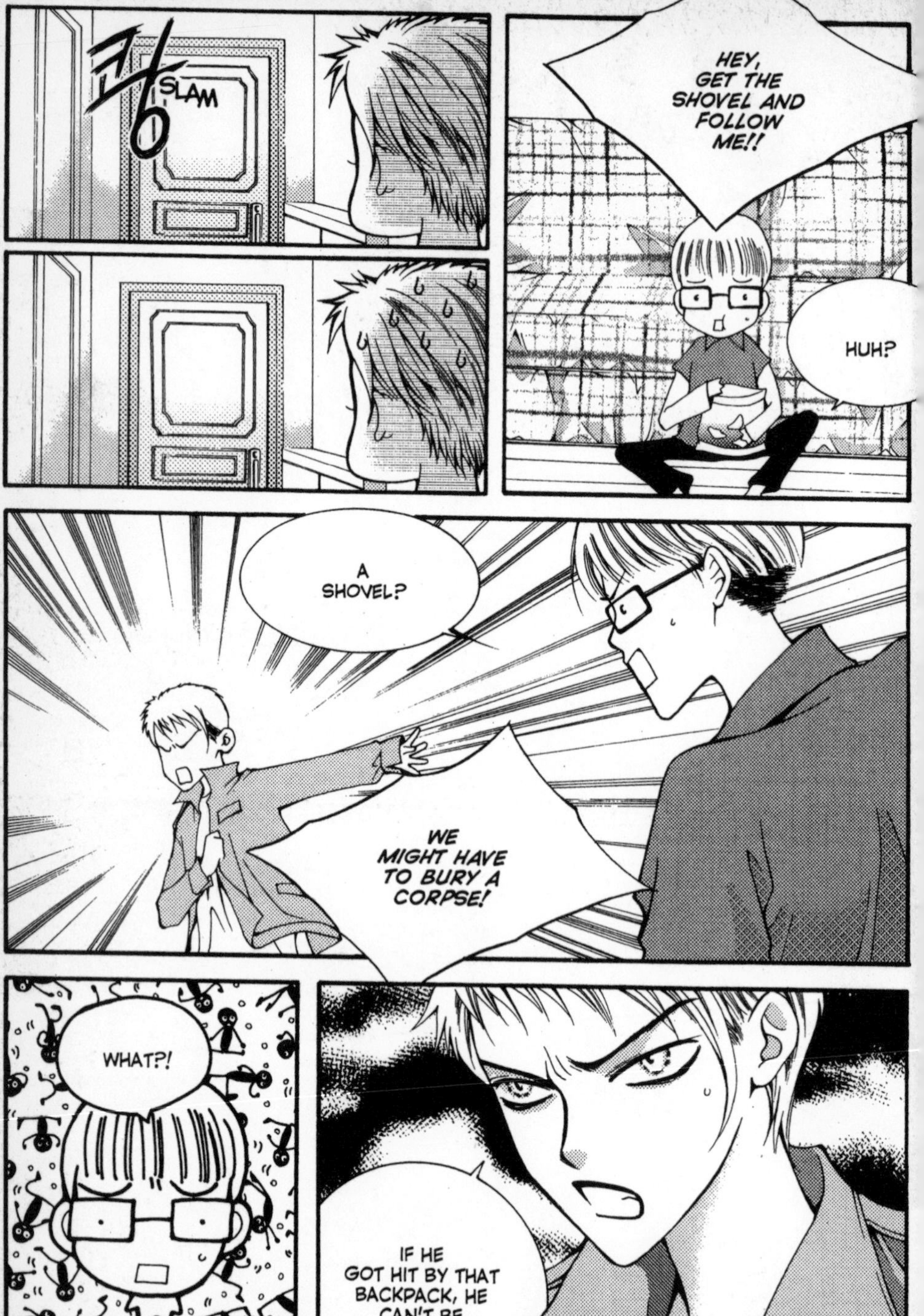
SLAM
HEY, GET THE SHOVEL AND FOLLOW ME!!
HUH?
A SHOVEL?
WE MIGHT HAVE TO BURY A CORPSE!
WHAT?!
IF HE GOT HIT BY THAT BACKPACK, HE CAN'T BE ALIVE.

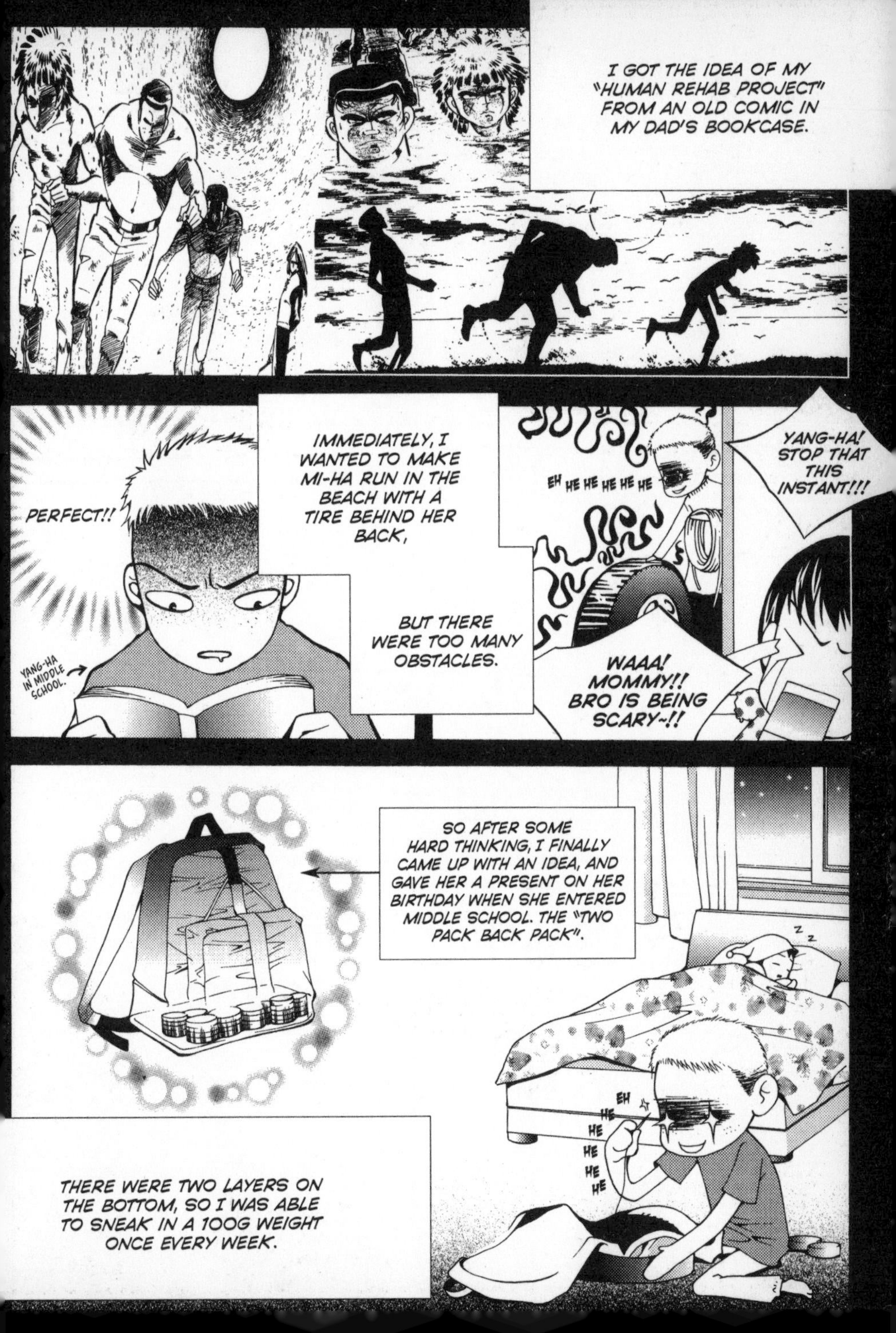
I GOT THE IDEA OF MY "HUMAN REHAB PROJECT" FROM AN OLD COMIC IN MY DAD'S BOOKCASE.
PERFECT!!
YANG-HA IN MIDDLE SCHOOL.
IMMEDIATELY, I WANTED TO MAKE MI-HA RUN IN THE BEACH WITH A TIRE BEHIND HER BACK,
BUT THERE WERE TOO MANY OBSTACLES.
EH HE HE HE HE HE
YANG-HA! STOP THAT THIS INSTANT!!!
WAAA! MOMMY!! BRO IS BEING SCARY~!!
SO AFTER SOME HARD THINKING, I FINALLY CAME UP WITH AN IDEA, AND GAVE HER A PRESENT ON HER BIRTHDAY WHEN SHE ENTERED MIDDLE SCHOOL. THE "TWO PACK BACK PACK".
Z Z
THERE WERE TWO LAYERS ON THE BOTTOM, SO I WAS ABLE TO SNEAK IN A 100G WEIGHT ONCE EVERY WEEK.
EH HE HE HE HE HE

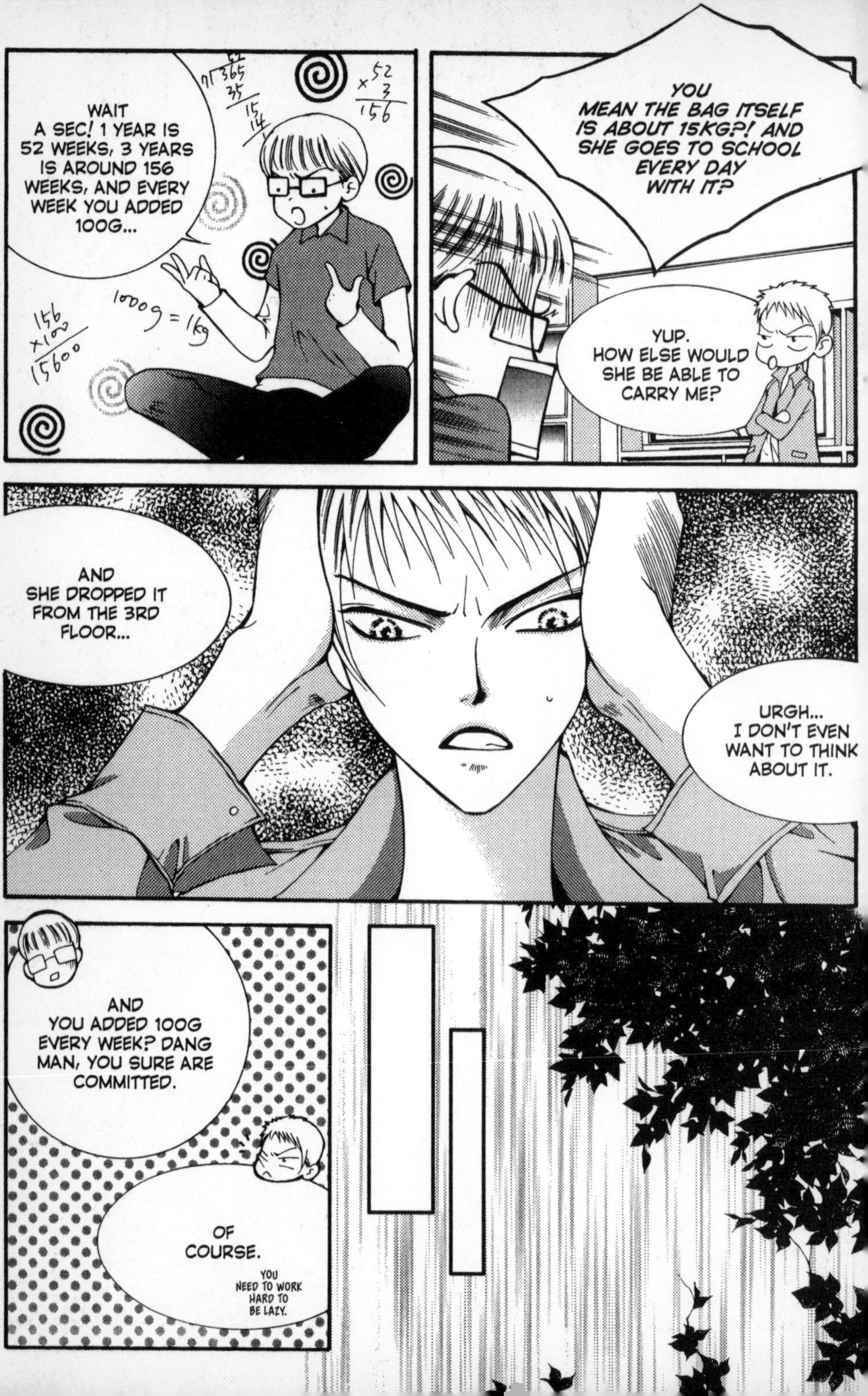
WAIT A SEC! 1 YEAR IS 52 WEEKS, 3 YEARS IS AROUND 156 WEEKS, AND EVERY WEEK YOU ADDED 100G...
1000g = 1kg
YOU MEAN THE BAG ITSELF IS ABOUT 15KG?! AND SHE GOES TO SCHOOL EVERY DAY WITH IT?
YUP. HOW ELSE WOULD SHE BE ABLE TO CARRY ME?
AND SHE DROPPED IT FROM THE 3RD FLOOR...
URGH... I DON'T EVEN WANT TO THINK ABOUT IT.
AND YOU ADDED 100G EVERY WEEK? DANG MAN, YOU SURE ARE COMMITTED.
OF COURSE.
YOU NEED TO WORK HARD TO BE LAZY.

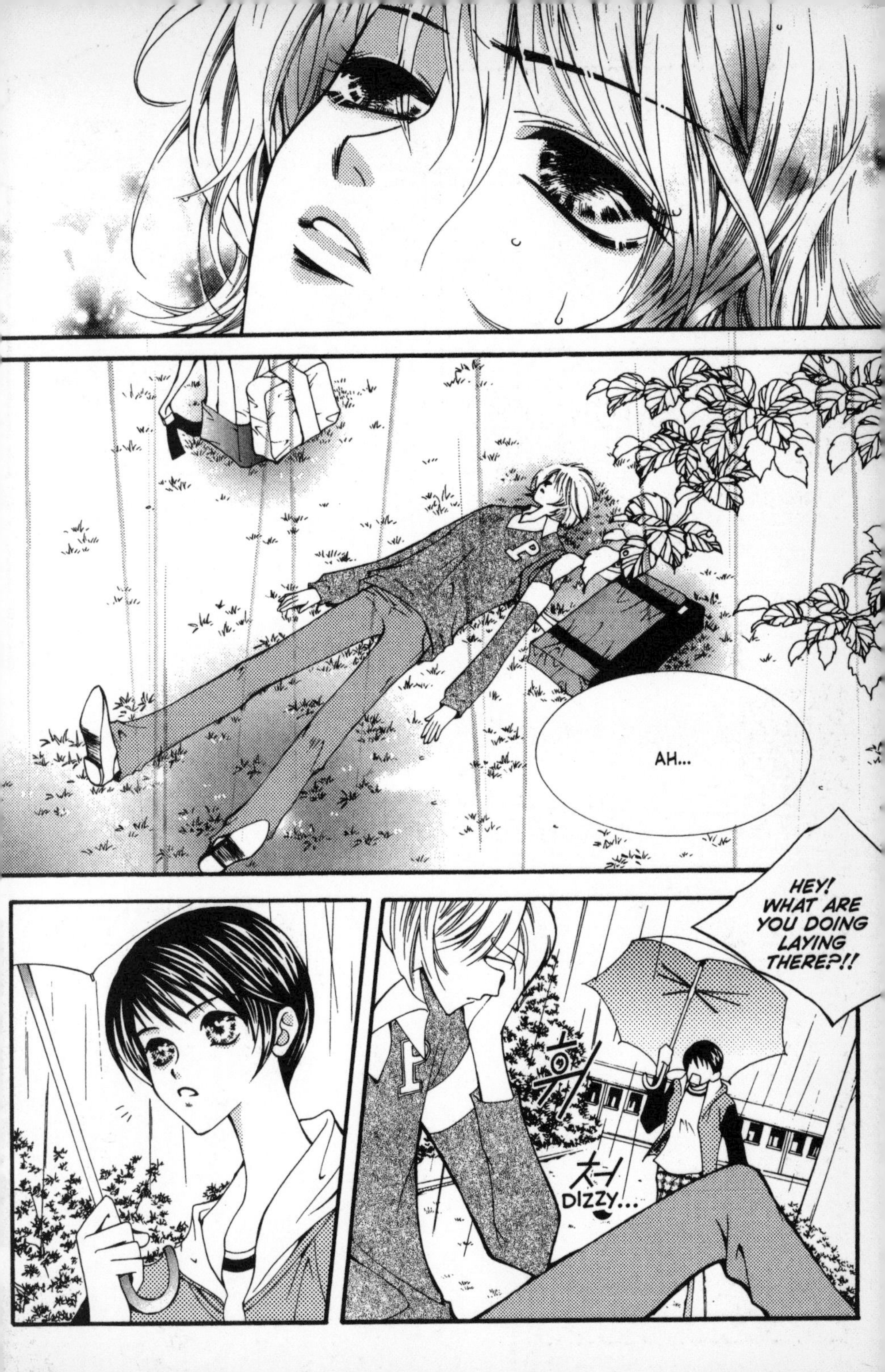
AH...
HEY! WHAT ARE YOU DOING LAYING THERE?!!
DIZZY...

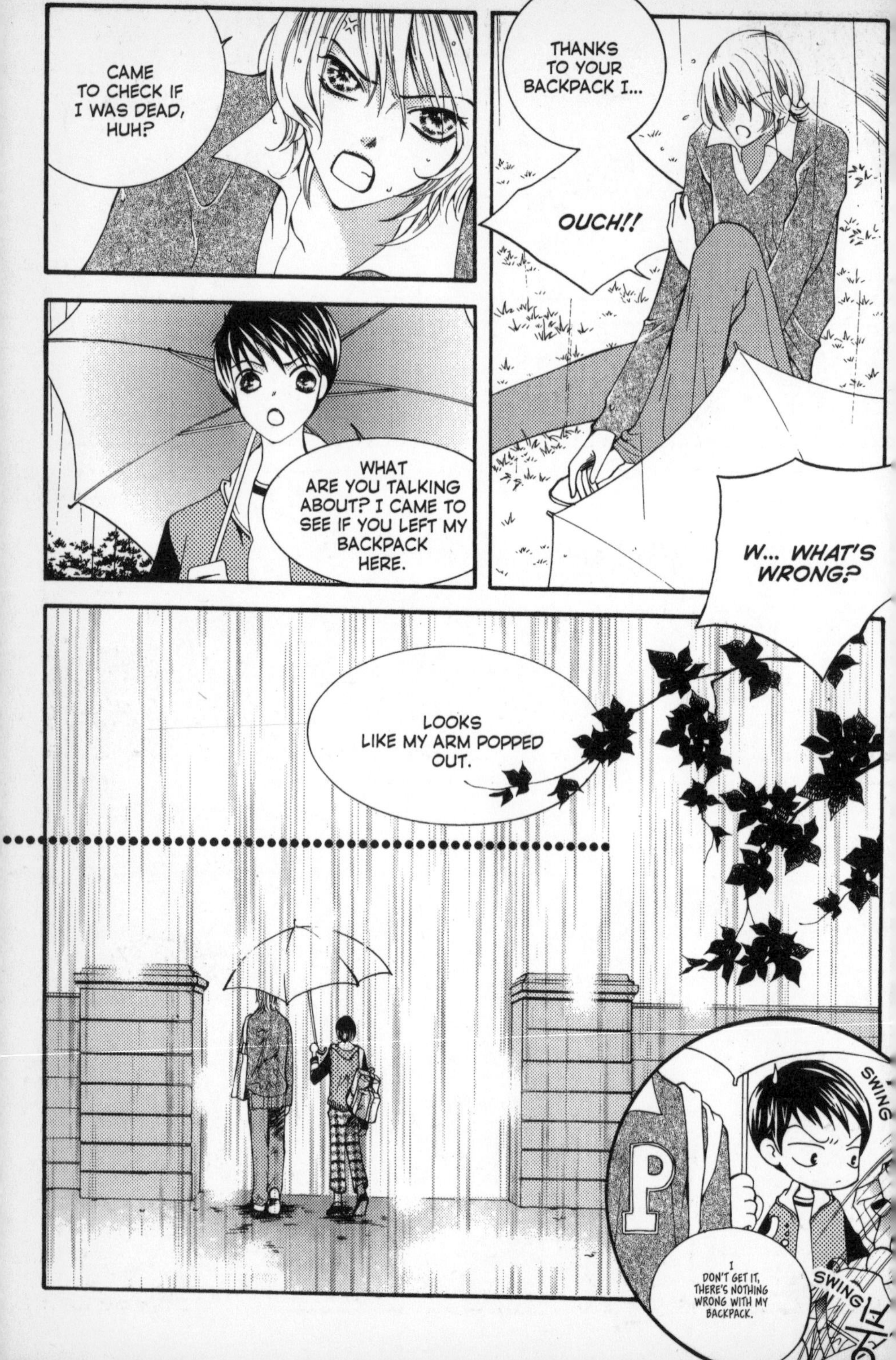
CAME TO CHECK IF I WAS DEAD, HUH?
WHAT ARE YOU TALKING ABOUT? I CAME TO SEE IF YOU LEFT MY BACKPACK HERE.
THANKS TO YOUR BACKPACK I...
OUCH!!
W... WHAT'S WRONG?
LOOKS LIKE MY ARM POPPED OUT.
SWING
I DON'T GET IT, THERE'S NOTHING WRONG WITH MY BACKPACK.
SWING

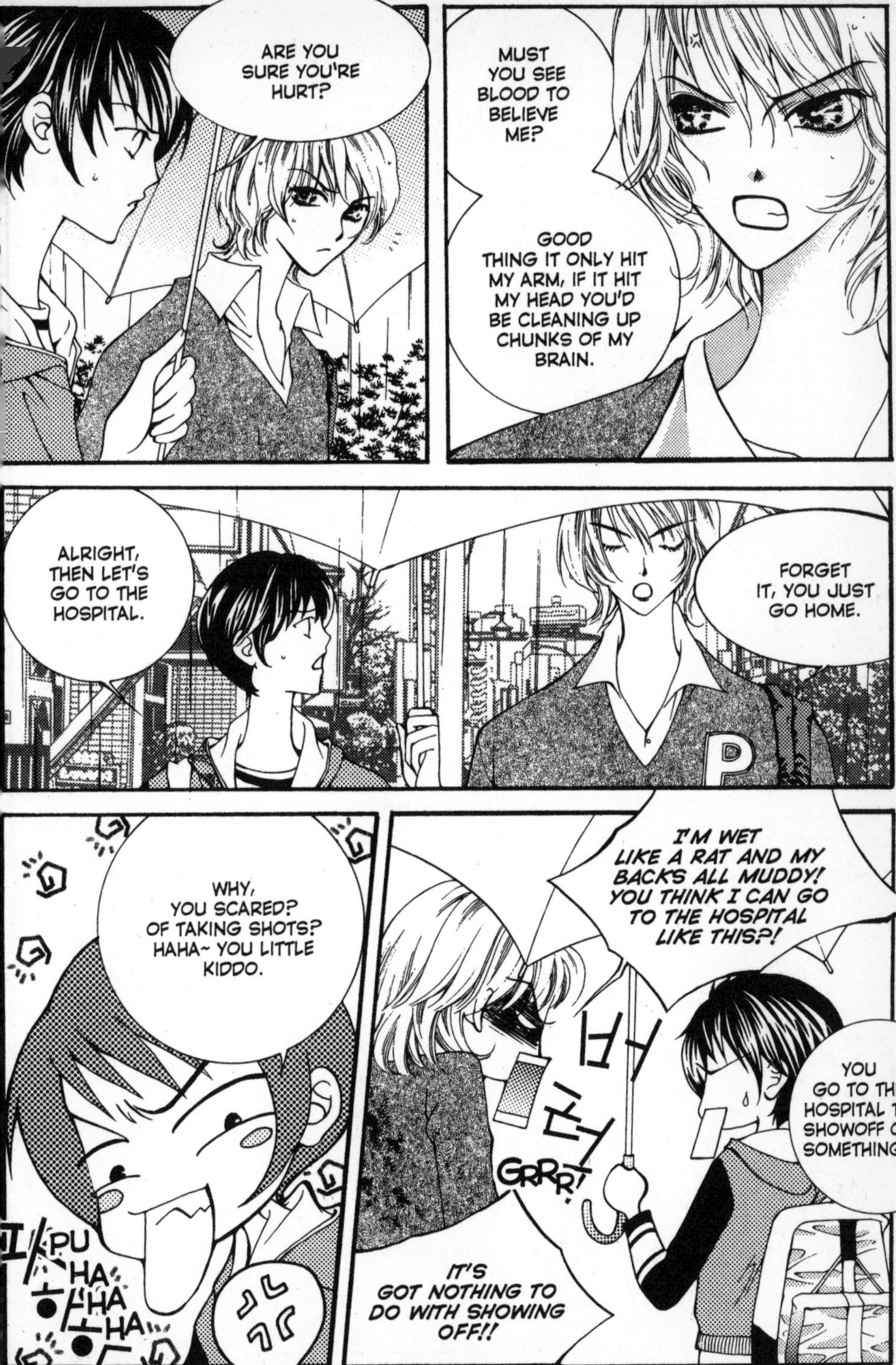
ARE YOU SURE YOU'RE HURT?
MUST YOU SEE BLOOD TO BELIEVE ME?
GOOD THING IT ONLY HIT MY ARM, IF IT HIT MY HEAD YOU'D BE CLEANING UP CHUNKS OF MY BRAIN.
ALRIGHT, THEN LET'S GO TO THE HOSPITAL.
FORGET IT, YOU JUST GO HOME.
WHY, YOU SCARED? OF TAKING SHOTS? HAHA~ YOU LITTLE KIDDO.
PU HA HA HA
I'M WET LIKE A RAT AND MY BACK'S ALL MUDDY! YOU THINK I CAN GO TO THE HOSPITAL LIKE THIS?!
YOU GO TO THE HOSPITAL TO SHOWOFF OR SOMETHING?
GRRR!
IT'S GOT NOTHING TO DO WITH SHOWING OFF!!

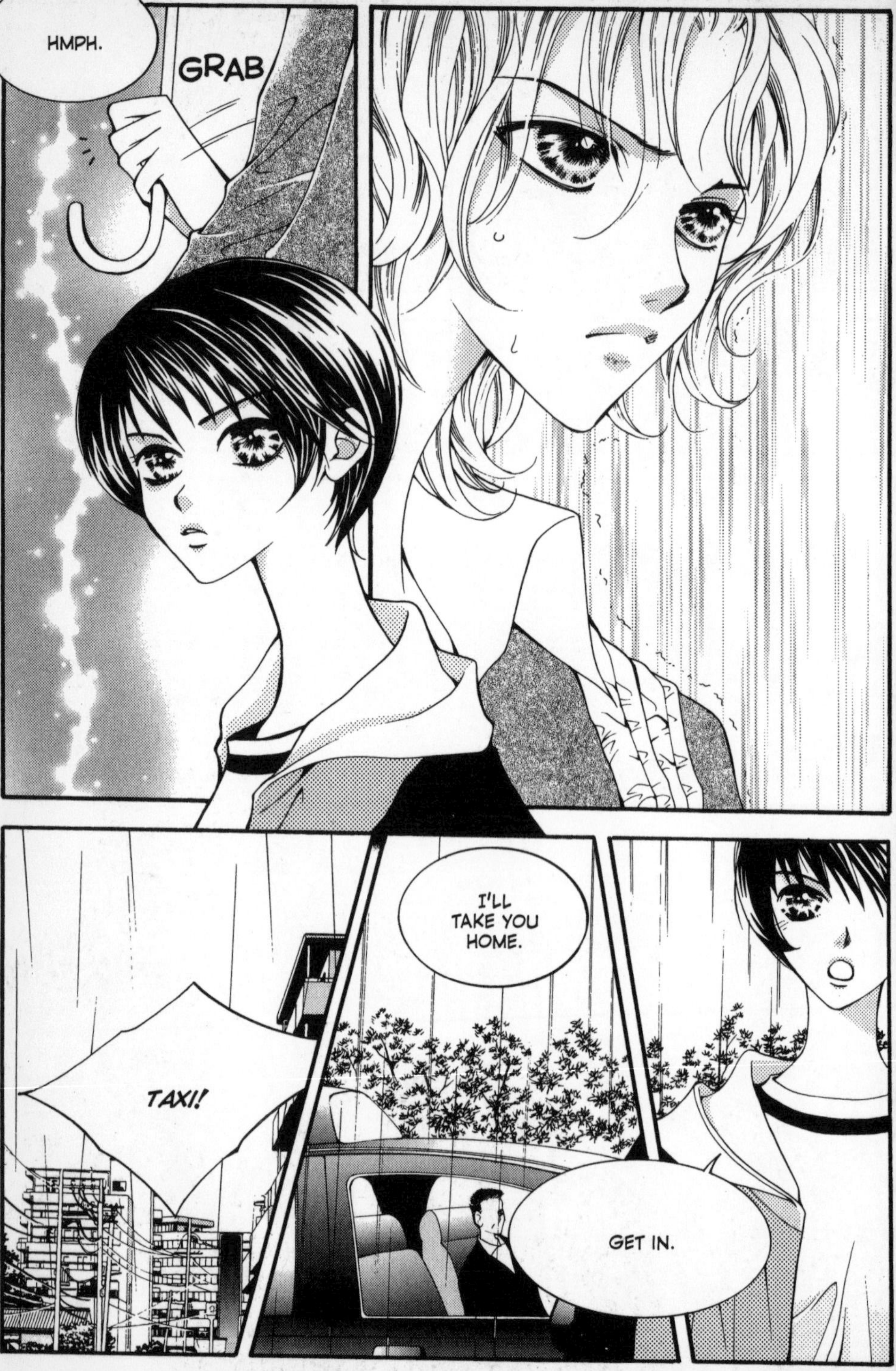
HMPH.
GRAB
TAXI!
I'LL TAKE YOU HOME.
GET IN.

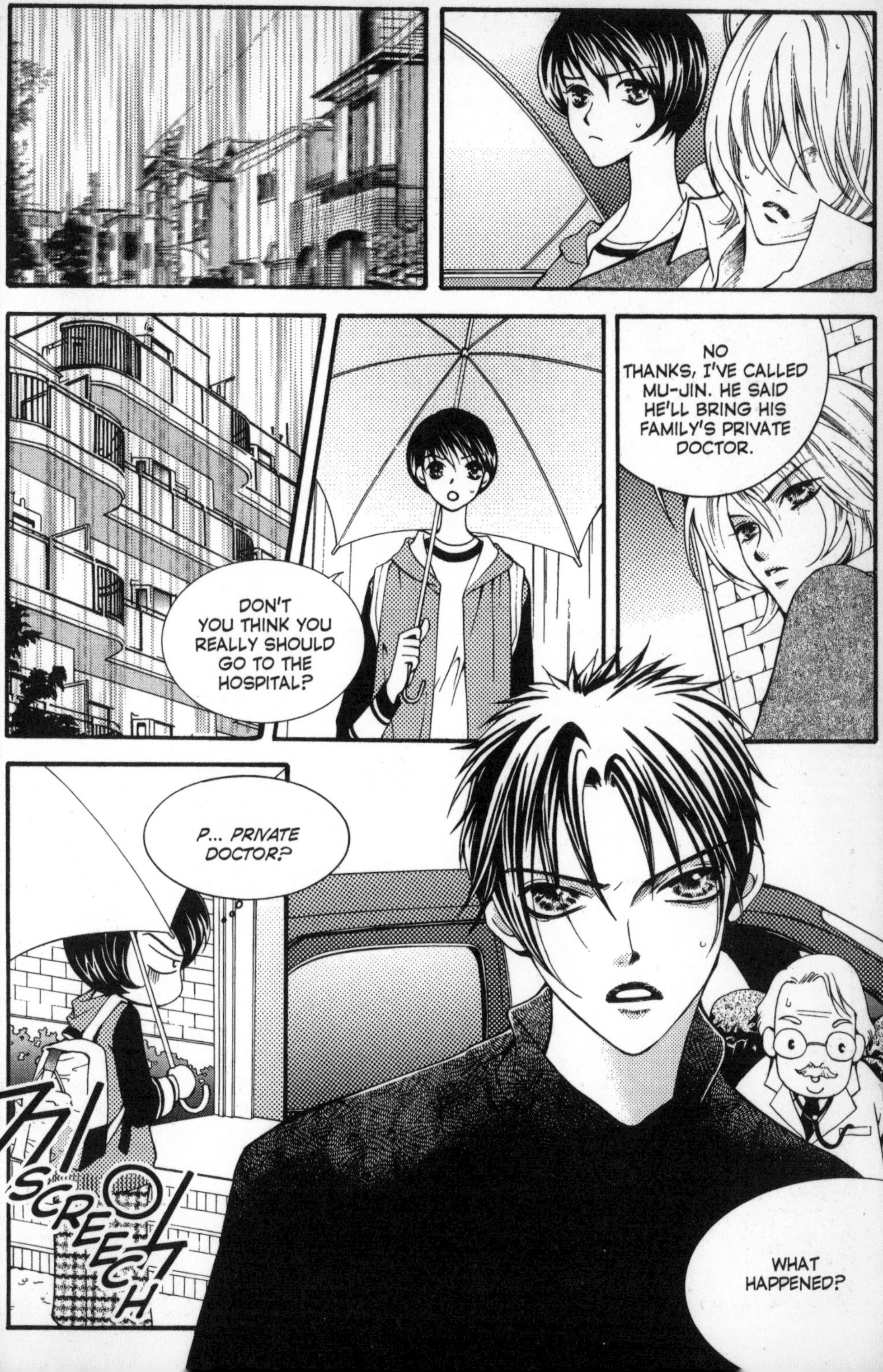
DON'T YOU THINK YOU REALLY SHOULD GO TO THE HOSPITAL?
NO THANKS, I'VE CALLED MU-JIN. HE SAID HE'LL BRING HIS FAMILY'S PRIVATE DOCTOR.
P... PRIVATE DOCTOR?
SCREEECH
WHAT HAPPENED?

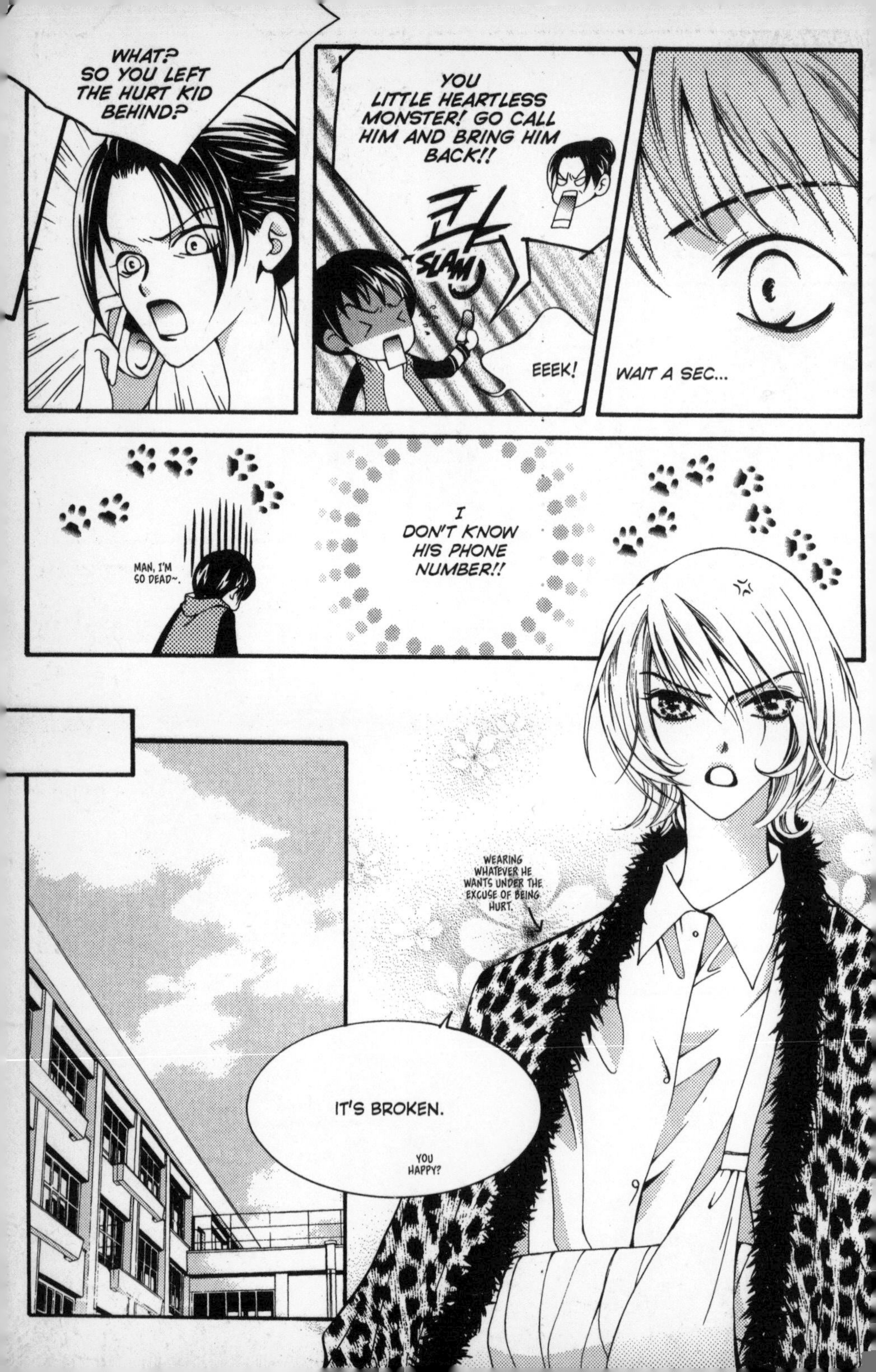
WHAT? SO YOU LEFT THE HURT KID BEHIND?
YOU LITTLE HEARTLESS MONSTER! GO CALL HIM AND BRING HIM BACK!!
SLAM
EEEK!
WAIT A SEC...
MAN, I'M SO DEAD~.
I DON'T KNOW HIS PHONE NUMBER!!
WEARING WHATEVER HE WANTS UNDER THE EXCUSE OF BEING HURT.
IT'S BROKEN.
YOU HAPPY?

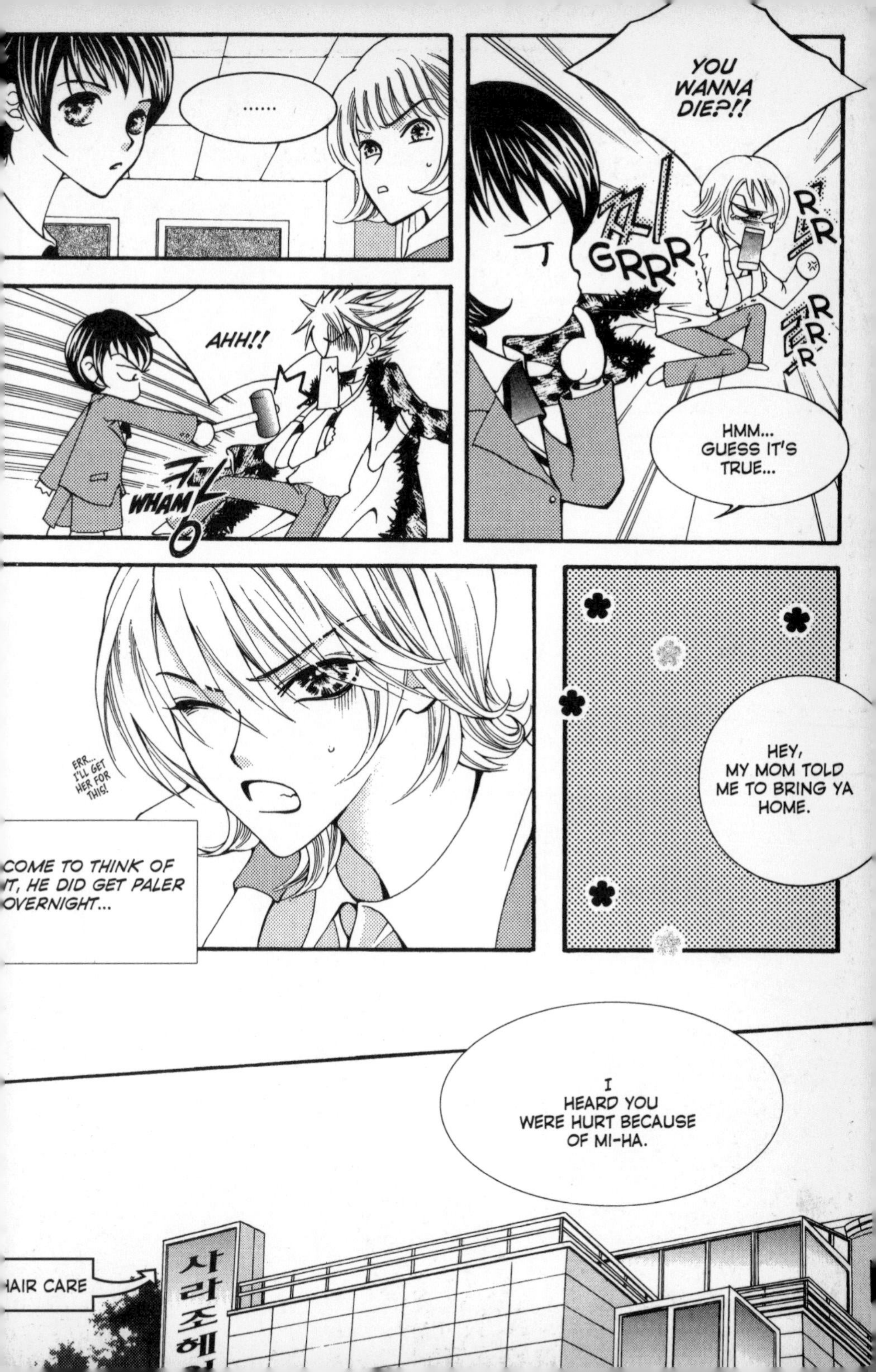

......
AHH!!
WHAM
YOU WANNA DIE?!!
GRRR
RRR
HMM... GUESS IT'S TRUE...
ERR... I'LL GET HER FOR THIS!
COME TO THINK OF IT, HE DID GET PALER OVERNIGHT...
HEY, MY MOM TOLD ME TO BRING YA HOME.
I HEARD YOU WERE HURT BECAUSE OF MI-HA.
HAIR CARE

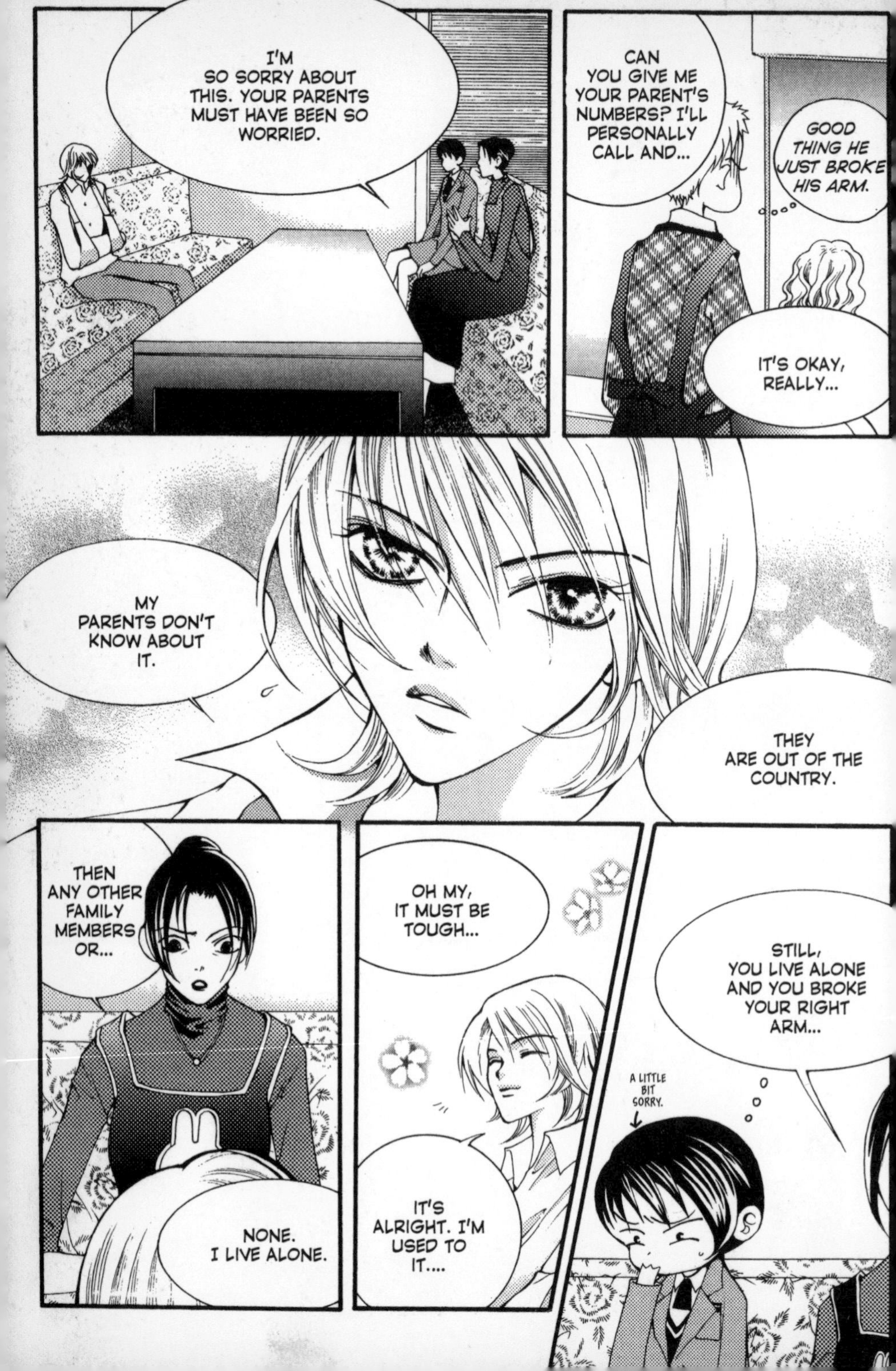
I'M SO SORRY ABOUT THIS. YOUR PARENTS MUST HAVE BEEN SO WORRIED.
CAN YOU GIVE ME YOUR PARENT'S NUMBERS? I'LL PERSONALLY CALL AND...
GOOD THING HE JUST BROKE HIS ARM.
IT'S OKAY, REALLY...
MY PARENTS DON'T KNOW ABOUT IT.
THEY ARE OUT OF THE COUNTRY.
THEN ANY OTHER FAMILY MEMBERS OR...
NONE. I LIVE ALONE.
OH MY, IT MUST BE TOUGH...
IT'S ALRIGHT. I'M USED TO IT....
STILL, YOU LIVE ALONE AND YOU BROKE YOUR RIGHT ARM...
A LITTLE BIT SORRY.

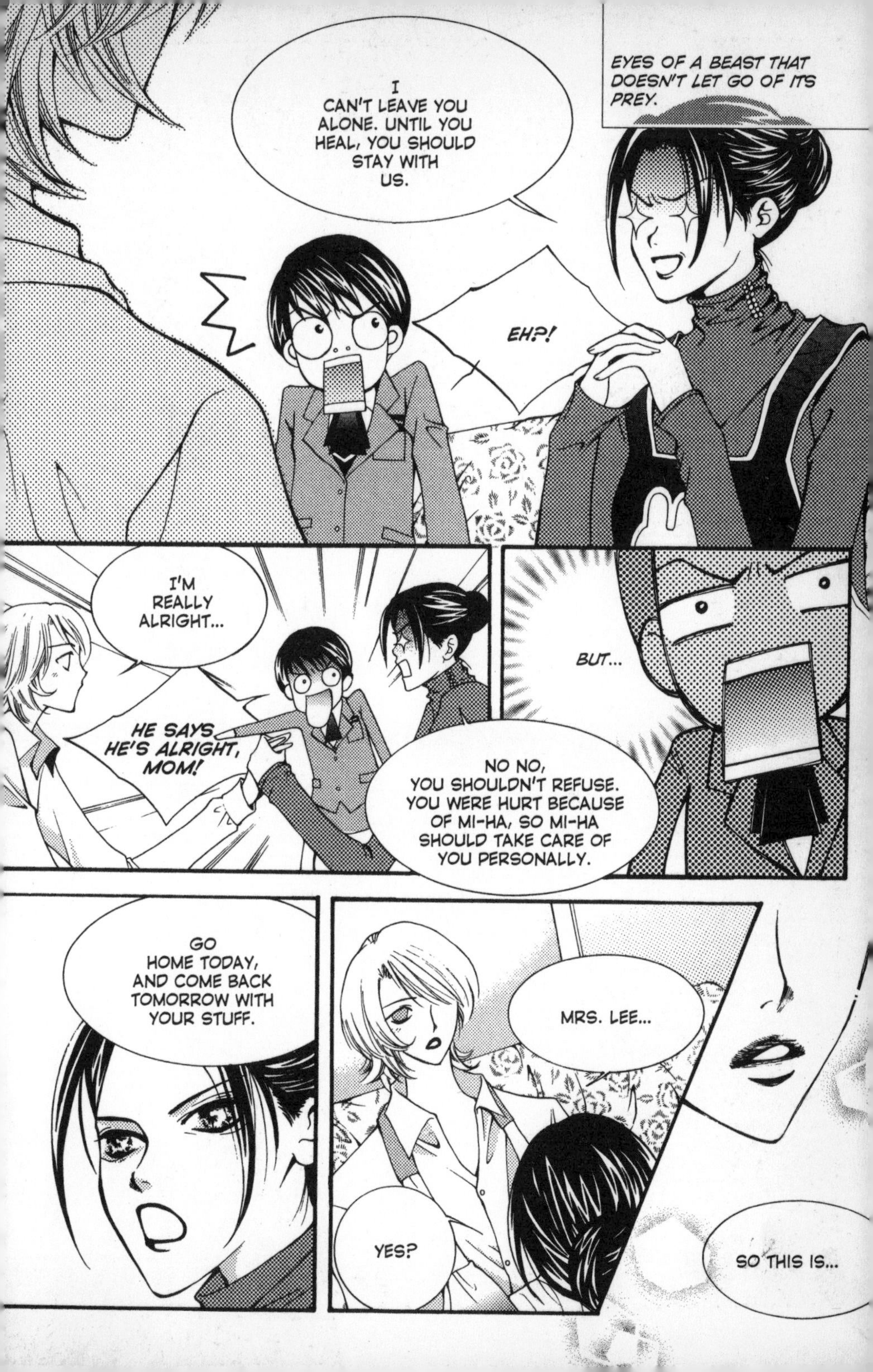
I CAN'T LEAVE YOU ALONE. UNTIL YOU HEAL, YOU SHOULD STAY WITH US.
EYES OF A BEAST THAT DOESN'T LET GO OF ITS PREY.
EH?!
I'M REALLY ALRIGHT...
HE SAYS HE'S ALRIGHT, MOM!
NO NO, YOU SHOULDN'T REFUSE. YOU WERE HURT BECAUSE OF MI-HA, SO MI-HA SHOULD TAKE CARE OF YOU PERSONALLY.
BUT...
GO HOME TODAY, AND COME BACK TOMORROW WITH YOUR STUFF.
MRS. LEE...
YES?
SO THIS IS...

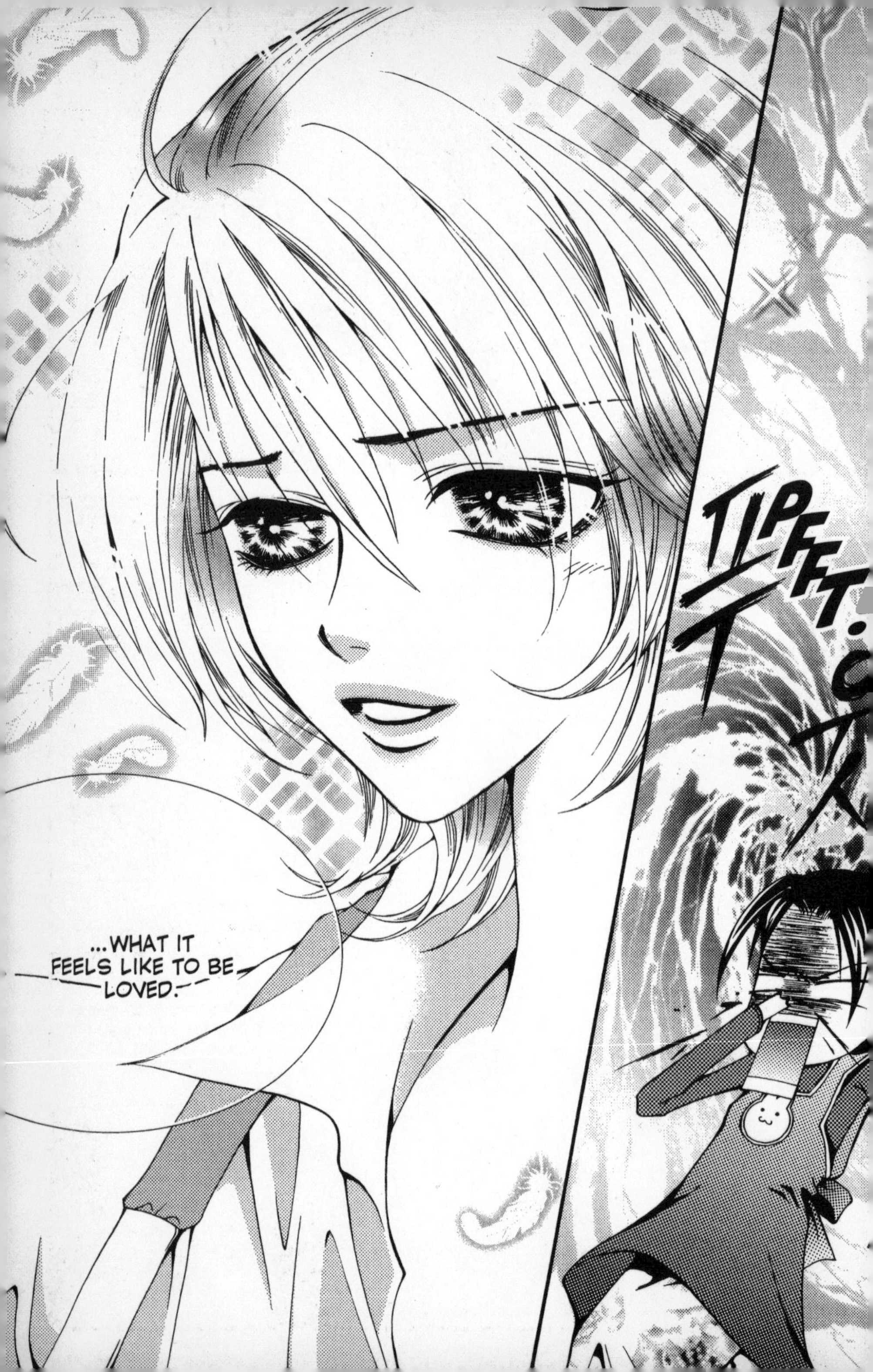
...WHAT IT FEELS LIKE TO BE LOVED.
TIPFFT

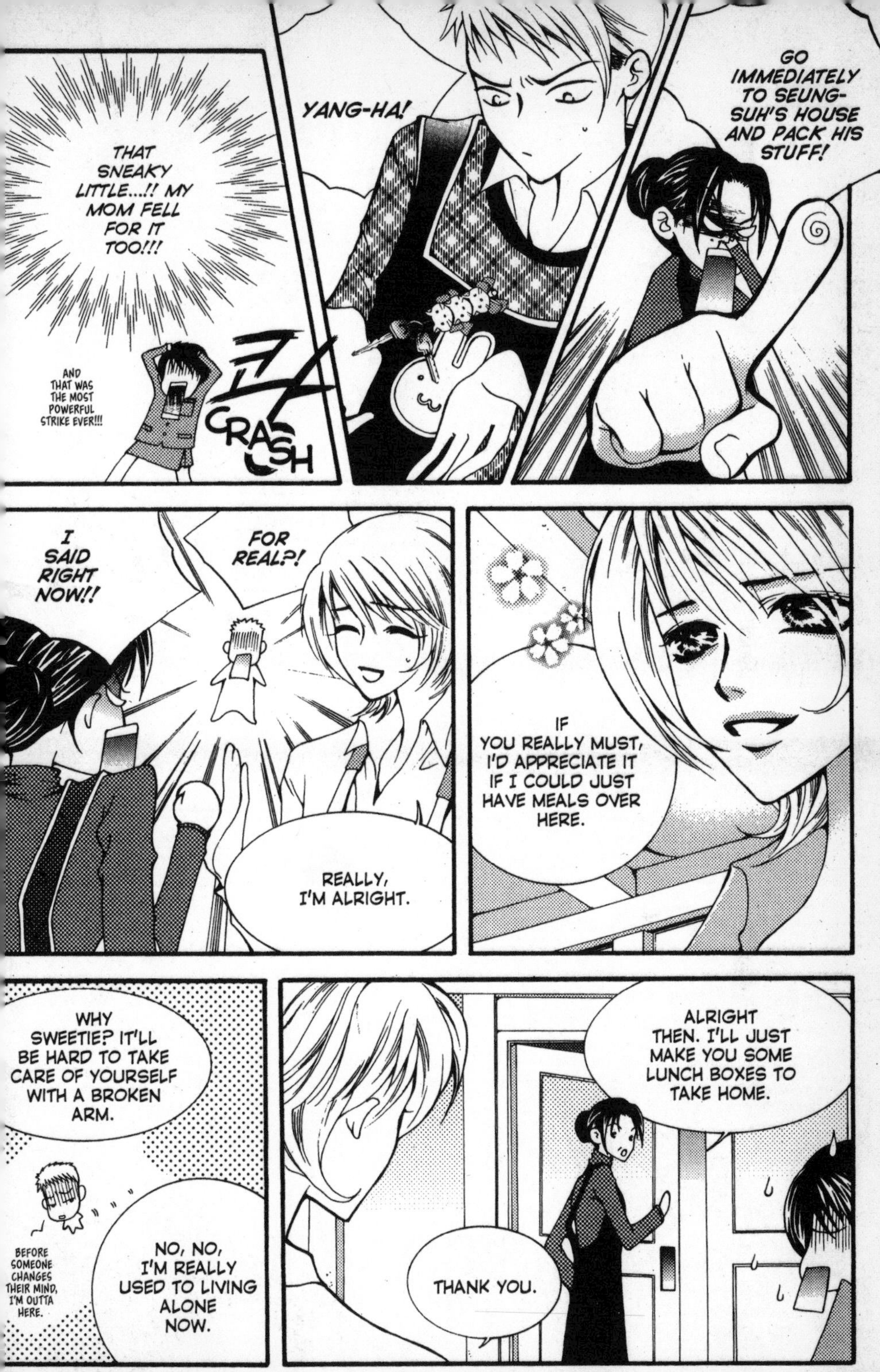
THAT SNEAKY LITTLE...!! MY MOM FELL FOR IT TOO!!!
AND THAT WAS THE MOST POWERFUL STRIKE EVER!!!
CRASH
YANG-HA!
GO IMMEDIATELY TO SEUNG-SUH'S HOUSE AND PACK HIS STUFF!
I SAID RIGHT NOW!!
FOR REAL?!
REALLY, I'M ALRIGHT.
IF YOU REALLY MUST, I'D APPRECIATE IT IF I COULD JUST HAVE MEALS OVER HERE.
WHY SWEETIE? IT'LL BE HARD TO TAKE CARE OF YOURSELF WITH A BROKEN ARM.
BEFORE SOMEONE CHANGES THEIR MIND, I'M OUTTA HERE.
NO, NO, I'M REALLY USED TO LIVING ALONE NOW.
ALRIGHT THEN. I'LL JUST MAKE YOU SOME LUNCH BOXES TO TAKE HOME.
THANK YOU.

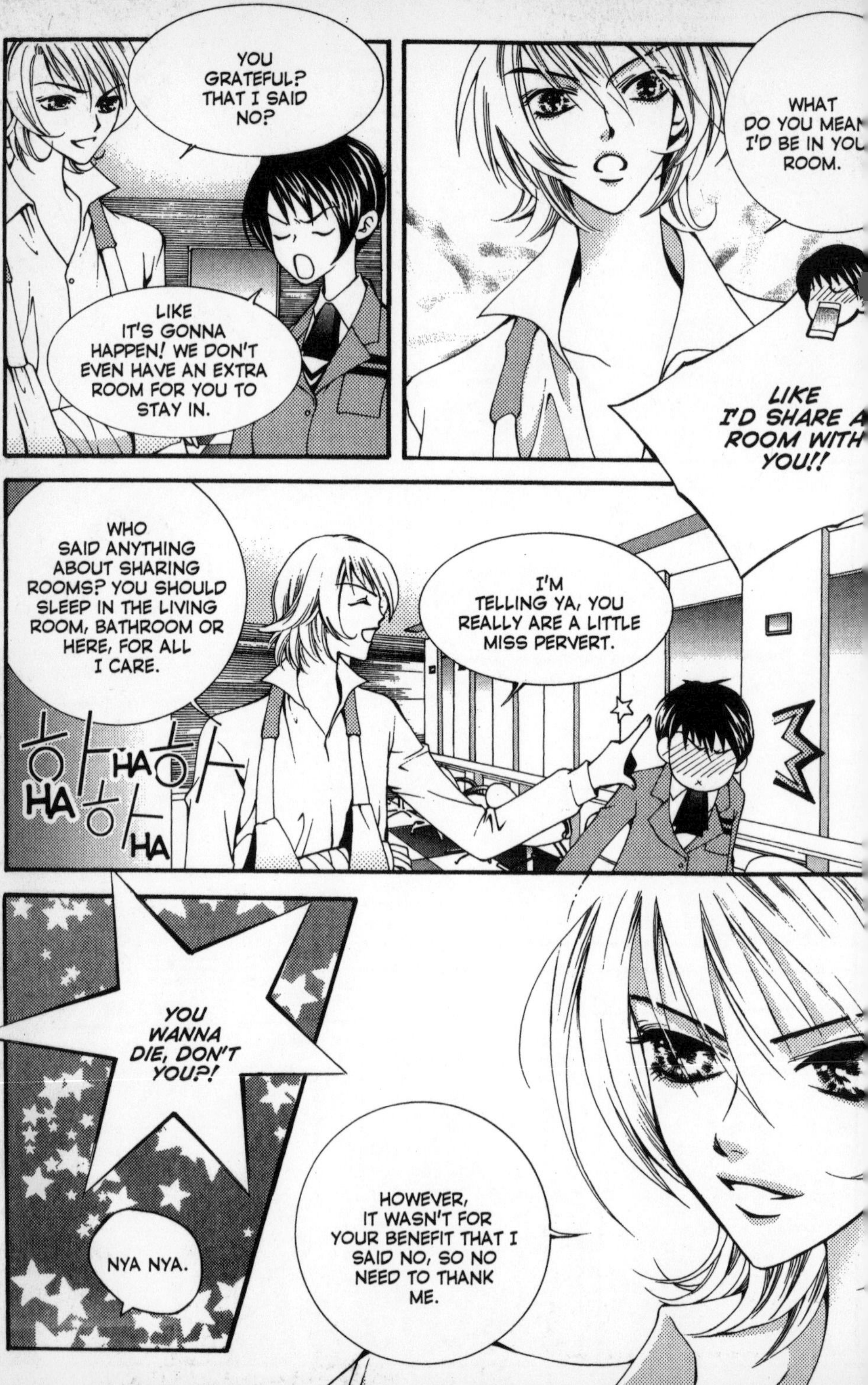
YOU GRATEFUL? THAT I SAID NO?
LIKE IT'S GONNA HAPPEN! WE DON'T EVEN HAVE AN EXTRA ROOM FOR YOU TO STAY IN.
WHAT DO YOU MEAN I'D BE IN YOU ROOM.
LIKE I'D SHARE A ROOM WITH YOU!!
WHO SAID ANYTHING ABOUT SHARING ROOMS? YOU SHOULD SLEEP IN THE LIVING ROOM, BATHROOM OR HERE, FOR ALL I CARE.
하 HA 하 HA 하 HA
I'M TELLING YA, YOU REALLY ARE A LITTLE MISS PERVERT.
YOU WANNA DIE, DON'T YOU?!
NYA NYA.
HOWEVER, IT WASN'T FOR YOUR BENEFIT THAT I SAID NO, SO NO NEED TO THANK ME.

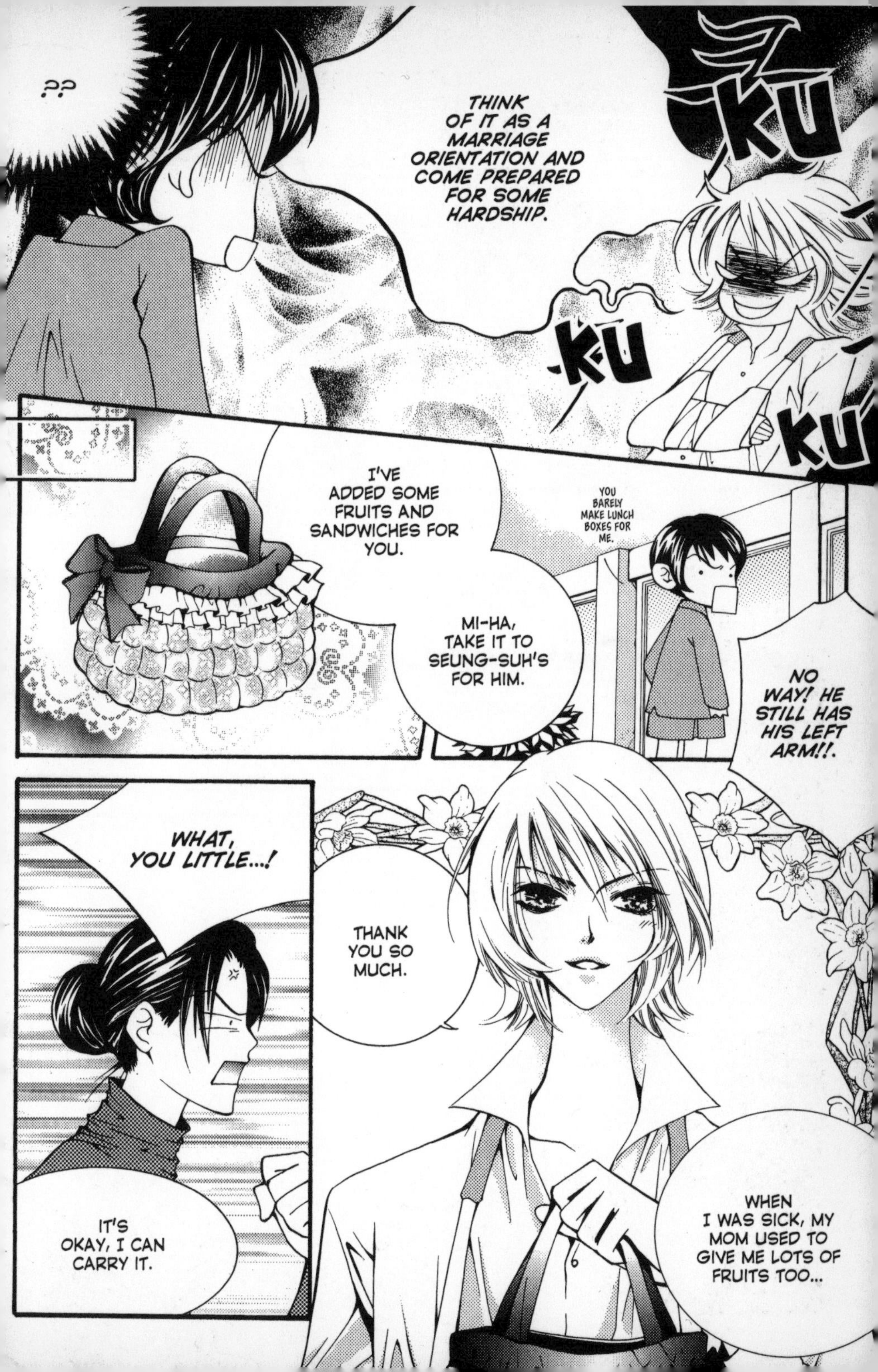
??
THINK OF IT AS A MARRIAGE ORIENTATION AND COME PREPARED FOR SOME HARDSHIP.
KU
KU
KU
I'VE ADDED SOME FRUITS AND SANDWICHES FOR YOU.
MI-HA, TAKE IT TO SEUNG-SUH'S FOR HIM.
YOU BARELY MAKE LUNCH BOXES FOR ME.
NO WAY! HE STILL HAS HIS LEFT ARM!!.
WHAT, YOU LITTLE...!
IT'S OKAY, I CAN CARRY IT.
THANK YOU SO MUCH.
WHEN I WAS SICK, MY MOM USED TO GIVE ME LOTS OF FRUITS TOO...

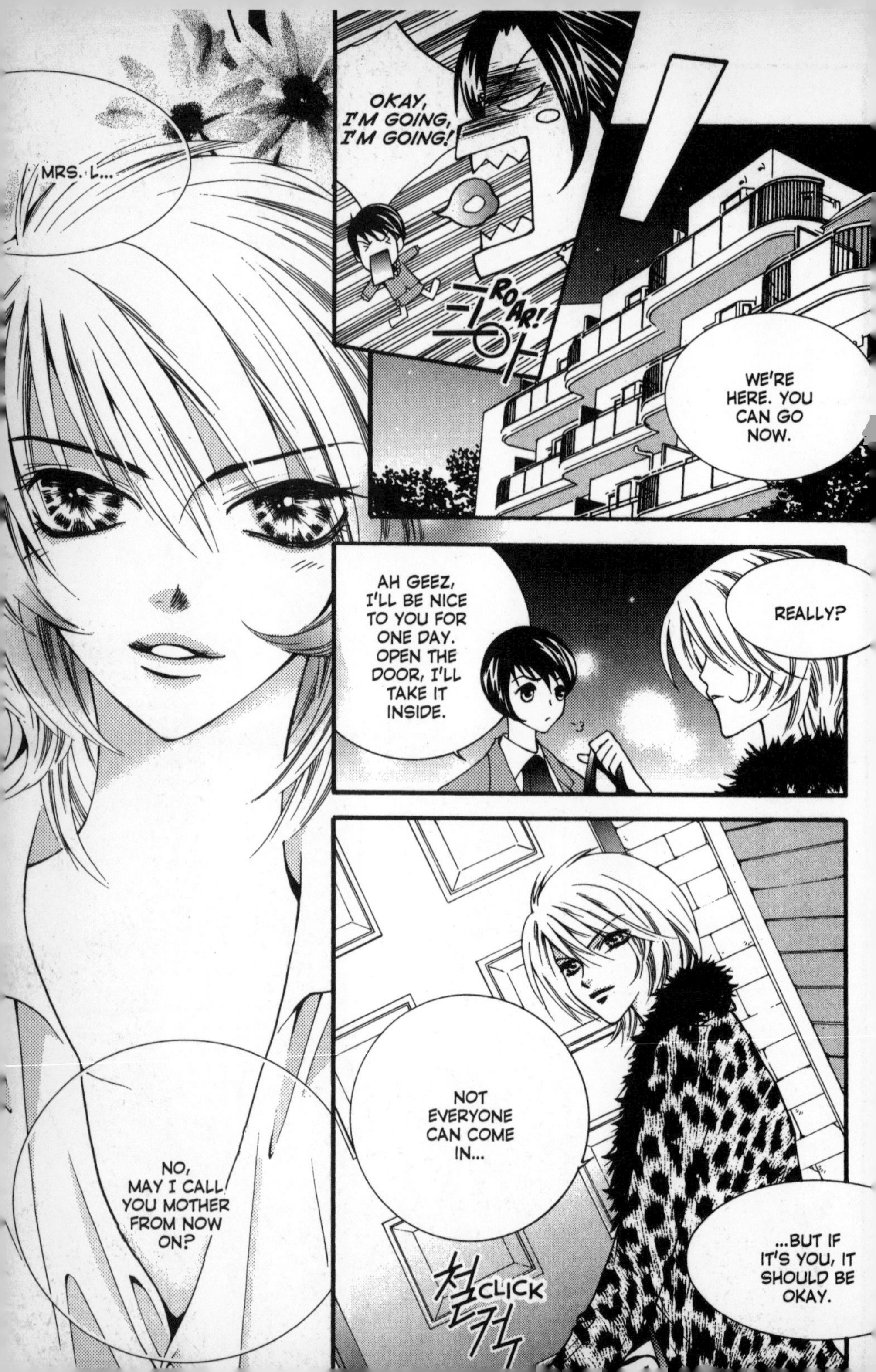
MRS. L...
NO, MAY I CALL YOU MOTHER FROM NOW ON?
OKAY, I'M GOING, I'M GOING!
ROAR!
WE'RE HERE. YOU CAN GO NOW.
AH GEEZ, I'LL BE NICE TO YOU FOR ONE DAY. OPEN THE DOOR, I'LL TAKE IT INSIDE.
REALLY?
NOT EVERYONE CAN COME IN...
CLICK
...BUT IF IT'S YOU, IT SHOULD BE OKAY.

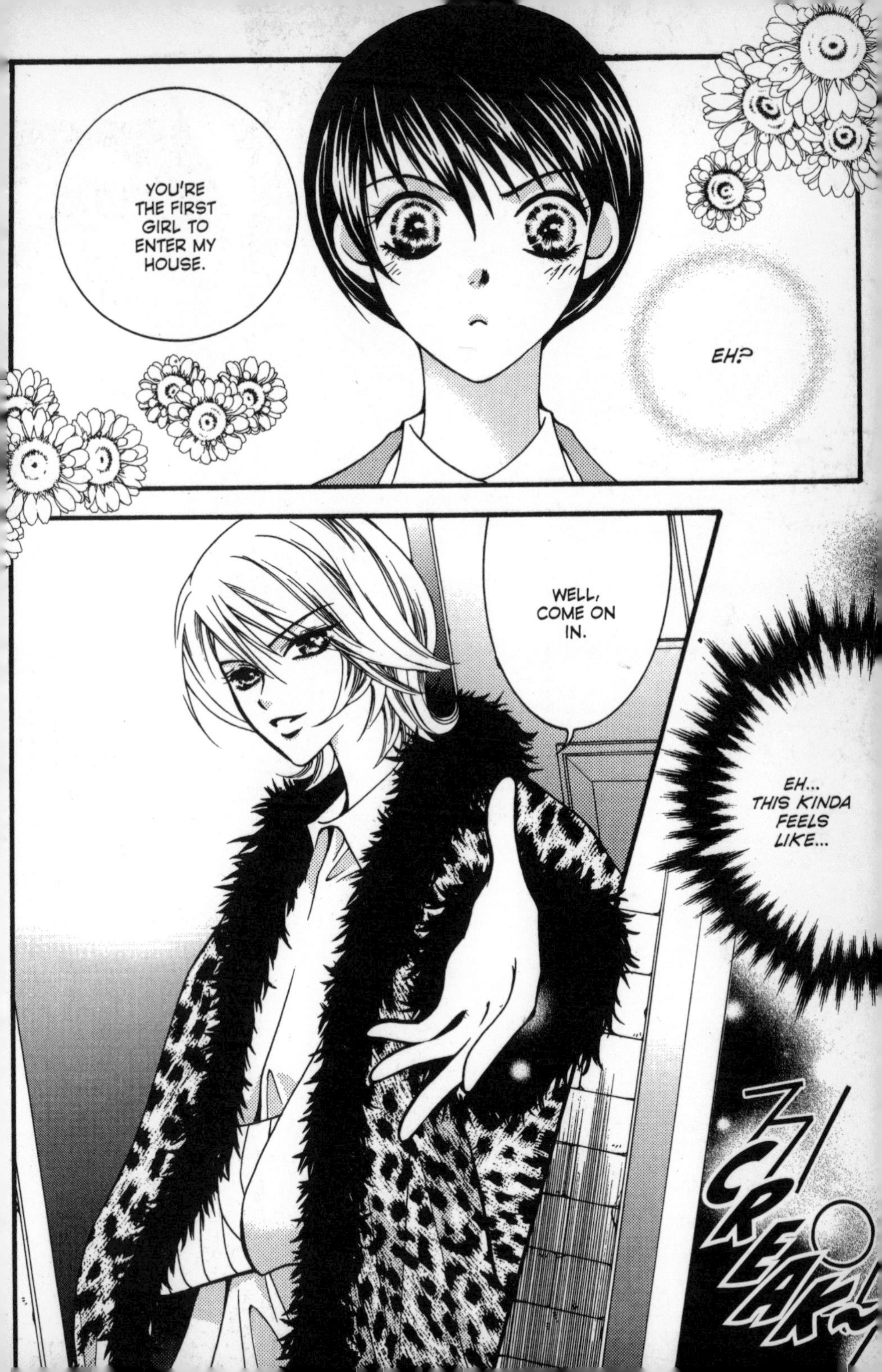
YOU'RE THE FIRST GIRL TO ENTER MY HOUSE.
EH?
WELL, COME ON IN.
EH... THIS KINDA FEELS LIKE...

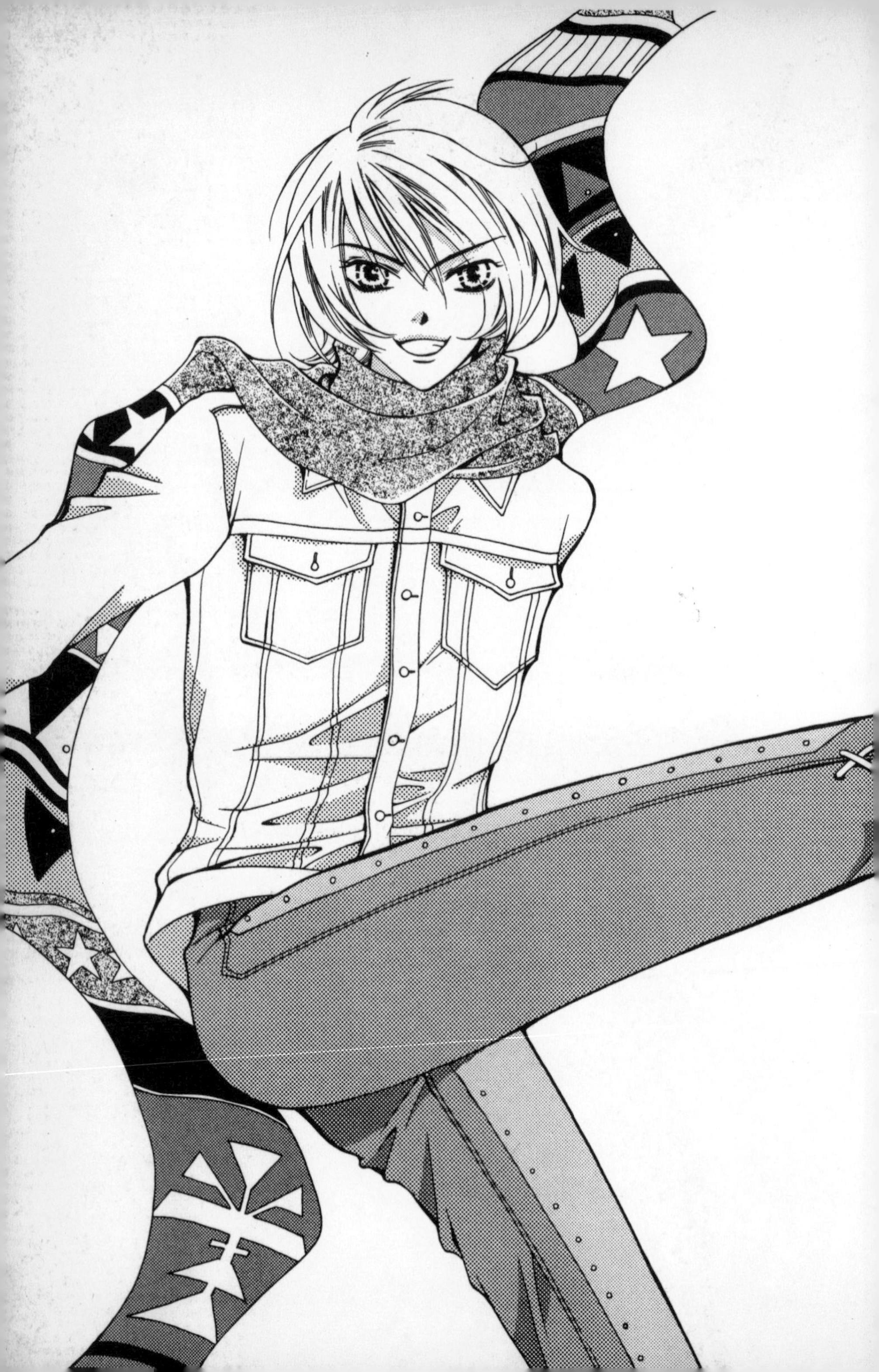

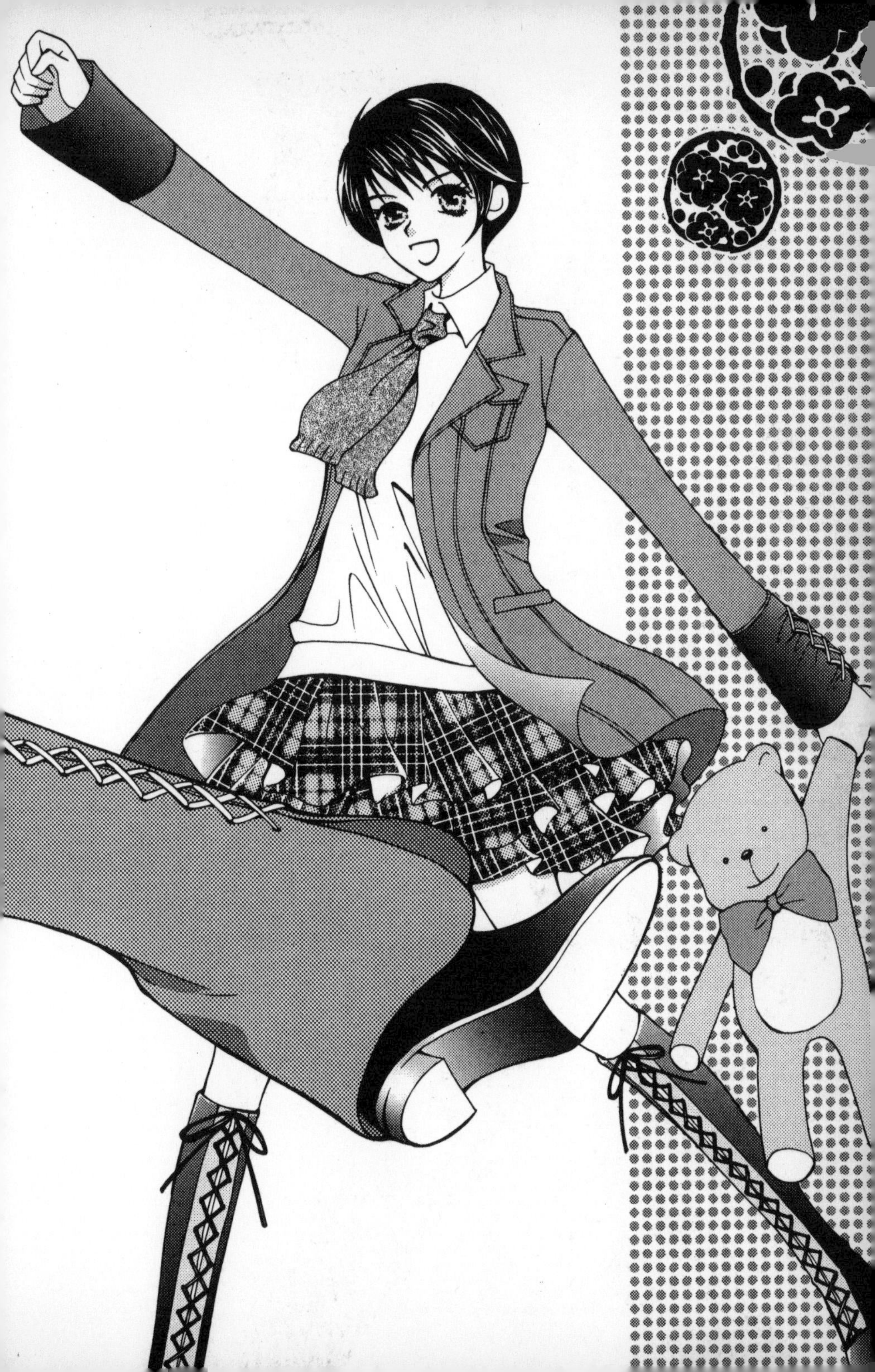

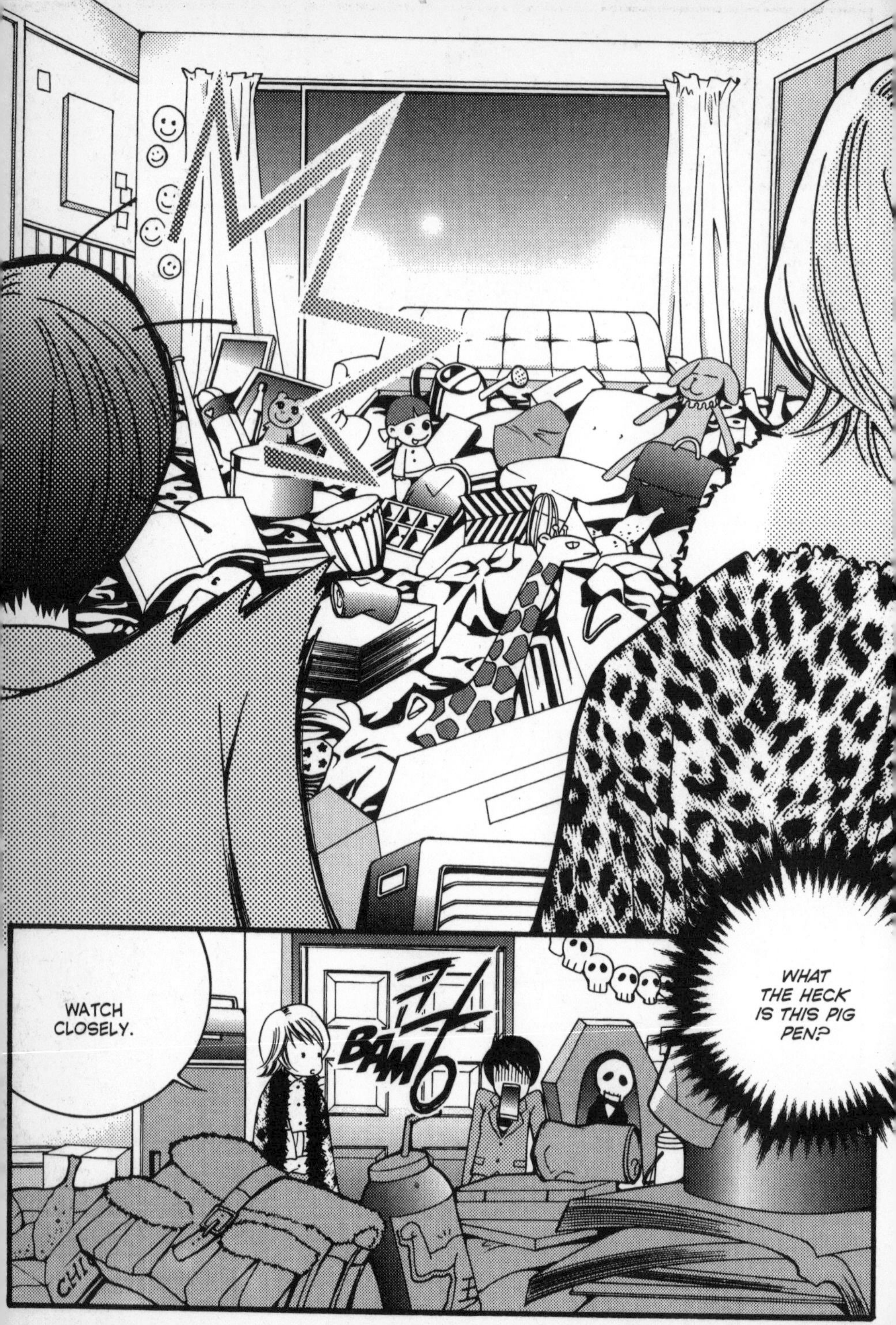
WATCH CLOSELY.
BAM
WHAT THE HECK IS THIS PIG PEN?

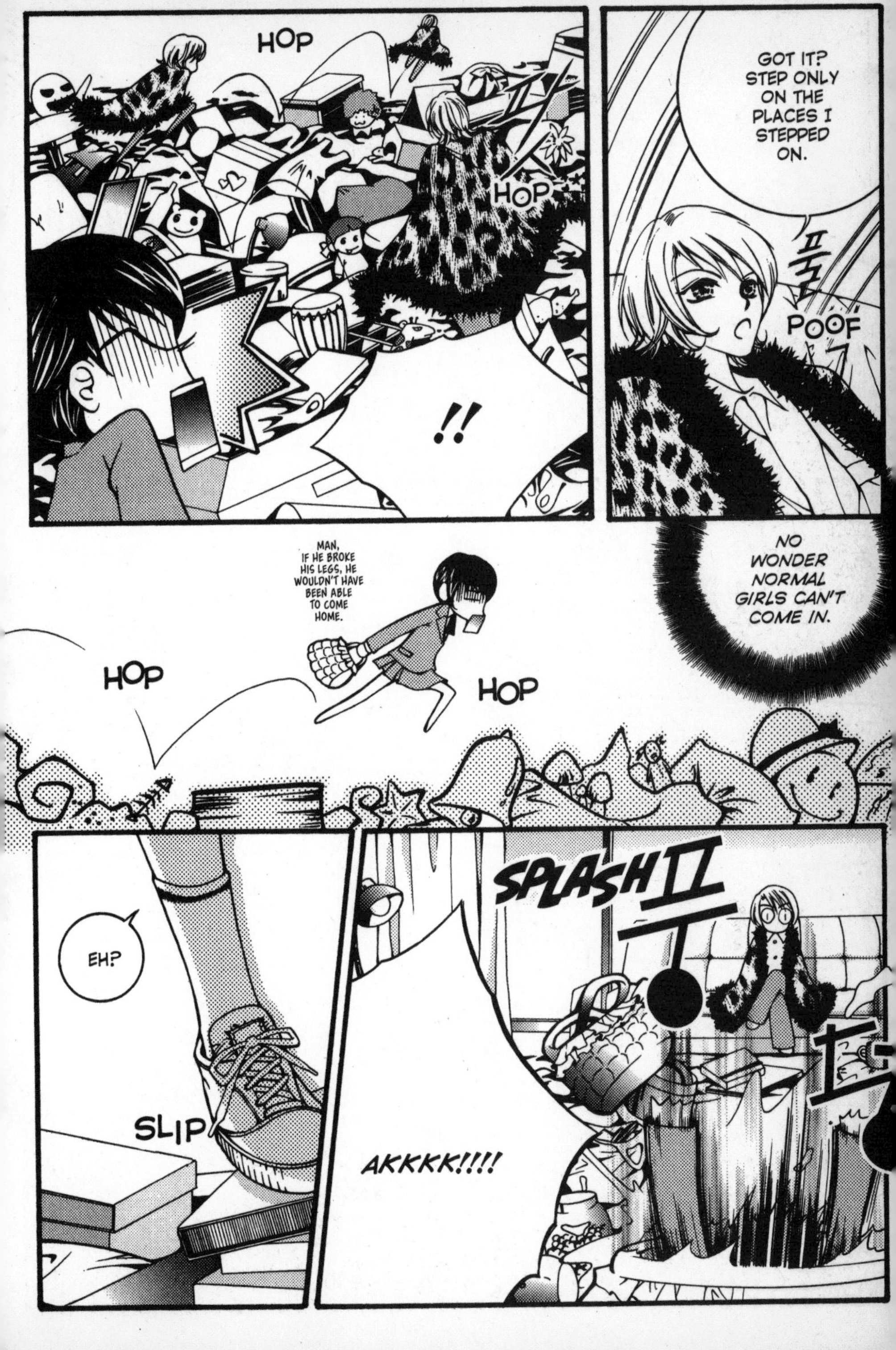
HOP
HOP
!!
GOT IT? STEP ONLY ON THE PLACES I STEPPED ON.
POOF
NO WONDER NORMAL GIRLS CAN'T COME IN.
HOP
MAN, IF HE BROKE HIS LEGS, HE WOULDN'T HAVE BEEN ABLE TO COME HOME.
HOP
EH?
SLIP
AKKKK!!!!
SPLASH

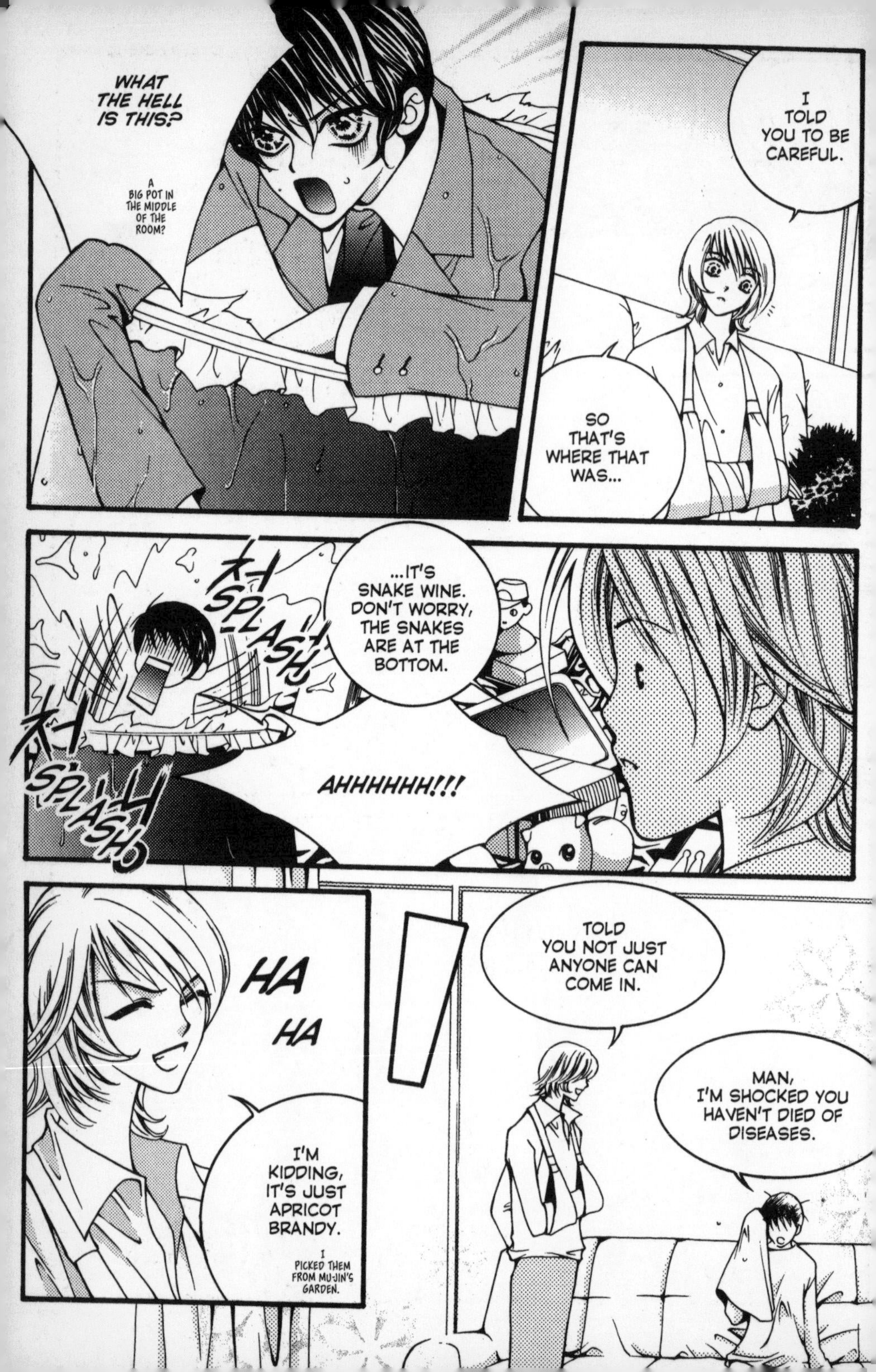
WHAT THE HELL IS THIS?
A BIG POT IN THE MIDDLE OF THE ROOM?
I TOLD YOU TO BE CAREFUL.
SO THAT'S WHERE THAT WAS...
SPLASH!
...IT'S SNAKE WINE. DON'T WORRY, THE SNAKES ARE AT THE BOTTOM.
SPLASH!
AHHHHHH!!!
HA HA
I'M KIDDING, IT'S JUST APRICOT BRANDY.
I PICKED THEM FROM MU-JIN'S GARDEN.
!
TOLD YOU NOT JUST ANYONE CAN COME IN.
MAN, I'M SHOCKED YOU HAVEN'T DIED OF DISEASES.

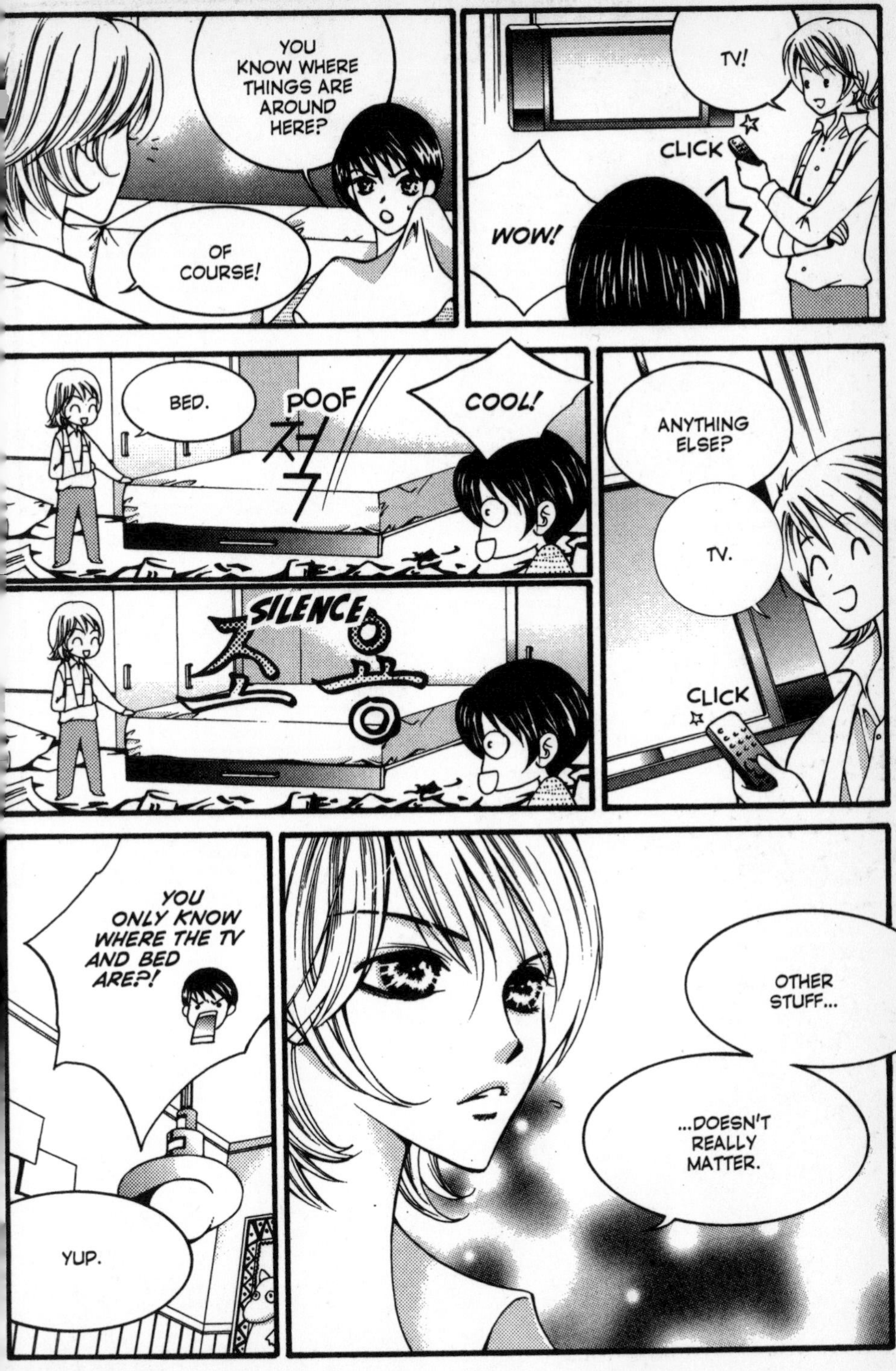
YOU KNOW WHERE THINGS ARE AROUND HERE?
OF COURSE!
TV!
CLICK
WOW!
BED.
POOF
COOL!
SILENCE
ANYTHING ELSE?
TV.
CLICK
YOU ONLY KNOW WHERE THE TV AND BED ARE?!
YUP.
OTHER STUFF...
...DOESN'T REALLY MATTER.

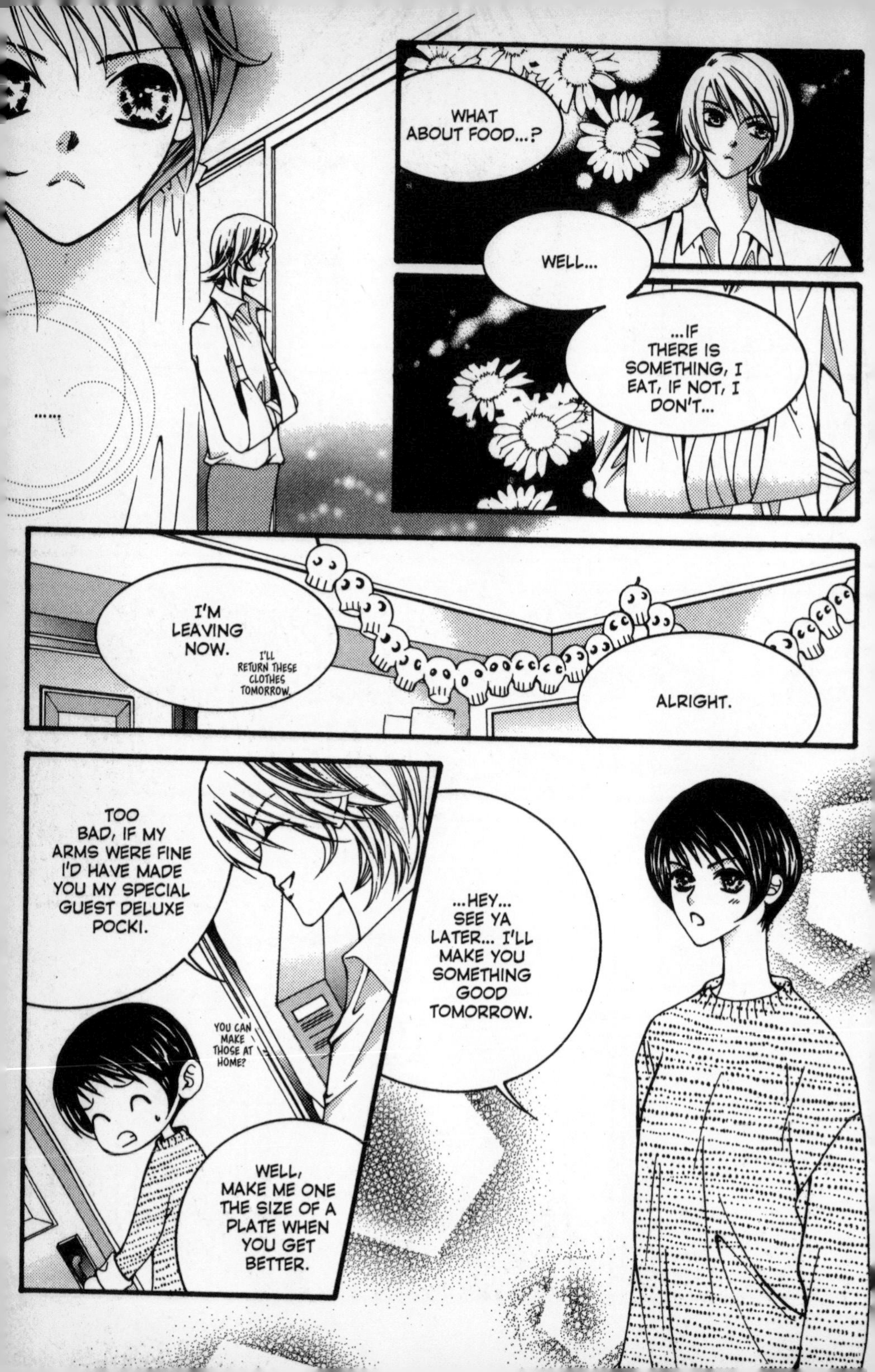
......
WHAT ABOUT FOOD...?
WELL...
...IF THERE IS SOMETHING, I EAT, IF NOT, I DON'T...
I'M LEAVING NOW.
I'LL RETURN THESE CLOTHES TOMORROW.
ALRIGHT.
TOO BAD, IF MY ARMS WERE FINE I'D HAVE MADE YOU MY SPECIAL GUEST DELUXE POCKI.
YOU CAN MAKE THOSE AT HOME?
WELL, MAKE ME ONE THE SIZE OF A PLATE WHEN YOU GET BETTER.
...HEY... SEE YA LATER... I'LL MAKE YOU SOMETHING GOOD TOMORROW.

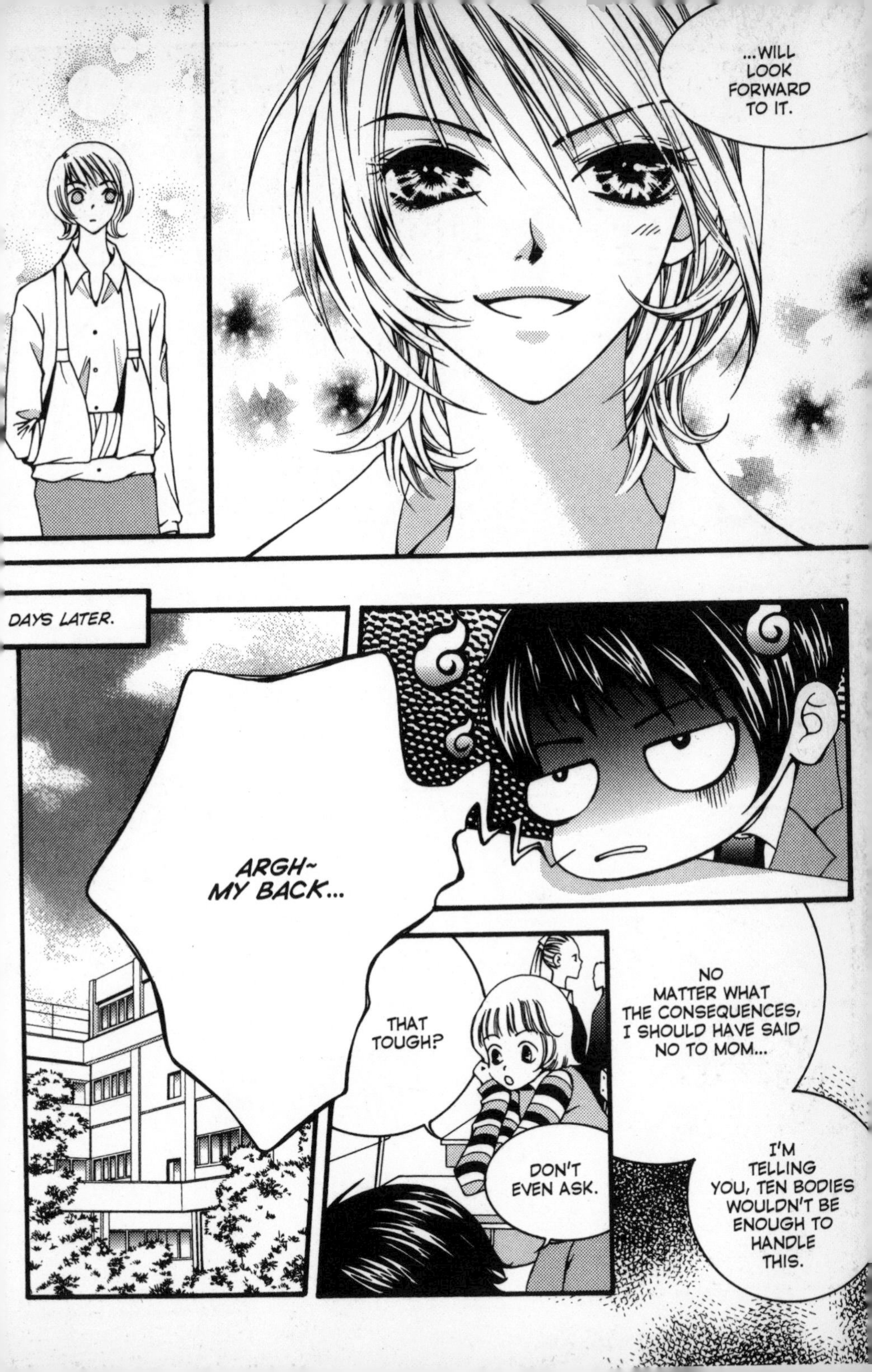
...WILL LOOK FORWARD TO IT.
DAYS LATER.
ARGH~ MY BACK...
THAT TOUGH?
NO MATTER WHAT THE CONSEQUENCES, I SHOULD HAVE SAID NO TO MOM...
DON'T EVEN ASK.
I'M TELLING YOU, TEN BODIES WOULDN'T BE ENOUGH TO HANDLE THIS.

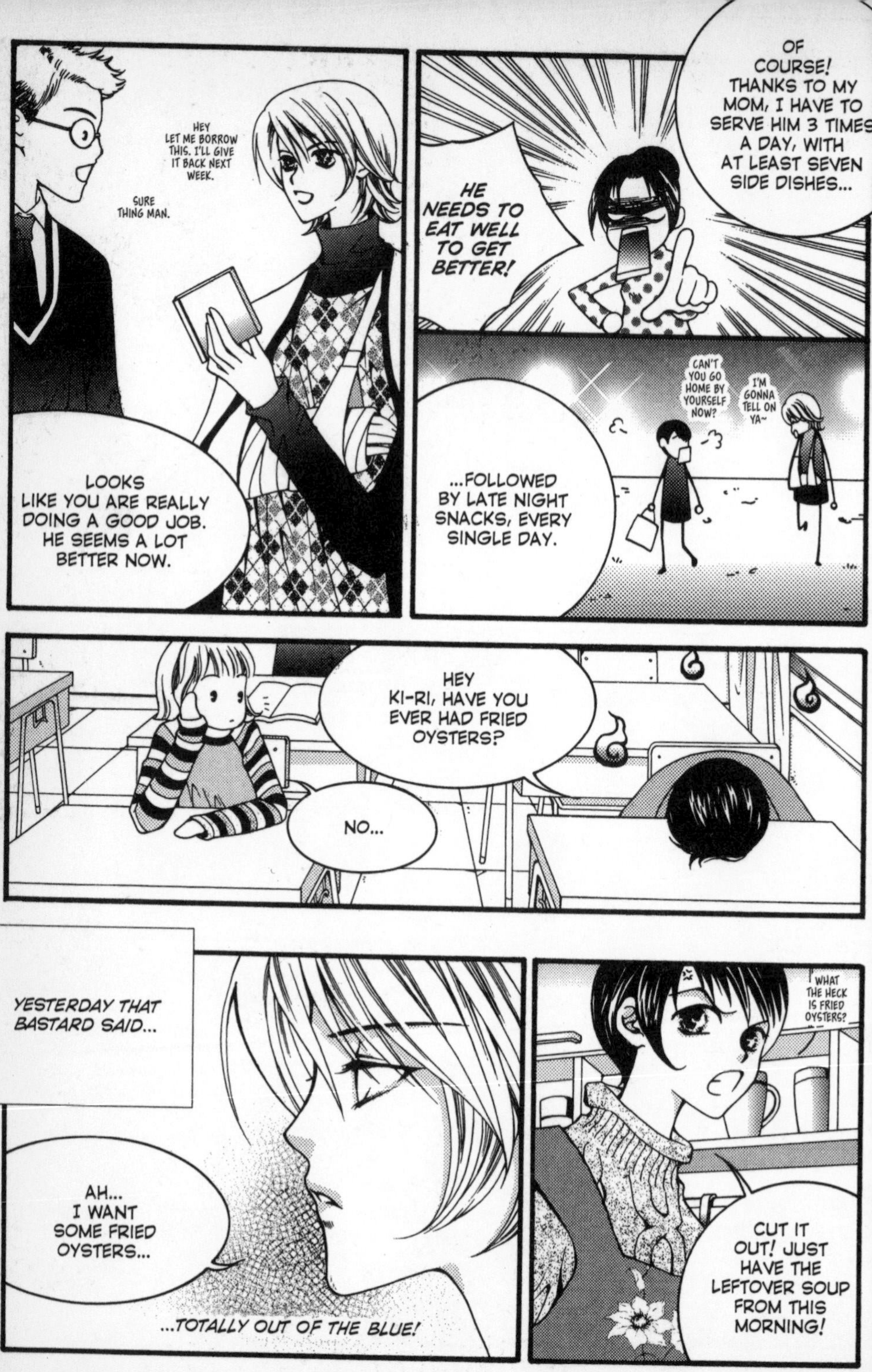
HEY LET ME BORROW THIS. I'LL GIVE IT BACK NEXT WEEK.
SURE THING MAN.
LOOKS LIKE YOU ARE REALLY DOING A GOOD JOB. HE SEEMS A LOT BETTER NOW.
HE NEEDS TO EAT WELL TO GET BETTER!
OF COURSE! THANKS TO MY MOM, I HAVE TO SERVE HIM 3 TIMES A DAY, WITH AT LEAST SEVEN SIDE DISHES...
...FOLLOWED BY LATE NIGHT SNACKS, EVERY SINGLE DAY.
CAN'T YOU GO HOME BY YOURSELF NOW?
I'M GONNA TELL ON YA~
HEY KI-RI, HAVE YOU EVER HAD FRIED OYSTERS?
NO...
YESTERDAY THAT BASTARD SAID...
AH... I WANT SOME FRIED OYSTERS...
...TOTALLY OUT OF THE BLUE!
WHAT THE HECK IS FRIED OYSTERS?
CUT IT OUT! JUST HAVE THE LEFTOVER SOUP FROM THIS MORNING!

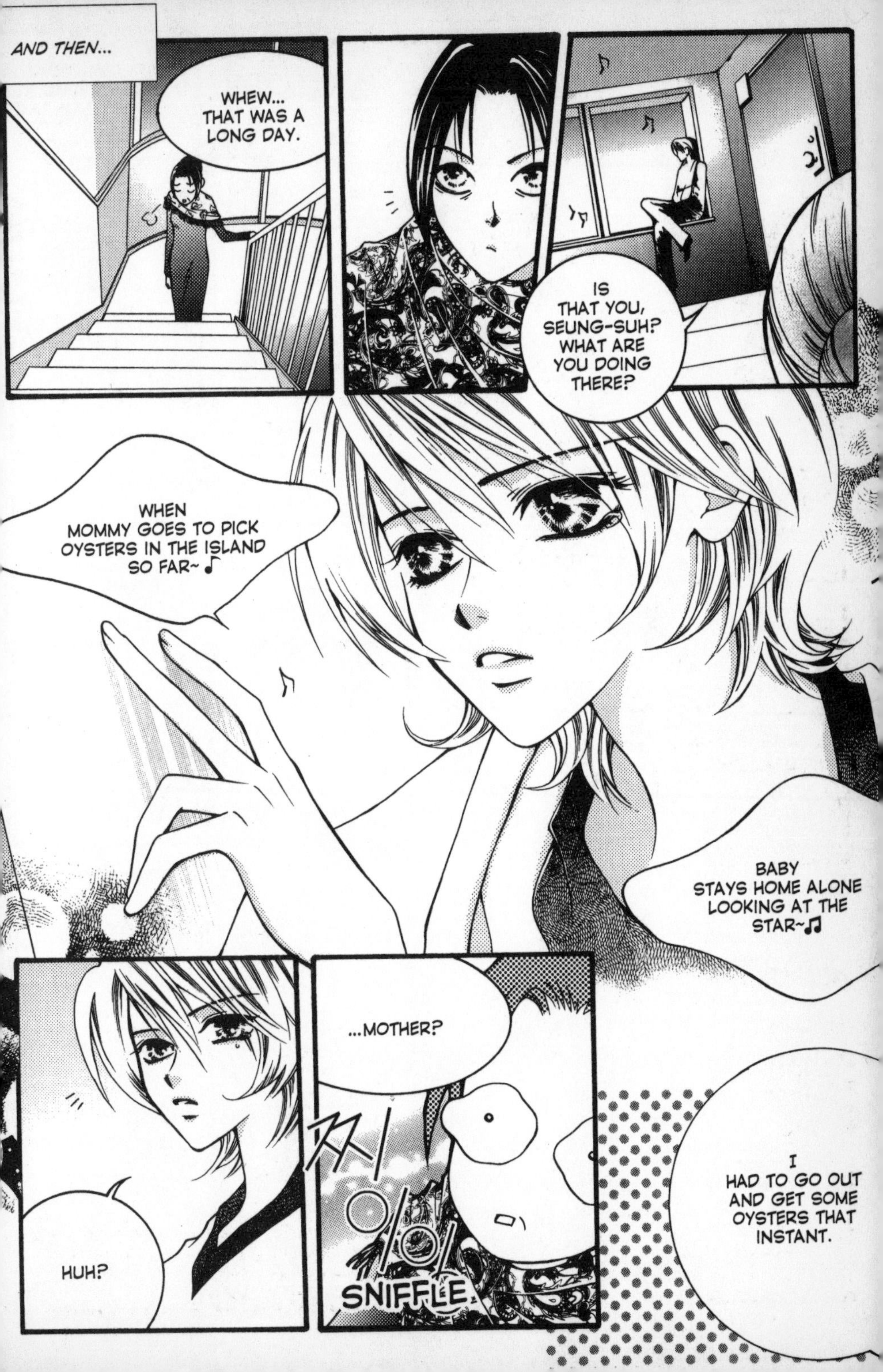
AND THEN...
WHEW... THAT WAS A LONG DAY.
IS THAT YOU, SEUNG-SUH? WHAT ARE YOU DOING THERE?
WHEN MOMMY GOES TO PICK OYSTERS IN THE ISLAND SO FAR~ ♪
BABY STAYS HOME ALONE LOOKING AT THE STAR~ ♫
HUH?
...MOTHER?
SNIFFLE
I HAD TO GO OUT AND GET SOME OYSTERS THAT INSTANT.

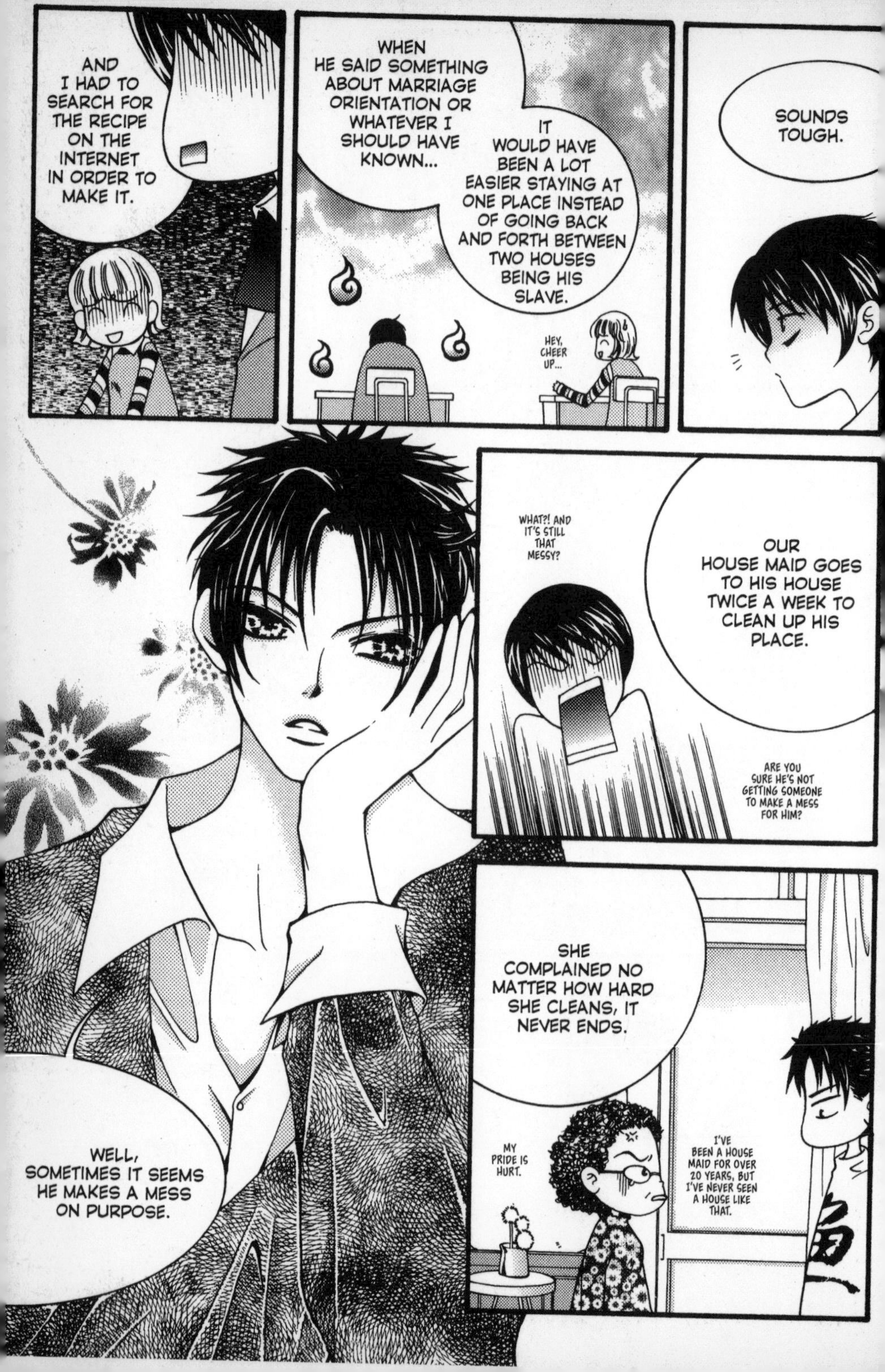
AND I HAD TO SEARCH FOR THE RECIPE ON THE INTERNET IN ORDER TO MAKE IT.
WHEN HE SAID SOMETHING ABOUT MARRIAGE ORIENTATION OR WHATEVER I SHOULD HAVE KNOWN...
IT WOULD HAVE BEEN A LOT EASIER STAYING AT ONE PLACE INSTEAD OF GOING BACK AND FORTH BETWEEN TWO HOUSES BEING HIS SLAVE.
HEY, CHEER UP...
SOUNDS TOUGH.
WELL, SOMETIMES IT SEEMS HE MAKES A MESS ON PURPOSE.
WHAT?! AND IT'S STILL THAT MESSY?
OUR HOUSE MAID GOES TO HIS HOUSE TWICE A WEEK TO CLEAN UP HIS PLACE.
ARE YOU SURE HE'S NOT GETTING SOMEONE TO MAKE A MESS FOR HIM?
SHE COMPLAINED NO MATTER HOW HARD SHE CLEANS, IT NEVER ENDS.
MY PRIDE IS HURT.
I'VE BEEN A HOUSE MAID FOR OVER 20 YEARS, BUT I'VE NEVER SEEN A HOUSE LIKE THAT.

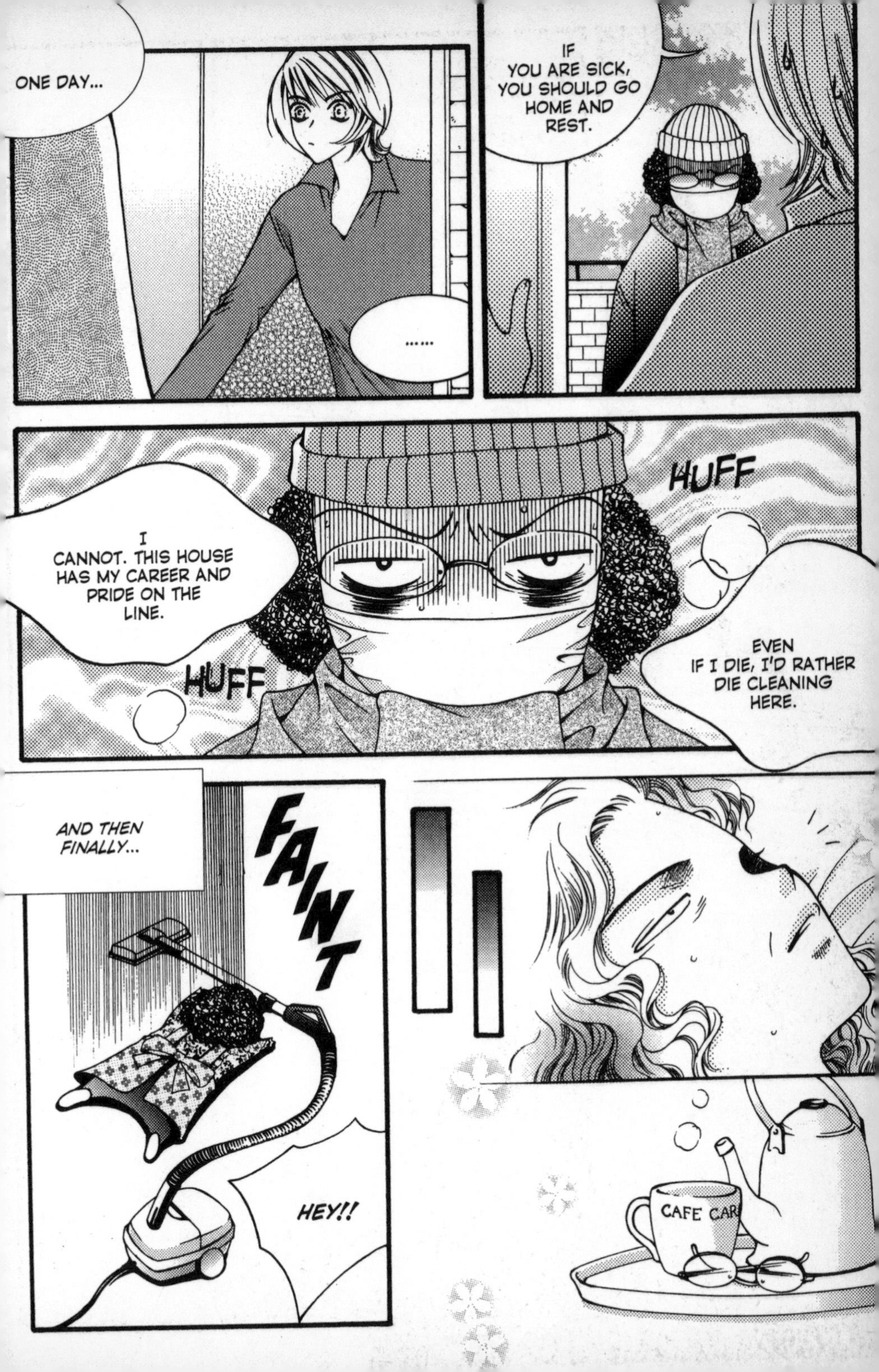
ONE DAY...
......
IF YOU ARE SICK, YOU SHOULD GO HOME AND REST.
I CANNOT. THIS HOUSE HAS MY CAREER AND PRIDE ON THE LINE.
HUFF
HUFF
EVEN IF I DIE, I'D RATHER DIE CLEANING HERE.
AND THEN FINALLY...
FAINT
HEY!!
CAFE CAR

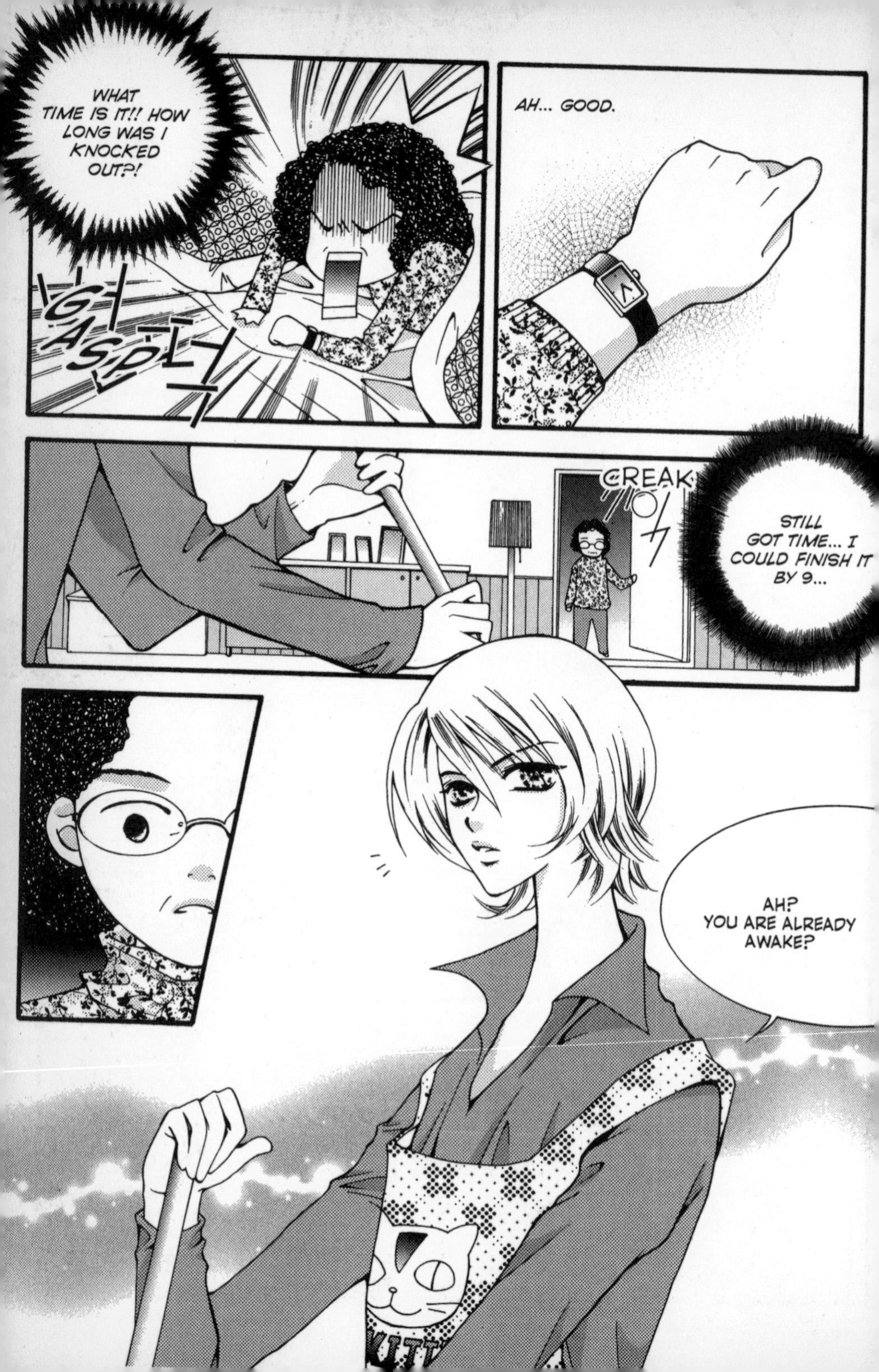
WHAT TIME IS IT!! HOW LONG WAS I KNOCKED OUT?!
GASP
AH... GOOD.
CREAK
STILL GOT TIME... I COULD FINISH IT BY 9...
AH? YOU ARE ALREADY AWAKE?

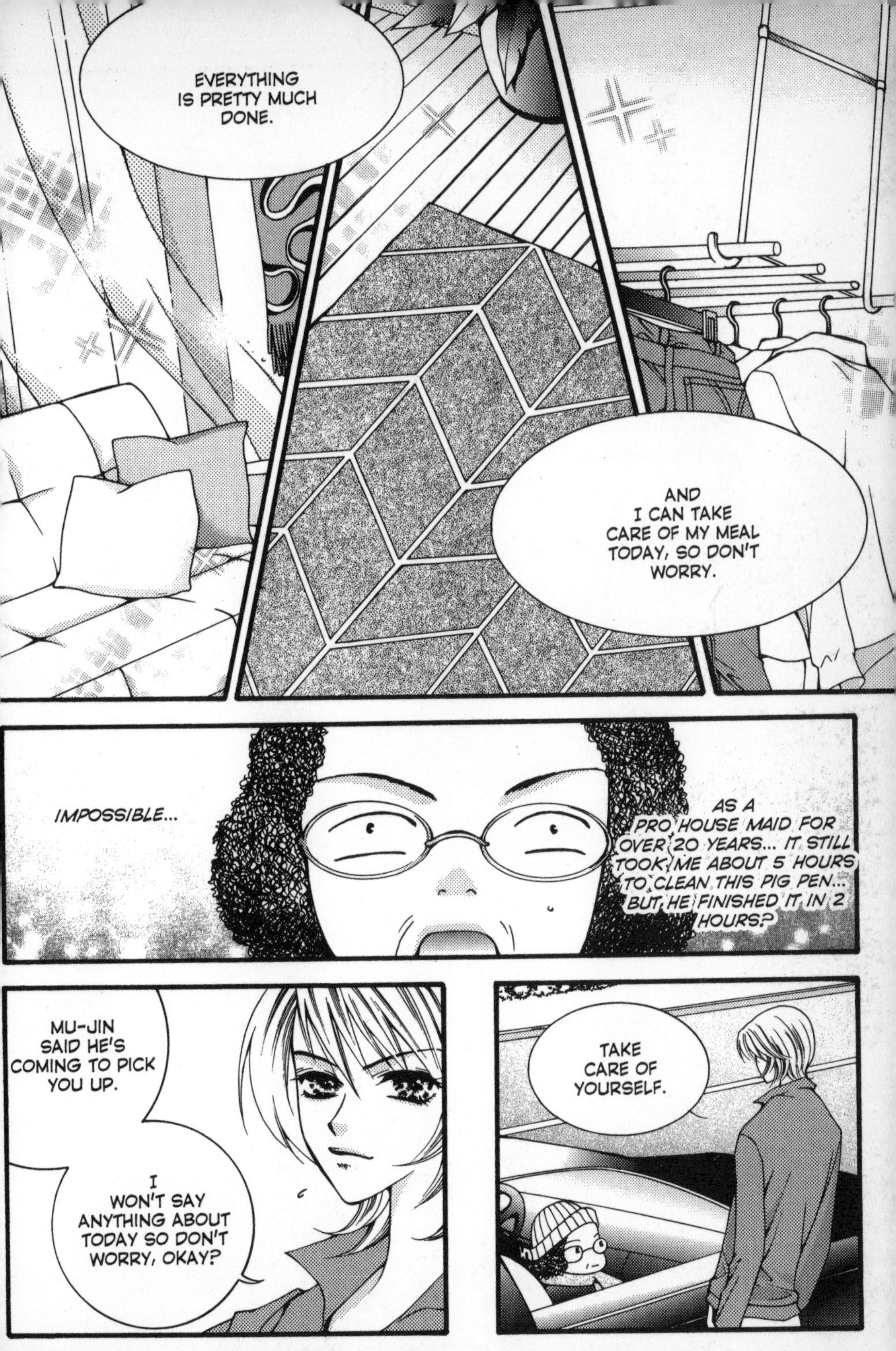
EVERYTHING IS PRETTY MUCH DONE.
AND I CAN TAKE CARE OF MY MEAL TODAY, SO DON'T WORRY.
IMPOSSIBLE...
AS A PRO HOUSE MAID FOR OVER 20 YEARS... IT STILL TOOK ME ABOUT 5 HOURS TO CLEAN THIS PIG PEN... BUT HE FINISHED IT IN 2 HOURS?
MU-JIN SAID HE'S COMING TO PICK YOU UP.
I WON'T SAY ANYTHING ABOUT TODAY SO DON'T WORRY, OKAY?
TAKE CARE OF YOURSELF.

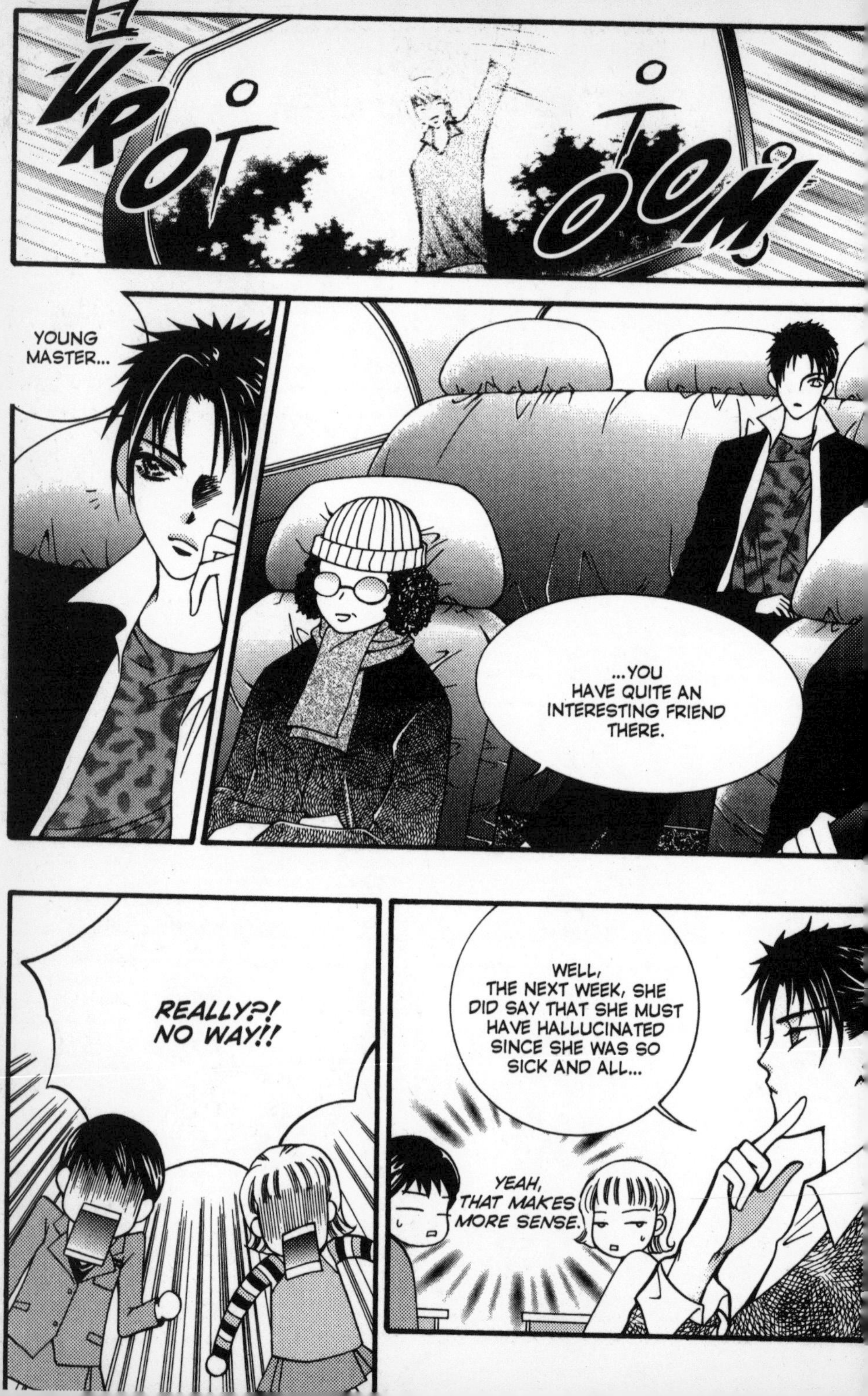
VROOOOM!
YOUNG MASTER...
...YOU HAVE QUITE AN INTERESTING FRIEND THERE.
REALLY?! NO WAY!!
WELL, THE NEXT WEEK, SHE DID SAY THAT SHE MUST HAVE HALLUCINATED SINCE SHE WAS SO SICK AND ALL...
YEAH, THAT MAKES MORE SENSE.

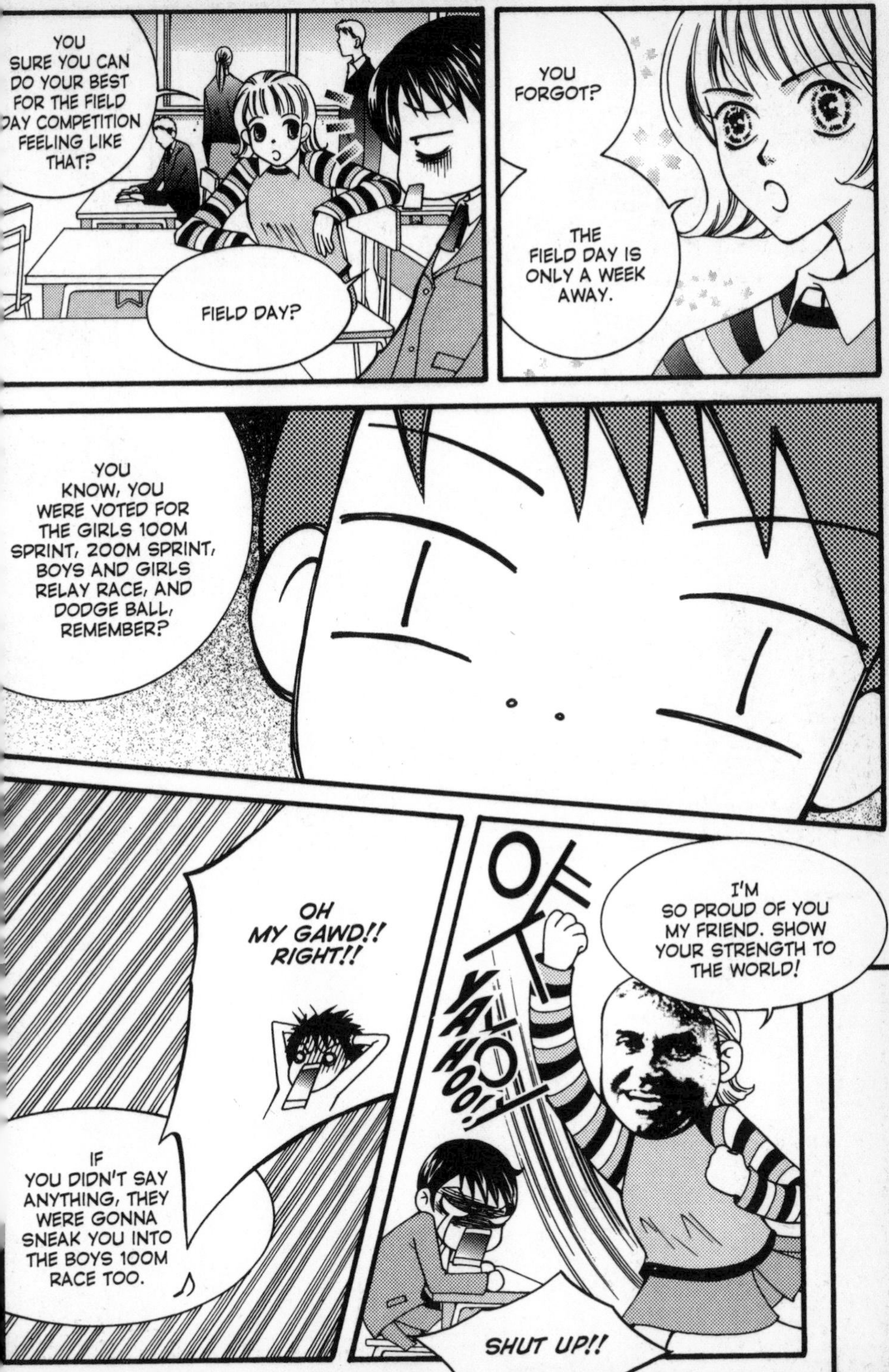
YOU SURE YOU CAN DO YOUR BEST FOR THE FIELD DAY COMPETITION FEELING LIKE THAT?
FIELD DAY?
YOU FORGOT?
THE FIELD DAY IS ONLY A WEEK AWAY.
YOU KNOW, YOU WERE VOTED FOR THE GIRLS 100M SPRINT, 200M SPRINT, BOYS AND GIRLS RELAY RACE, AND DODGE BALL, REMEMBER?
OH MY GAWD!! RIGHT!!
IF YOU DIDN'T SAY ANYTHING, THEY WERE GONNA SNEAK YOU INTO THE BOYS 100M RACE TOO.
I'M SO PROUD OF YOU MY FRIEND. SHOW YOUR STRENGTH TO THE WORLD!
YAHOO!!
SHUT UP!!

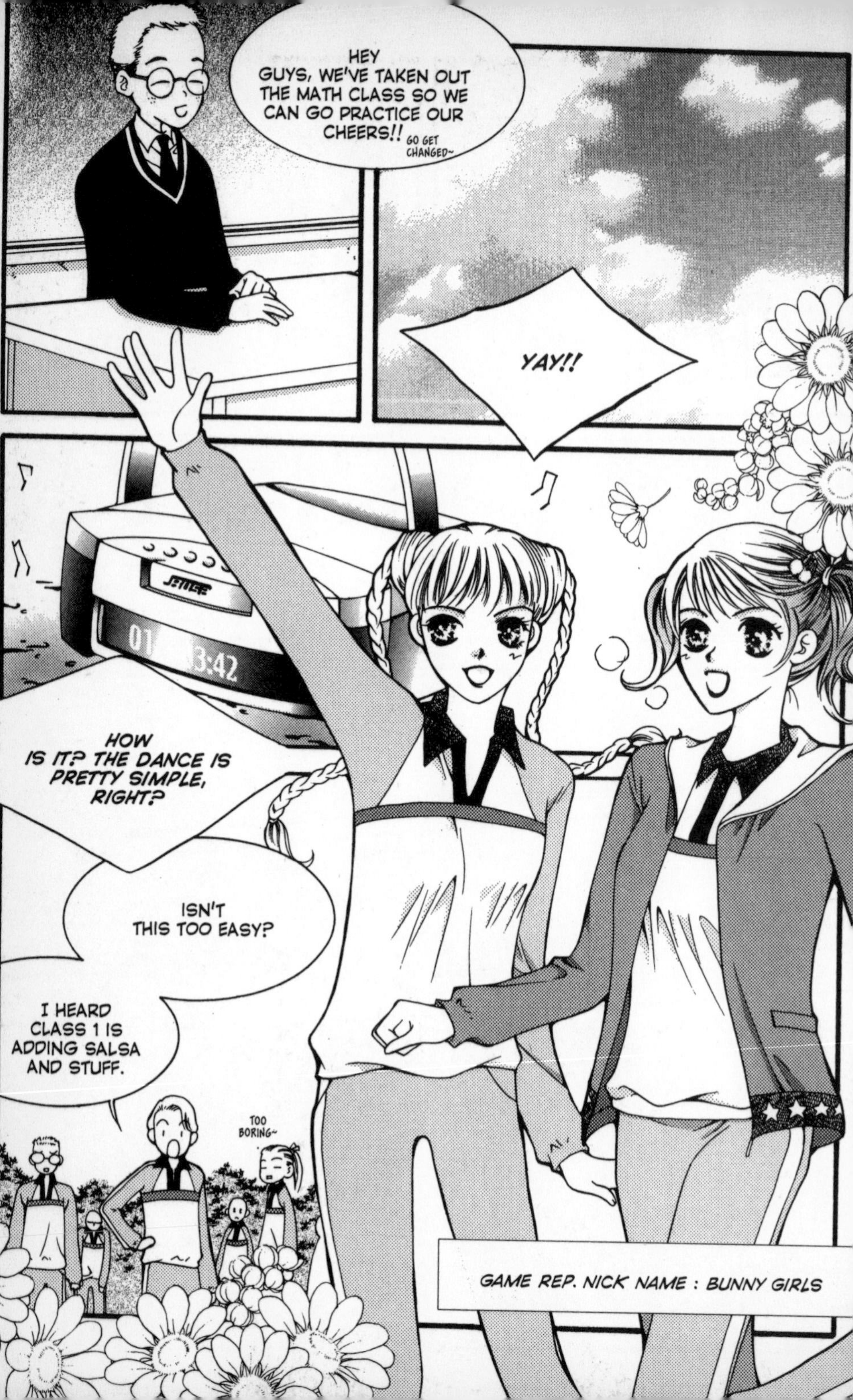
HEY GUYS, WE'VE TAKEN OUT THE MATH CLASS SO WE CAN GO PRACTICE OUR CHEERS!!
GO GET CHANGED~
YAY!!
HOW IS IT? THE DANCE IS PRETTY SIMPLE, RIGHT?
ISN'T THIS TOO EASY?
I HEARD CLASS 1 IS ADDING SALSA AND STUFF.
TOO BORING~
GAME REP. NICK NAME : BUNNY GIRLS

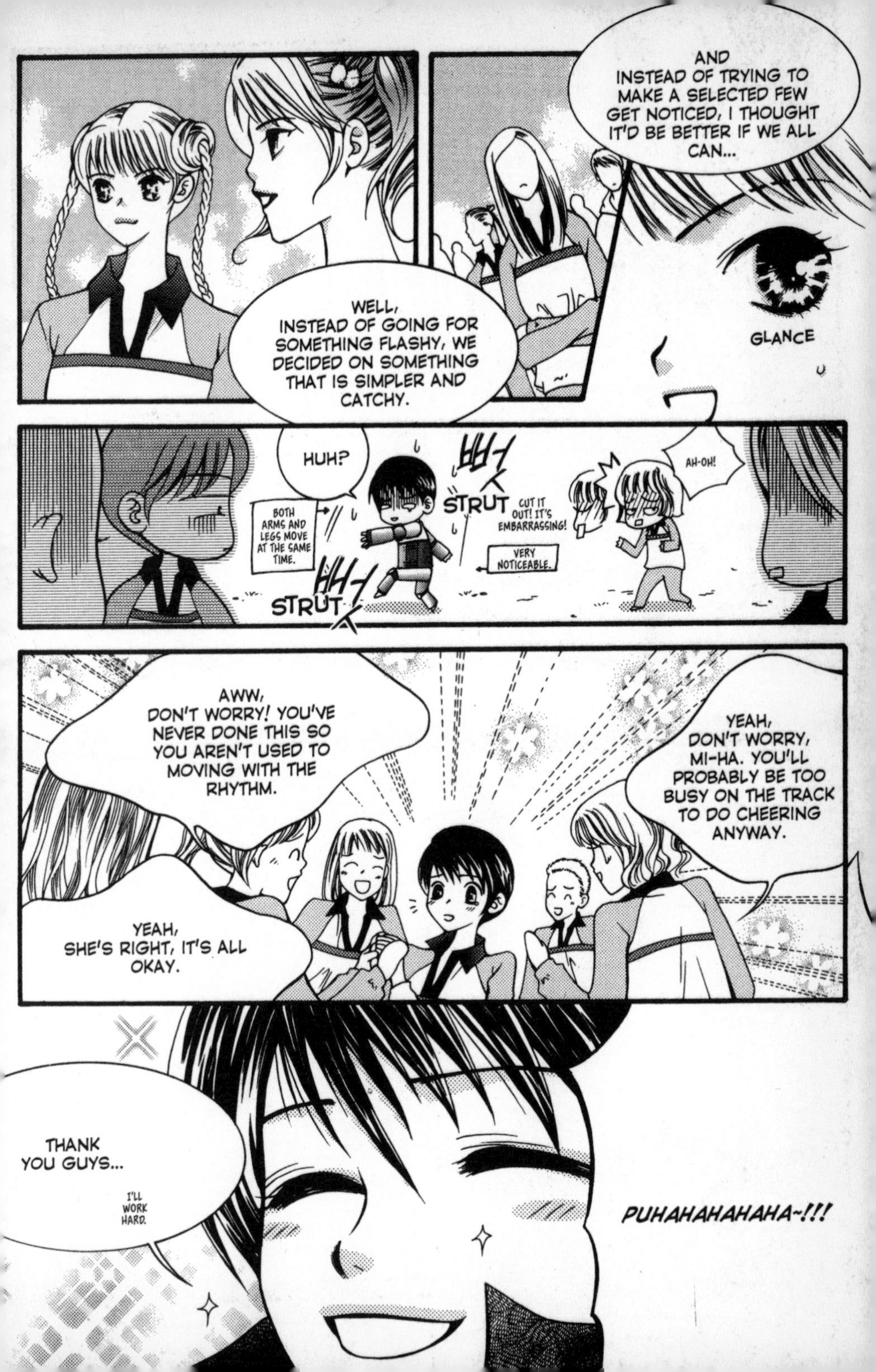
WELL, INSTEAD OF GOING FOR SOMETHING FLASHY, WE DECIDED ON SOMETHING THAT IS SIMPLER AND CATCHY.
AND INSTEAD OF TRYING TO MAKE A SELECTED FEW GET NOTICED, I THOUGHT IT'D BE BETTER IF WE ALL CAN...
GLANCE
HUH?
BOTH ARMS AND LEGS MOVE AT THE SAME TIME.
STRUT
STRUT
CUT IT OUT! IT'S EMBARRASSING!
VERY NOTICEABLE.
AH-OH!
AWW, DON'T WORRY! YOU'VE NEVER DONE THIS SO YOU AREN'T USED TO MOVING WITH THE RHYTHM.
YEAH, SHE'S RIGHT, IT'S ALL OKAY.
YEAH, DON'T WORRY, MI-HA. YOU'LL PROBABLY BE TOO BUSY ON THE TRACK TO DO CHEERING ANYWAY.
THANK YOU GUYS...
I'LL WORK HARD.
PUHAHAHAHAHA~!!!

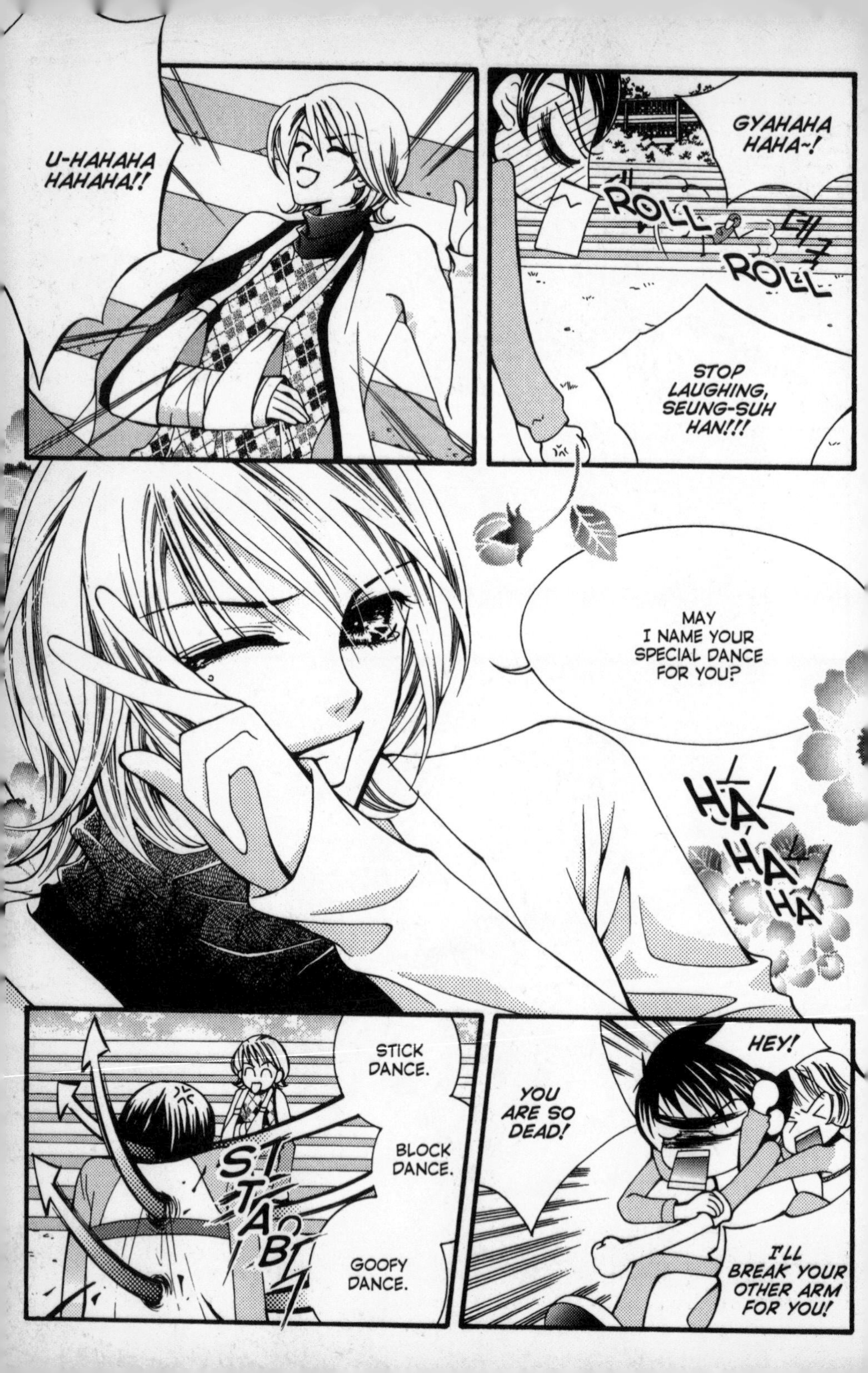
U-HAHAHA HAHAHA!!
GYAHAHA HAHA~!
ROLL
ROLL
STOP LAUGHING, SEUNG-SUH HAN!!!
MAY I NAME YOUR SPECIAL DANCE FOR YOU?
HA HA HA HA
STICK DANCE.
BLOCK DANCE.
STAB
GOOFY DANCE.
HEY!
YOU ARE SO DEAD!
I'LL BREAK YOUR OTHER ARM FOR YOU!

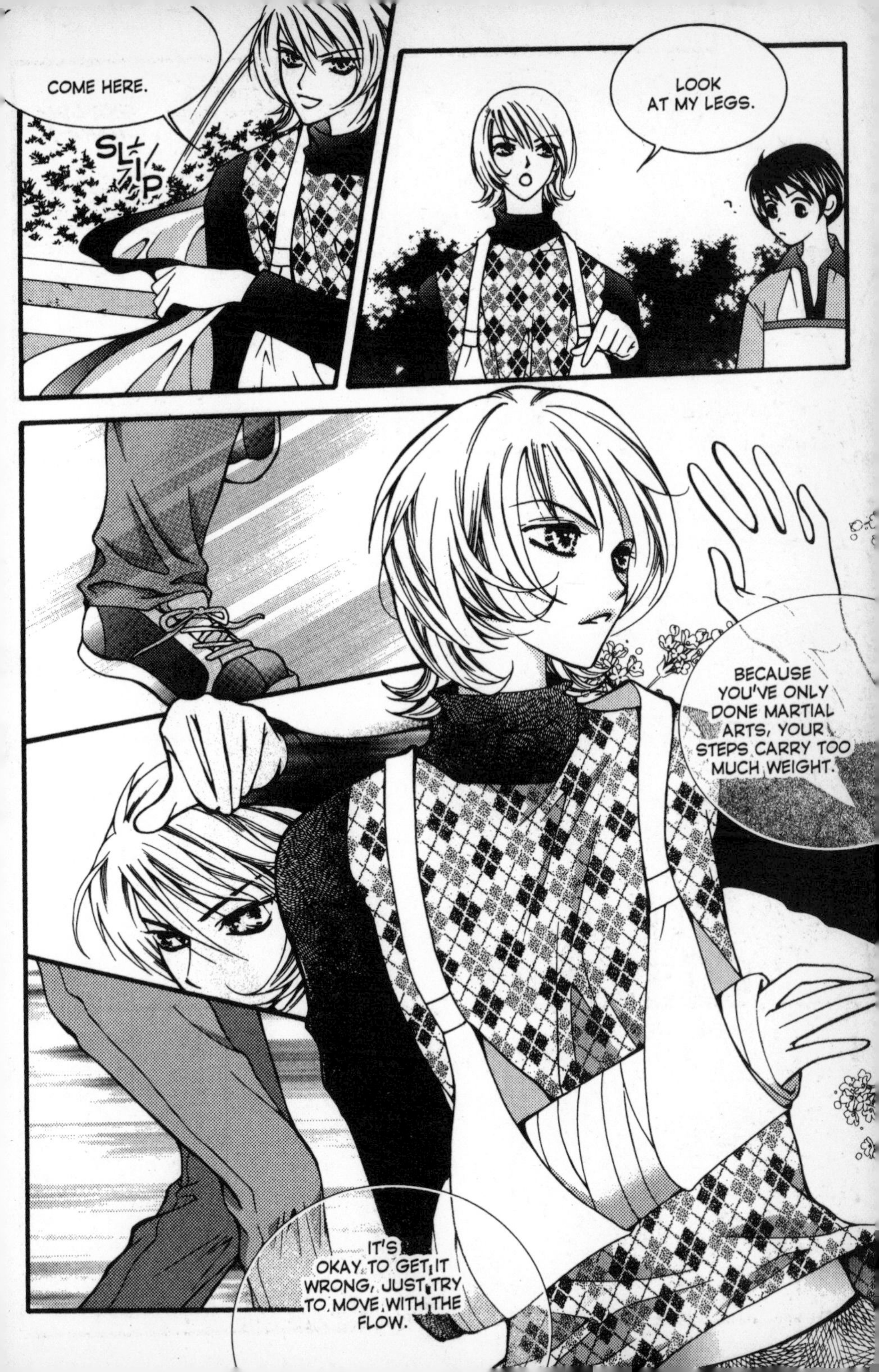
COME HERE.
SLIP
LOOK AT MY LEGS.
?
BECAUSE YOU'VE ONLY DONE MARTIAL ARTS, YOUR STEPS CARRY TOO MUCH WEIGHT.
IT'S OKAY TO GET IT WRONG, JUST TRY TO MOVE WITH THE FLOW.

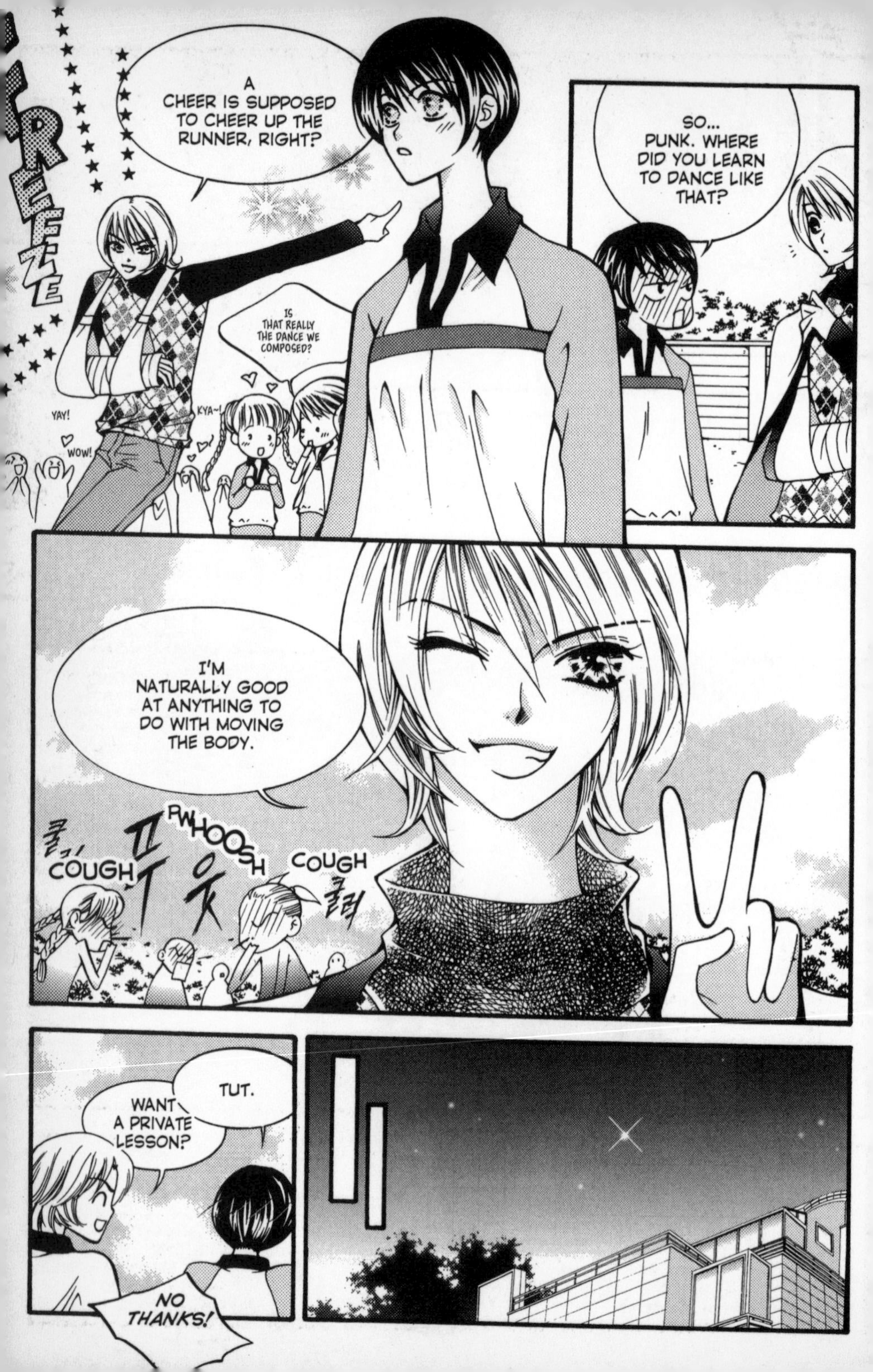
A CHEER IS SUPPOSED TO CHEER UP THE RUNNER, RIGHT?
IS THAT REALLY THE DANCE WE COMPOSED?
YAY!
WOW!
KYA~!
SO... PUNK. WHERE DID YOU LEARN TO DANCE LIKE THAT?
I'M NATURALLY GOOD AT ANYTHING TO DO WITH MOVING THE BODY.
COUGH
PWHOOSH
COUGH
WANT A PRIVATE LESSON?
TUT.
NO THANKS!

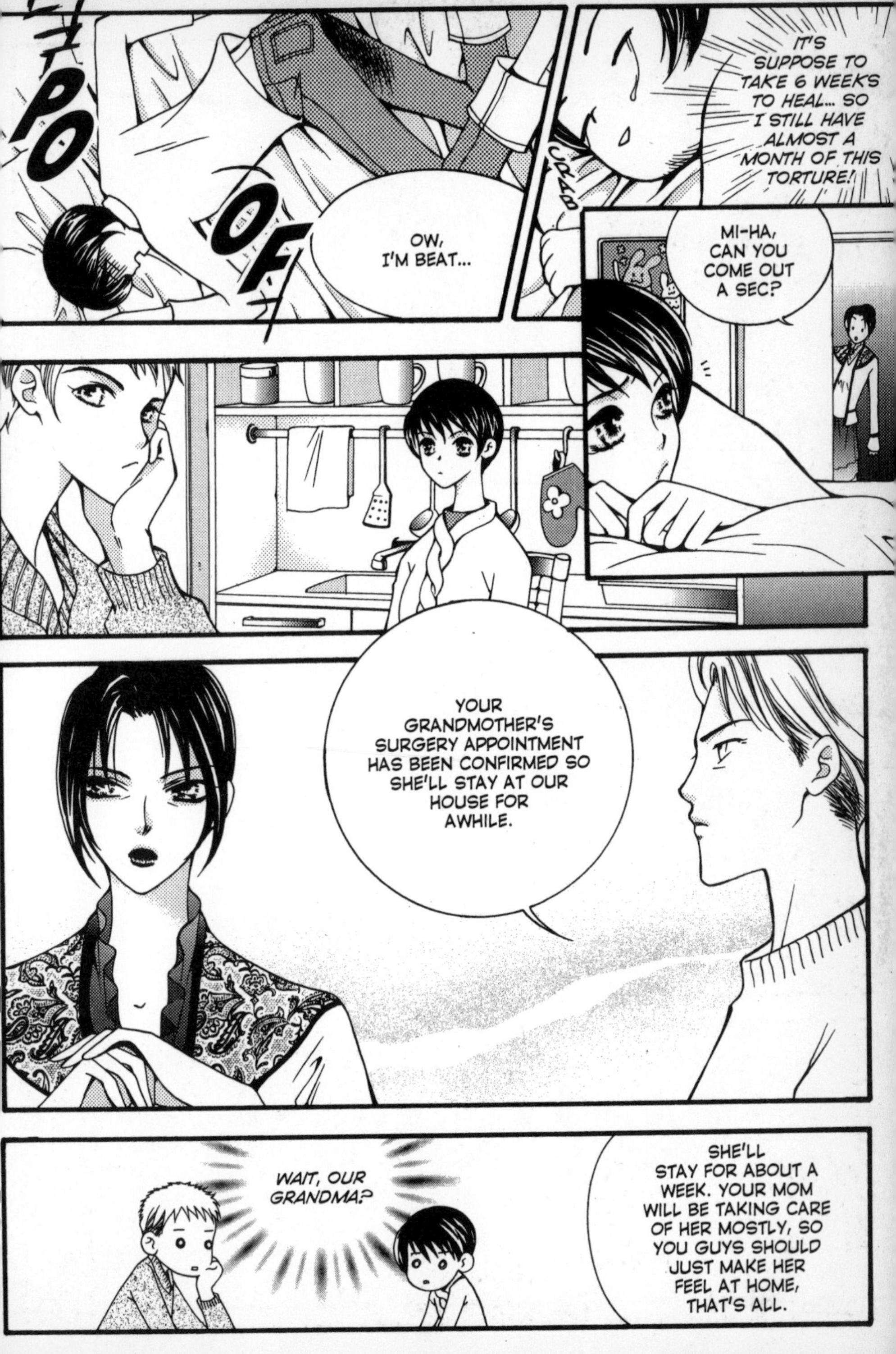
POOF
OW, I'M BEAT...
IT'S SUPPOSE TO TAKE 6 WEEKS TO HEAL... SO I STILL HAVE ALMOST A MONTH OF THIS TORTURE!
MI-HA, CAN YOU COME OUT A SEC?
YOUR GRANDMOTHER'S SURGERY APPOINTMENT HAS BEEN CONFIRMED SO SHE'LL STAY AT OUR HOUSE FOR AWHILE.
WAIT, OUR GRANDMA?
SHE'LL STAY FOR ABOUT A WEEK. YOUR MOM WILL BE TAKING CARE OF HER MOSTLY, SO YOU GUYS SHOULD JUST MAKE HER FEEL AT HOME, THAT'S ALL.

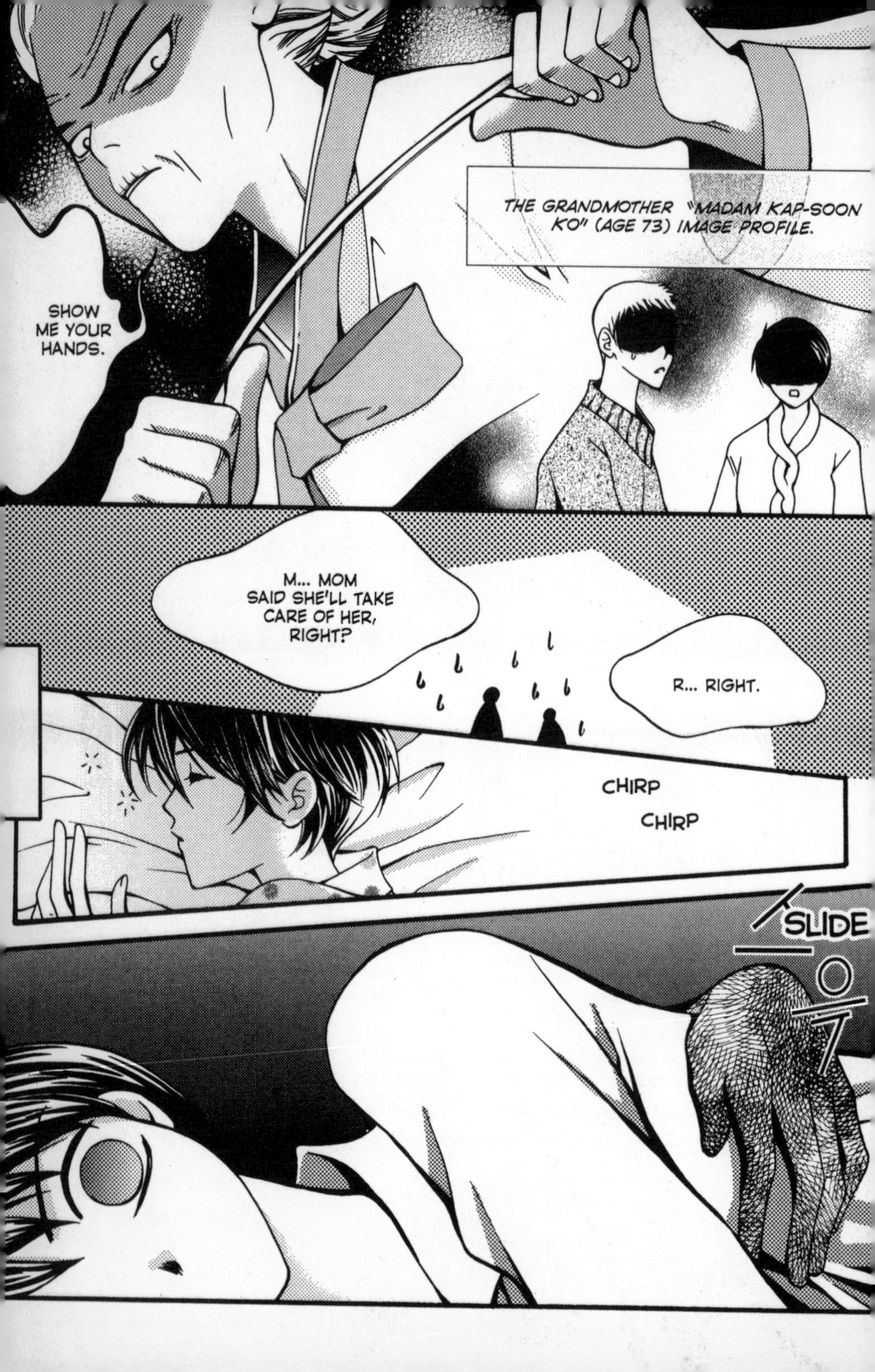
THE GRANDMOTHER "MADAM KAP-SOON KO" (AGE 73) IMAGE PROFILE.
SHOW ME YOUR HANDS.
M... MOM SAID SHE'LL TAKE CARE OF HER, RIGHT?
R... RIGHT.
CHIRP
CHIRP
SLIDE

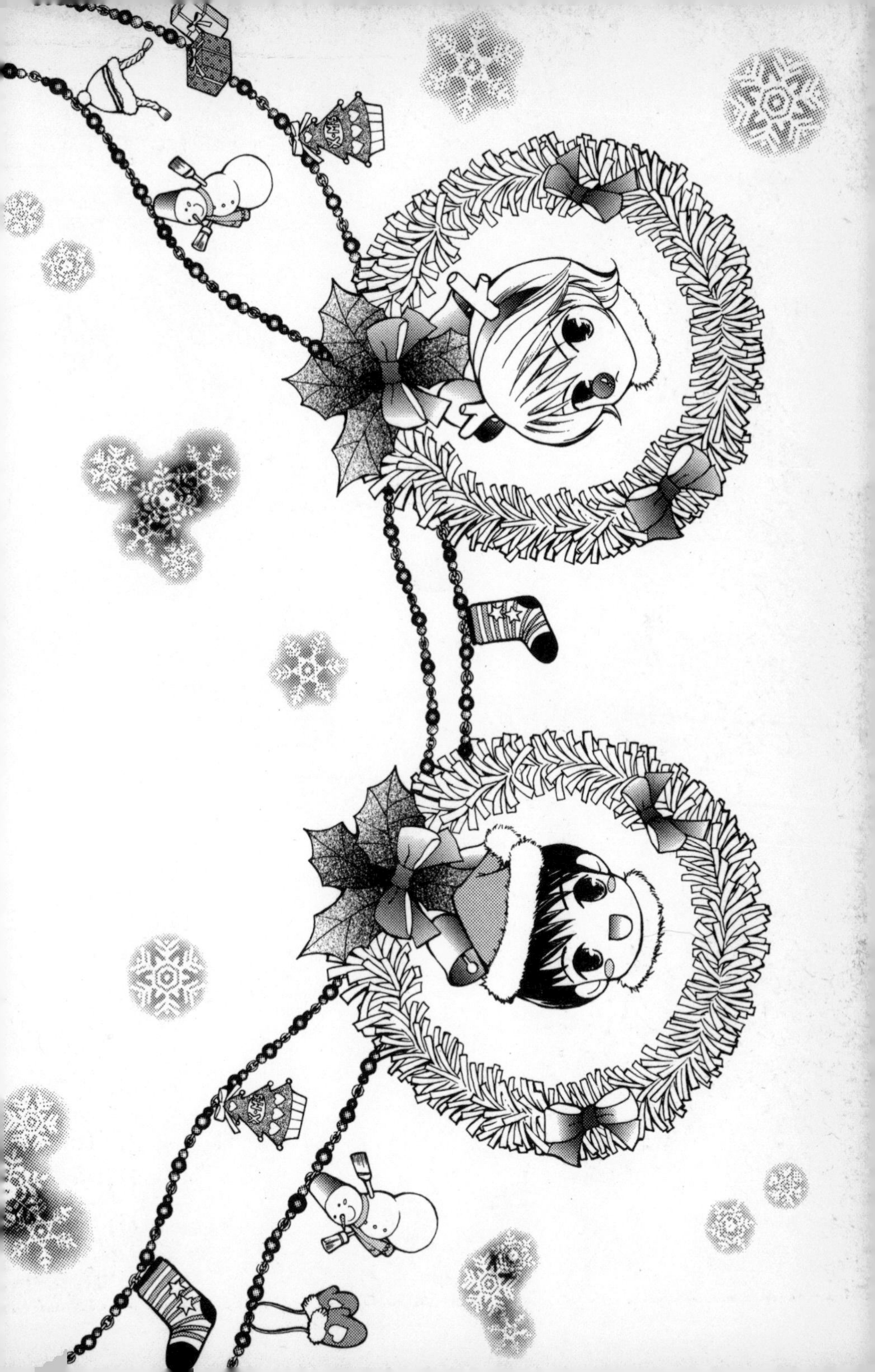

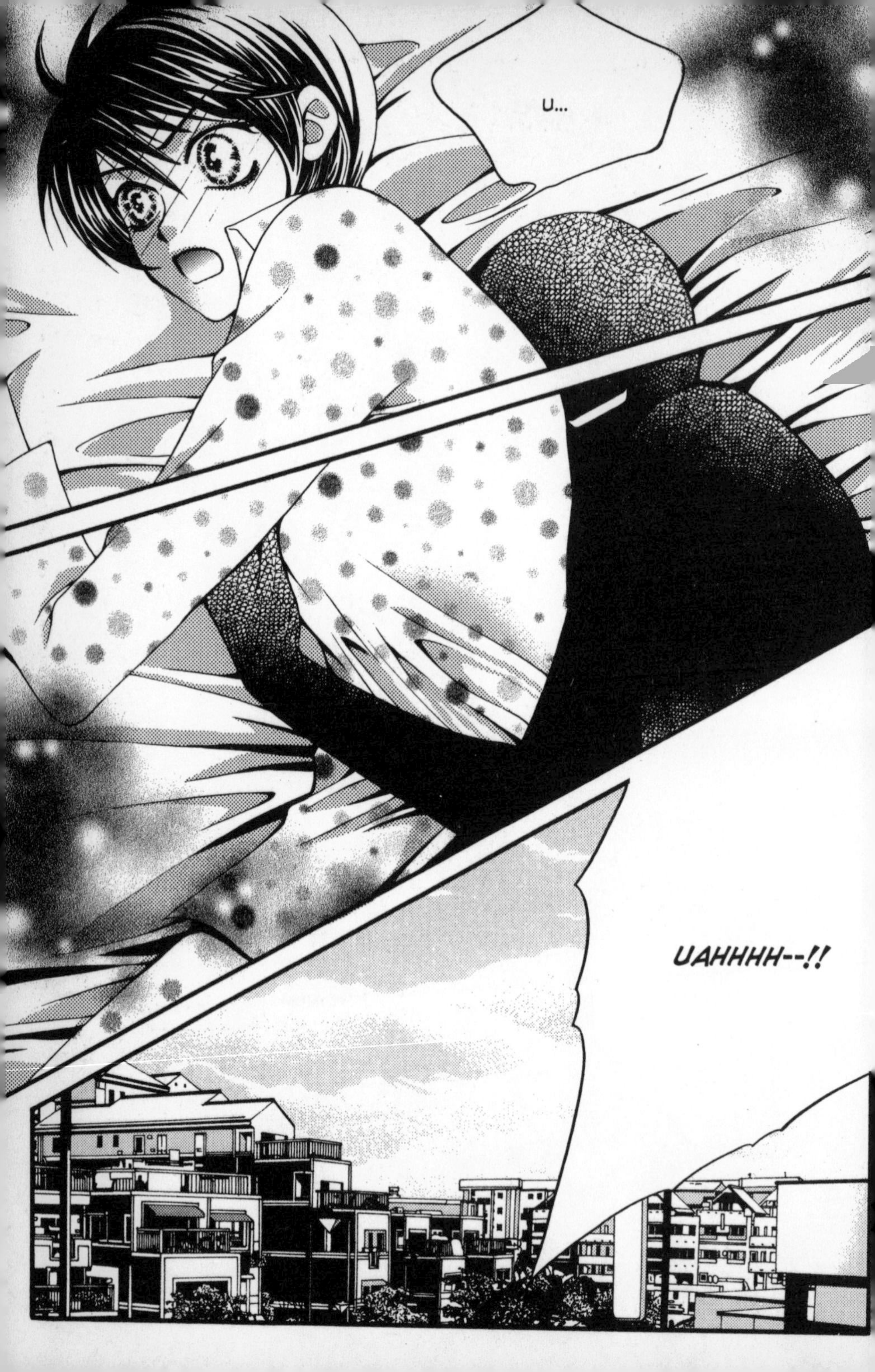

U...
UAHHHH--!!

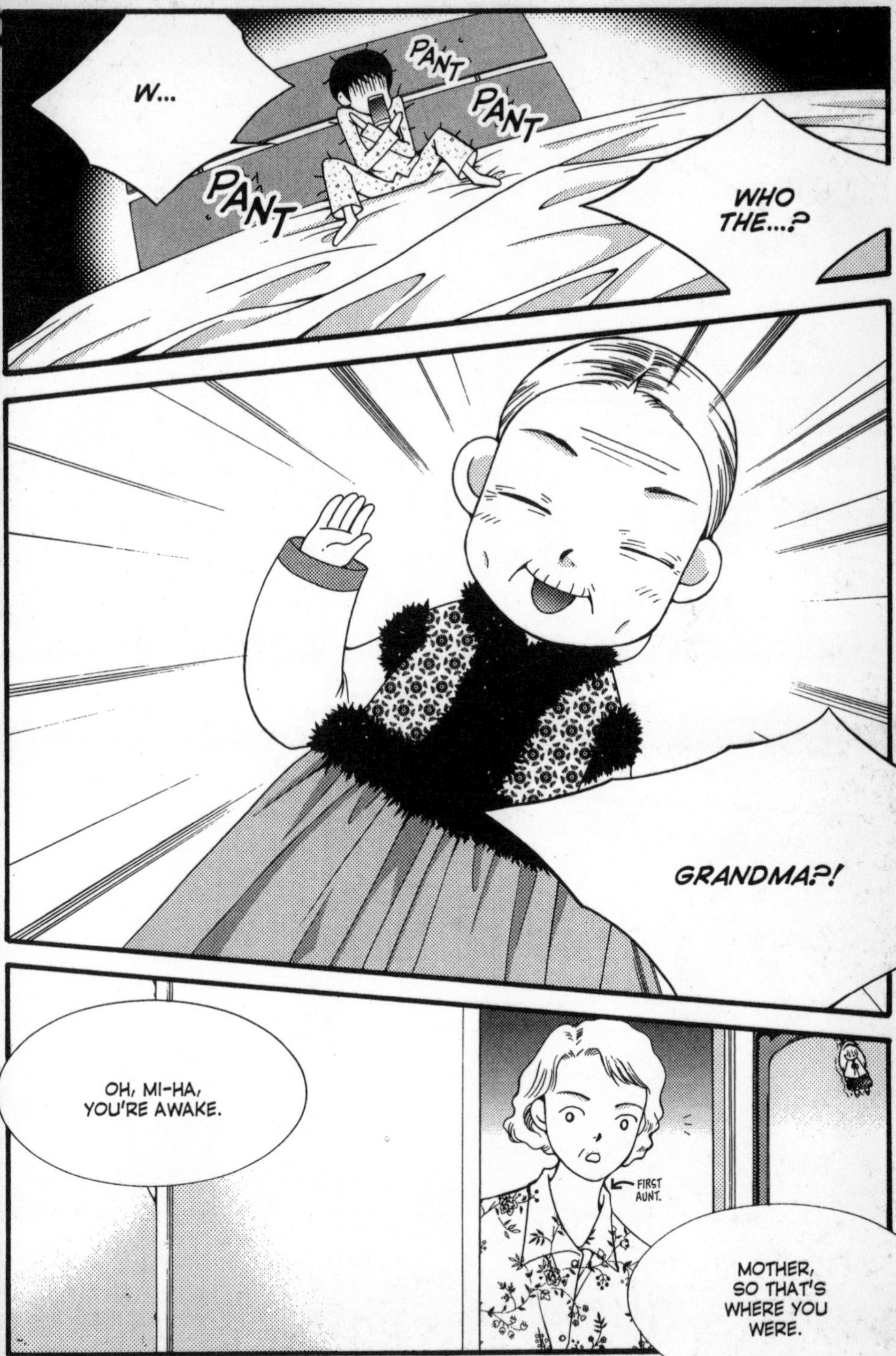
W...
PANT
PANT
PANT
WHO THE...?
GRANDMA?!
OH, MI-HA, YOU'RE AWAKE.
FIRST AUNT.
MOTHER, SO THAT'S WHERE YOU WERE.

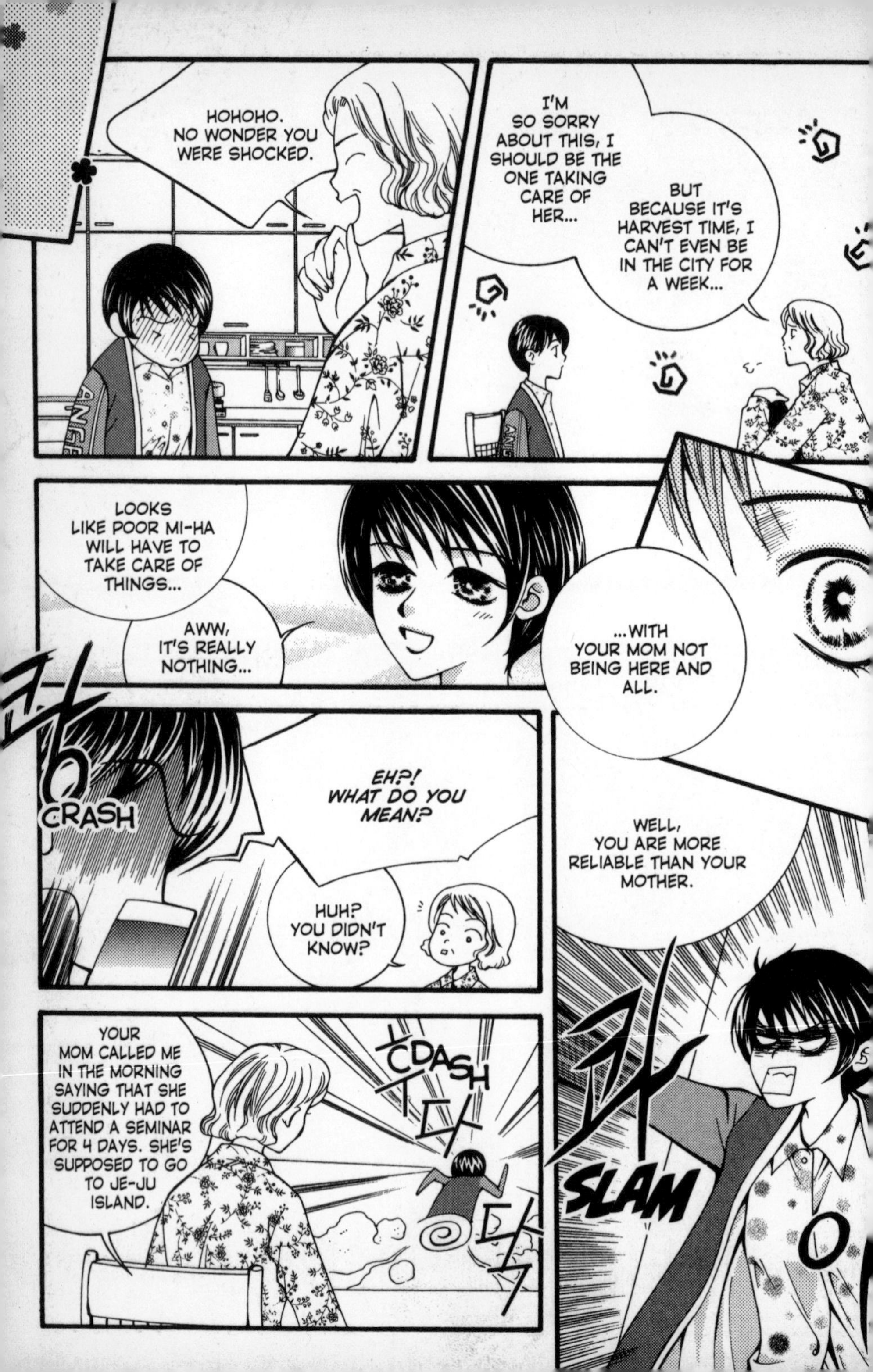
HOHOHO. NO WONDER YOU WERE SHOCKED.
I'M SO SORRY ABOUT THIS, I SHOULD BE THE ONE TAKING CARE OF HER...
BUT BECAUSE IT'S HARVEST TIME, I CAN'T EVEN BE IN THE CITY FOR A WEEK...
LOOKS LIKE POOR MI-HA WILL HAVE TO TAKE CARE OF THINGS...
AWW, IT'S REALLY NOTHING...
...WITH YOUR MOM NOT BEING HERE AND ALL.
CRASH
EH?! WHAT DO YOU MEAN?
HUH? YOU DIDN'T KNOW?
YOUR MOM CALLED ME IN THE MORNING SAYING THAT SHE SUDDENLY HAD TO ATTEND A SEMINAR FOR 4 DAYS. SHE'S SUPPOSED TO GO TO JE-JU ISLAND.
DASH
WELL, YOU ARE MORE RELIABLE THAN YOUR MOTHER.
SLAM

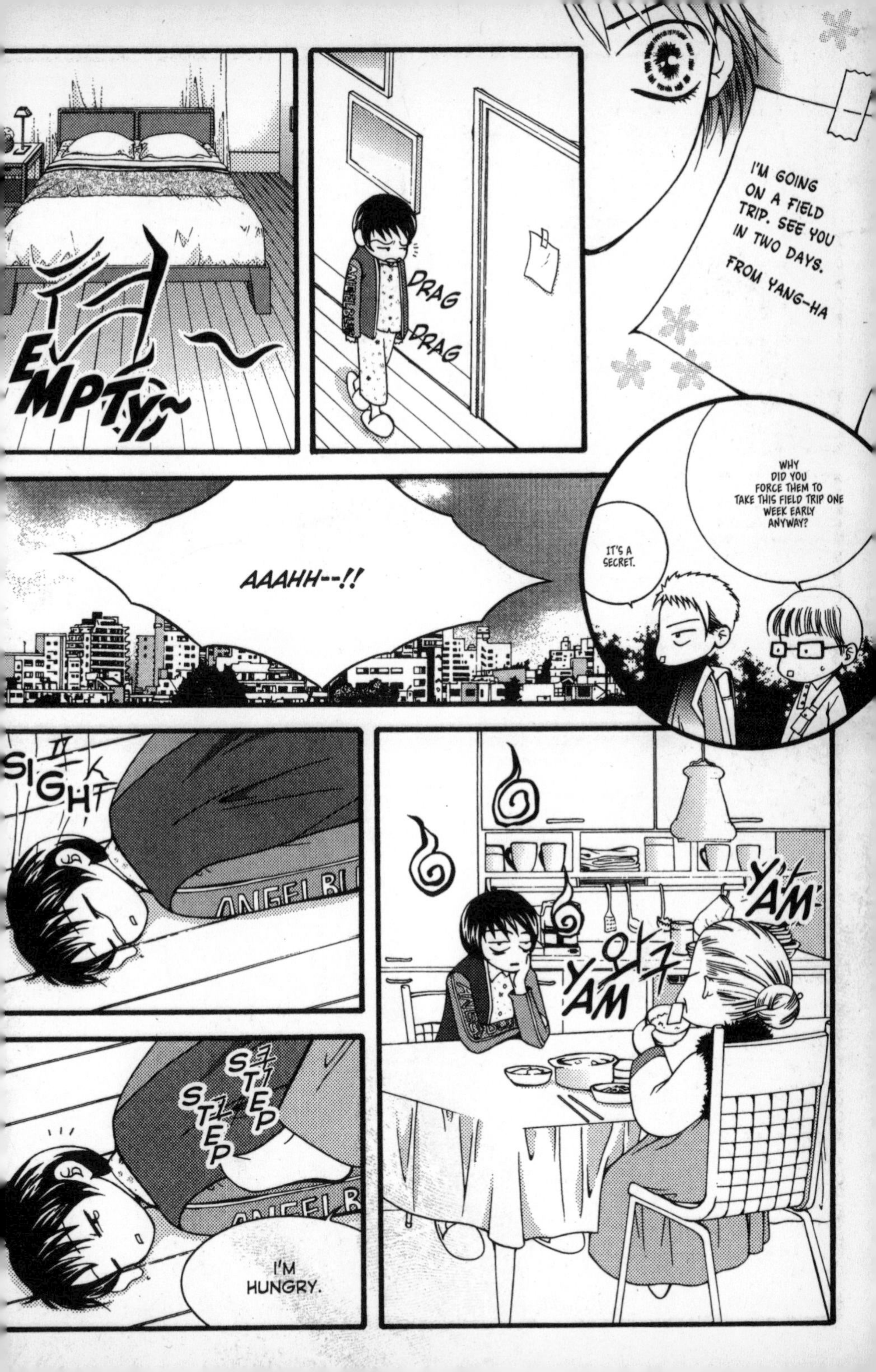
EMPTY~
DRAG
DRAG
I'M GOING ON A FIELD TRIP. SEE YOU IN TWO DAYS.
FROM YANG-HA
AAAHH--!!
WHY DID YOU FORCE THEM TO TAKE THIS FIELD TRIP ONE WEEK EARLY ANYWAY?
IT'S A SECRET.
SIGH
YAM
YAM
STEP
STEP
I'M HUNGRY.

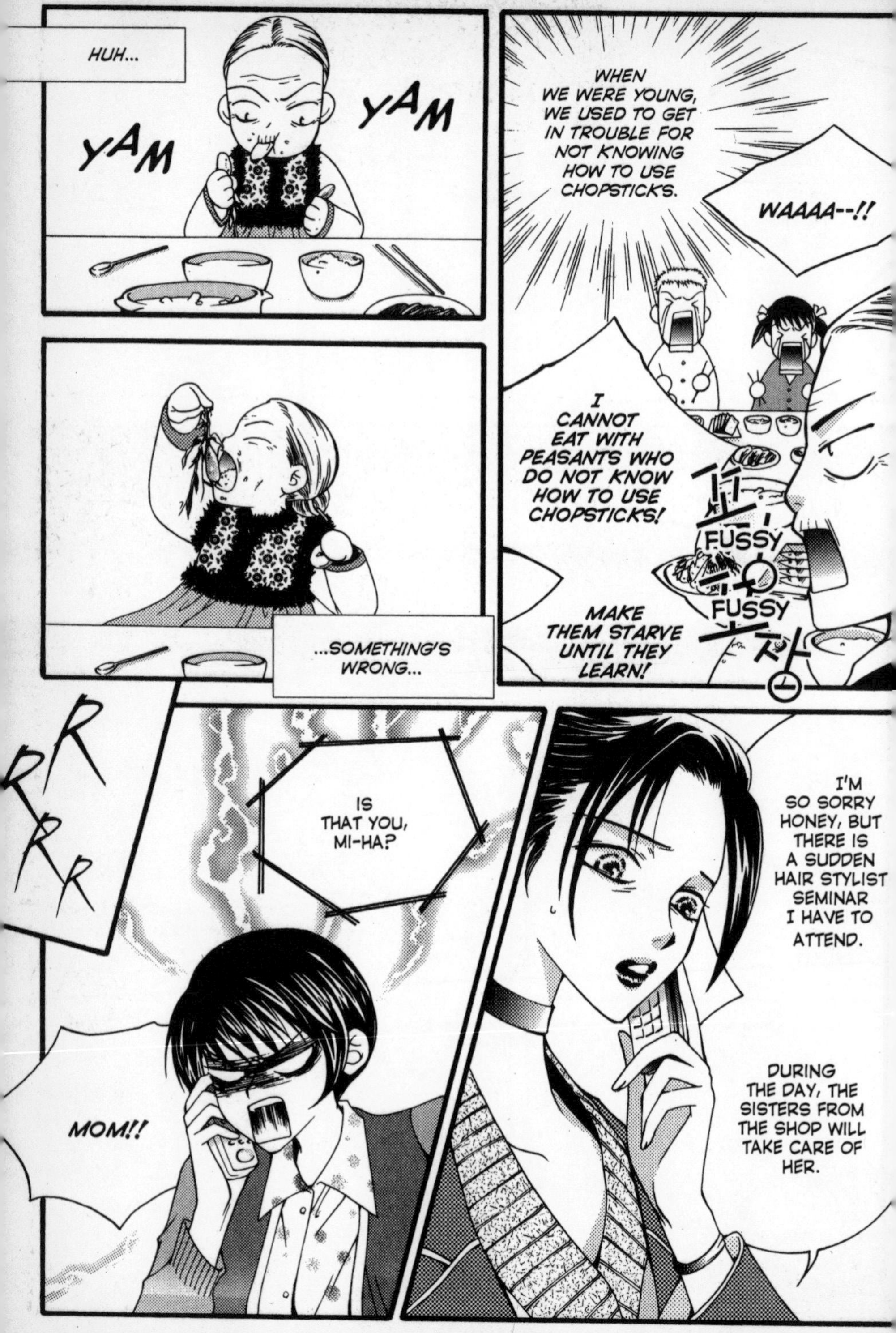
HUH...
YAM
YAM
...SOMETHING'S WRONG...
WHEN WE WERE YOUNG, WE USED TO GET IN TROUBLE FOR NOT KNOWING HOW TO USE CHOPSTICKS.
WAAAA--!!
I CANNOT EAT WITH PEASANTS WHO DO NOT KNOW HOW TO USE CHOPSTICKS!
FUSSY
FUSSY
MAKE THEM STARVE UNTIL THEY LEARN!
RRRRR
IS THAT YOU, MI-HA?
MOM!!
I'M SO SORRY HONEY, BUT THERE IS A SUDDEN HAIR STYLIST SEMINAR I HAVE TO ATTEND.
DURING THE DAY, THE SISTERS FROM THE SHOP WILL TAKE CARE OF HER.

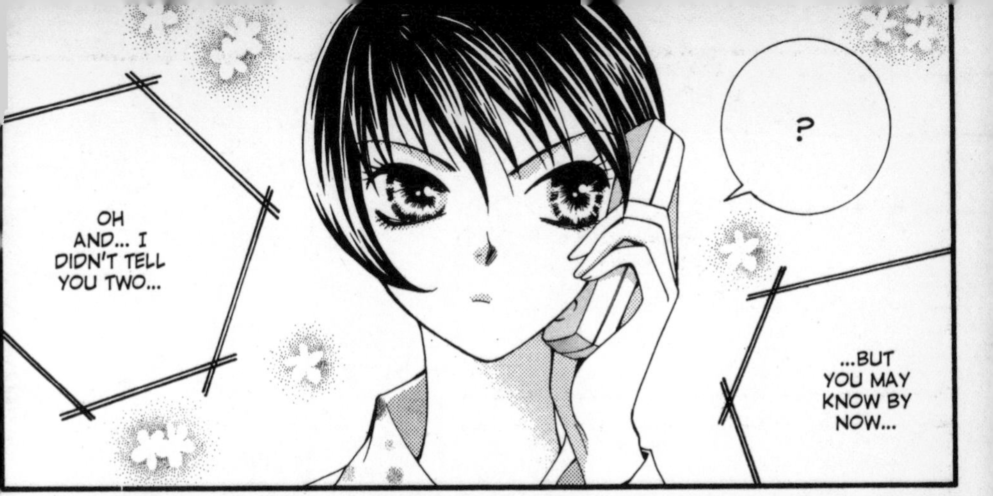
OH AND... I DIDN'T TELL YOU TWO...
?
...BUT YOU MAY KNOW BY NOW...

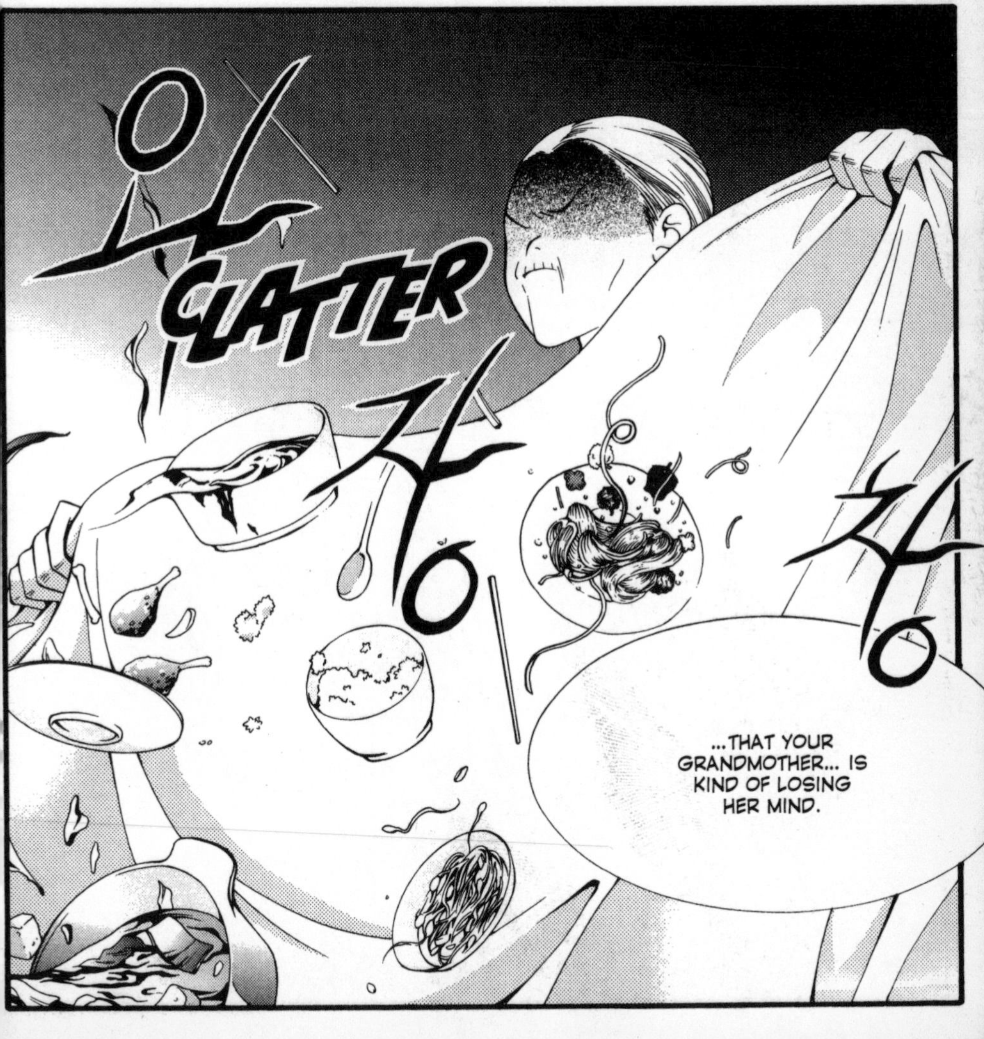
CLATTER
...THAT YOUR GRANDMOTHER... IS KIND OF LOSING HER MIND.

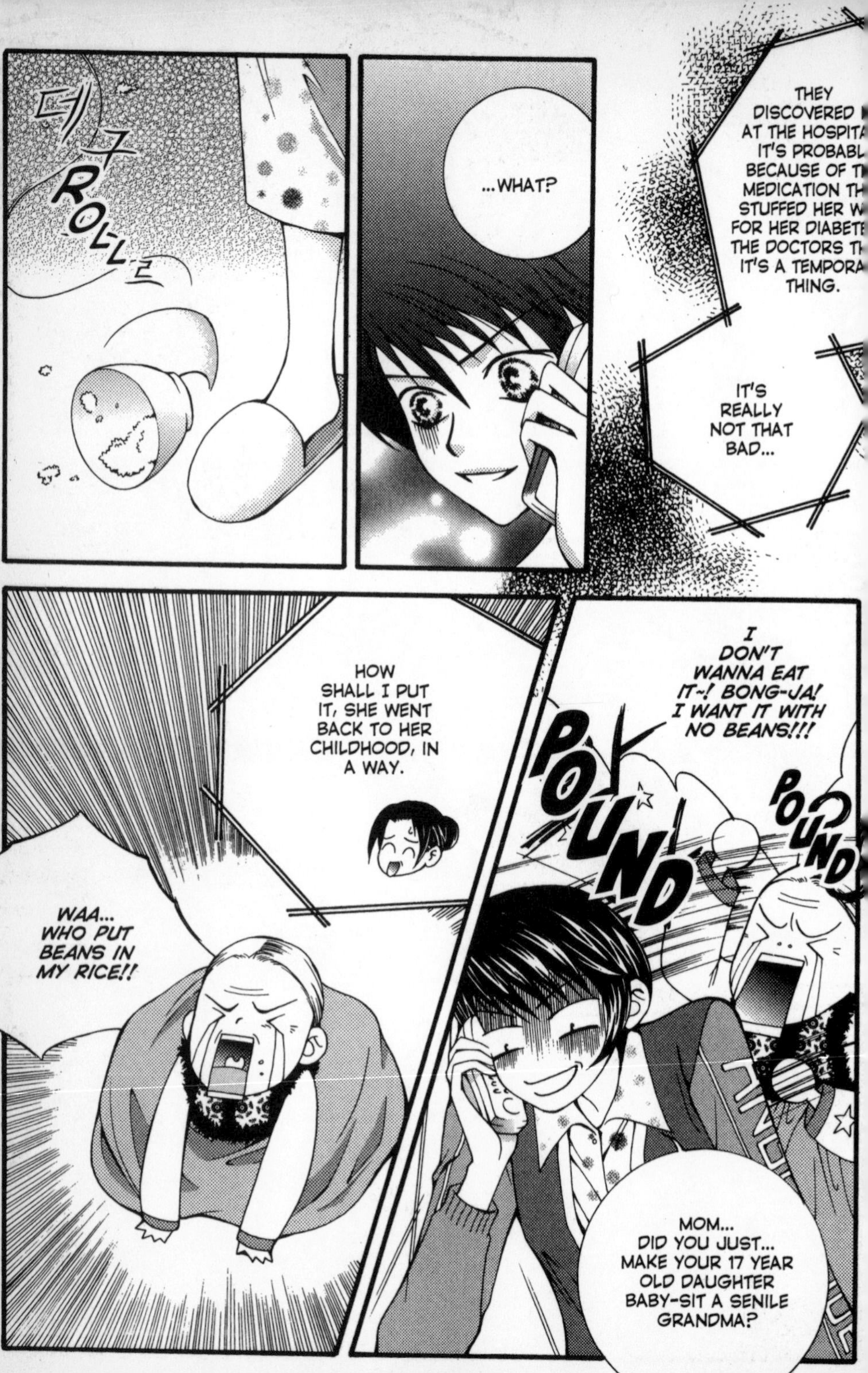
데구르
ROLL
...WHAT?
THEY
DISCOVERED
AT THE HOSPITA
IT'S PROBABL
BECAUSE OF T
MEDICATION TH
STUFFED HER W
FOR HER DIABETE
THE DOCTORS T
IT'S A TEMPORA
THING.
IT'S REALLY NOT THAT BAD...
HOW SHALL I PUT IT, SHE WENT BACK TO HER CHILDHOOD, IN A WAY.
WAA... WHO PUT BEANS IN MY RICE!!
I DON'T WANNA EAT IT~! BONG-JA! I WANT IT WITH NO BEANS!!!
POUND
POUND
MOM... DID YOU JUST... MAKE YOUR 17 YEAR OLD DAUGHTER BABY-SIT A SENILE GRANDMA?

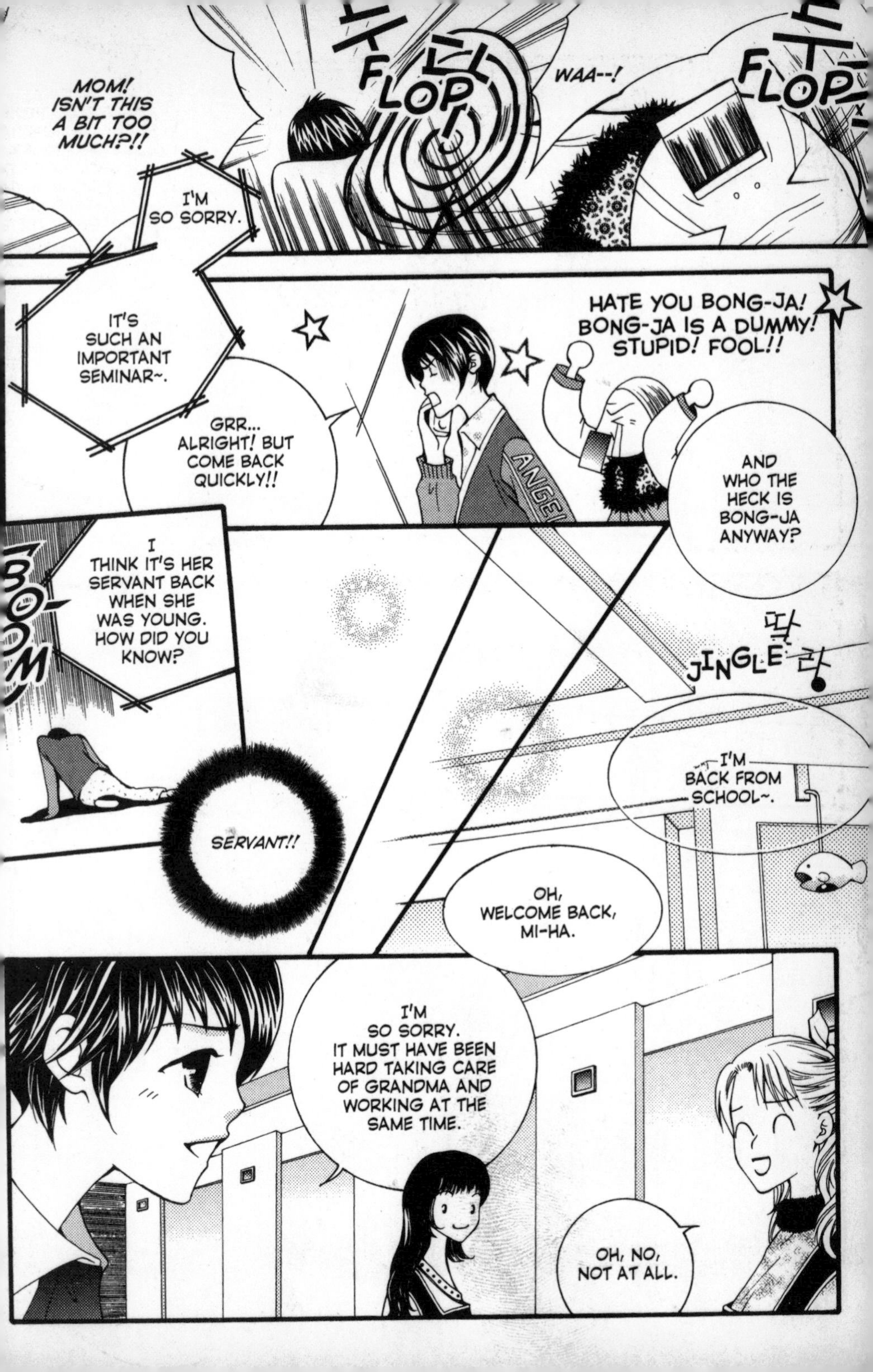
MOM! ISN'T THIS A BIT TOO MUCH?!!
FLOP!
WAA--!
FLOP!
I'M SO SORRY.
IT'S SUCH AN IMPORTANT SEMINAR~.
GRR... ALRIGHT! BUT COME BACK QUICKLY!!
HATE YOU BONG-JA! BONG-JA IS A DUMMY! STUPID! FOOL!!
AND WHO THE HECK IS BONG-JA ANYWAY?
I THINK IT'S HER SERVANT BACK WHEN SHE WAS YOUNG. HOW DID YOU KNOW?
BOOM
SERVANT!!
JINGLE
I'M BACK FROM SCHOOL~.
OH, WELCOME BACK, MI-HA.
I'M SO SORRY. IT MUST HAVE BEEN HARD TAKING CARE OF GRANDMA AND WORKING AT THE SAME TIME.
OH, NO, NOT AT ALL.

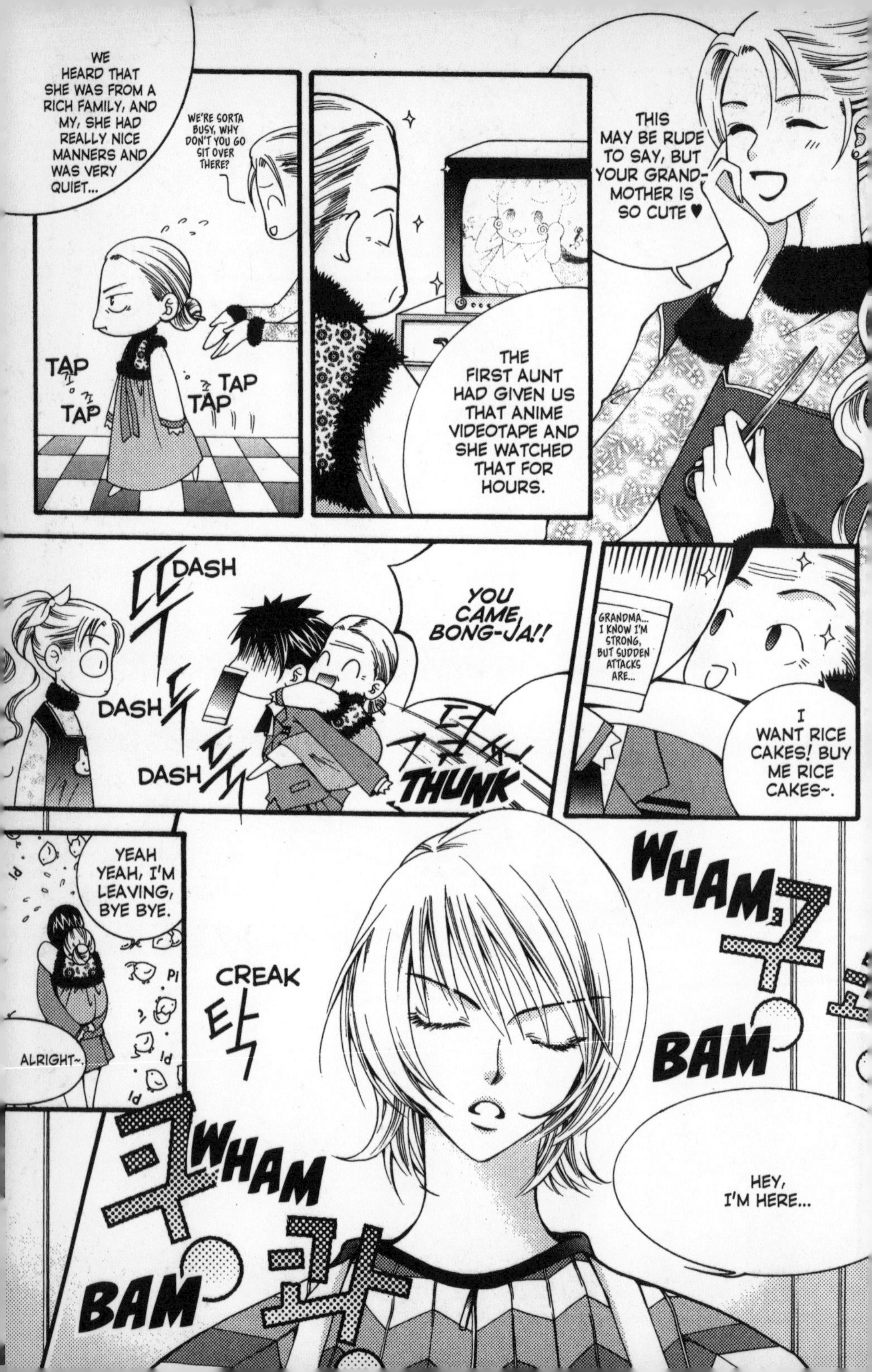
WE HEARD THAT SHE WAS FROM A RICH FAMILY, AND MY, SHE HAD REALLY NICE MANNERS AND WAS VERY QUIET...
WE'RE SORTA BUSY, WHY DON'T YOU GO SIT OVER THERE?
TAP
TAP
TAP
TAP
THE FIRST AUNT HAD GIVEN US THAT ANIME VIDEOTAPE AND SHE WATCHED THAT FOR HOURS.
THIS MAY BE RUDE TO SAY, BUT YOUR GRAND-MOTHER IS SO CUTE ♥
DASH
DASH
DASH
YOU CAME, BONG-JA!!
THUNK
GRANDMA... I KNOW I'M STRONG, BUT SUDDEN ATTACKS ARE...
I WANT RICE CAKES! BUY ME RICE CAKES~.
YEAH YEAH, I'M LEAVING, BYE BYE.
ALRIGHT~.
PI
PI
CREAK
WHAM
BAM
WHAM
BAM
HEY, I'M HERE...

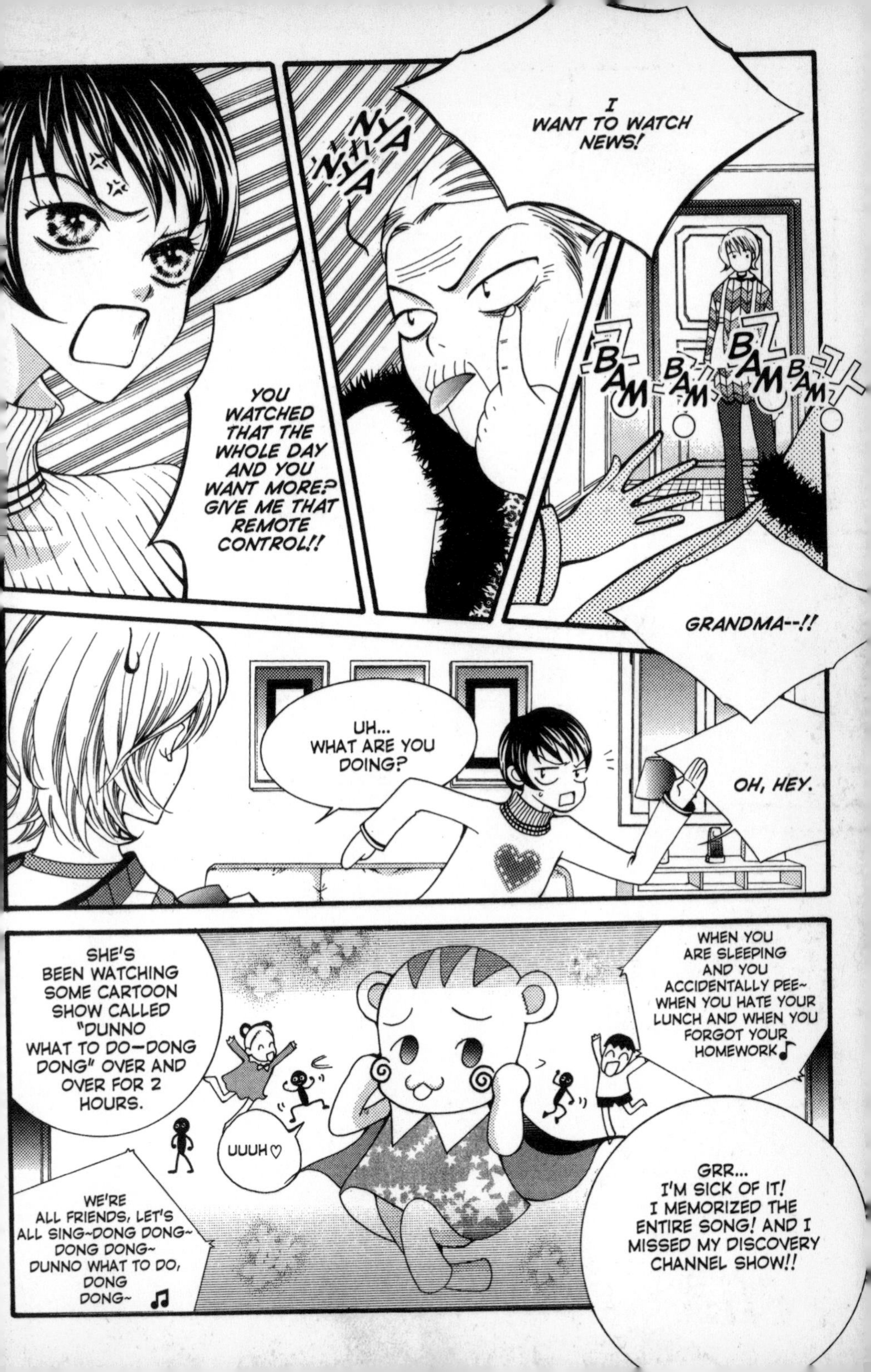
YOU WATCHED THAT THE WHOLE DAY AND YOU WANT MORE? GIVE ME THAT REMOTE CONTROL!!
NYA NYA
I WANT TO WATCH NEWS!
BAM BAM BAM BAM
GRANDMA--!!
UH... WHAT ARE YOU DOING?
OH, HEY.
SHE'S BEEN WATCHING SOME CARTOON SHOW CALLED "DUNNO WHAT TO DO—DONG DONG" OVER AND OVER FOR 2 HOURS.
UUUH♡
WE'RE ALL FRIENDS, LET'S ALL SING~DONG DONG~ DONG DONG~ DUNNO WHAT TO DO, DONG DONG~ ♫
WHEN YOU ARE SLEEPING AND YOU ACCIDENTALLY PEE~ WHEN YOU HATE YOUR LUNCH AND WHEN YOU FORGOT YOUR HOMEWORK♪
GRR... I'M SICK OF IT! I MEMORIZED THE ENTIRE SONG! AND I MISSED MY DISCOVERY CHANNEL SHOW!!

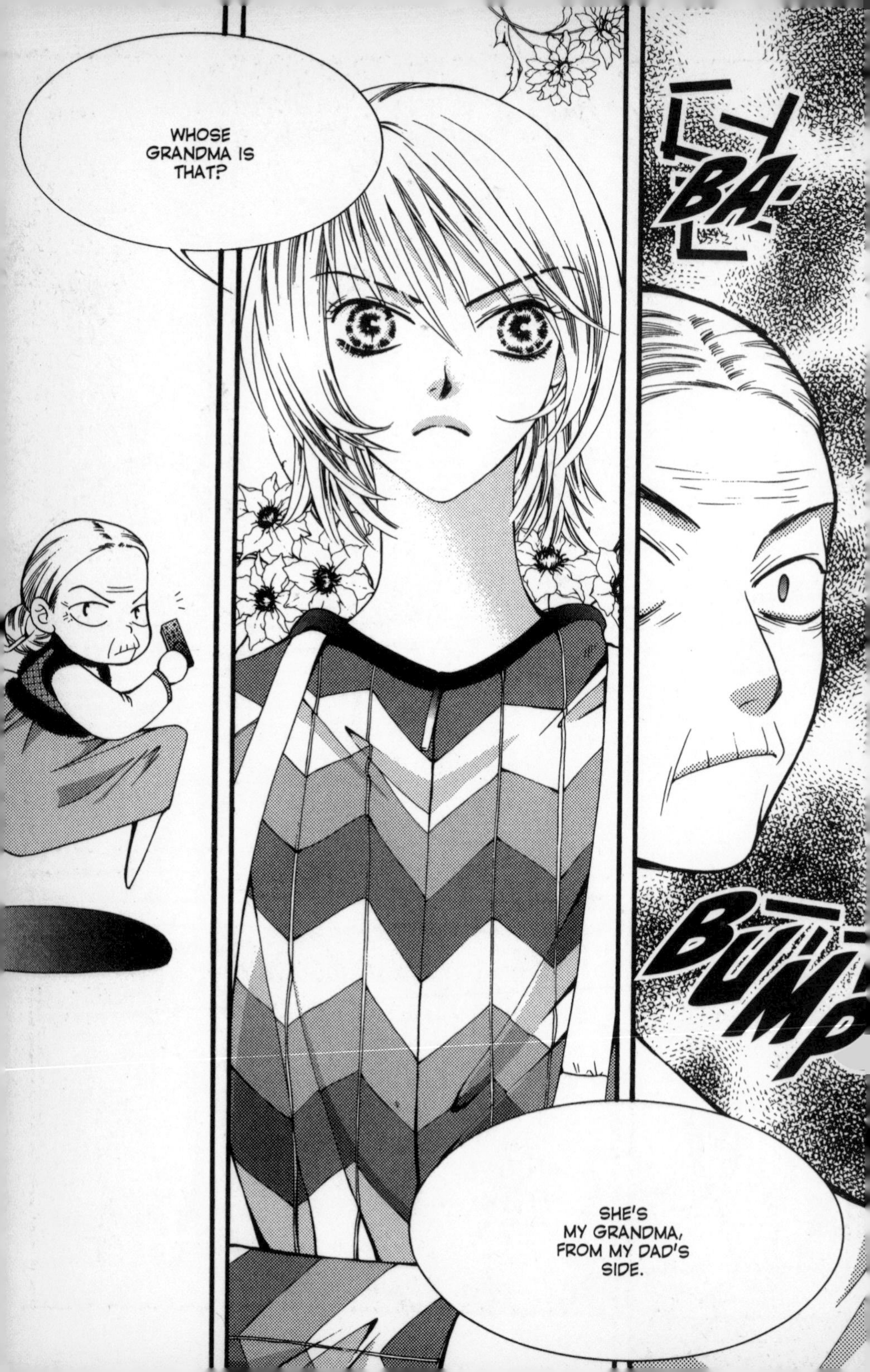
WHOSE GRANDMA IS THAT?
BA-
BUMP
SHE'S MY GRANDMA, FROM MY DAD'S SIDE.

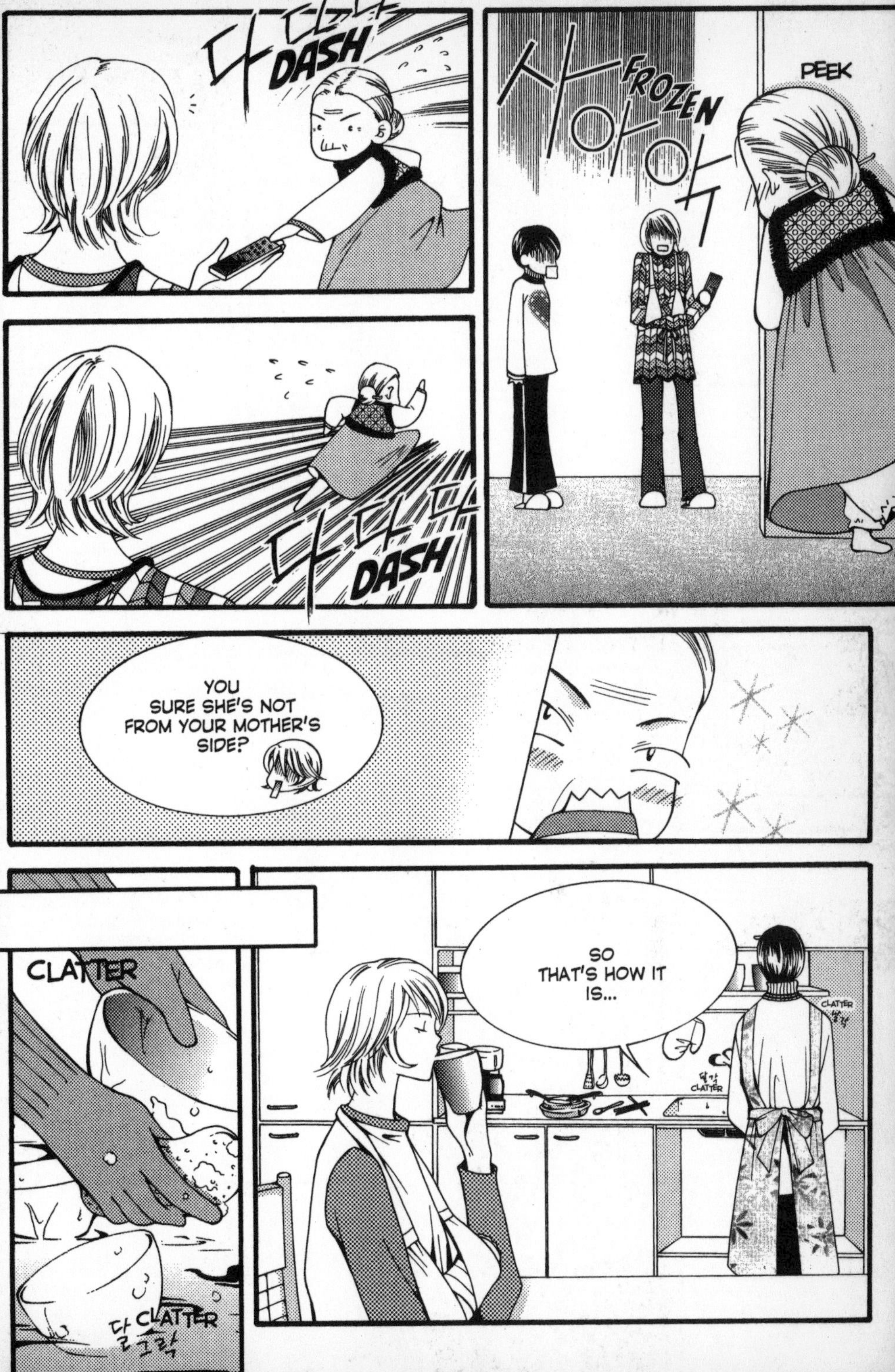
DASH
DASH
FROZEN
PEEK
YOU SURE SHE'S NOT FROM YOUR MOTHER'S SIDE?
CLATTER
CLATTER
달그락
SO THAT'S HOW IT IS...
CLATTER
CLATTER

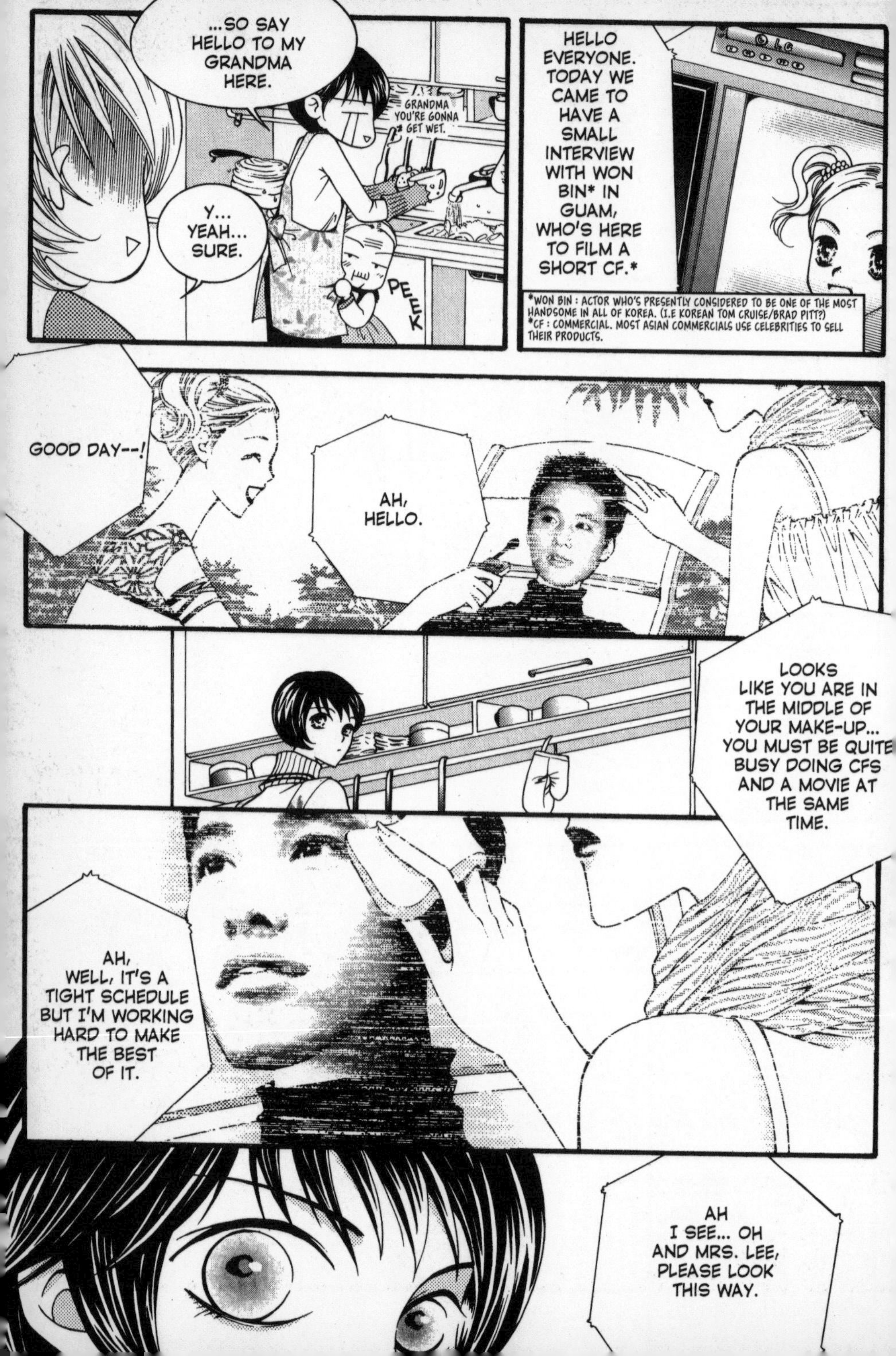
...SO SAY HELLO TO MY GRANDMA HERE.
GRANDMA YOU'RE GONNA GET WET.
Y... YEAH... SURE.
PEEK
HELLO EVERYONE. TODAY WE CAME TO HAVE A SMALL INTERVIEW WITH WON BIN* IN GUAM, WHO'S HERE TO FILM A SHORT CF.*
*WON BIN : ACTOR WHO'S PRESENTLY CONSIDERED TO BE ONE OF THE MOST HANDSOME IN ALL OF KOREA. (I.E KOREAN TOM CRUISE/BRAD PITT?)
*CF : COMMERCIAL. MOST ASIAN COMMERCIALS USE CELEBRITIES TO SELL THEIR PRODUCTS.
GOOD DAY--!
AH, HELLO.
LOOKS LIKE YOU ARE IN THE MIDDLE OF YOUR MAKE-UP... YOU MUST BE QUITE BUSY DOING CFS AND A MOVIE AT THE SAME TIME.
AH, WELL, IT'S A TIGHT SCHEDULE BUT I'M WORKING HARD TO MAKE THE BEST OF IT.
AH I SEE... OH AND MRS. LEE, PLEASE LOOK THIS WAY.

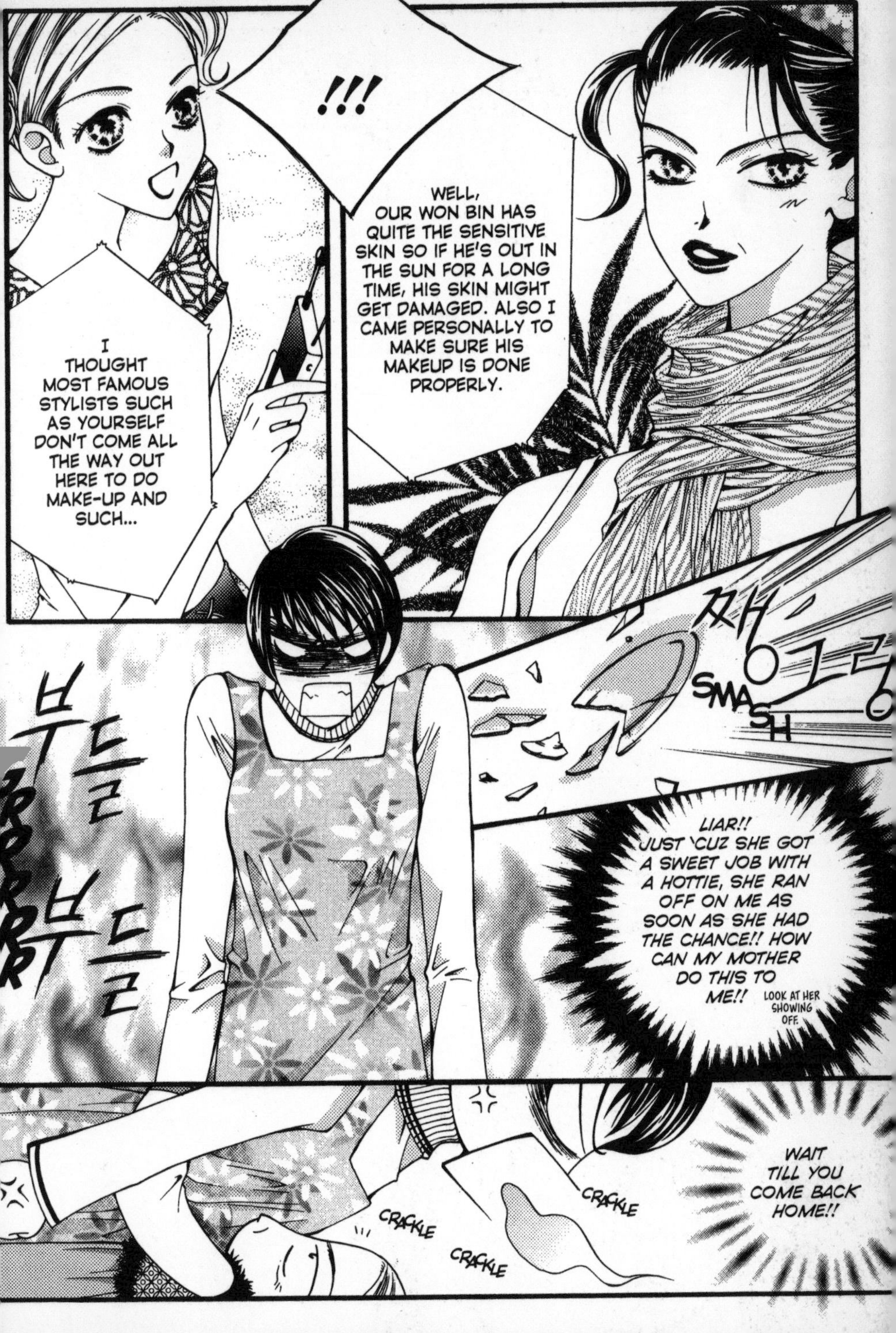

I THOUGHT MOST FAMOUS STYLISTS SUCH AS YOURSELF DON'T COME ALL THE WAY OUT HERE TO DO MAKE-UP AND SUCH...
!!!
WELL, OUR WON BIN HAS QUITE THE SENSITIVE SKIN SO IF HE'S OUT IN THE SUN FOR A LONG TIME, HIS SKIN MIGHT GET DAMAGED. ALSO I CAME PERSONALLY TO MAKE SURE HIS MAKEUP IS DONE PROPERLY.
부들 부들
쨍그랑
SMASH
LIAR!! JUST 'CUZ SHE GOT A SWEET JOB WITH A HOTTIE, SHE RAN OFF ON ME AS SOON AS SHE HAD THE CHANCE!! HOW CAN MY MOTHER DO THIS TO ME!!
LOOK AT HER SHOWING OFF.
CRACKLE
CRACKLE
CRACKLE
WAIT TILL YOU COME BACK HOME!!

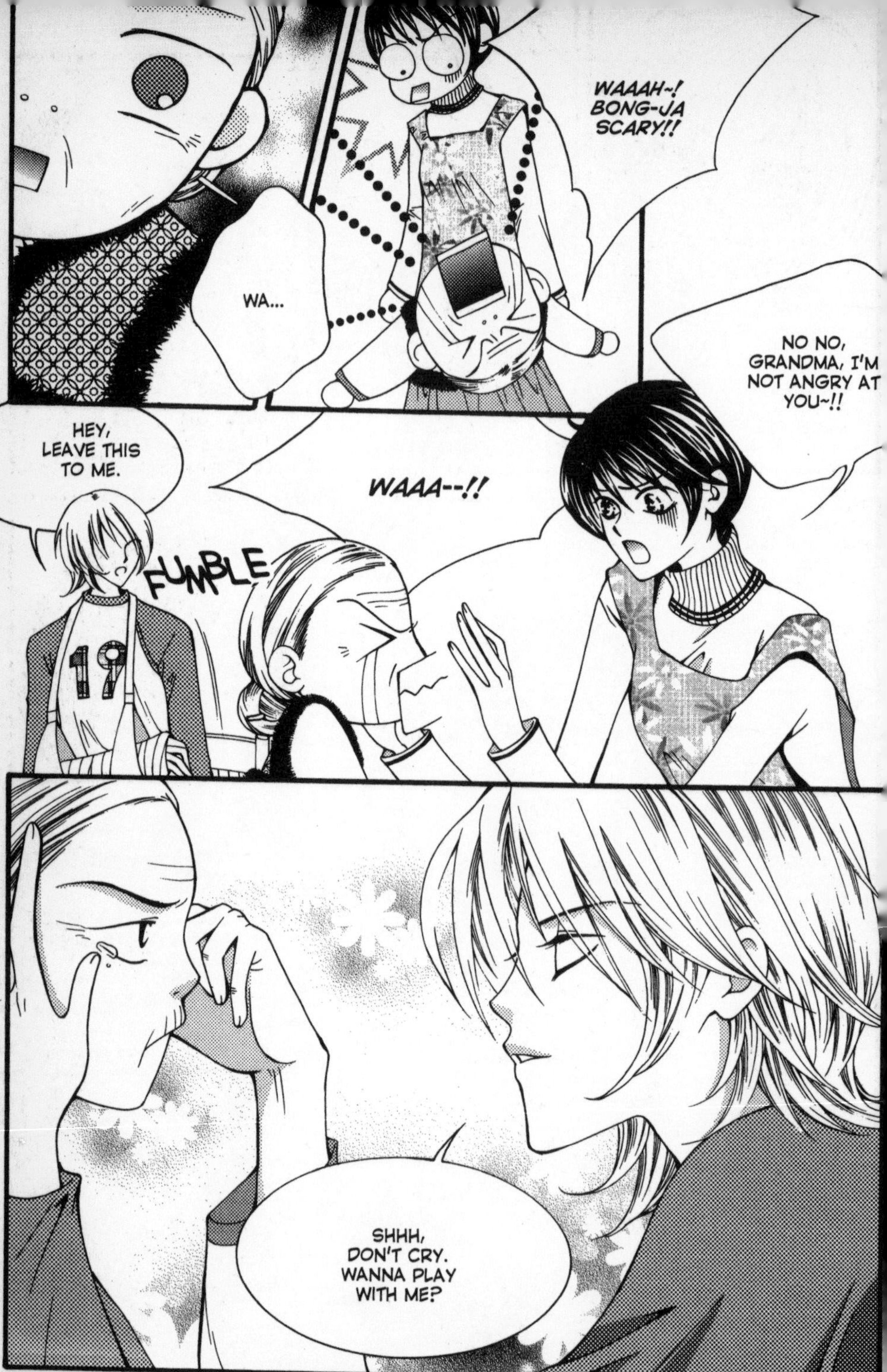
WA...
WAAAH~! BONG-JA SCARY!!
HEY, LEAVE THIS TO ME.
FUMBLE
WAAA--!!
NO NO, GRANDMA, I'M NOT ANGRY AT YOU~!!
SHHH, DON'T CRY. WANNA PLAY WITH ME?

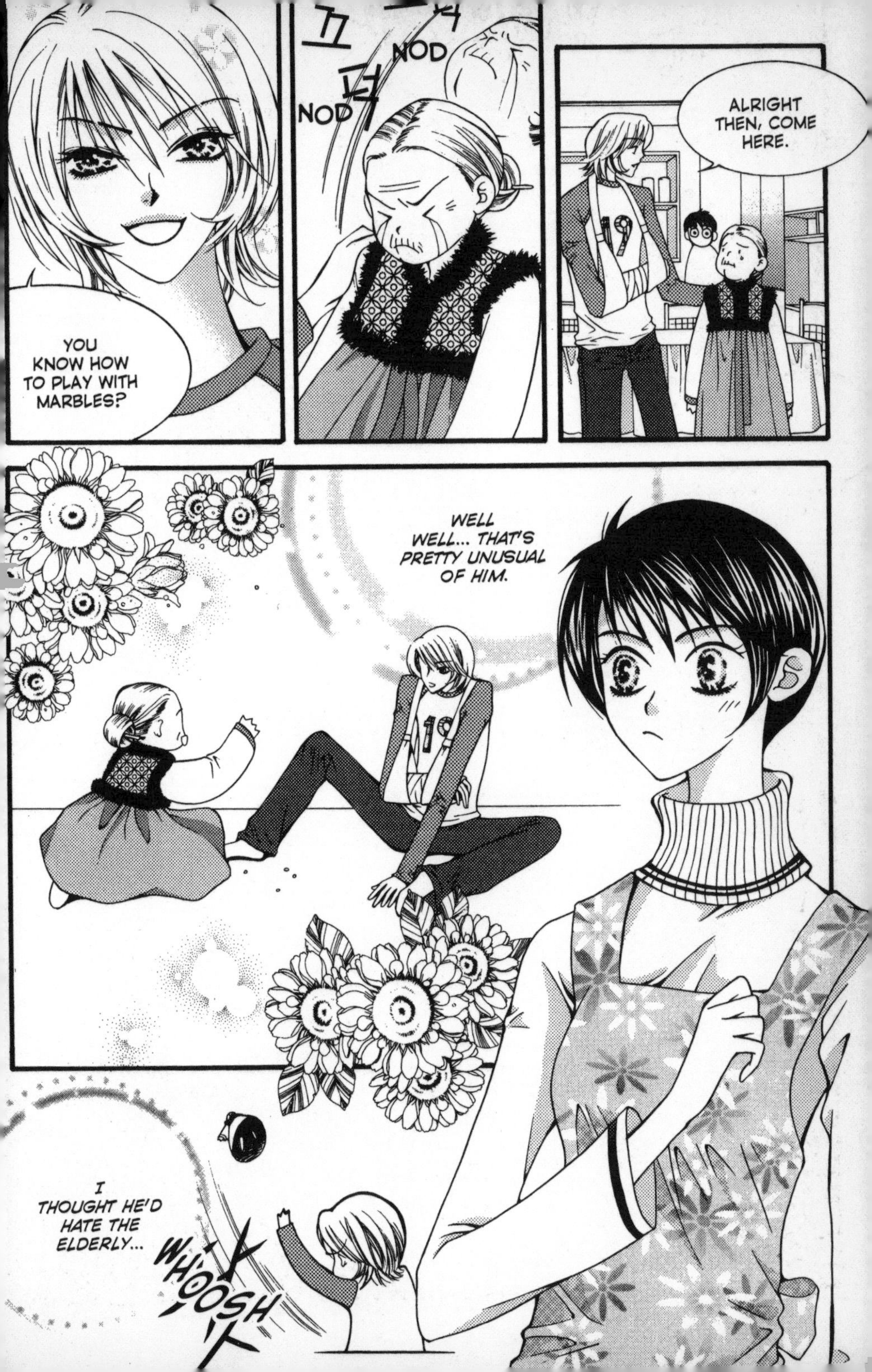
YOU KNOW HOW TO PLAY WITH MARBLES?
NOD
NOD
ALRIGHT THEN, COME HERE.
WELL WELL... THAT'S PRETTY UNUSUAL OF HIM.
I THOUGHT HE'D HATE THE ELDERLY...
WHOOSH

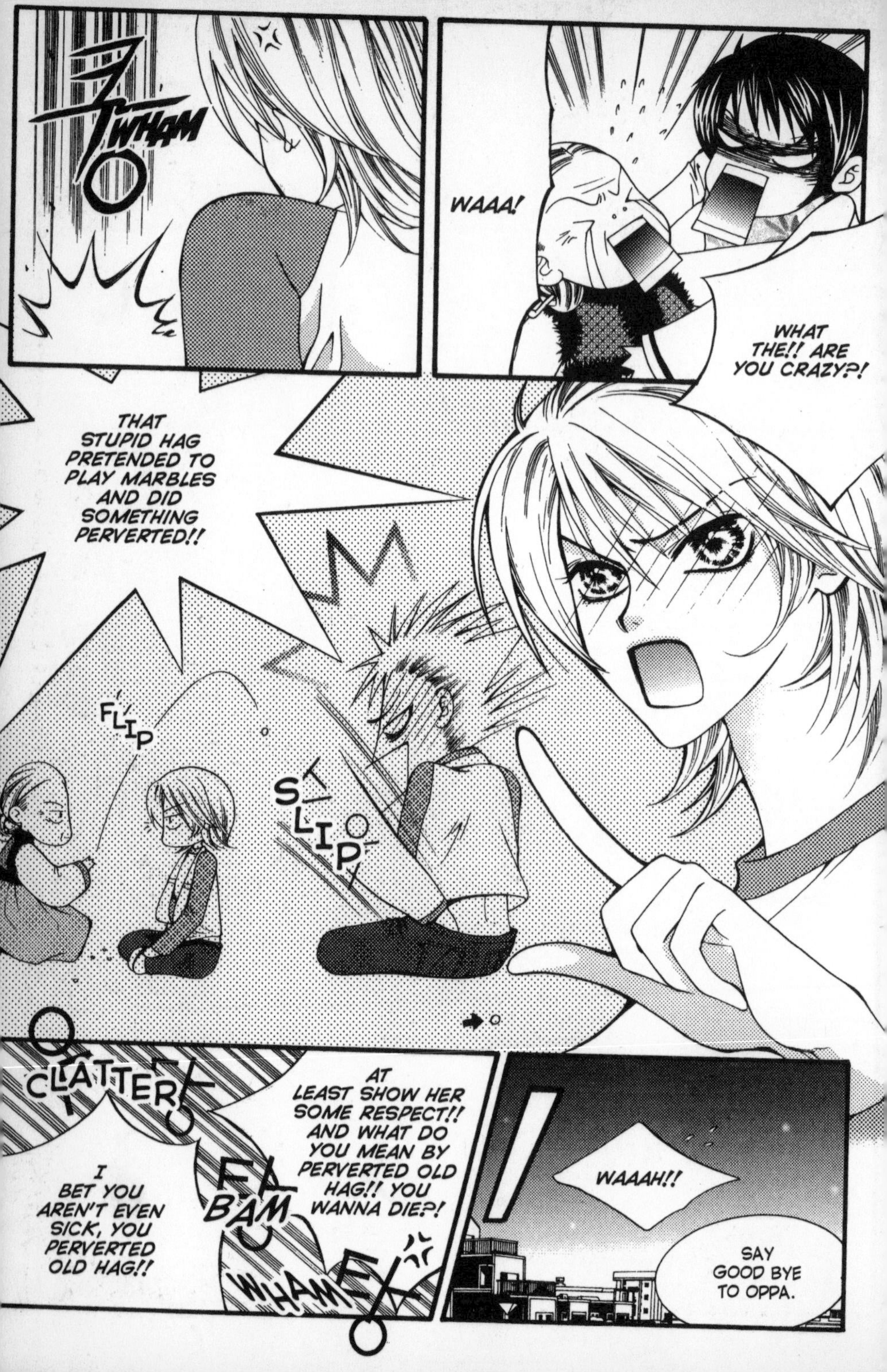
WHAM
WAAA!
WHAT THE!! ARE YOU CRAZY?!
THAT STUPID HAG PRETENDED TO PLAY MARBLES AND DID SOMETHING PERVERTED!!
FLIP
SLIP
CLATTER
I BET YOU AREN'T EVEN SICK, YOU PERVERTED OLD HAG!!
FLBAM
AT LEAST SHOW HER SOME RESPECT!! AND WHAT DO YOU MEAN BY PERVERTED OLD HAG!! YOU WANNA DIE?!
WHAM
WAAAH!!
SAY GOOD BYE TO OPPA.

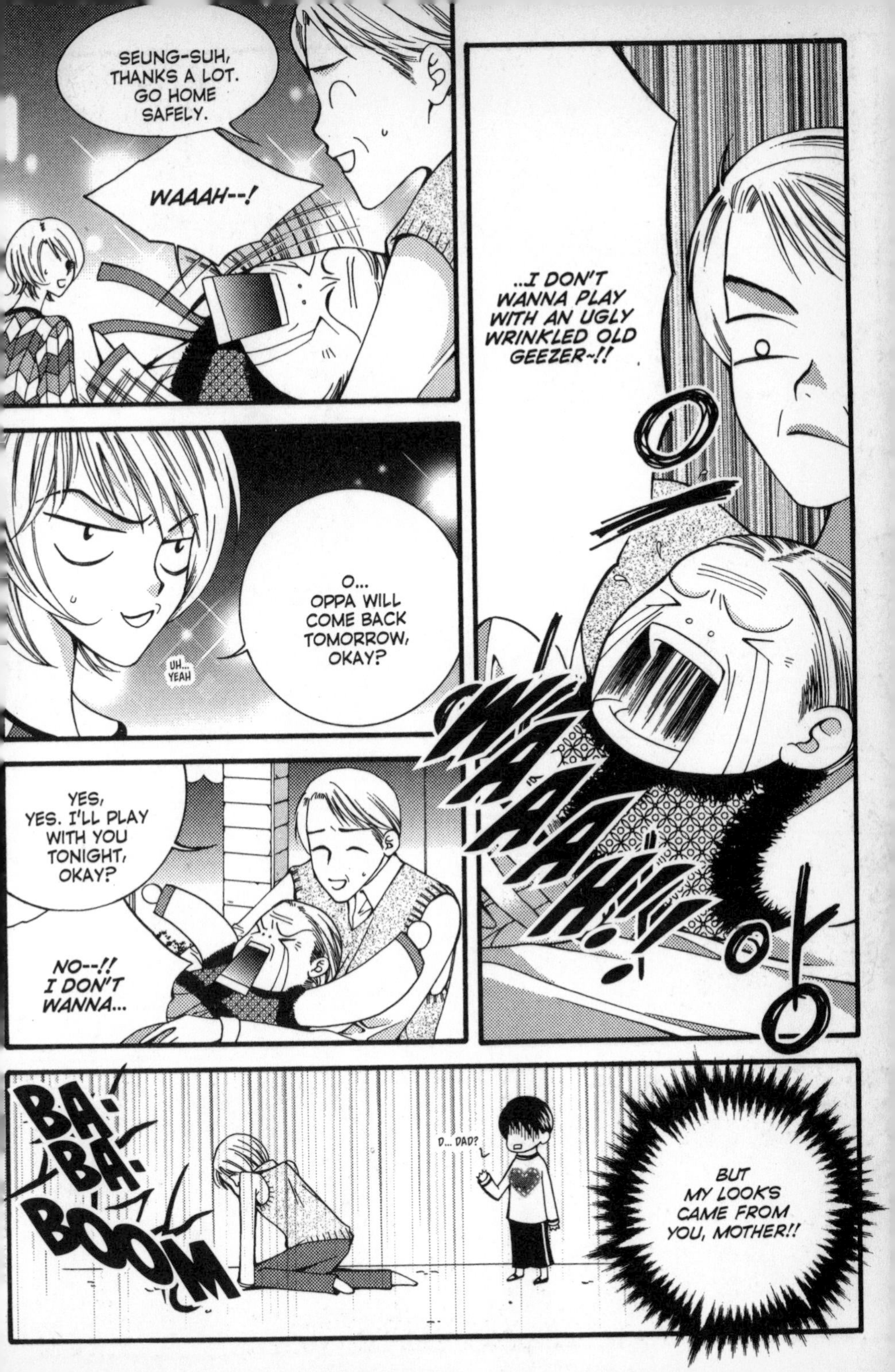
SEUNG-SUH, THANKS A LOT. GO HOME SAFELY.
WAAAH--!
O... OPPA WILL COME BACK TOMORROW, OKAY?
UH... YEAH
YES, YES. I'LL PLAY WITH YOU TONIGHT, OKAY?
NO--!! I DON'T WANNA...
...I DON'T WANNA PLAY WITH AN UGLY WRINKLED OLD GEEZER~!!
WAAAAH!!
BA-BA-BOOM
D... DAD?
BUT MY LOOKS CAME FROM YOU, MOTHER!!

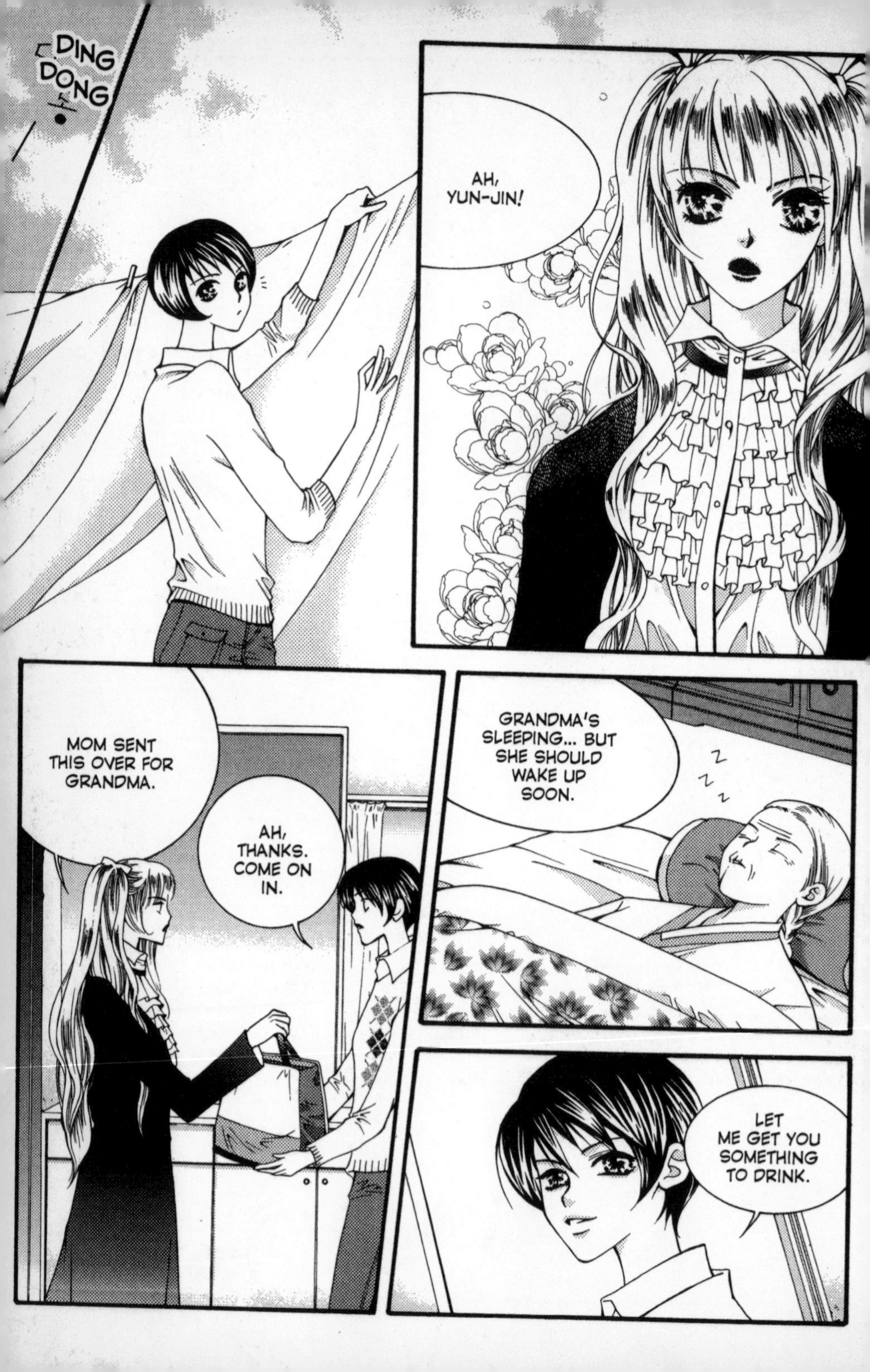
DING DONG
AH, YUN-JIN!
MOM SENT THIS OVER FOR GRANDMA.
AH, THANKS. COME ON IN.
GRANDMA'S SLEEPING... BUT SHE SHOULD WAKE UP SOON.
Z Z Z
LET ME GET YOU SOMETHING TO DRINK.

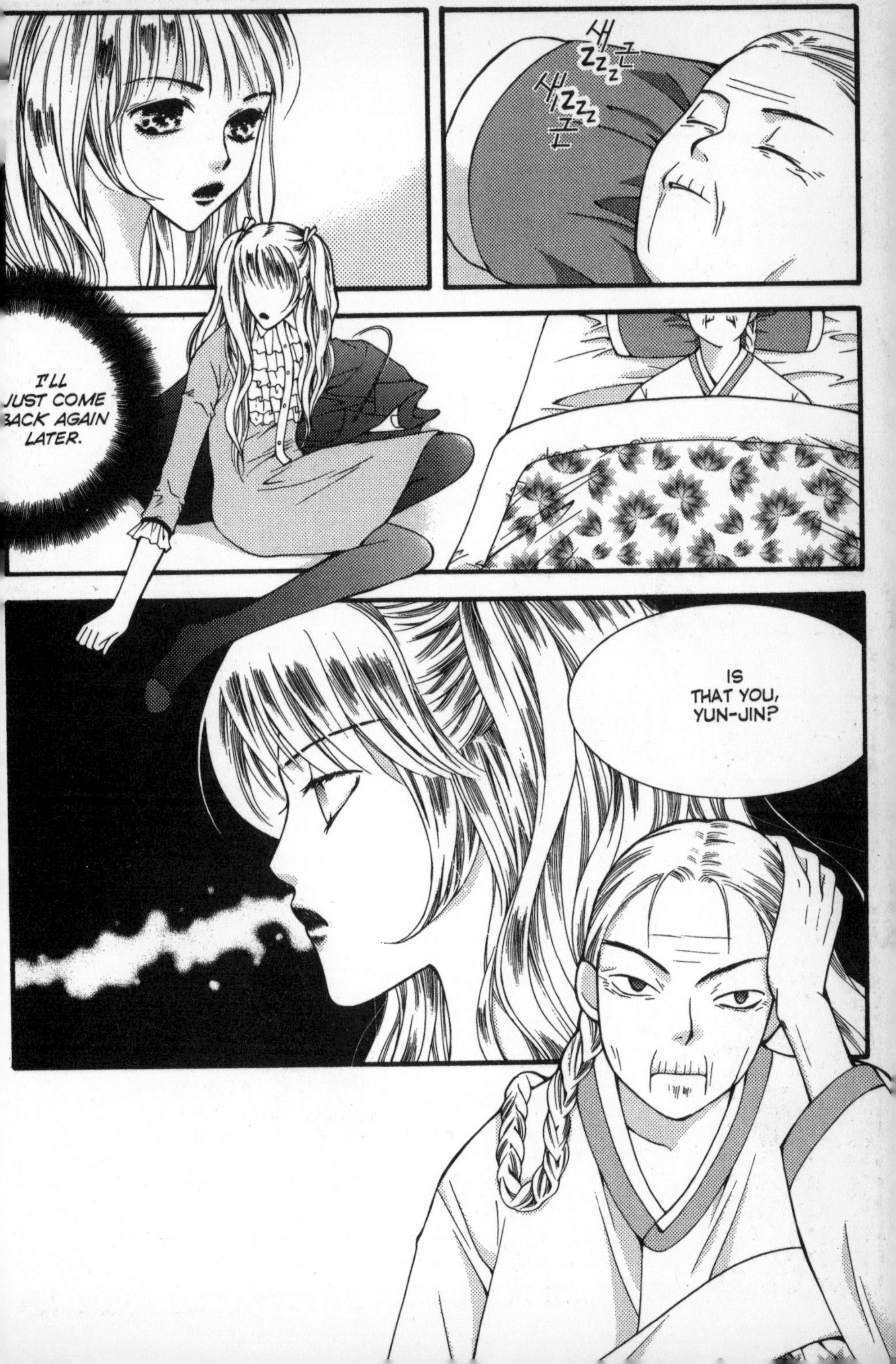
새근 zzz
새근 zzz
I'LL JUST COME BACK AGAIN LATER.
IS THAT YOU, YUN-JIN?

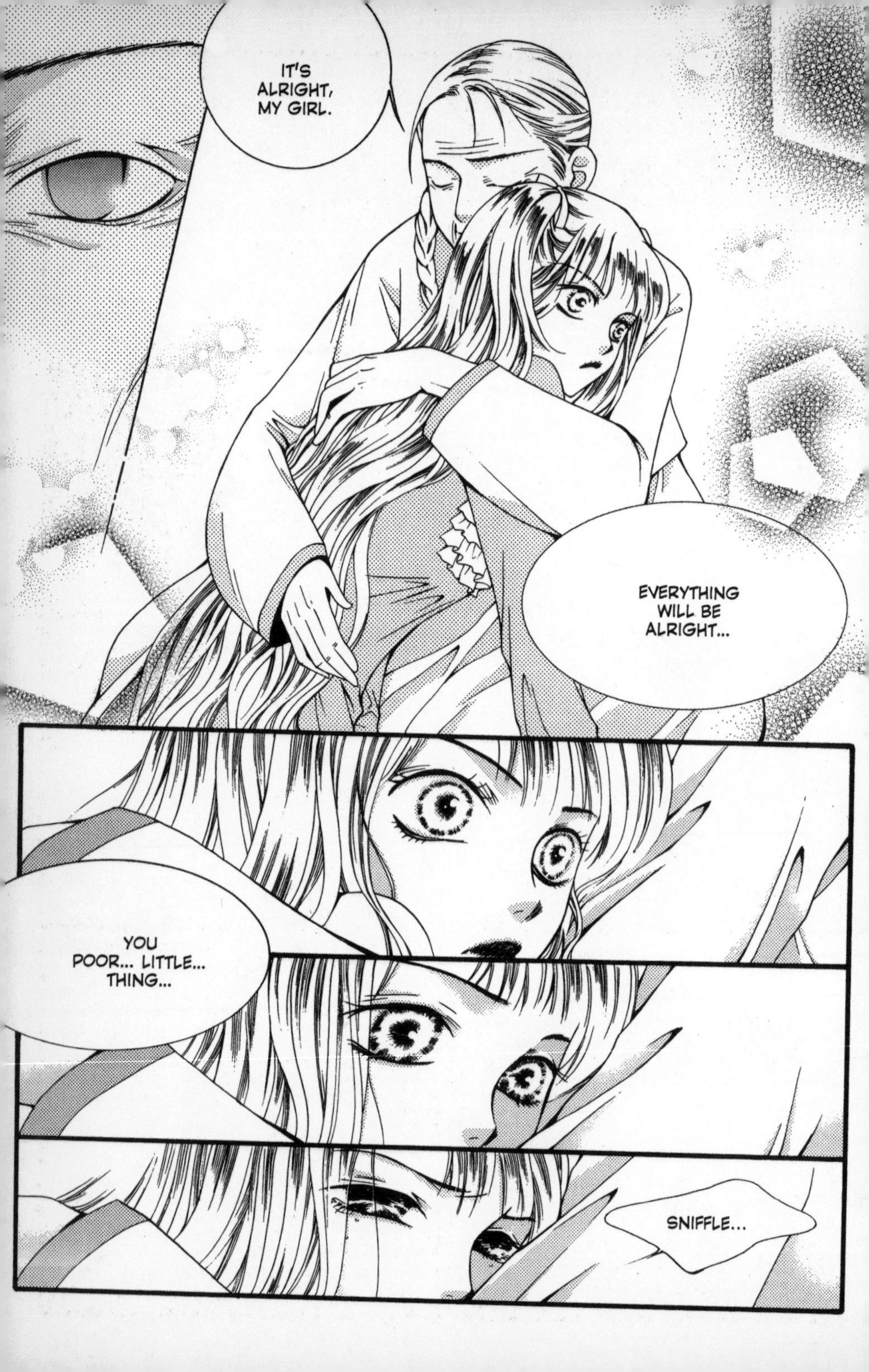
IT'S ALRIGHT, MY GIRL.
EVERYTHING WILL BE ALRIGHT...
YOU POOR... LITTLE... THING...
SNIFFLE...

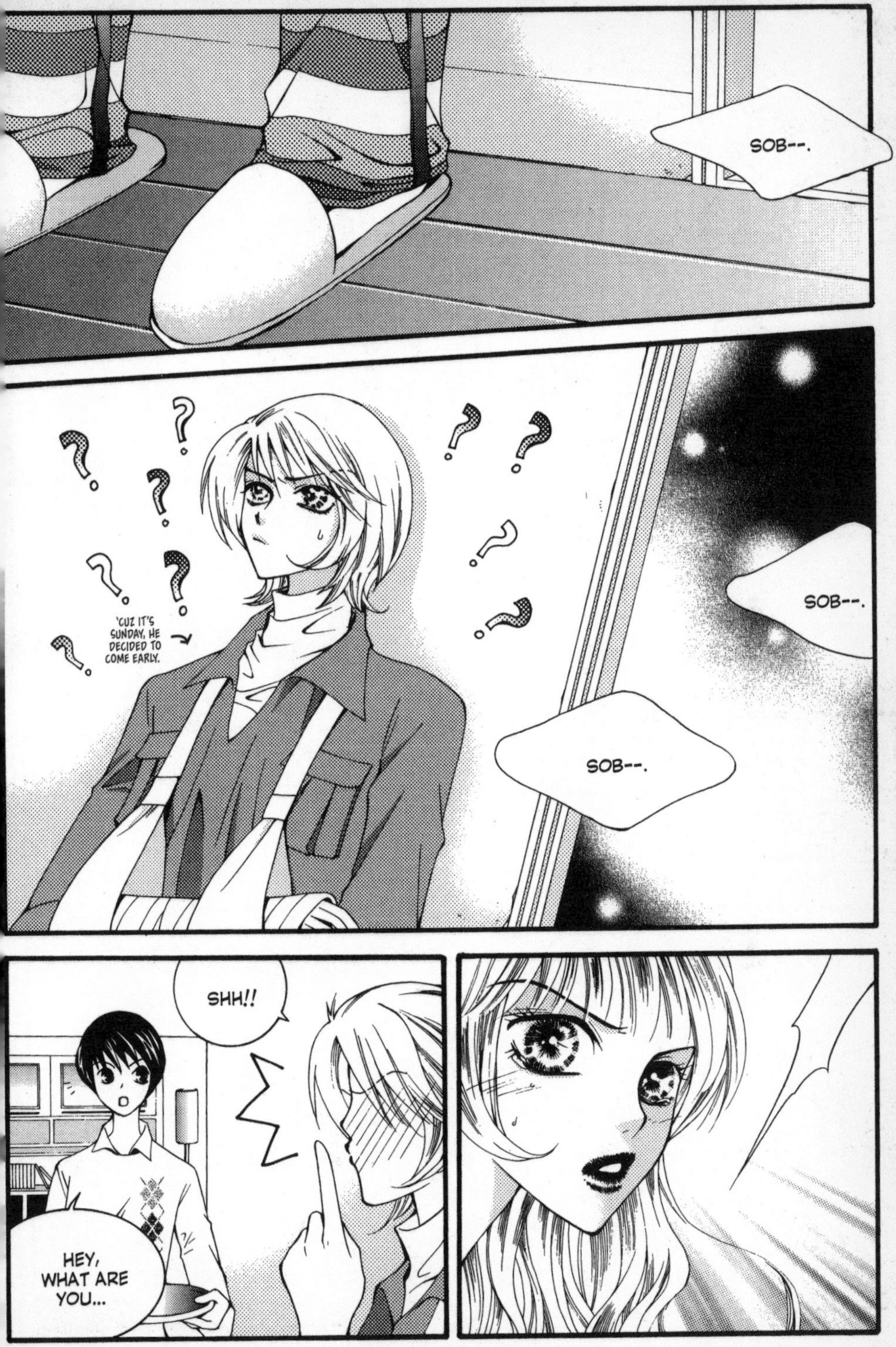
SOB--.
'CUZ IT'S SUNDAY, HE DECIDED TO COME EARLY.
SOB--.
SOB--.
HEY, WHAT ARE YOU...
SHH!!

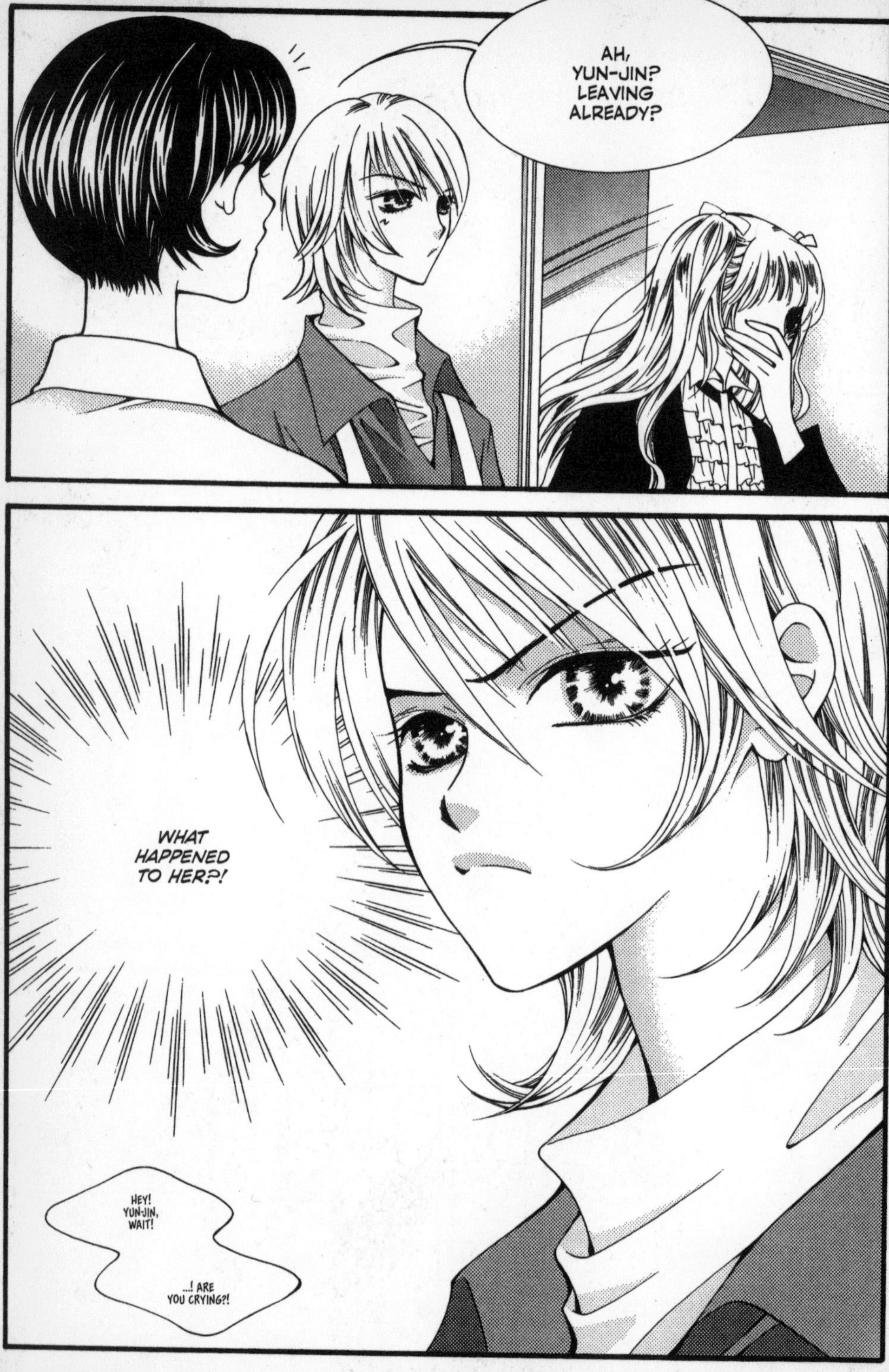
AH, YUN-JIN? LEAVING ALREADY?
WHAT HAPPENED TO HER?!
HEY! YUN-JIN, WAIT!
...! ARE YOU CRYING?!

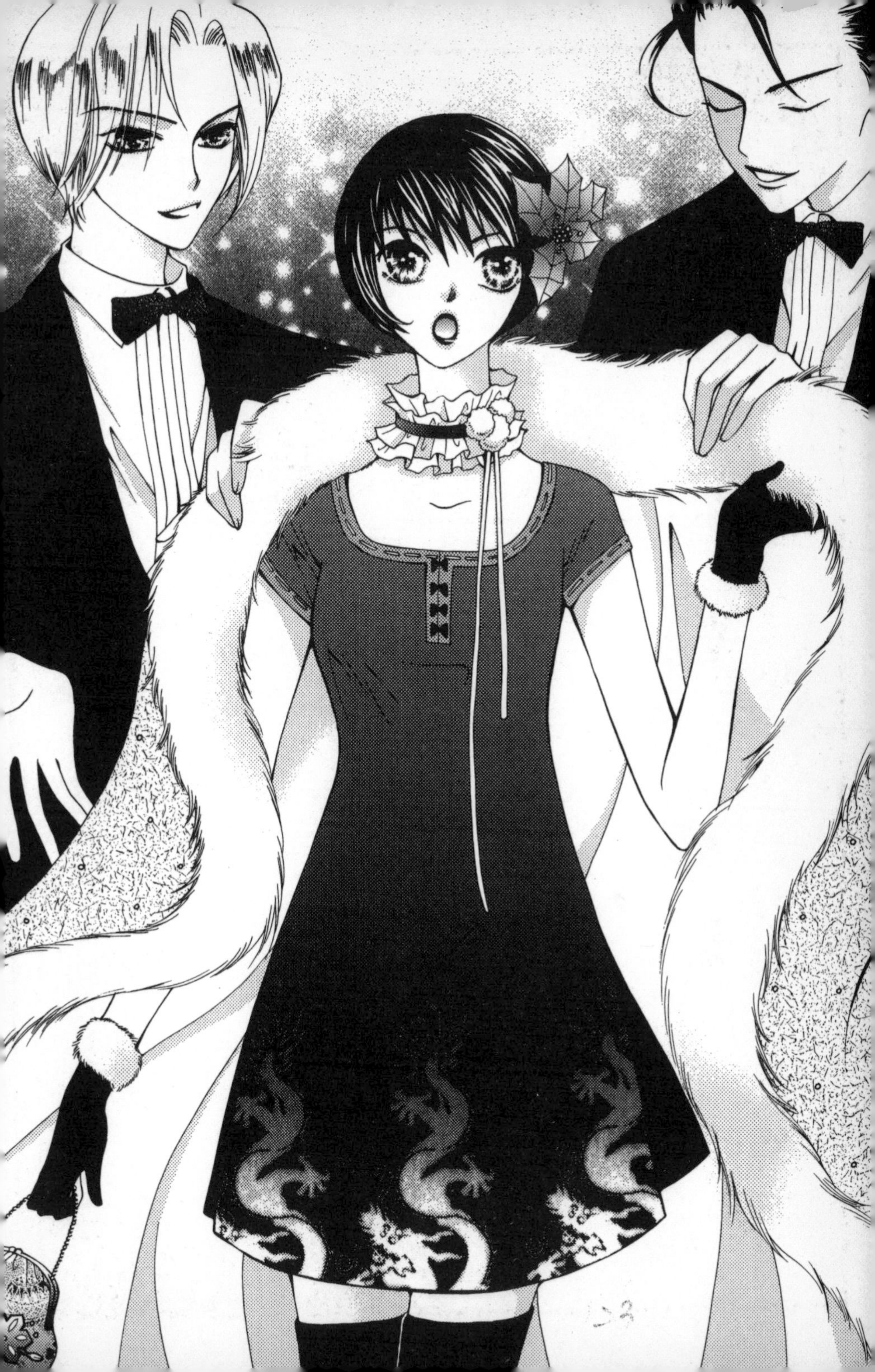

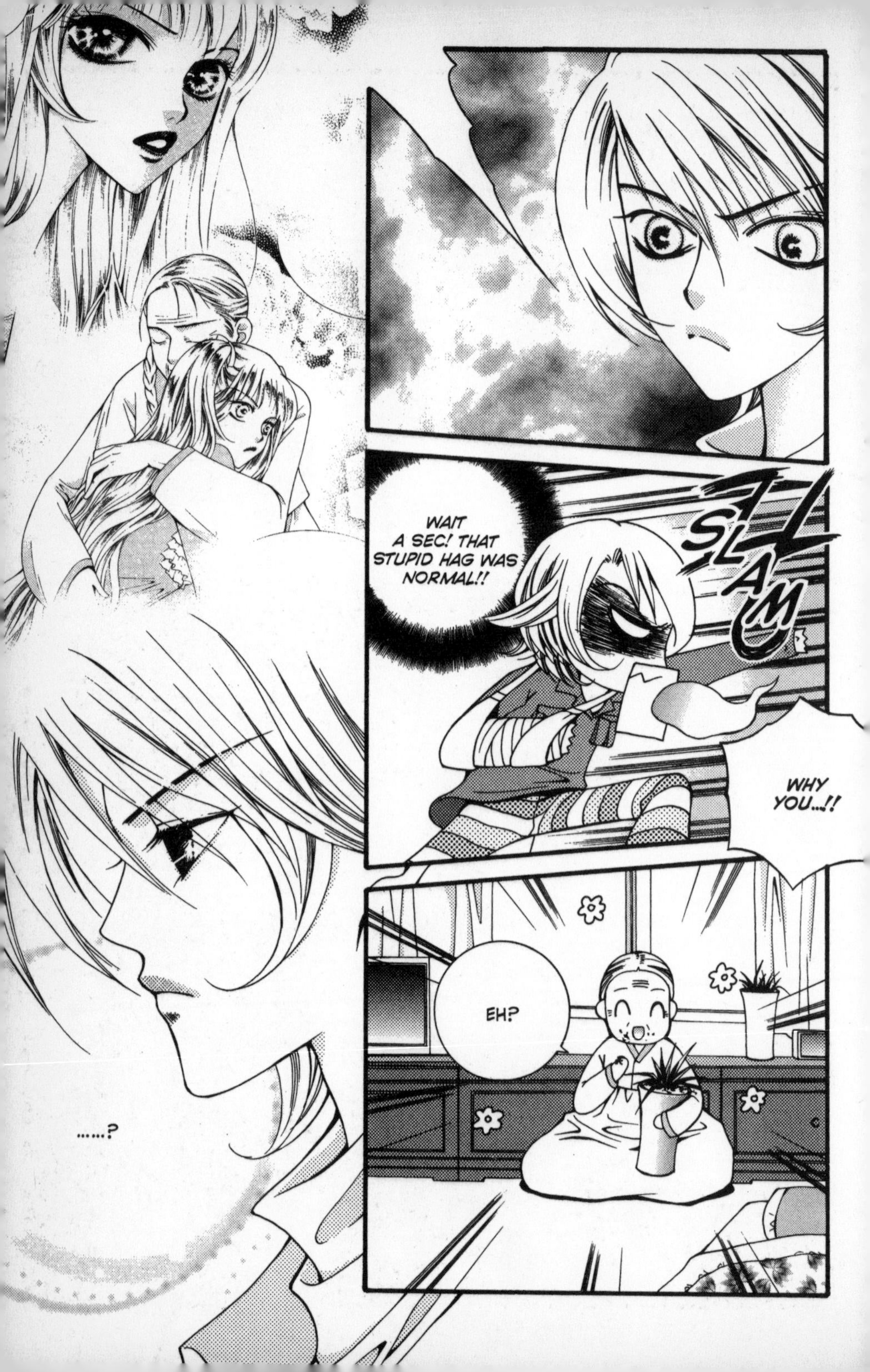
......?
WAIT A SEC! THAT STUPID HAG WAS NORMAL!!
SLAM
WHY YOU...!!
EH?

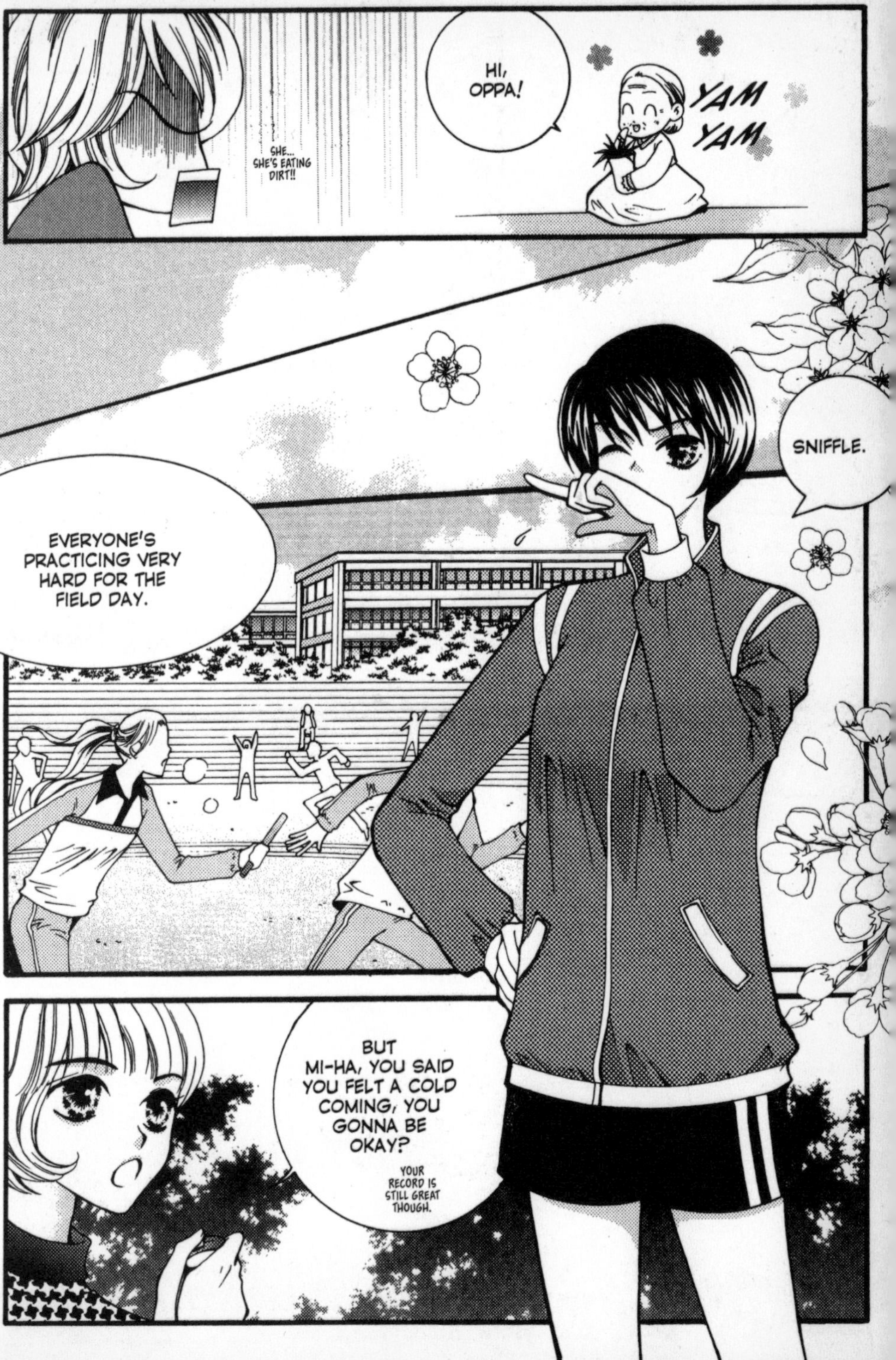
SHE... SHE'S EATING DIRT!!
HI, OPPA!
YAM YAM
EVERYONE'S PRACTICING VERY HARD FOR THE FIELD DAY.
SNIFFLE.
BUT MI-HA, YOU SAID YOU FELT A COLD COMING, YOU GONNA BE OKAY?
YOUR RECORD IS STILL GREAT THOUGH.

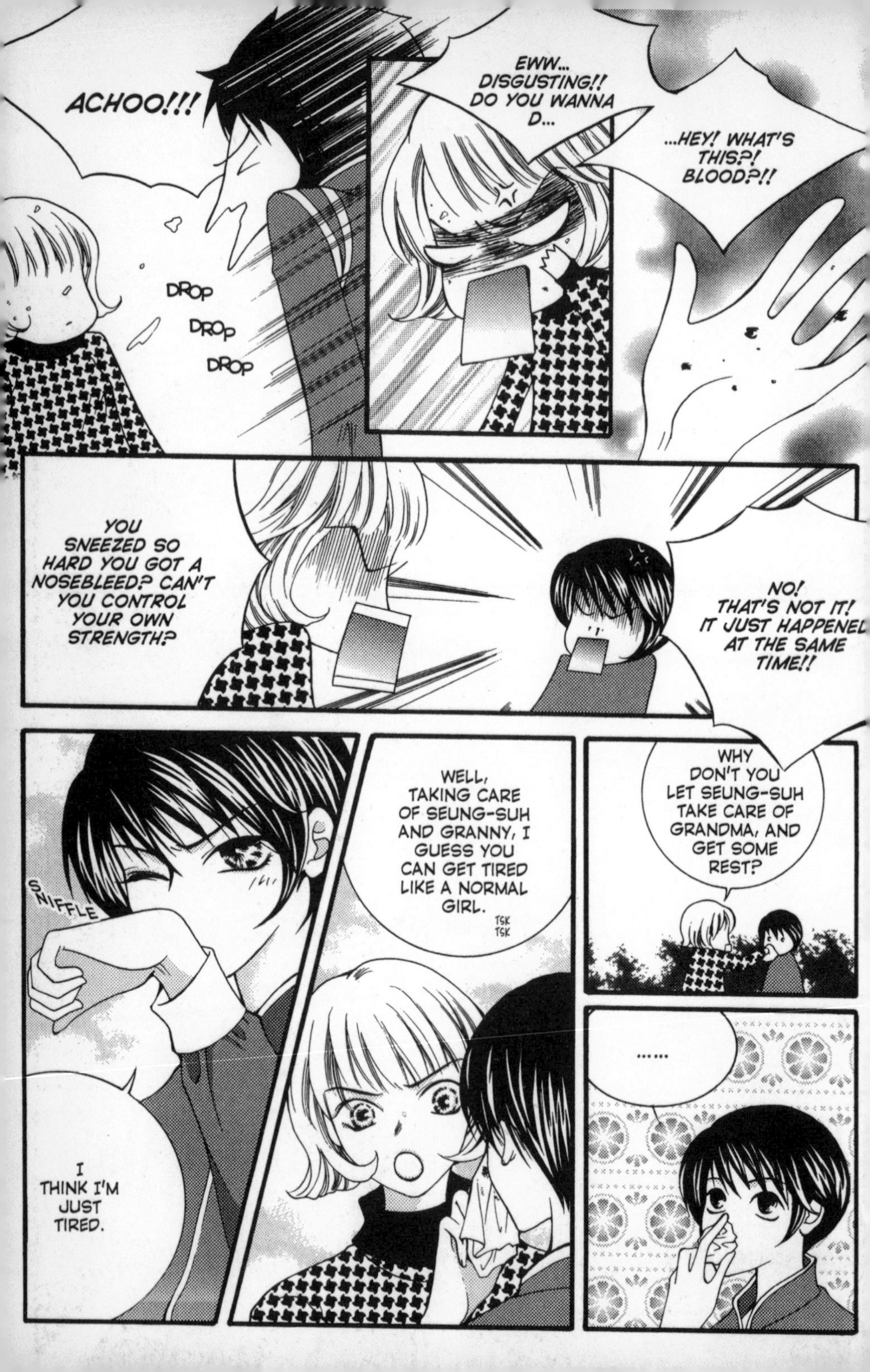
ACHOO!!!
DROP
DROP
DROP
EWW... DISGUSTING!! DO YOU WANNA D...
...HEY! WHAT'S THIS?! BLOOD?!!
YOU SNEEZED SO HARD YOU GOT A NOSEBLEED? CAN'T YOU CONTROL YOUR OWN STRENGTH?
NO! THAT'S NOT IT! IT JUST HAPPENE AT THE SAME TIME!!
SNIFFLE
I THINK I'M JUST TIRED.
WELL, TAKING CARE OF SEUNG-SUH AND GRANNY, I GUESS YOU CAN GET TIRED LIKE A NORMAL GIRL.
TSK TSK
WHY DON'T YOU LET SEUNG-SUH TAKE CARE OF GRANDMA, AND GET SOME REST?
......

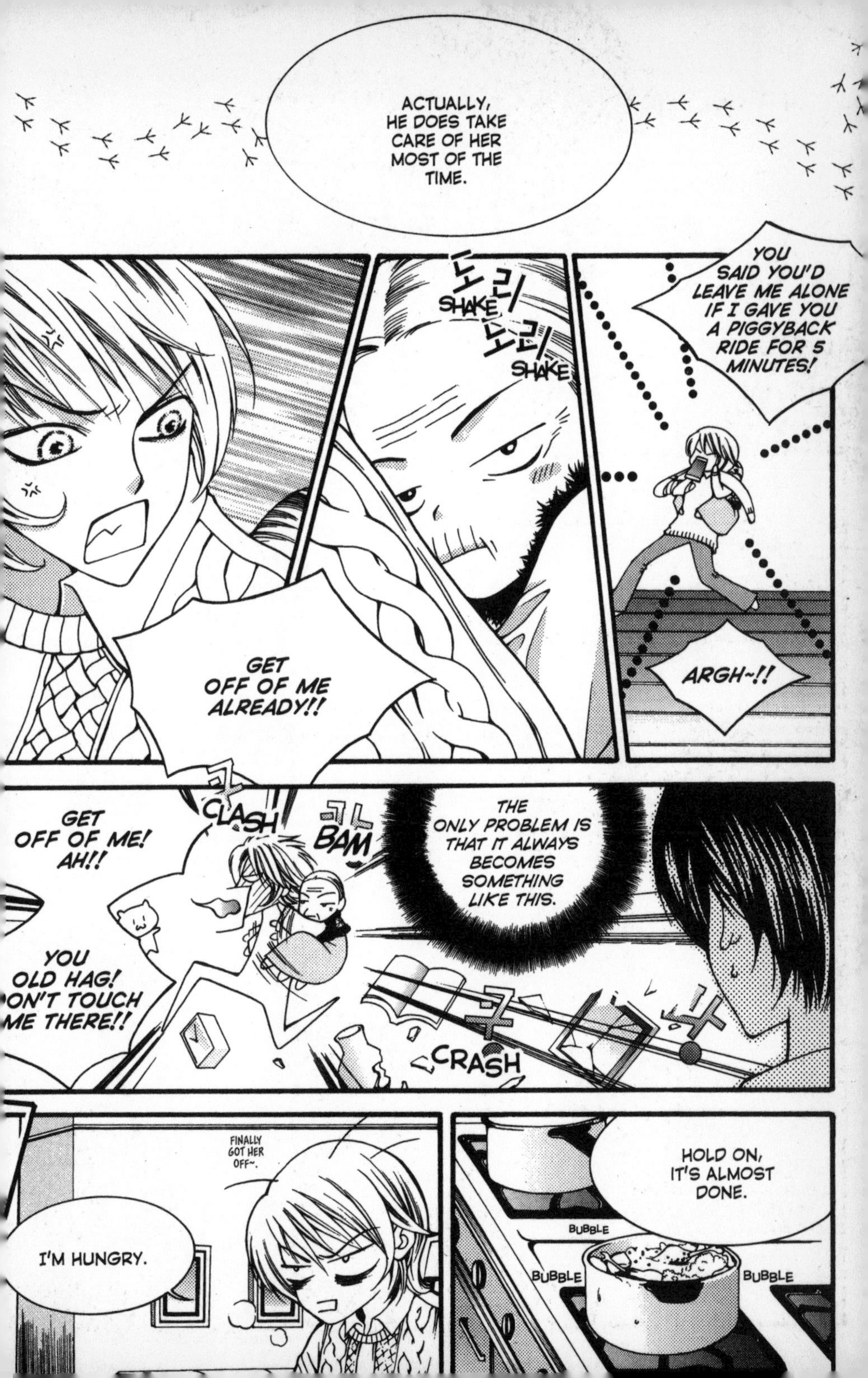
ACTUALLY, HE DOES TAKE CARE OF HER MOST OF THE TIME.
GET OFF OF ME ALREADY!!
SHAKE
SHAKE
YOU SAID YOU'D LEAVE ME ALONE IF I GAVE YOU A PIGGYBACK RIDE FOR 5 MINUTES!
ARGH~!!
GET OFF OF ME! AH!!
YOU OLD HAG! ON'T TOUCH ME THERE!!
CLASH
BAM
THE ONLY PROBLEM IS THAT IT ALWAYS BECOMES SOMETHING LIKE THIS.
CRASH
I'M HUNGRY.
FINALLY GOT HER OFF~.
HOLD ON, IT'S ALMOST DONE.
BUBBLE
BUBBLE
BUBBLE

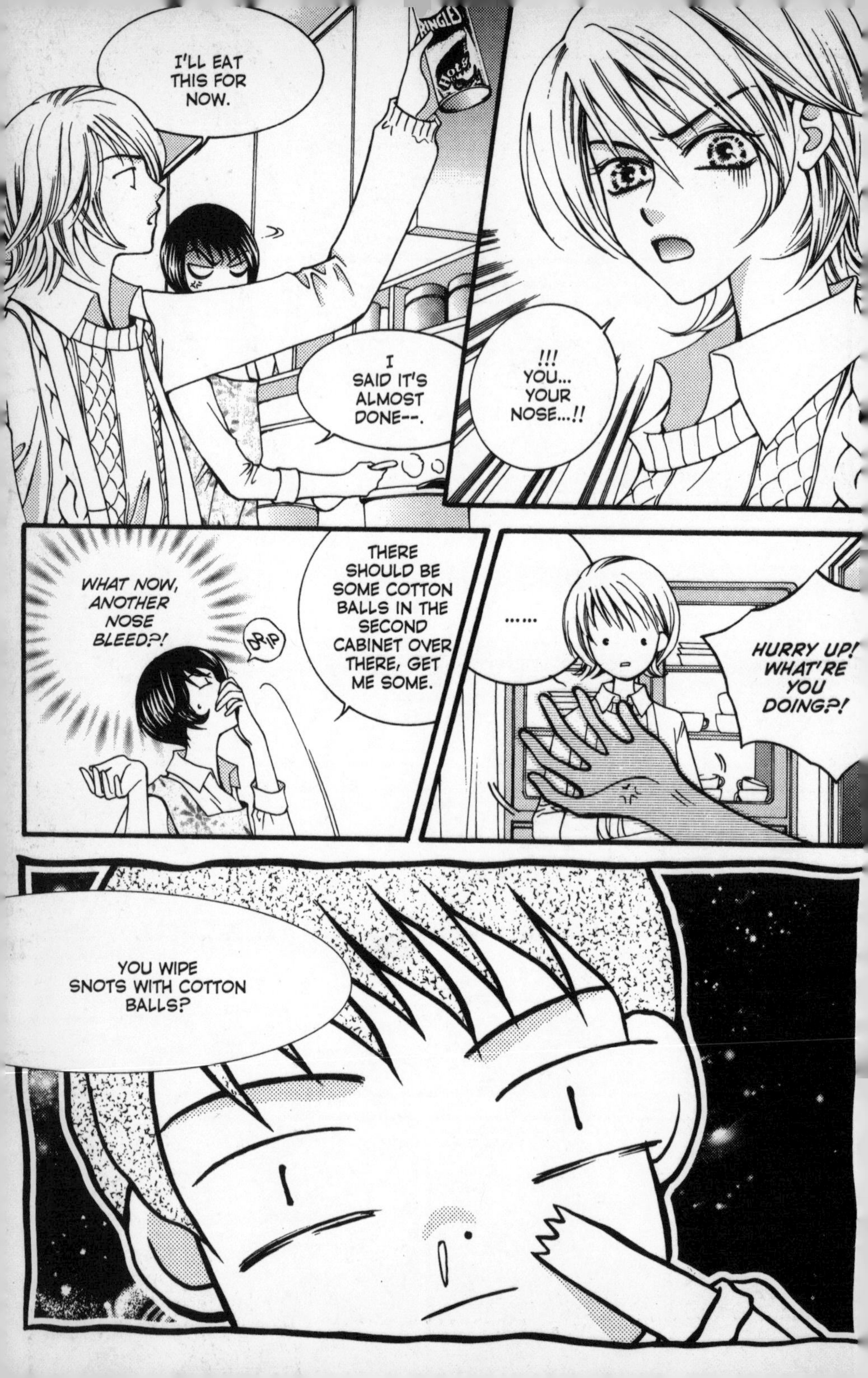
I'LL EAT THIS FOR NOW.
I SAID IT'S ALMOST DONE--.
!!! YOU... YOUR NOSE...!!
WHAT NOW, ANOTHER NOSE BLEED?!
DRIP
THERE SHOULD BE SOME COTTON BALLS IN THE SECOND CABINET OVER THERE, GET ME SOME.
......
HURRY UP! WHAT'RE YOU DOING?!
YOU WIPE SNOTS WITH COTTON BALLS?

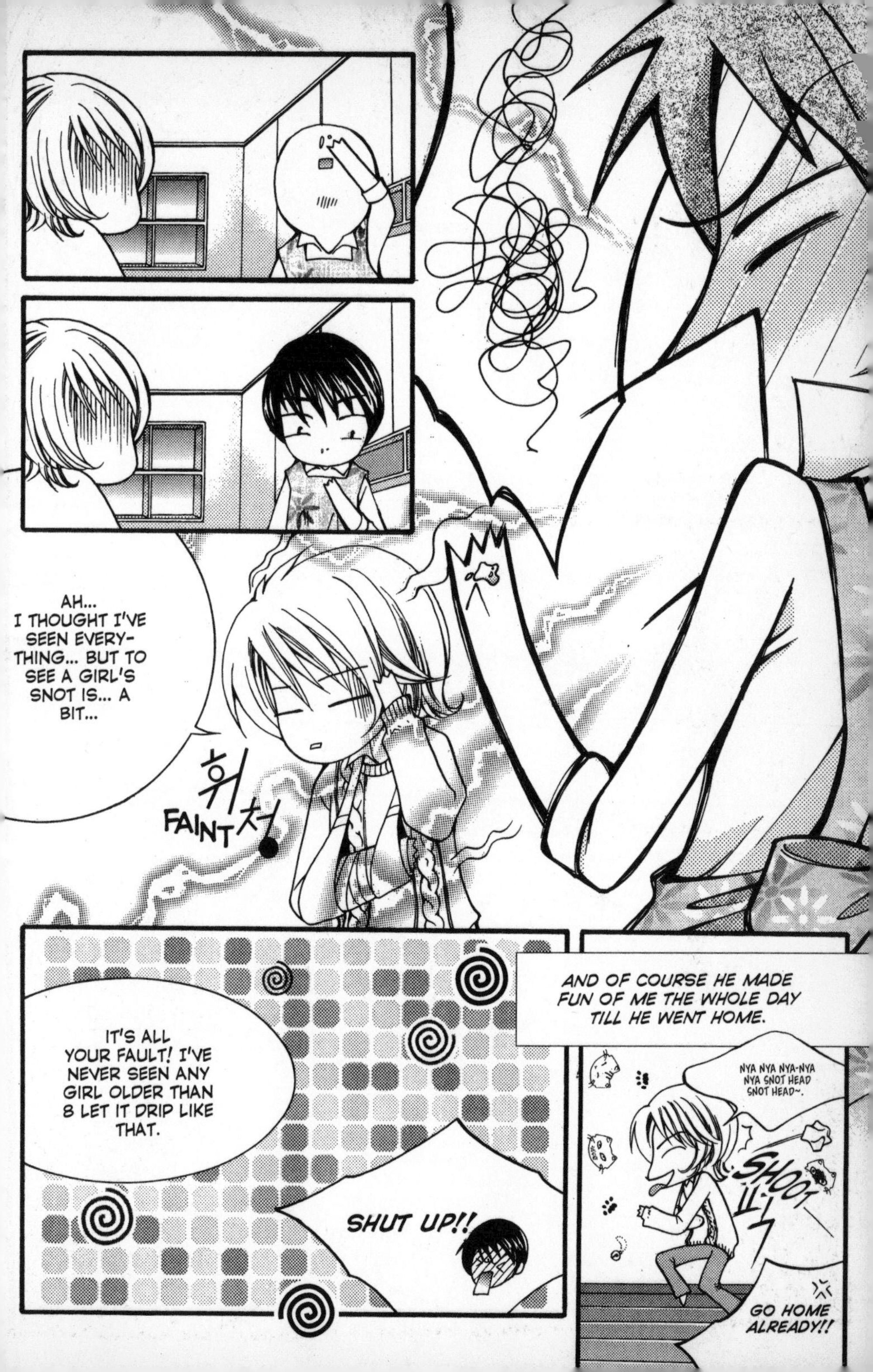
AH... I THOUGHT I'VE SEEN EVERY-THING... BUT TO SEE A GIRL'S SNOT IS... A BIT...
휘청
FAINT
IT'S ALL YOUR FAULT! I'VE NEVER SEEN ANY GIRL OLDER THAN 8 LET IT DRIP LIKE THAT.
SHUT UP!!
AND OF COURSE HE MADE FUN OF ME THE WHOLE DAY TILL HE WENT HOME.
NYA NYA NYA-NYA NYA SNOT HEAD SNOT HEAD~.
SHOOT
GO HOME ALREADY!!

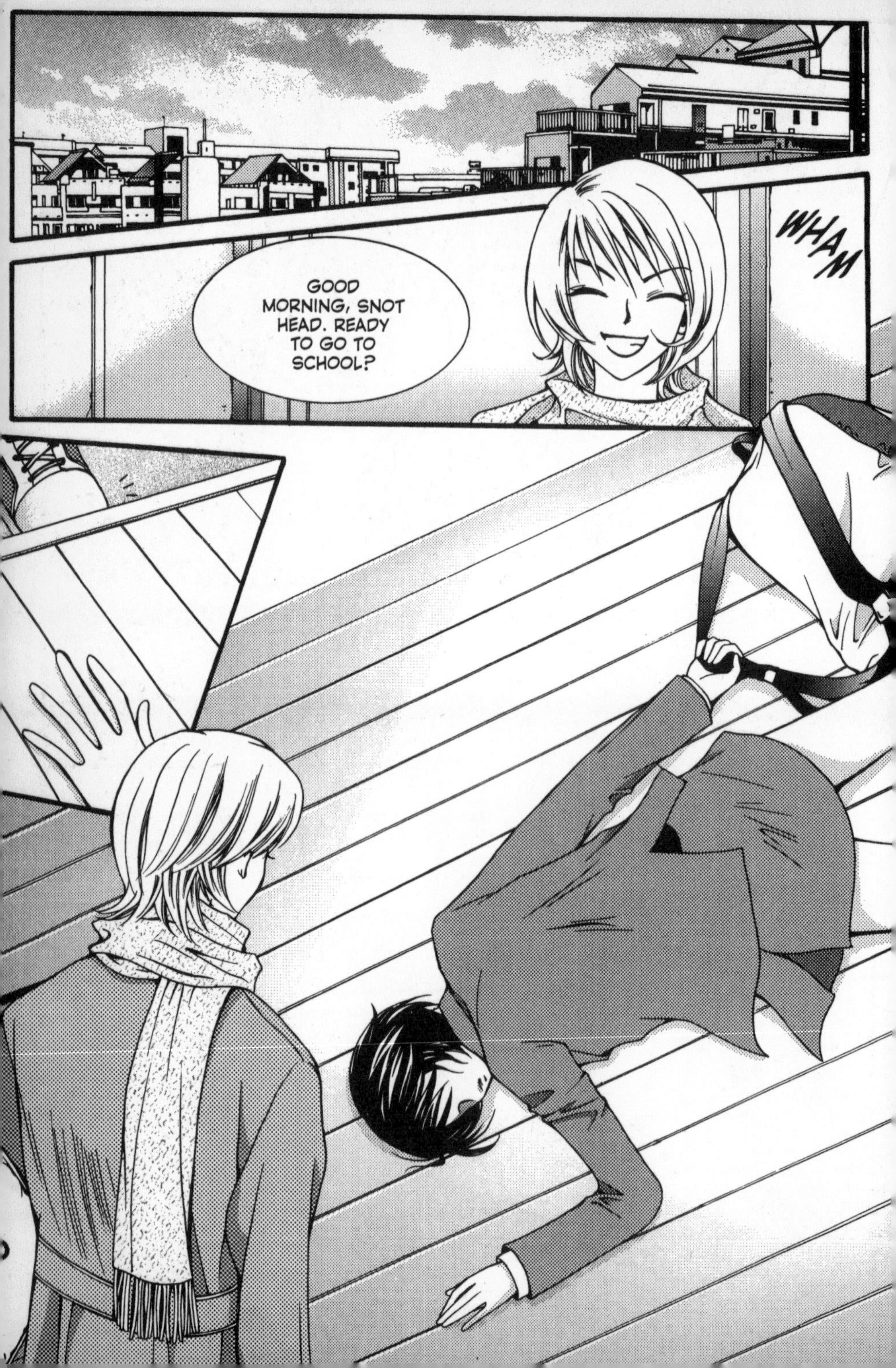
GOOD MORNING, SNOT HEAD. READY TO GO TO SCHOOL?
WHAM

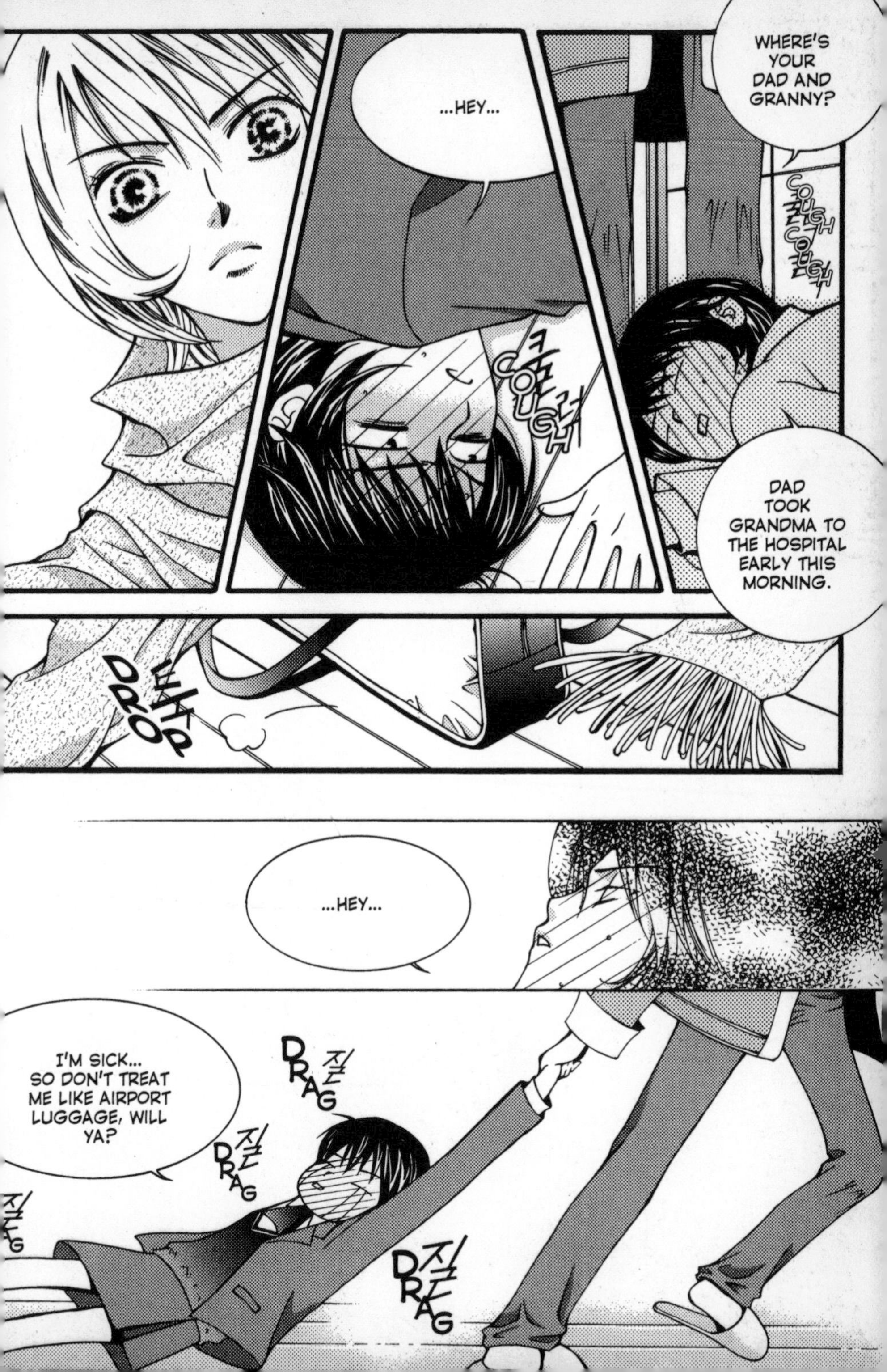
...HEY...
COUGH
WHERE'S YOUR DAD AND GRANNY?
COUGH COUGH
DAD TOOK GRANDMA TO THE HOSPITAL EARLY THIS MORNING.
DROP
...HEY...
I'M SICK... SO DON'T TREAT ME LIKE AIRPORT LUGGAGE, WILL YA?
DRAG
DRAG
DRAG
DRAG

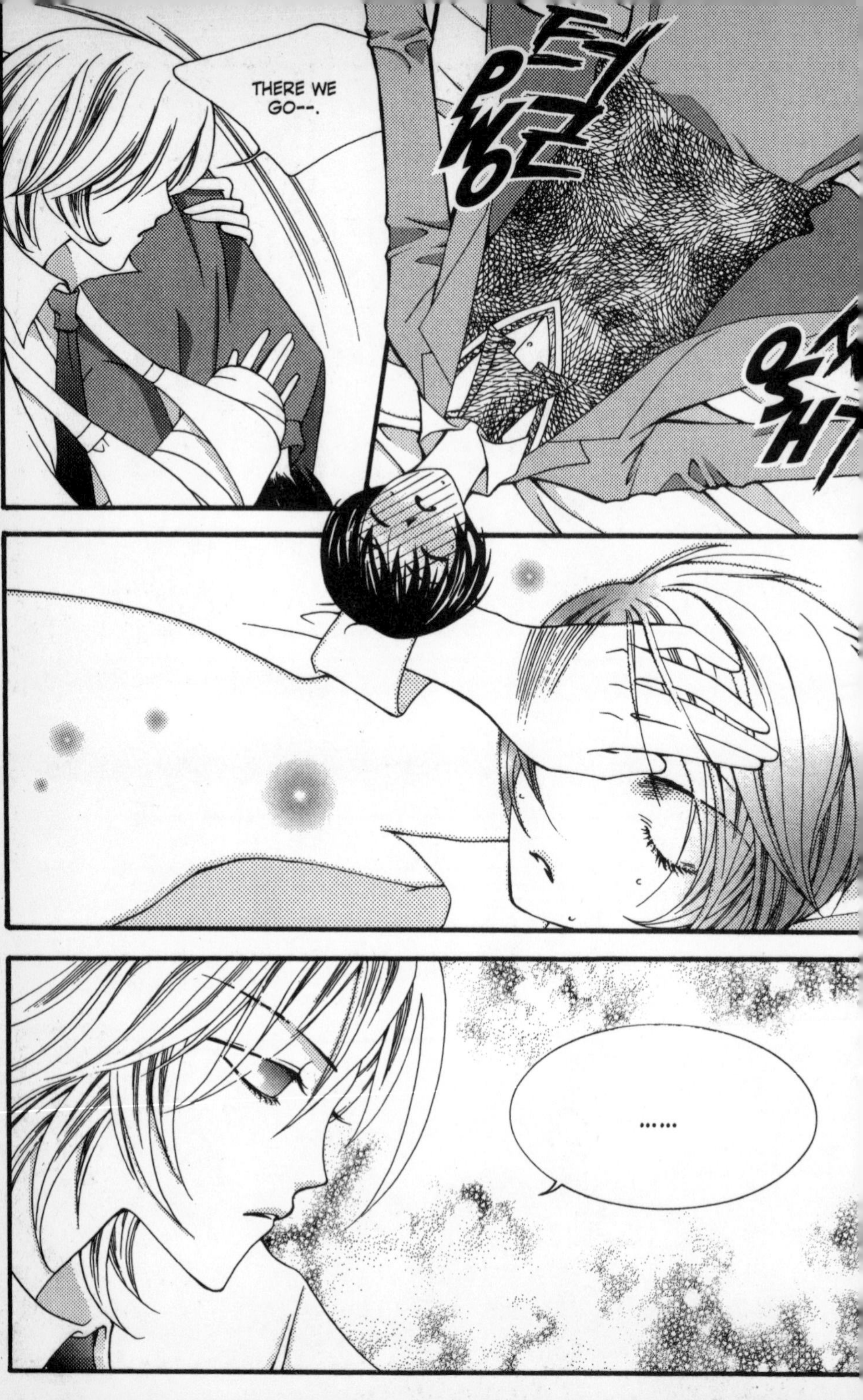
THERE WE GO--.
......

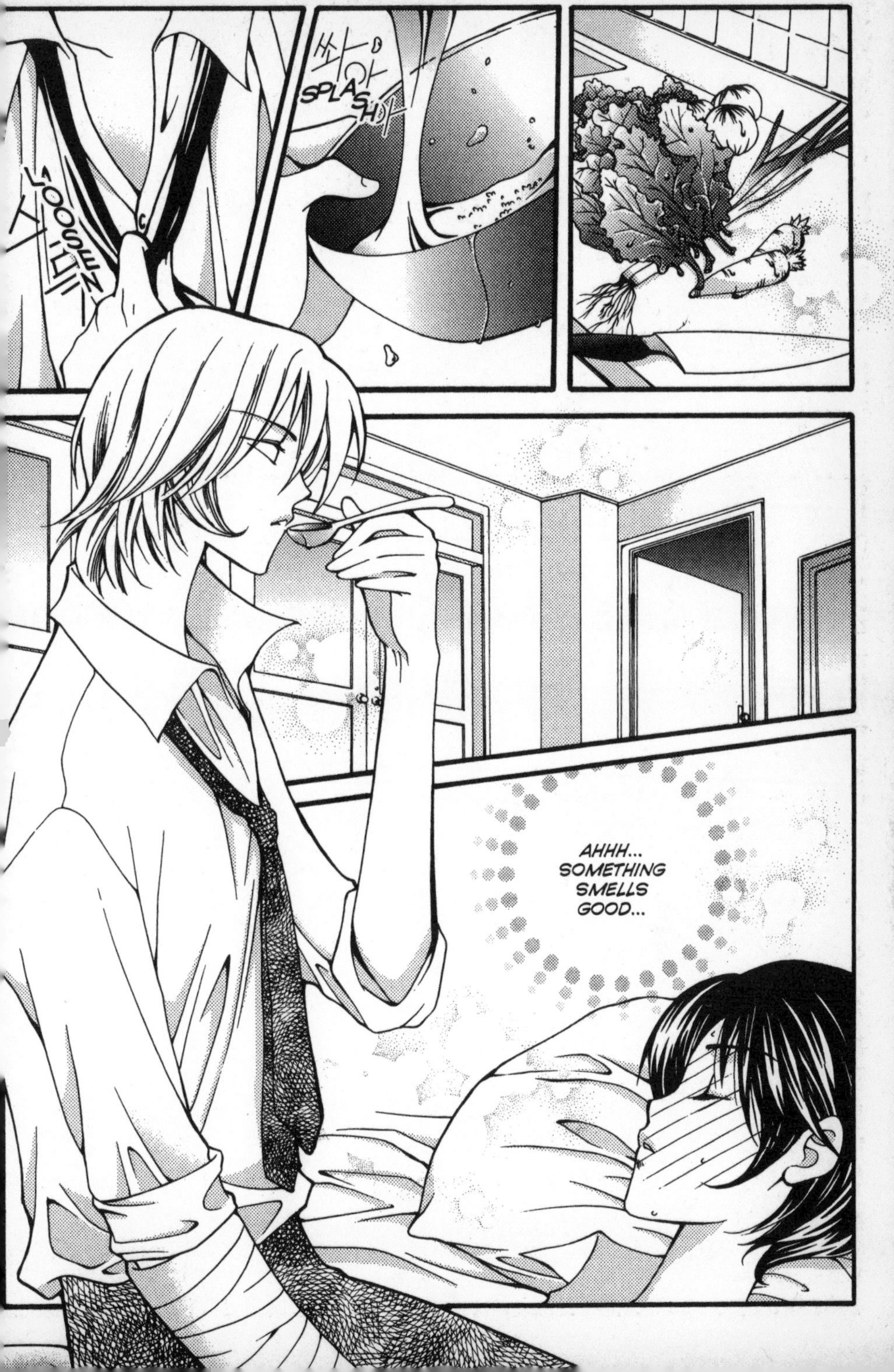
LOOSEN
쏴아
SPLASH
AHHH... SOMETHING SMELLS GOOD...

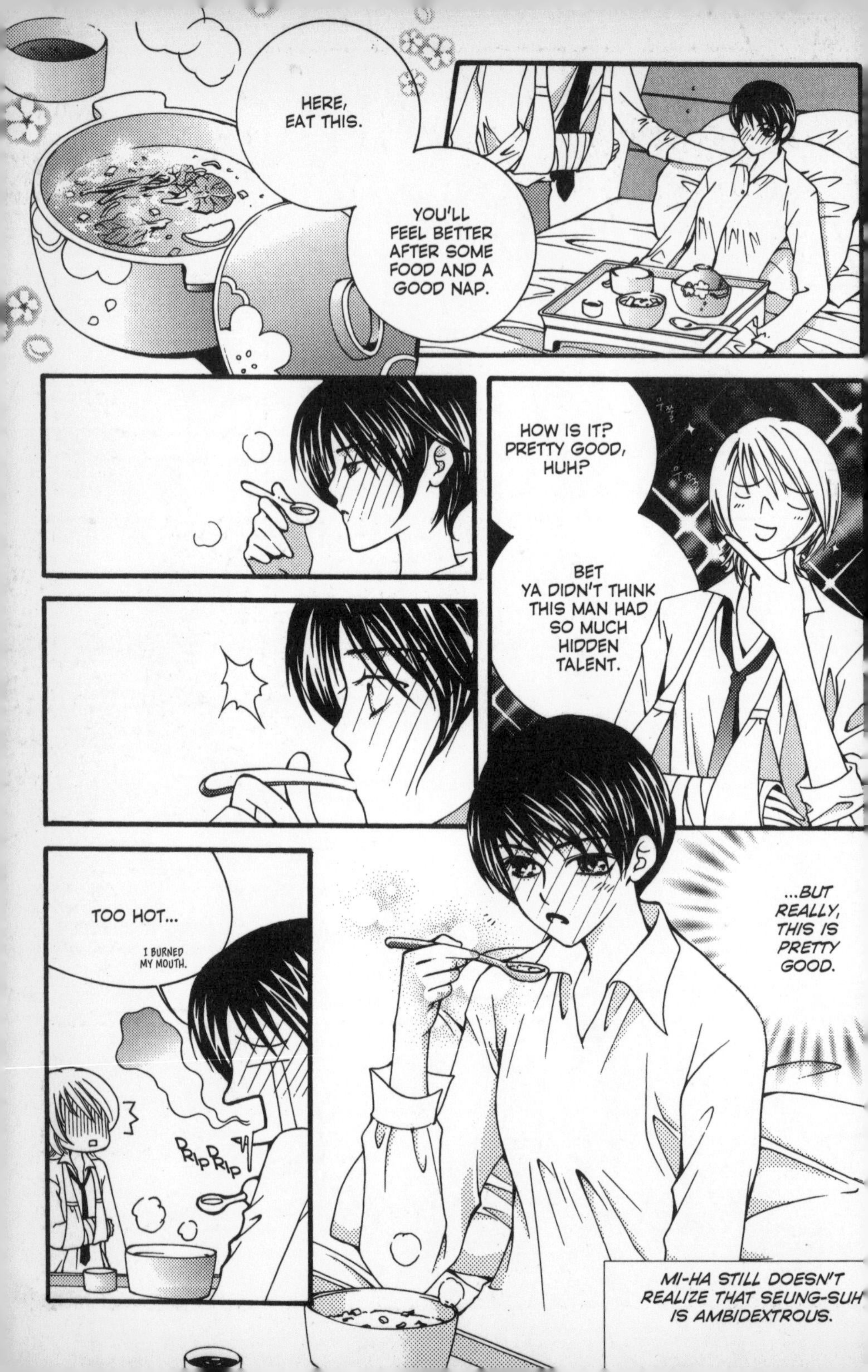
HERE, EAT THIS.
YOU'LL FEEL BETTER AFTER SOME FOOD AND A GOOD NAP.
HOW IS IT? PRETTY GOOD, HUH?
BET YA DIDN'T THINK THIS MAN HAD SO MUCH HIDDEN TALENT.
TOO HOT...
I BURNED MY MOUTH.
DRIP DRIP
...BUT REALLY, THIS IS PRETTY GOOD.
MI-HA STILL DOESN'T REALIZE THAT SEUNG-SUH IS AMBIDEXTROUS.

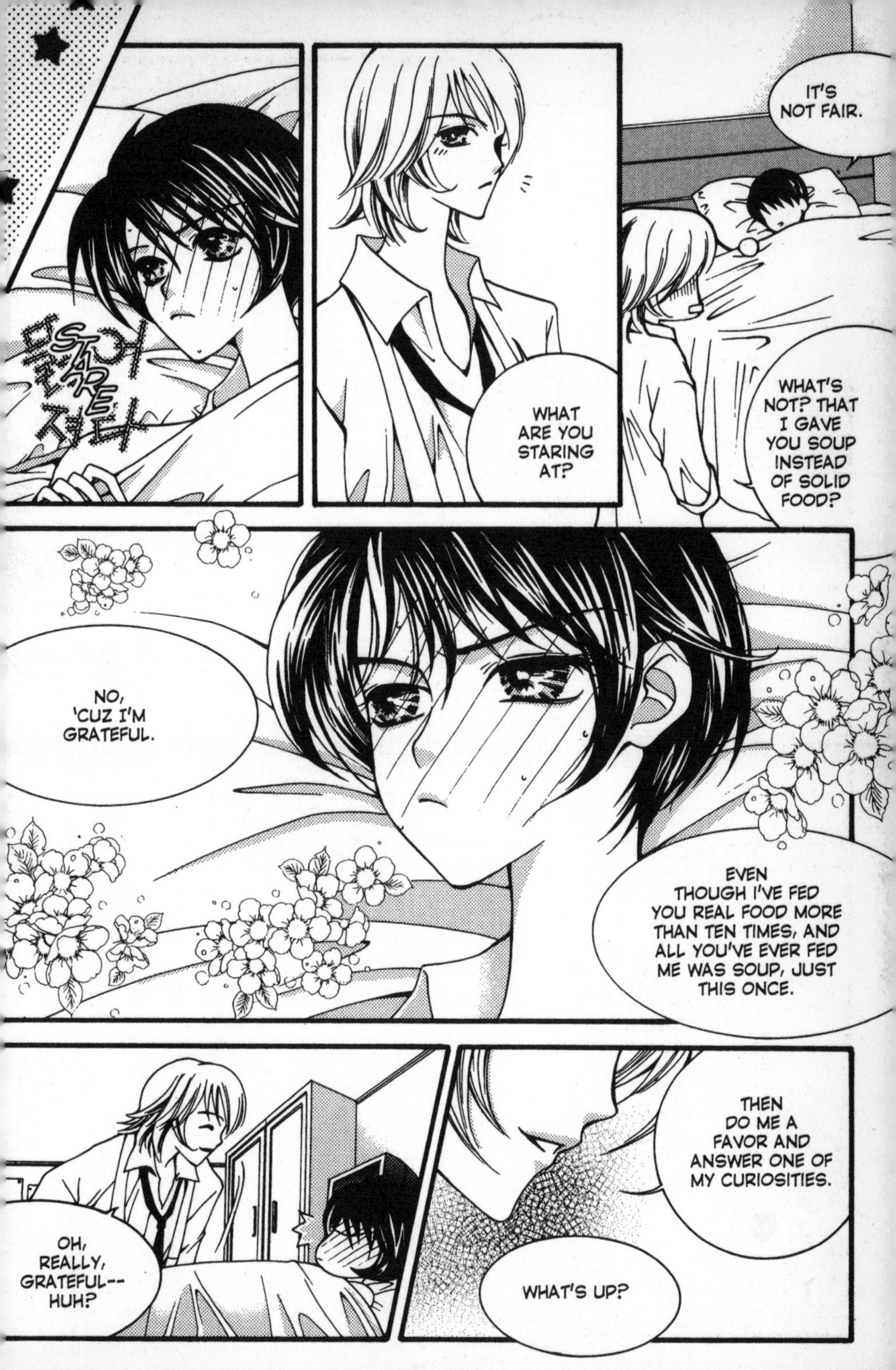
STARE
WHAT ARE YOU STARING AT?
IT'S NOT FAIR.
WHAT'S NOT? THAT I GAVE YOU SOUP INSTEAD OF SOLID FOOD?
NO, 'CUZ I'M GRATEFUL.
EVEN THOUGH I'VE FED YOU REAL FOOD MORE THAN TEN TIMES, AND ALL YOU'VE EVER FED ME WAS SOUP, JUST THIS ONCE.
OH, REALLY, GRATEFUL-- HUH?
THEN DO ME A FAVOR AND ANSWER ONE OF MY CURIOSITIES.
WHAT'S UP?

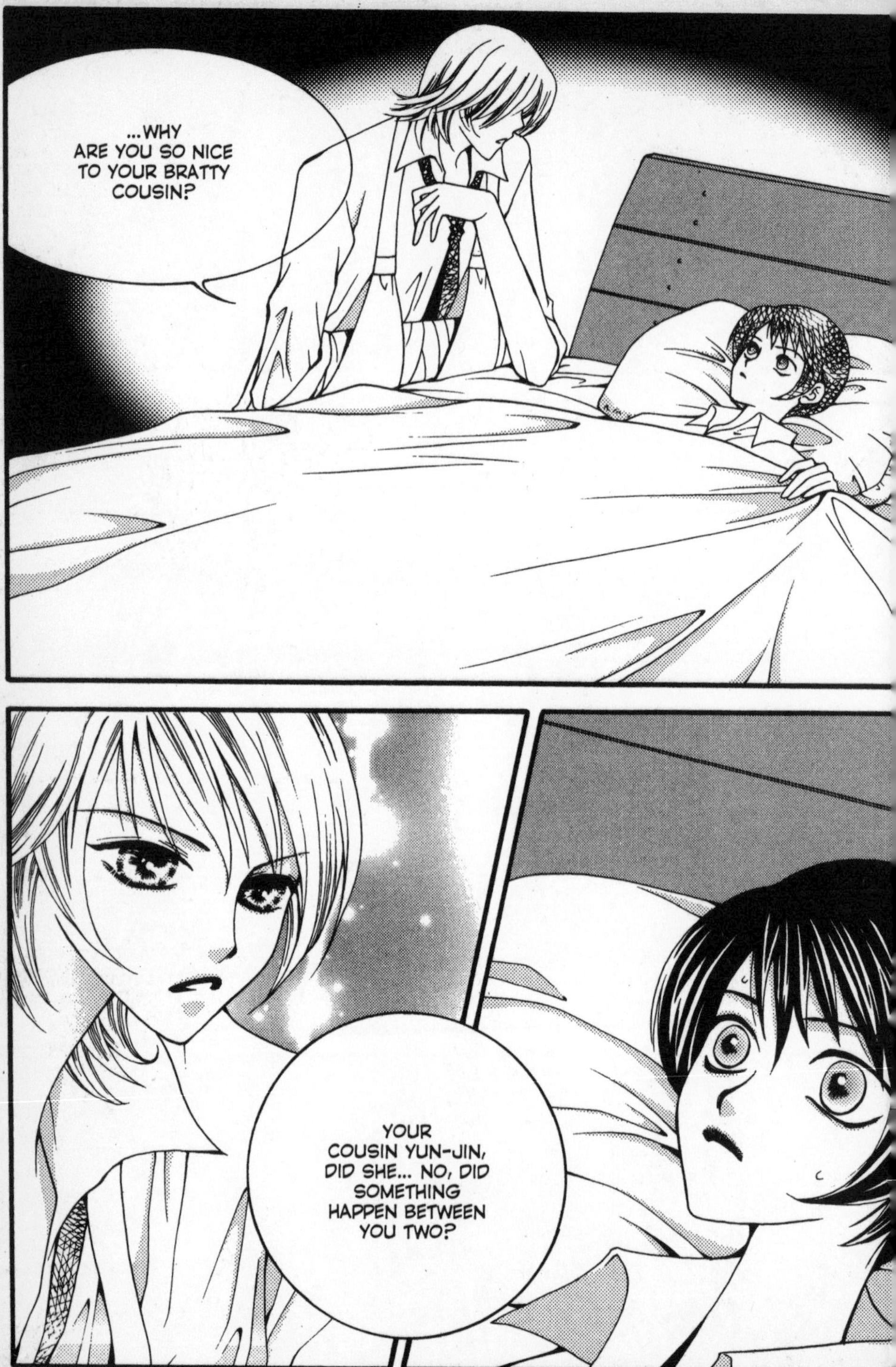
...WHY ARE YOU SO NICE TO YOUR BRATTY COUSIN?
YOUR COUSIN YUN-JIN, DID SHE... NO, DID SOMETHING HAPPEN BETWEEN YOU TWO?

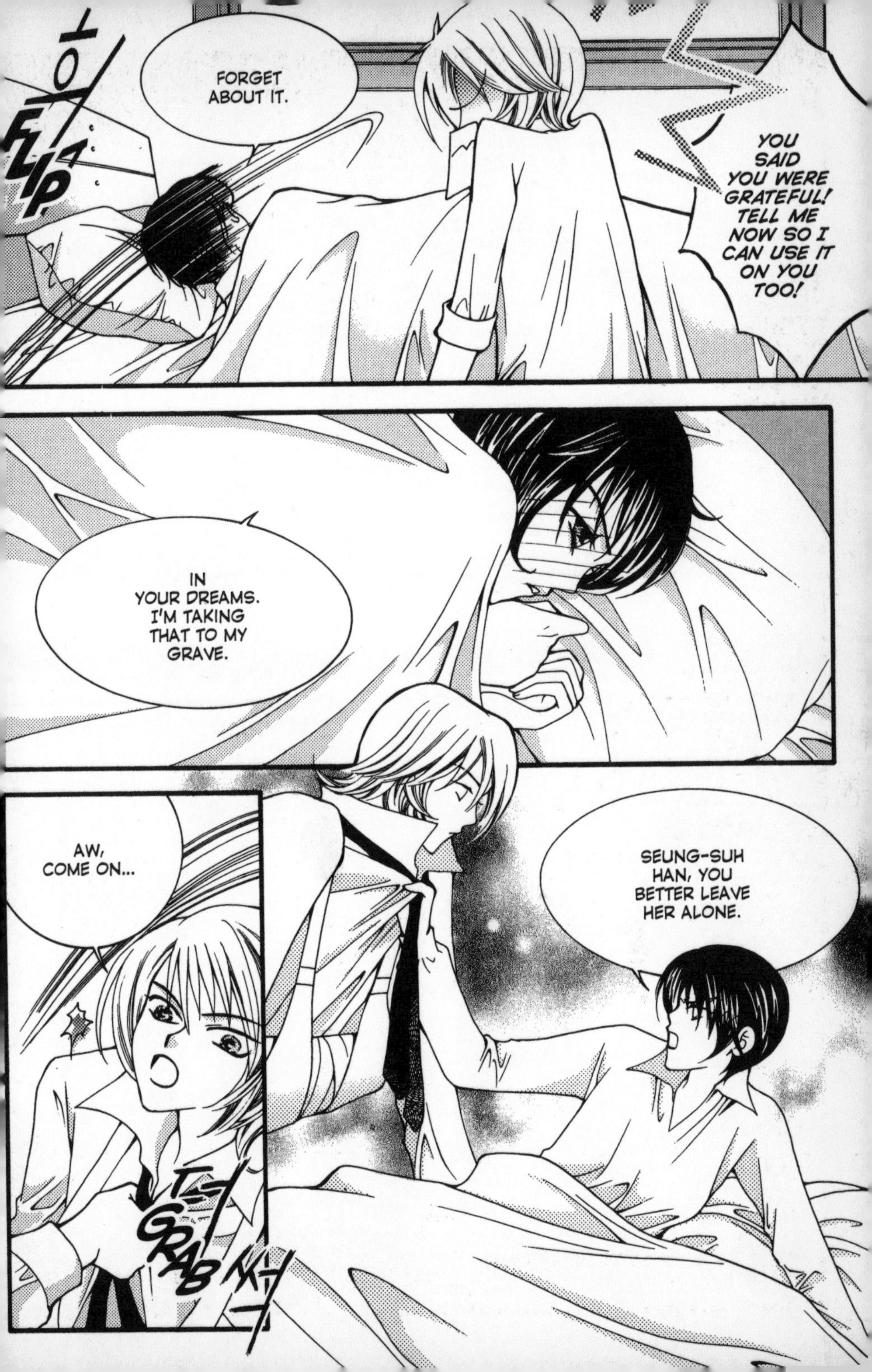
FLIP
FORGET ABOUT IT.
YOU SAID YOU WERE GRATEFUL! TELL ME NOW SO I CAN USE IT ON YOU TOO!
IN YOUR DREAMS. I'M TAKING THAT TO MY GRAVE.
AW, COME ON...
GRAB
SEUNG-SUH HAN, YOU BETTER LEAVE HER ALONE.

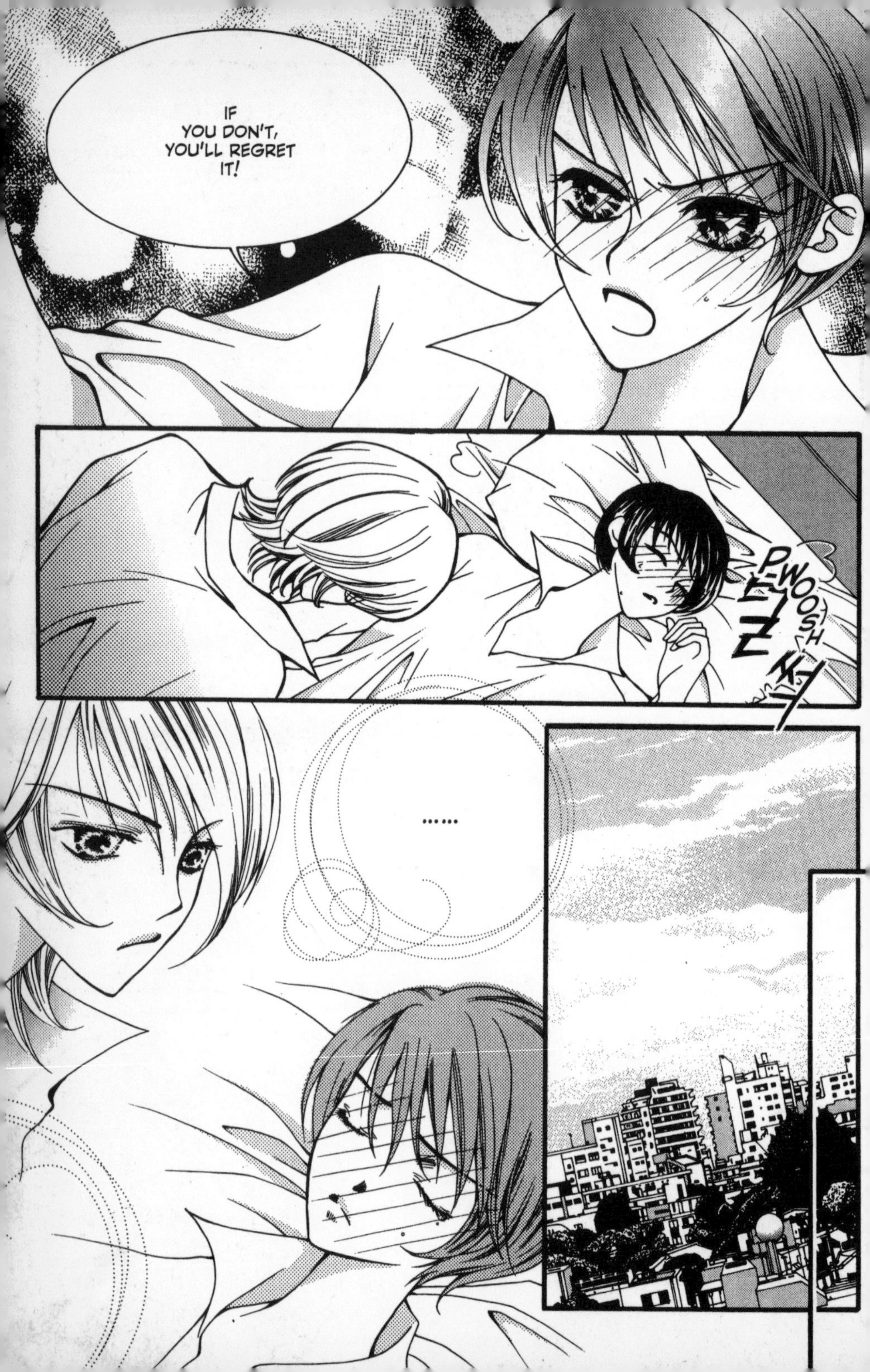
IF YOU DON'T, YOU'LL REGRET IT!
P-WOOSH
......

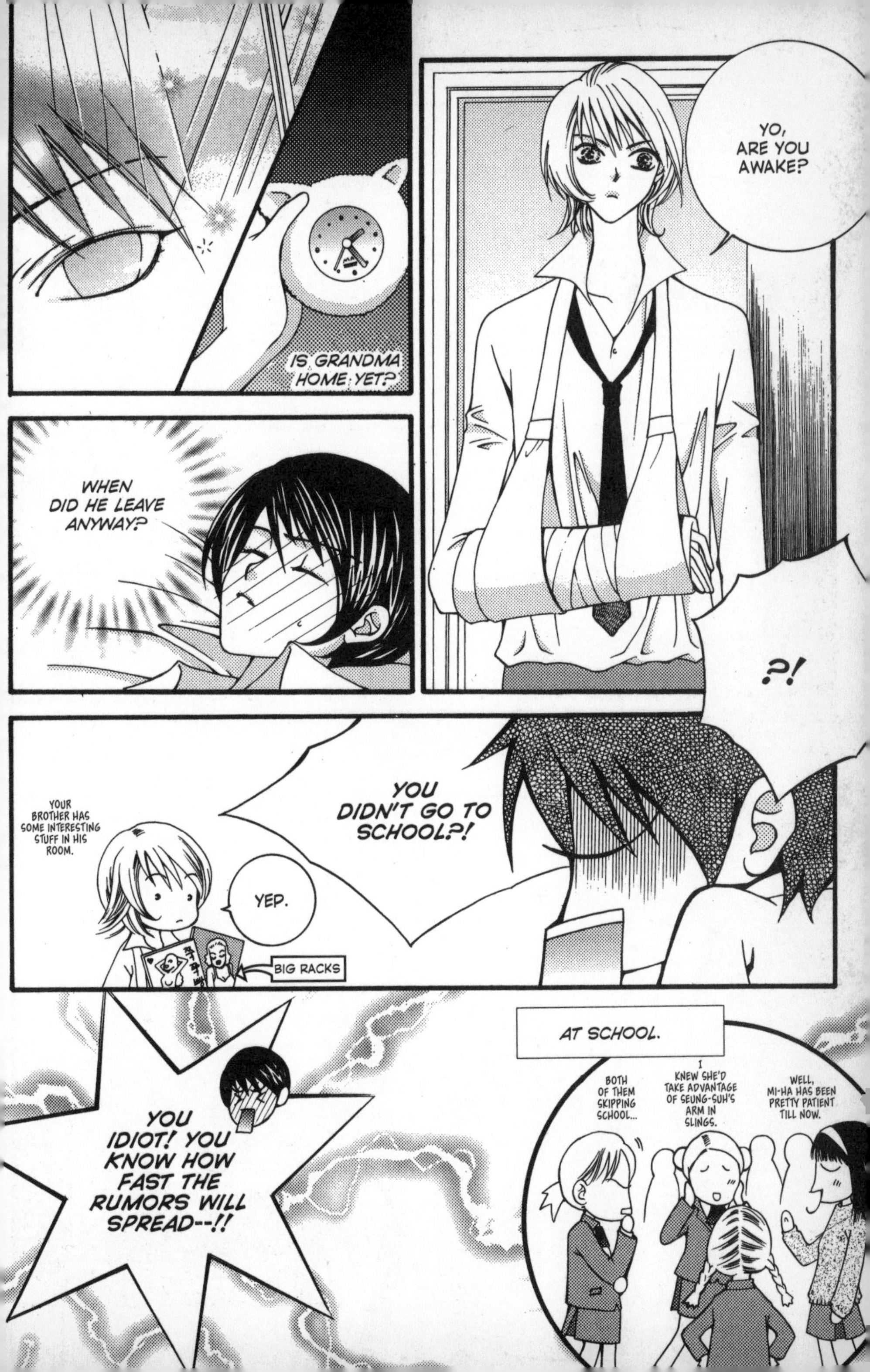
IS GRANDMA HOME YET?
WHEN DID HE LEAVE ANYWAY?
YO, ARE YOU AWAKE?
?!
YOU DIDN'T GO TO SCHOOL?!
YOUR BROTHER HAS SOME INTERESTING STUFF IN HIS ROOM.
YEP.
BIG RACKS
YOU IDIOT! YOU KNOW HOW FAST THE RUMORS WILL SPREAD--!!
AT SCHOOL.
BOTH OF THEM SKIPPING SCHOOL...
I KNEW SHE'D TAKE ADVANTAGE OF SEUNG-SUH'S ARM IN SLINGS.
WELL, MI-HA HAS BEEN PRETTY PATIENT TILL NOW.

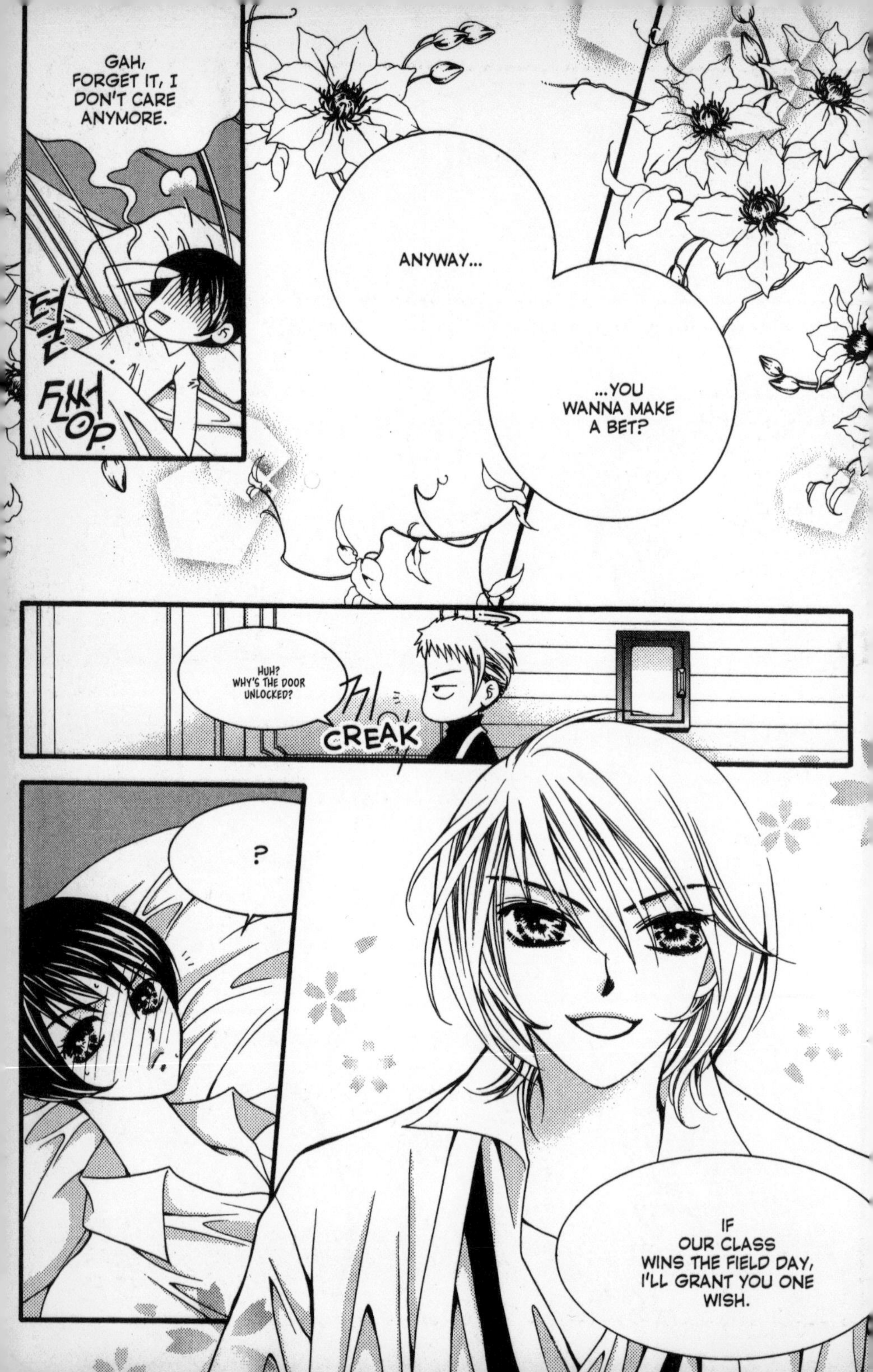
GAH, FORGET IT, I DON'T CARE ANYMORE.
FLOP
ANYWAY...
...YOU WANNA MAKE A BET?
HUH? WHY'S THE DOOR UNLOCKED?
CREAK
?
IF OUR CLASS WINS THE FIELD DAY, I'LL GRANT YOU ONE WISH.

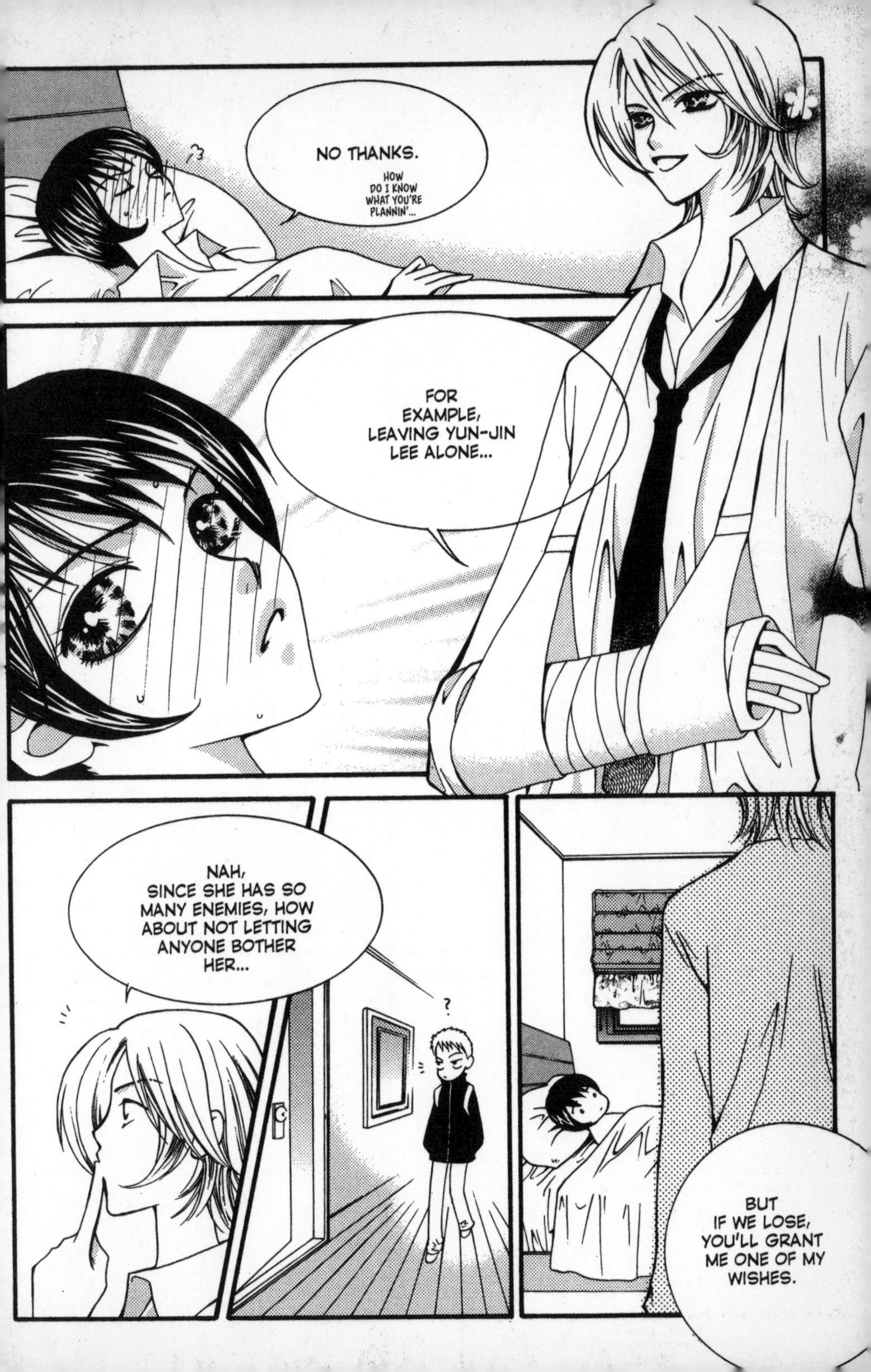
NO THANKS.
HOW DO I KNOW WHAT YOU'RE PLANNIN'...
FOR EXAMPLE, LEAVING YUN-JIN LEE ALONE...
NAH, SINCE SHE HAS SO MANY ENEMIES, HOW ABOUT NOT LETTING ANYONE BOTHER HER...
?
BUT IF WE LOSE, YOU'LL GRANT ME ONE OF MY WISHES.

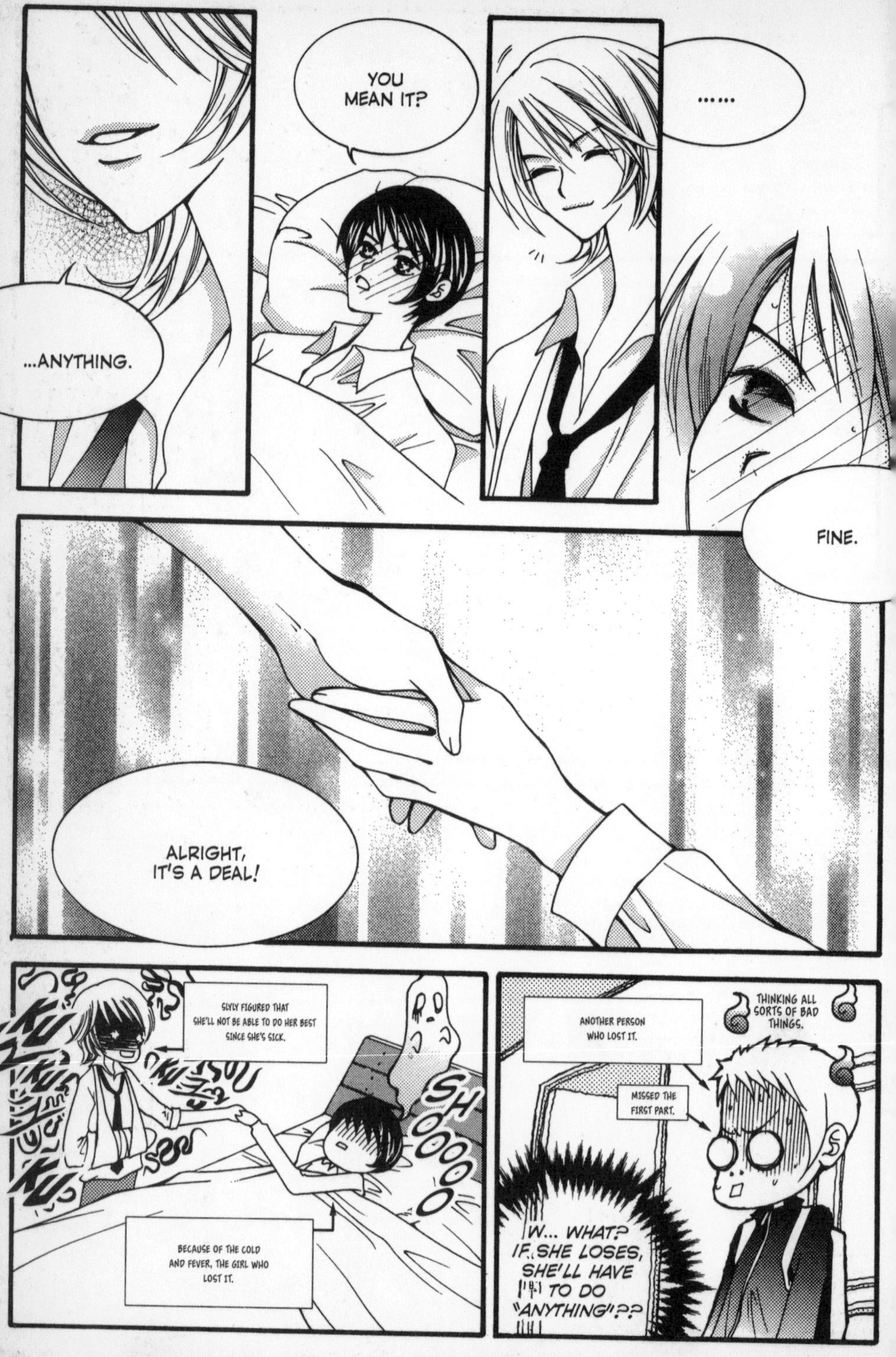
...ANYTHING.
YOU MEAN IT?
......
FINE.
ALRIGHT, IT'S A DEAL!
SLYLY FIGURED THAT SHE'LL NOT BE ABLE TO DO HER BEST SINCE SHE'S SICK.
SHOOOOOO
BECAUSE OF THE COLD AND FEVER, THE GIRL WHO LOST IT.
ANOTHER PERSON WHO LOST IT.
THINKING ALL SORTS OF BAD THINGS.
MISSED THE FIRST PART.
W... WHAT? IF SHE LOSES, SHE'LL HAVE TO DO "ANYTHING"??

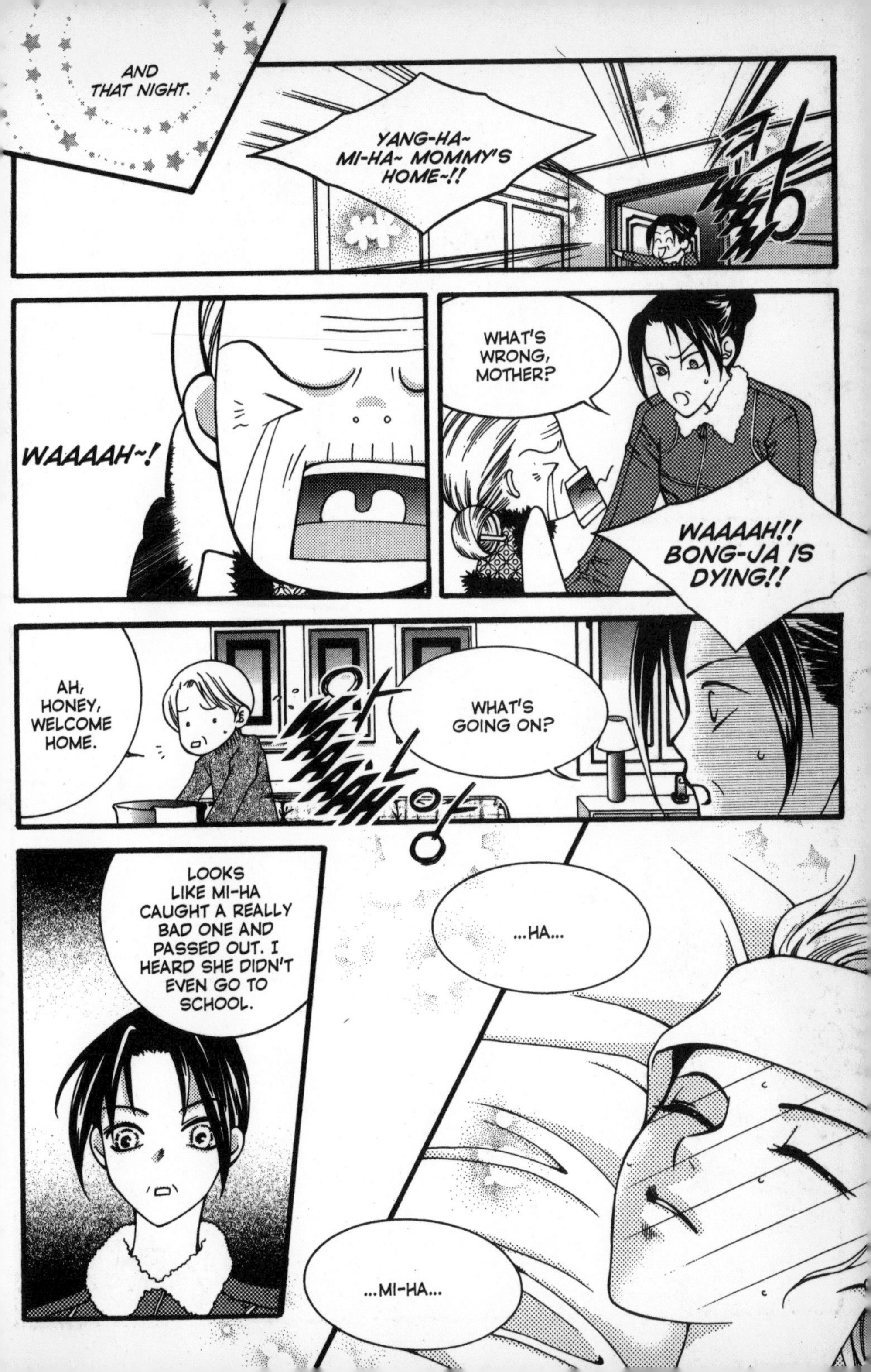
AND THAT NIGHT.
YANG-HA~ MI-HA~ MOMMY'S HOME~!!
WAAAAH~!
WHAT'S WRONG, MOTHER?
WAAAAH!! BONG-JA IS DYING!!
AH, HONEY, WELCOME HOME.
WHAT'S GOING ON?
LOOKS LIKE MI-HA CAUGHT A REALLY BAD ONE AND PASSED OUT. I HEARD SHE DIDN'T EVEN GO TO SCHOOL.
...HA...
...MI-HA...

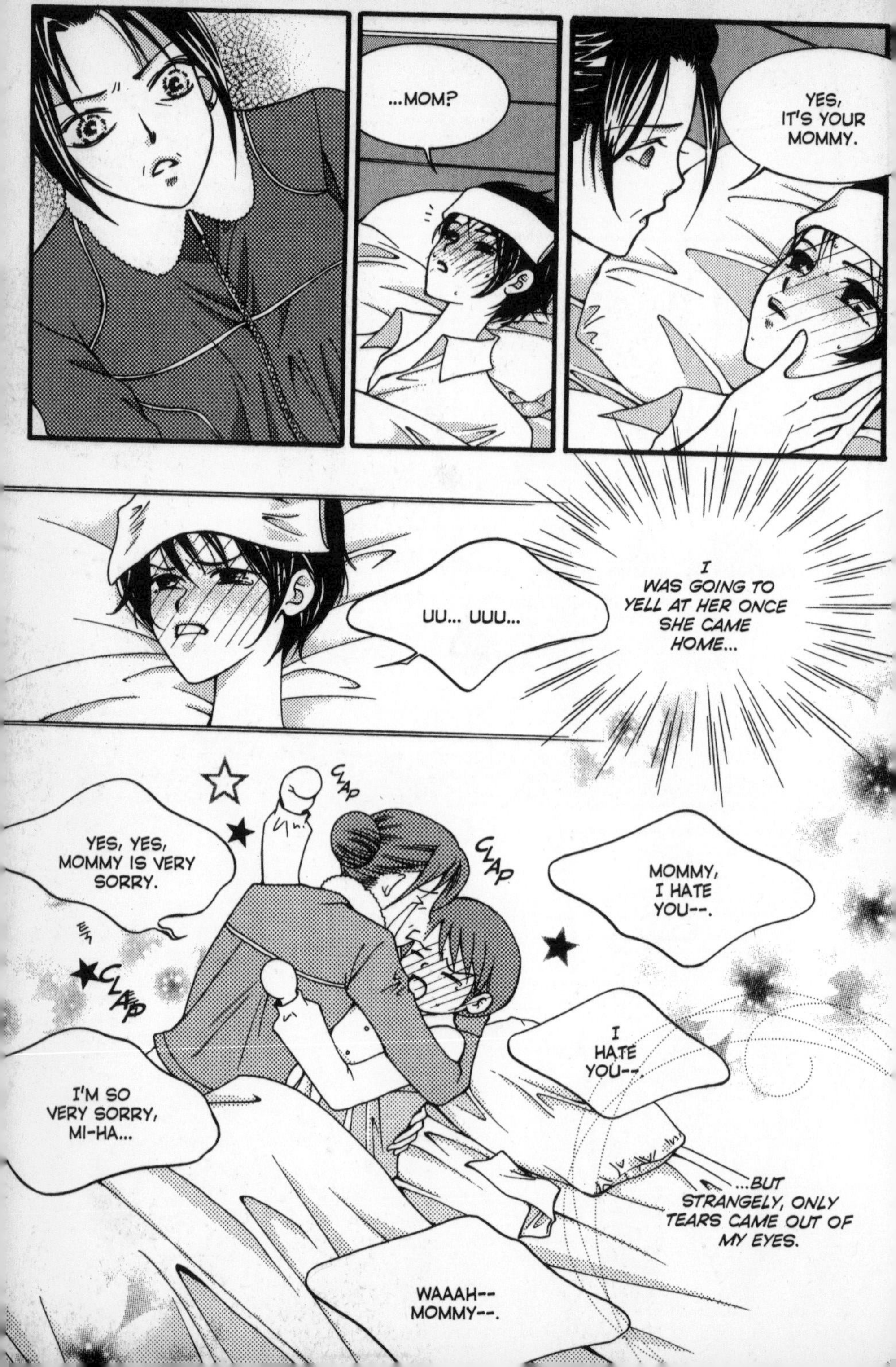
...MOM?
YES, IT'S YOUR MOMMY.
UU... UUU...
I WAS GOING TO YELL AT HER ONCE SHE CAME HOME...
CLAP
YES, YES, MOMMY IS VERY SORRY.
CLAP
MOMMY, I HATE YOU--.
CLAP
I'M SO VERY SORRY, MI-HA...
I HATE YOU--.
...BUT STRANGELY, ONLY TEARS CAME OUT OF MY EYES.
WAAAH-- MOMMY--.

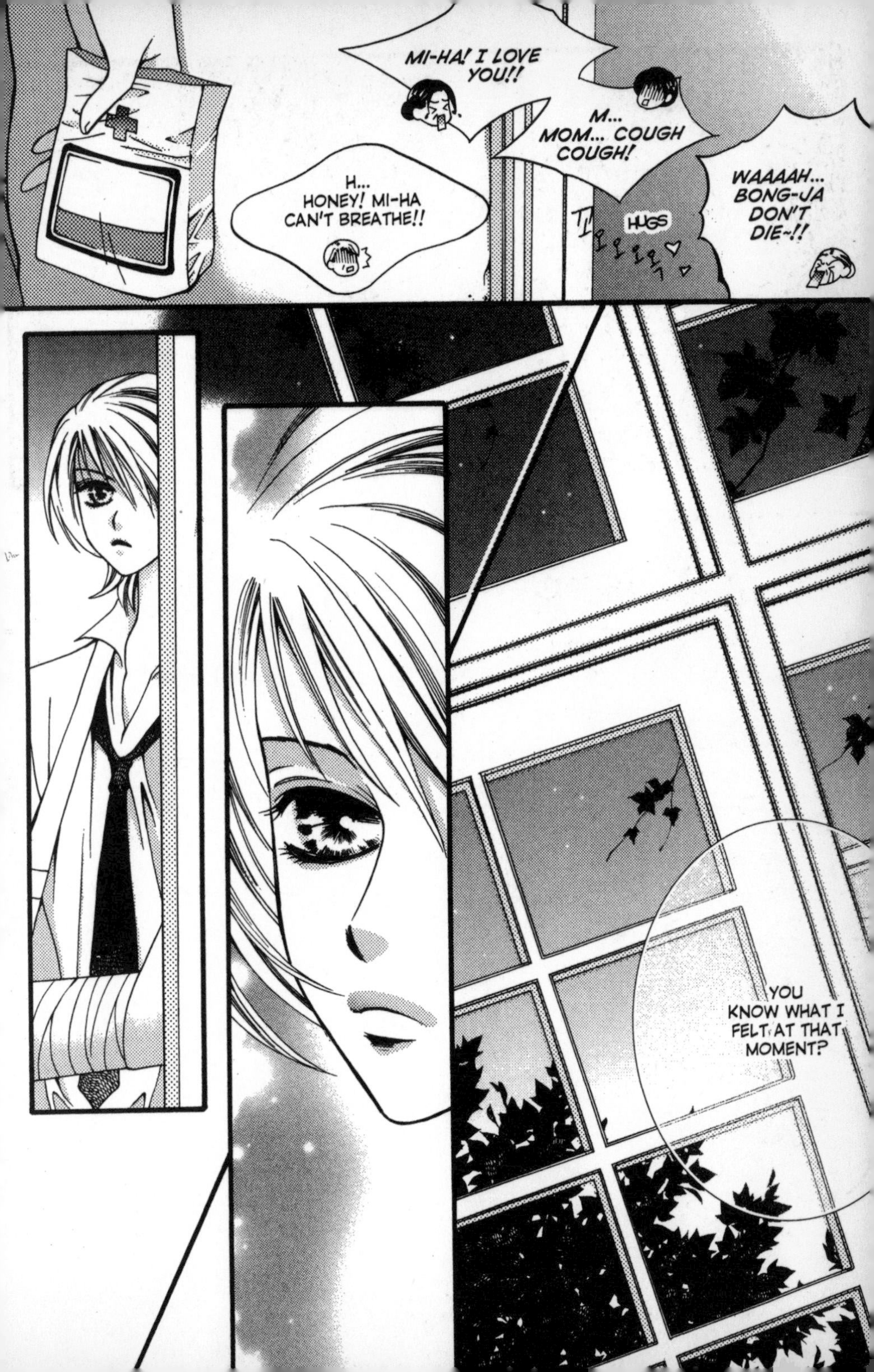
MI-HA! I LOVE YOU!!
M... MOM... COUGH COUGH!
H... HONEY! MI-HA CAN'T BREATHE!!
HUGS
WAAAAH... BONG-JA DON'T DIE~!!
YOU KNOW WHAT I FELT AT THAT MOMENT?

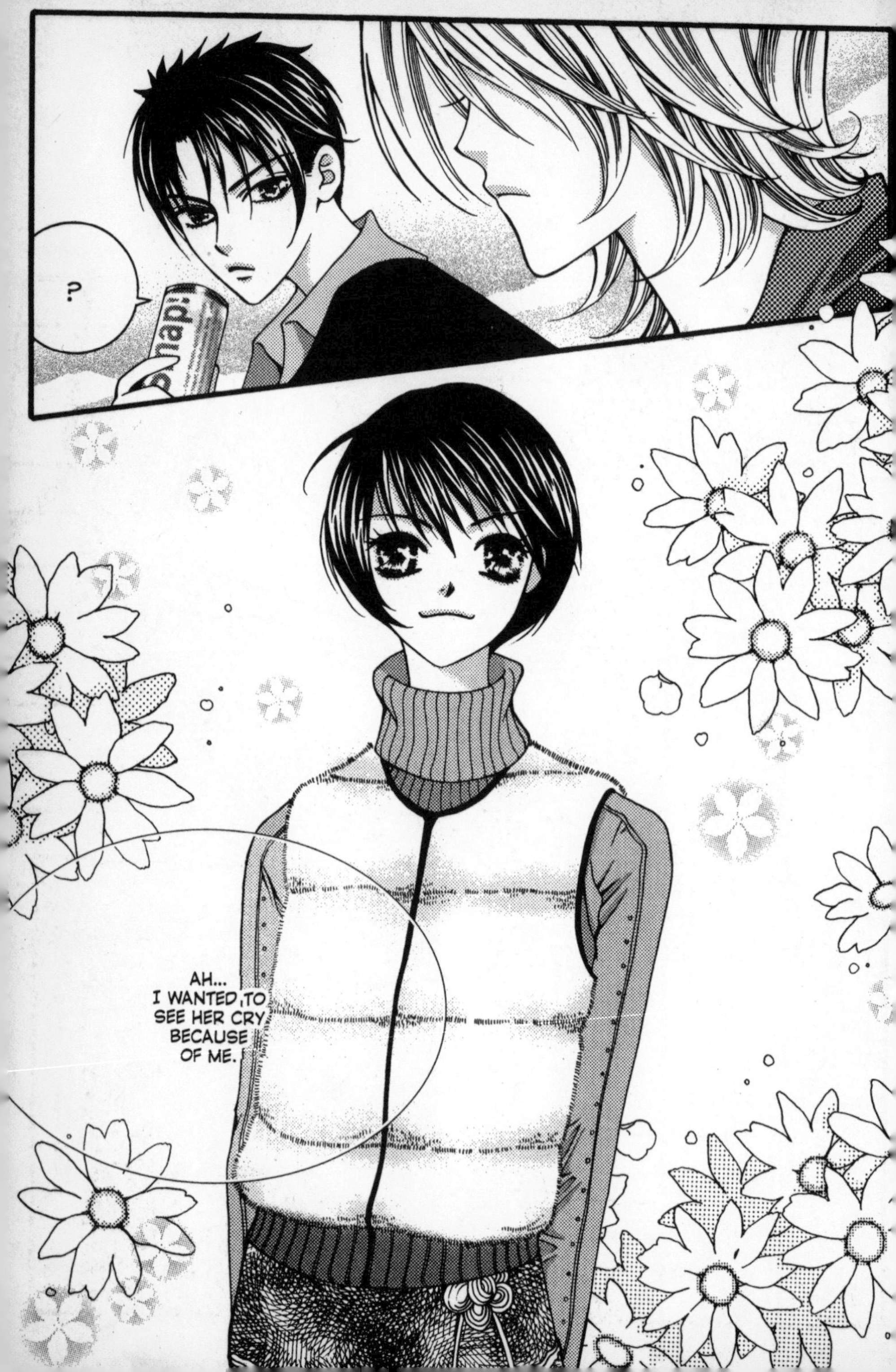
?
Snap!
AH... I WANTED TO SEE HER CRY BECAUSE OF ME.

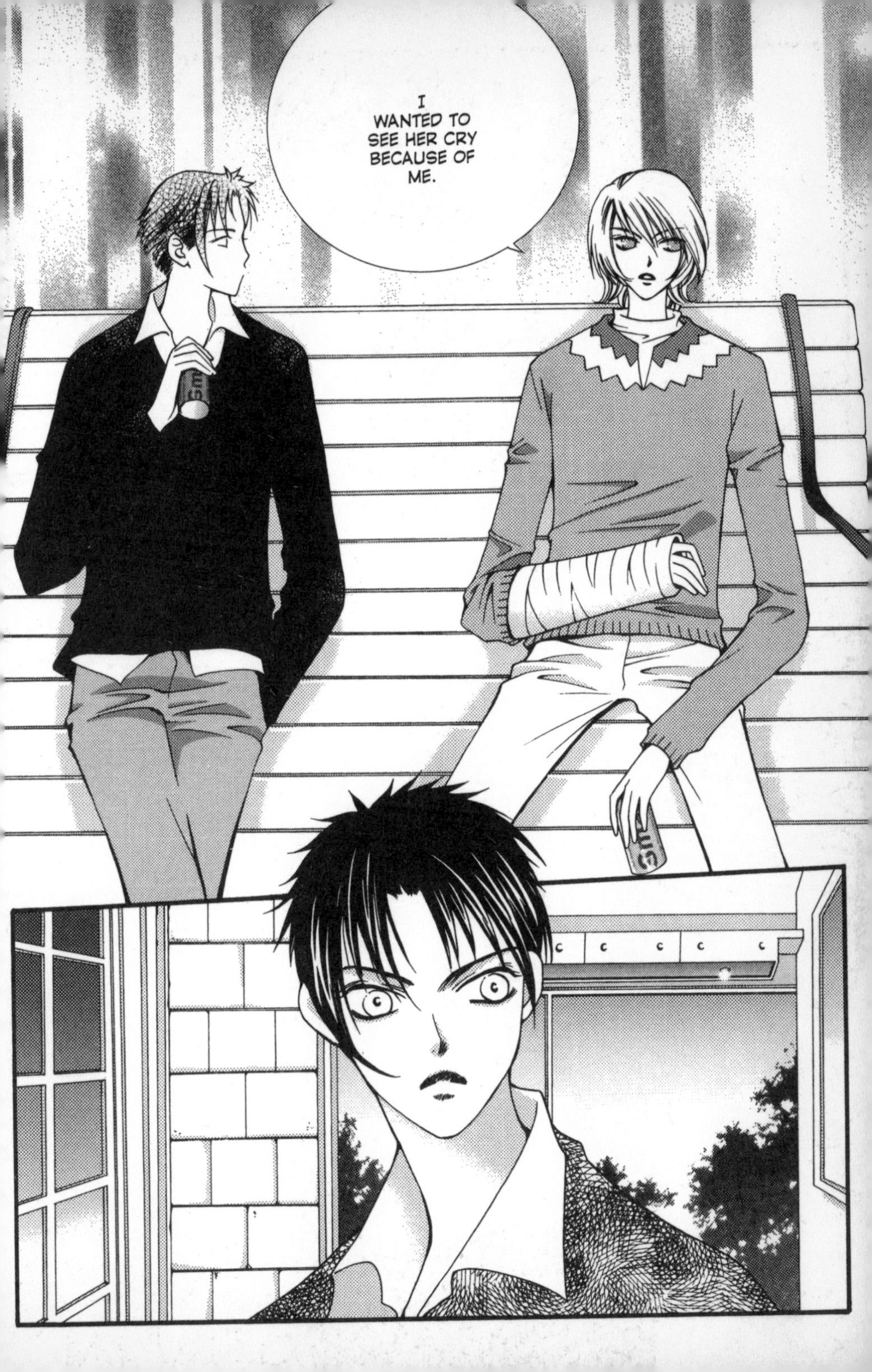
I WANTED TO SEE HER CRY BECAUSE OF ME.

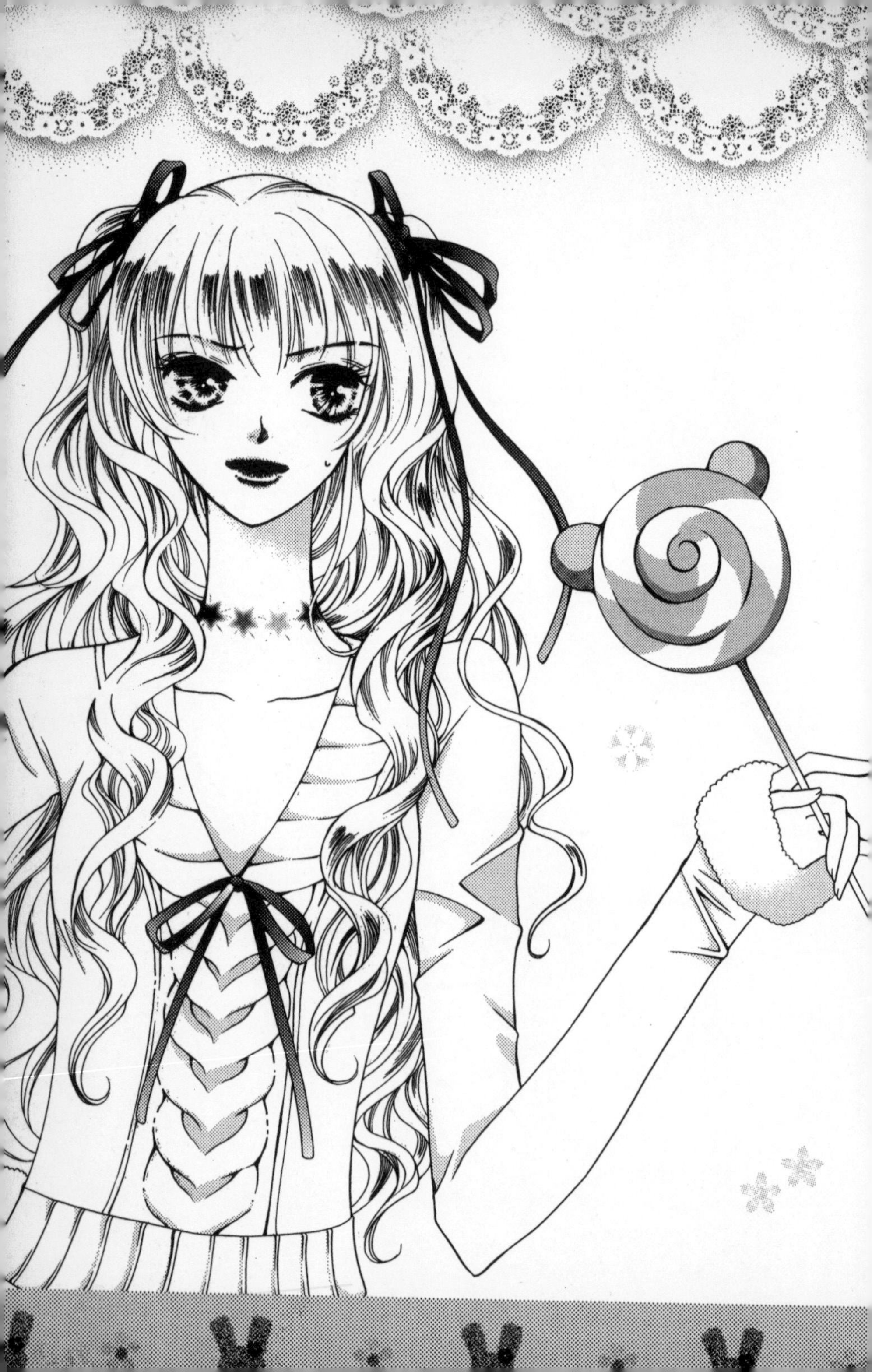

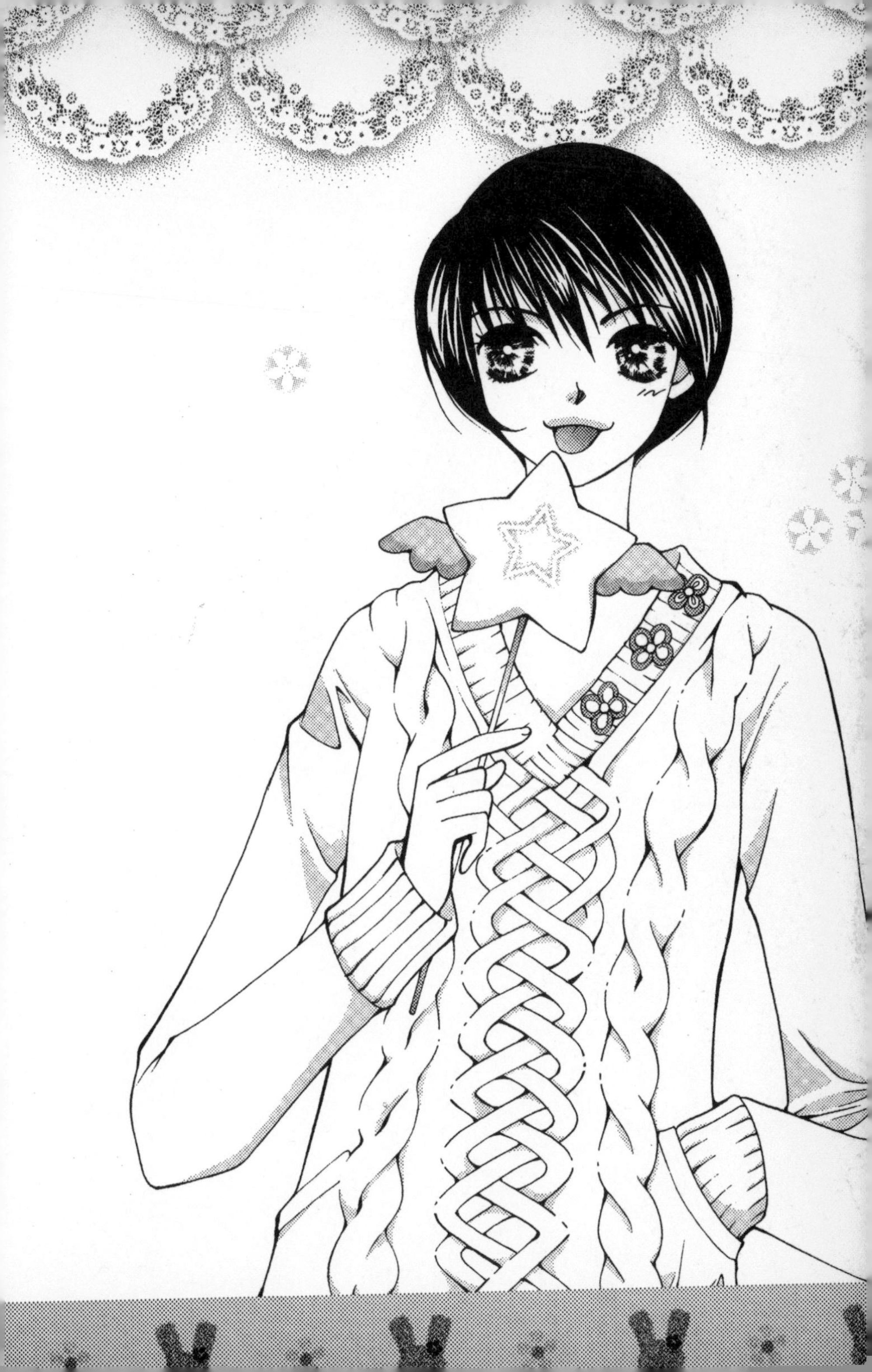

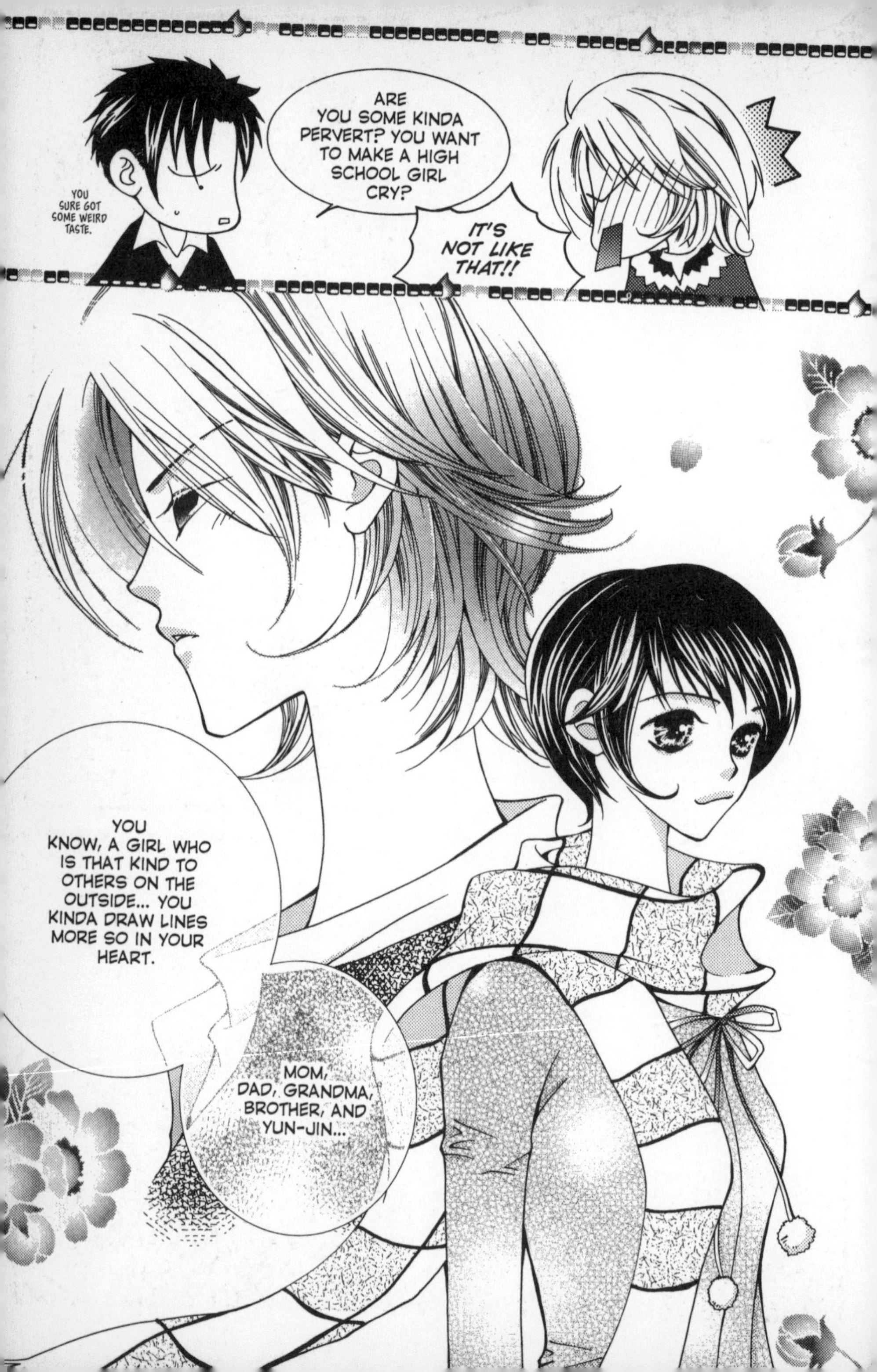
YOU SURE GOT SOME WEIRD TASTE.
ARE YOU SOME KINDA PERVERT? YOU WANT TO MAKE A HIGH SCHOOL GIRL CRY?
IT'S NOT LIKE THAT!!
YOU KNOW, A GIRL WHO IS THAT KIND TO OTHERS ON THE OUTSIDE... YOU KINDA DRAW LINES MORE SO IN YOUR HEART.
MOM, DAD, GRANDMA, BROTHER, AND YUN-JIN...

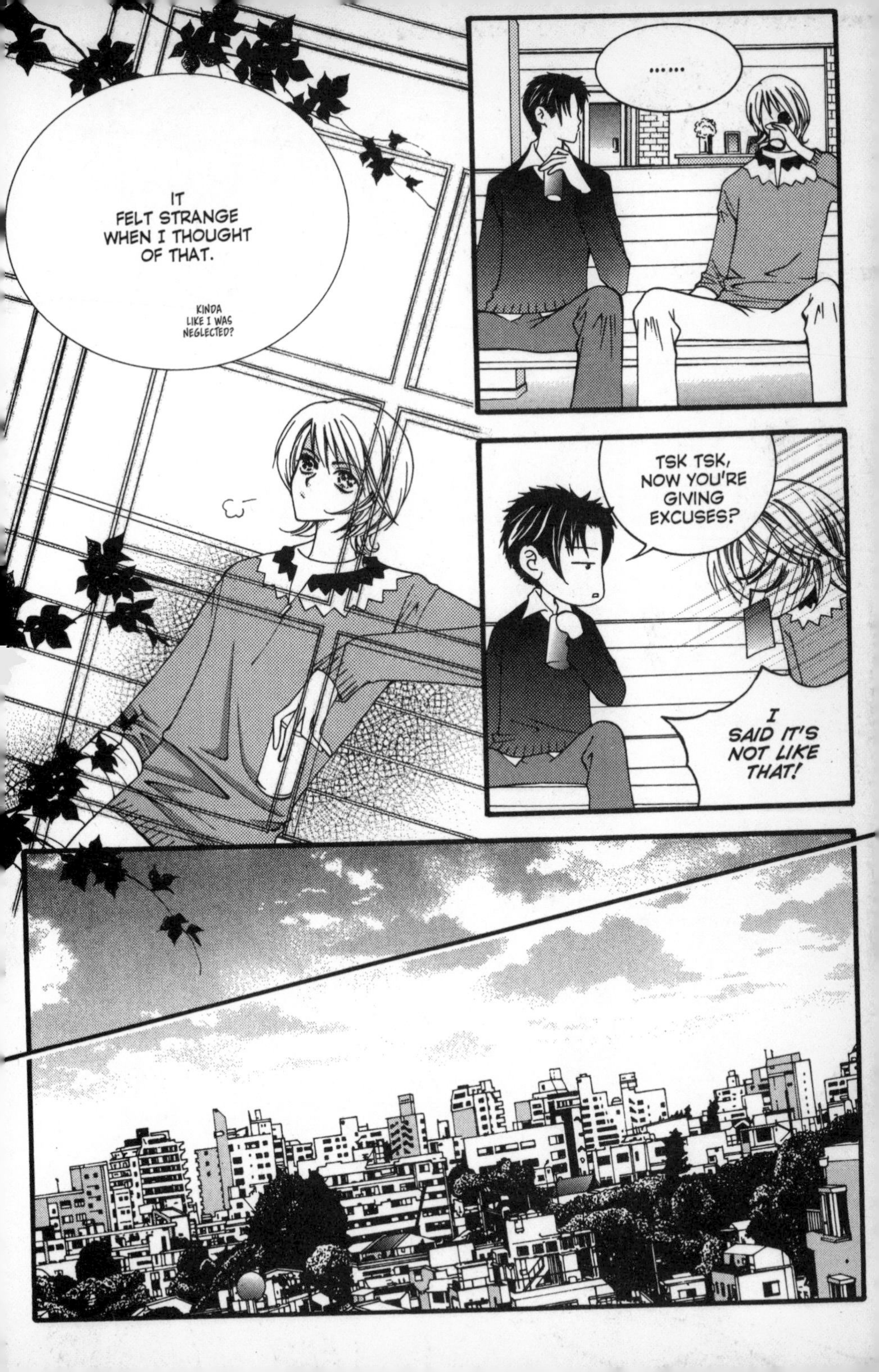
IT FELT STRANGE WHEN I THOUGHT OF THAT.
KINDA LIKE I WAS NEGLECTED?
......
TSK TSK, NOW YOU'RE GIVING EXCUSES?
I SAID IT'S NOT LIKE THAT!

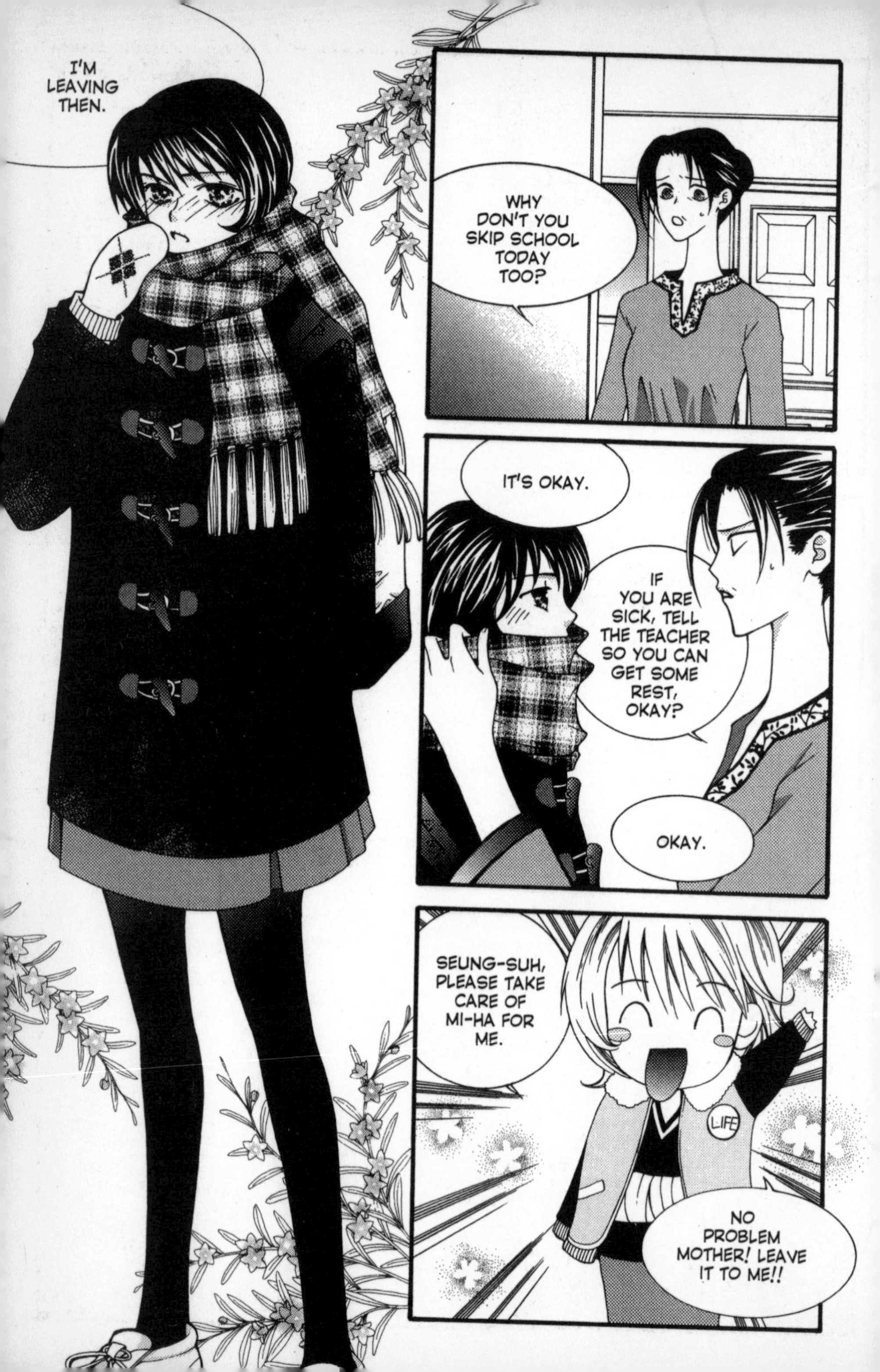
I'M LEAVING THEN.
WHY DON'T YOU SKIP SCHOOL TODAY TOO?
IT'S OKAY.
IF YOU ARE SICK, TELL THE TEACHER SO YOU CAN GET SOME REST, OKAY?
OKAY.
SEUNG-SUH, PLEASE TAKE CARE OF MI-HA FOR ME.
LIFE
NO PROBLEM MOTHER! LEAVE IT TO ME!!

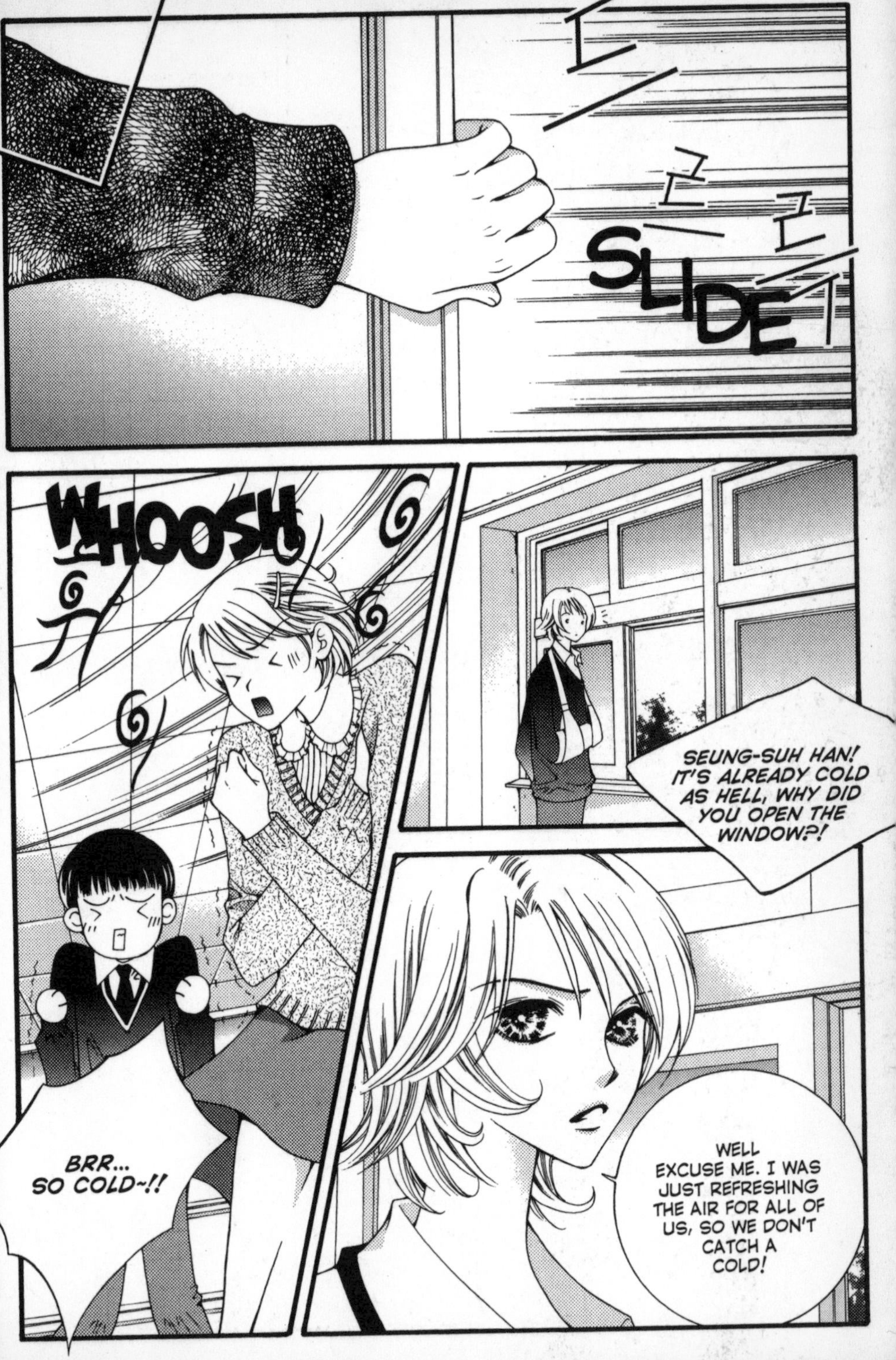
SLIDE
WHOOSH
BRR... SO COLD~!!
SEUNG-SUH HAN! IT'S ALREADY COLD AS HELL, WHY DID YOU OPEN THE WINDOW?!
WELL EXCUSE ME. I WAS JUST REFRESHING THE AIR FOR ALL OF US, SO WE DON'T CATCH A COLD!

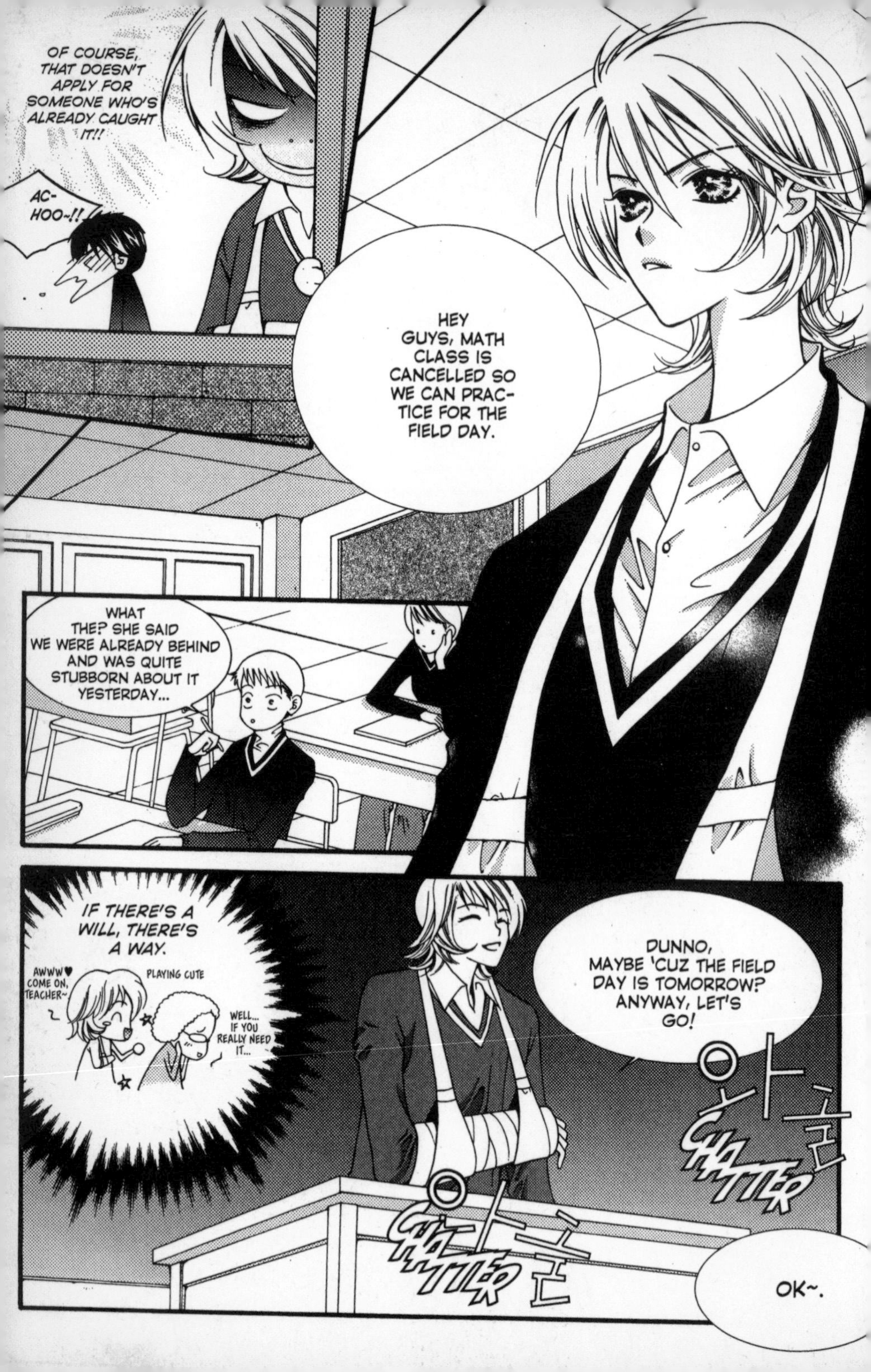
OF COURSE, THAT DOESN'T APPLY FOR SOMEONE WHO'S ALREADY CAUGHT IT!!
AC-HOO~!!
HEY GUYS, MATH CLASS IS CANCELLED SO WE CAN PRAC-TICE FOR THE FIELD DAY.
WHAT THE? SHE SAID WE WERE ALREADY BEHIND AND WAS QUITE STUBBORN ABOUT IT YESTERDAY...
IF THERE'S A WILL, THERE'S A WAY.
AWWW♥ COME ON, TEACHER~
PLAYING CUTE
WELL... IF YOU REALLY NEED IT...
DUNNO, MAYBE 'CUZ THE FIELD DAY IS TOMORROW? ANYWAY, LET'S GO!
와글
CHATTER
와글
CHATTER
OK~.

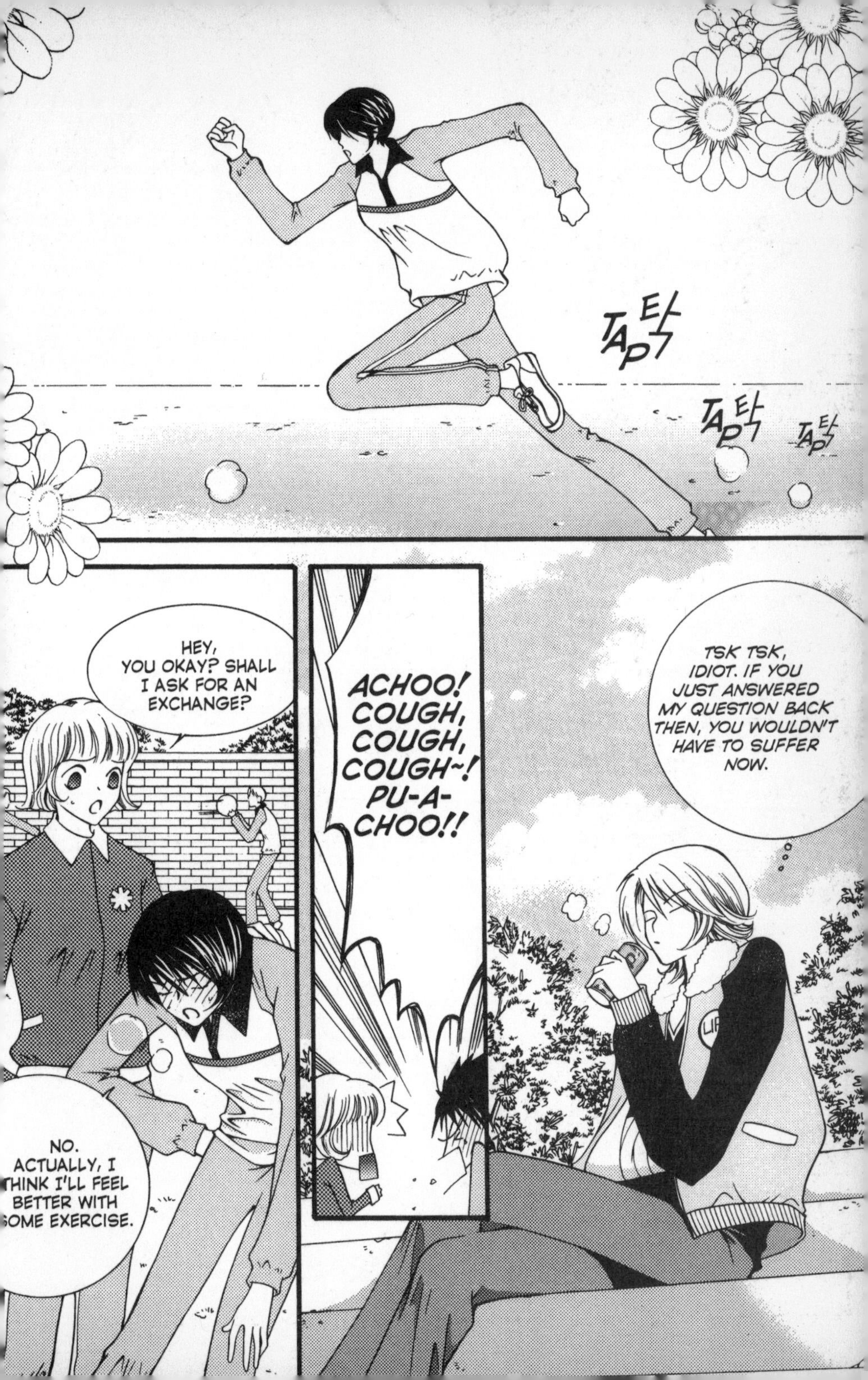
TAP 탁
TAP 탁
TAP 탁
HEY, YOU OKAY? SHALL I ASK FOR AN EXCHANGE?
NO. ACTUALLY, I THINK I'LL FEEL BETTER WITH SOME EXERCISE.
ACHOO! COUGH, COUGH, COUGH~! PU-A-CHOO!!
TSK TSK, IDIOT. IF YOU JUST ANSWERED MY QUESTION BACK THEN, YOU WOULDN'T HAVE TO SUFFER NOW.

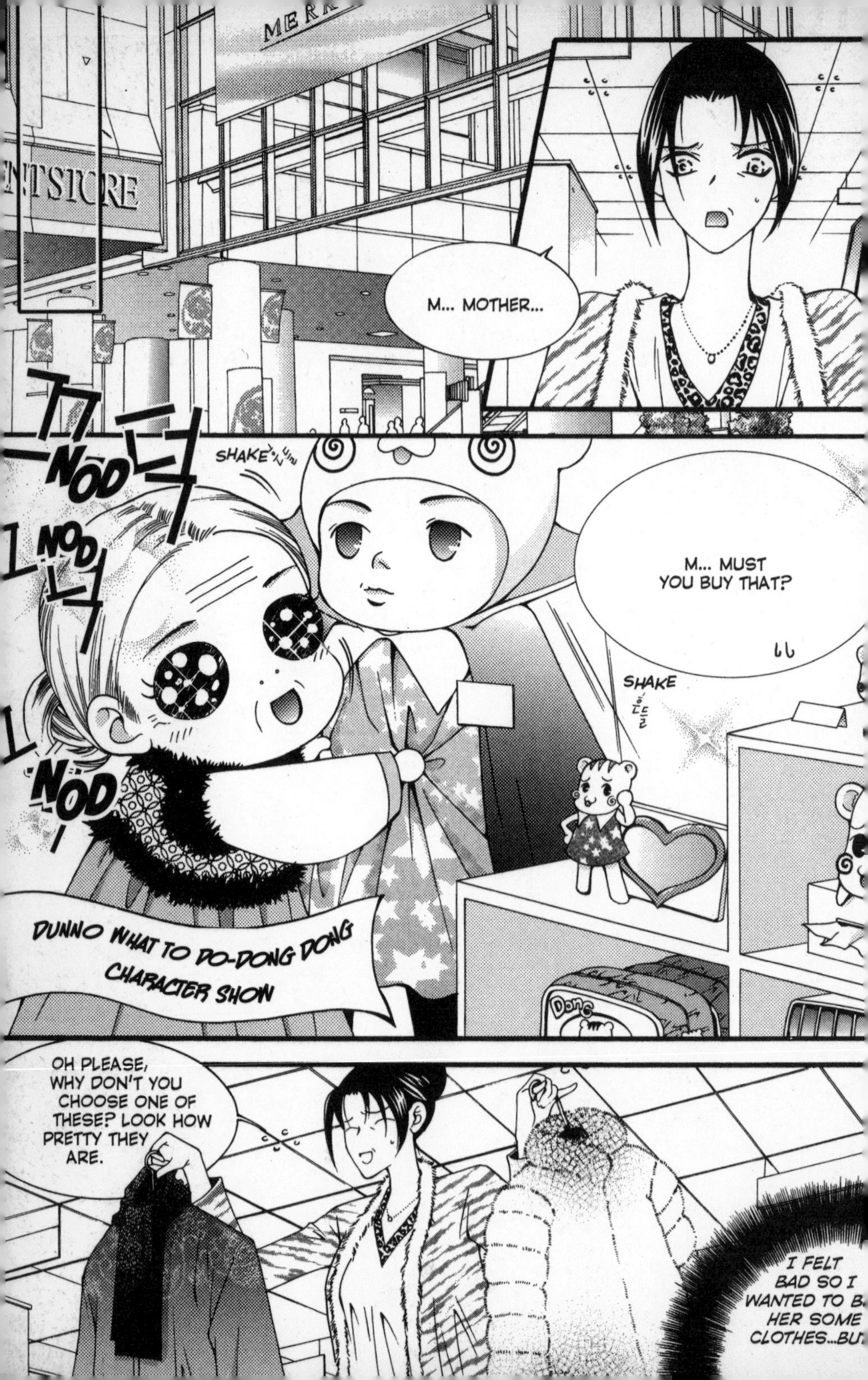
MERR
NTSTORE
M... MOTHER...
NOD
NOD
NOD
SHAKE
M... MUST YOU BUY THAT?
SHAKE
DUNNO WHAT TO DO-DONG DONG CHARACTER SHOW
Dong
OH PLEASE, WHY DON'T YOU CHOOSE ONE OF THESE? LOOK HOW PRETTY THEY ARE.
I FELT BAD SO I WANTED TO B HER SOME CLOTHES...BU

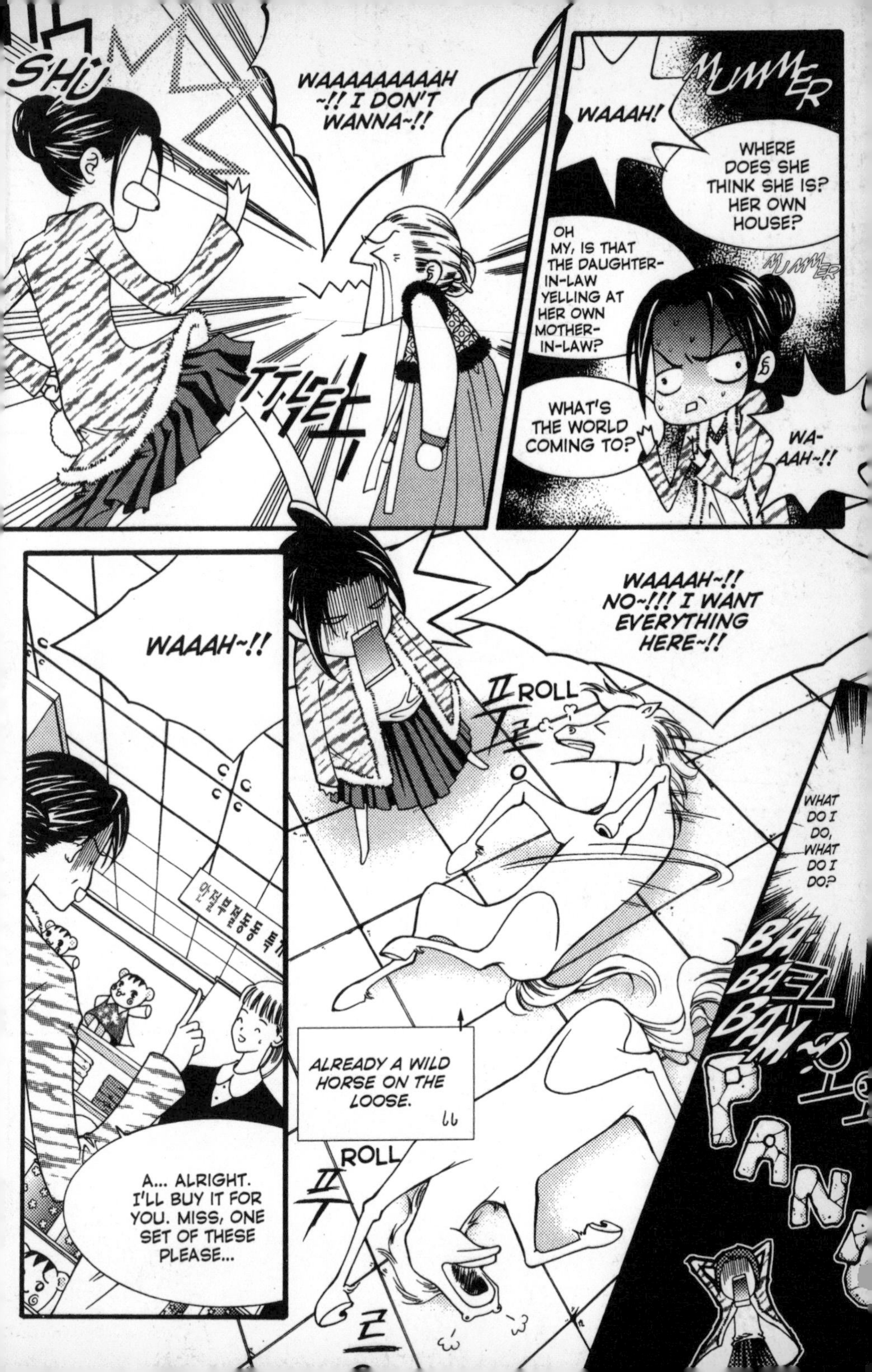
SHU
WAAAAAAAAAH ~!! I DON'T WANNA~!!
MUMMER
WAAAH!
WHERE DOES SHE THINK SHE IS? HER OWN HOUSE?
OH MY, IS THAT THE DAUGHTER-IN-LAW YELLING AT HER OWN MOTHER-IN-LAW?
MUMMER
WHAT'S THE WORLD COMING TO?
WA-AAH~!!
WAAAH~!!
A... ALRIGHT. I'LL BUY IT FOR YOU. MISS, ONE SET OF THESE PLEASE...
WAAAAH~!! NO~!!! I WANT EVERYTHING HERE~!!
ROLL
ALREADY A WILD HORSE ON THE LOOSE.
ROLL
WHAT DO I DO, WHAT DO I DO?
BA BA BAM
PAN

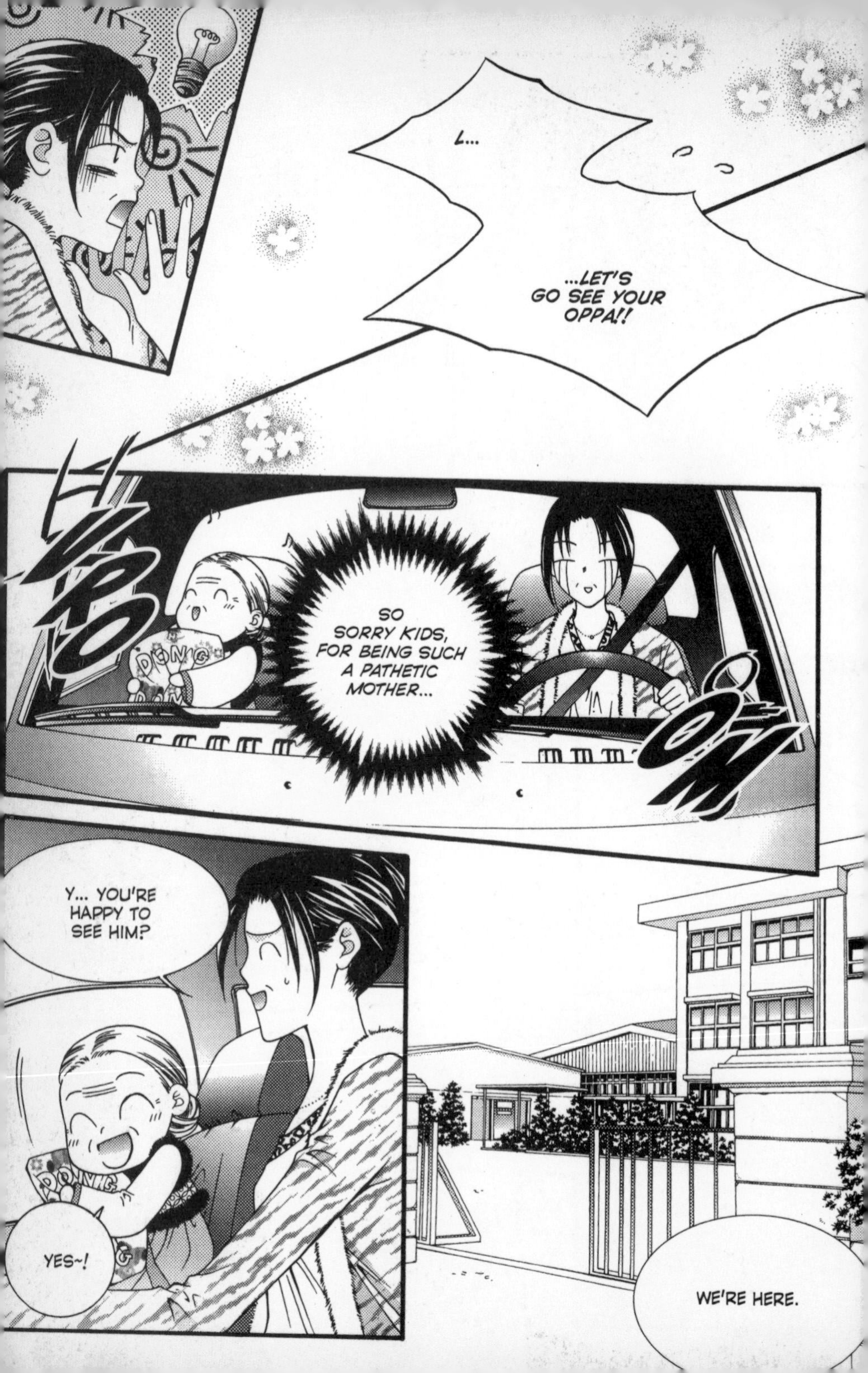
L...
...LET'S GO SEE YOUR OPPA!!
SO SORRY KIDS, FOR BEING SUCH A PATHETIC MOTHER...
Y... YOU'RE HAPPY TO SEE HIM?
YES~!
WE'RE HERE.

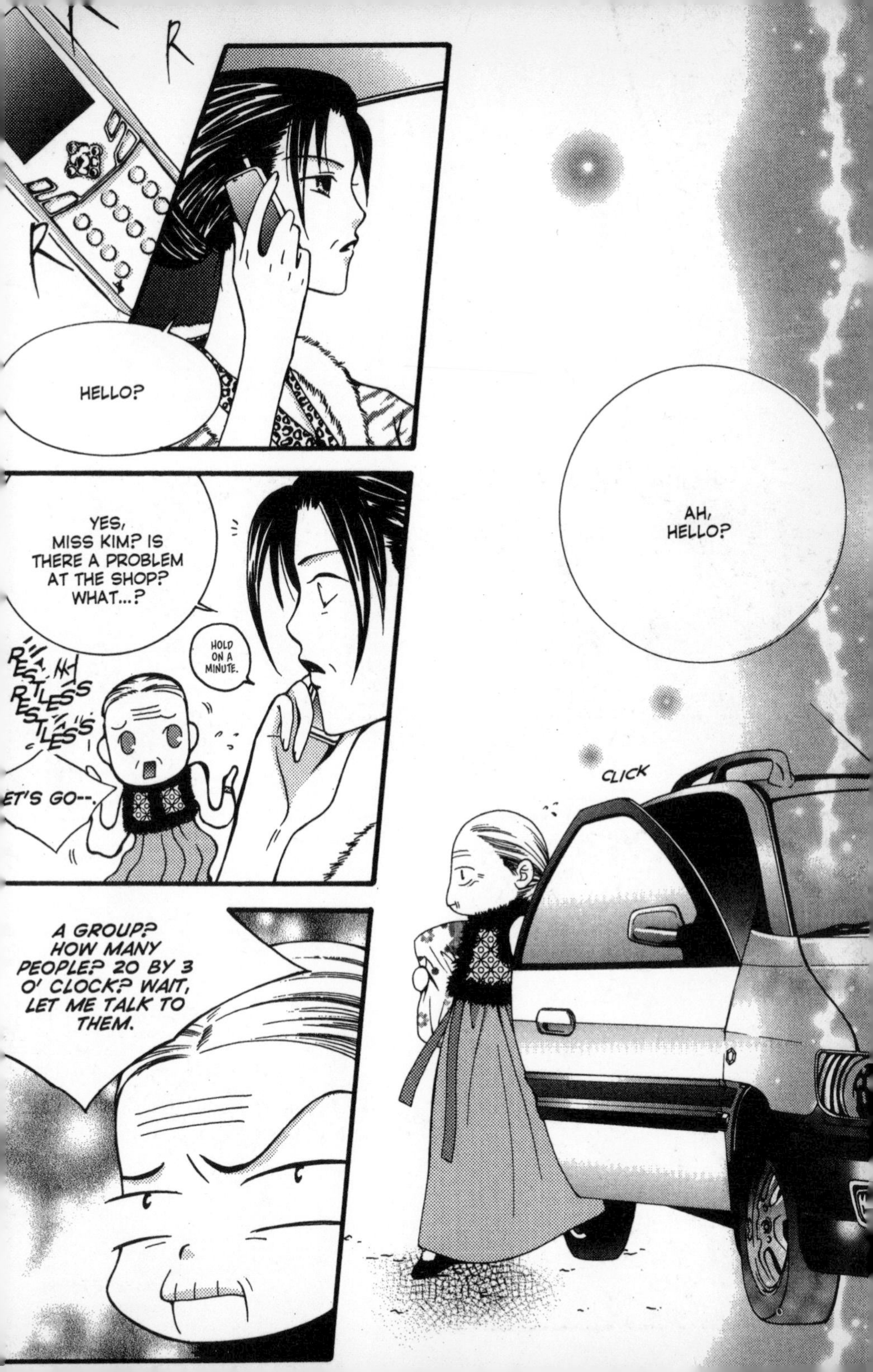
R
R
HELLO?
YES, MISS KIM? IS THERE A PROBLEM AT THE SHOP? WHAT...?
HOLD ON A MINUTE.
RESTLESS
RESTLESS
ET'S GO--.
A GROUP? HOW MANY PEOPLE? 20 BY 3 O' CLOCK? WAIT, LET ME TALK TO THEM.
AH, HELLO?
CLICK

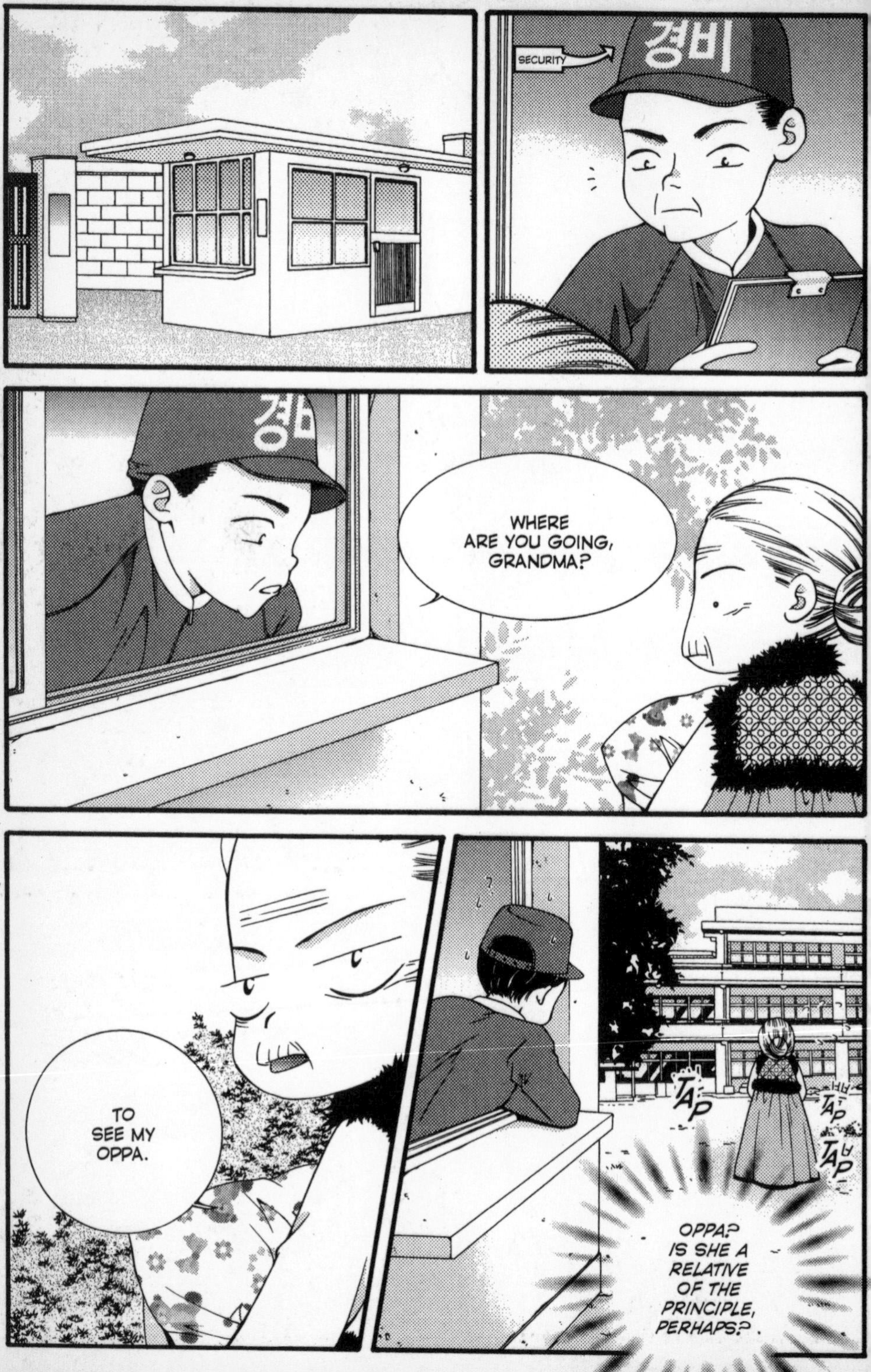
경비
SECURITY
WHERE ARE YOU GOING, GRANDMA?
TO SEE MY OPPA.
TAP
TAP
TAP
OPPA? IS SHE A RELATIVE OF THE PRINCIPLE, PERHAPS?

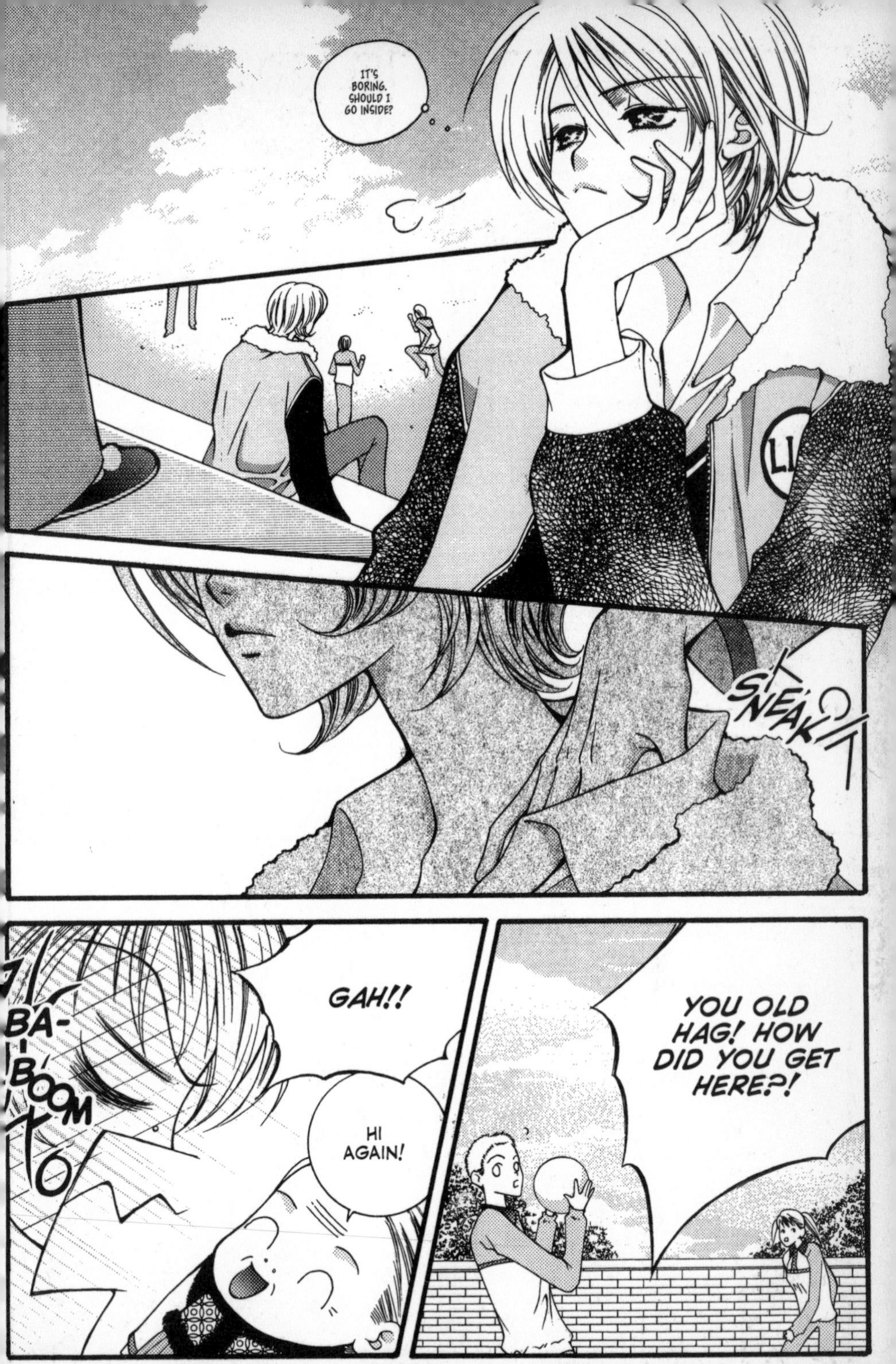
IT'S BORING. SHOULD I GO INSIDE?
SNEAK
BA-BOOM
GAH!!
HI AGAIN!
YOU OLD HAG! HOW DID YOU GET HERE?!

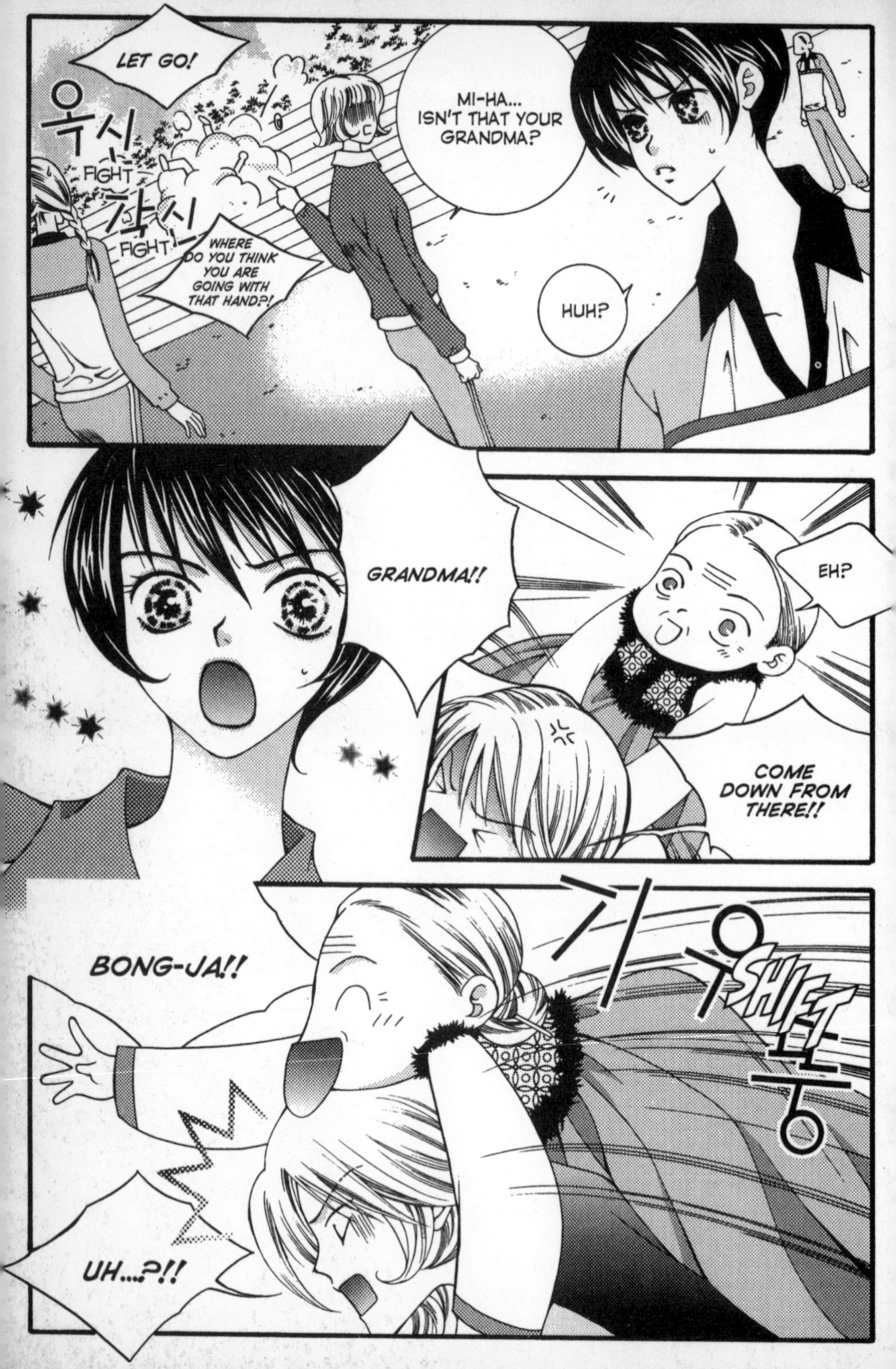
LET GO!
FIGHT
FIGHT
WHERE DO YOU THINK YOU ARE GOING WITH THAT HAND?!
MI-HA... ISN'T THAT YOUR GRANDMA?
HUH?
GRANDMA!!
EH?
COME DOWN FROM THERE!!
BONG-JA!!
SHIFT
UH...?!!

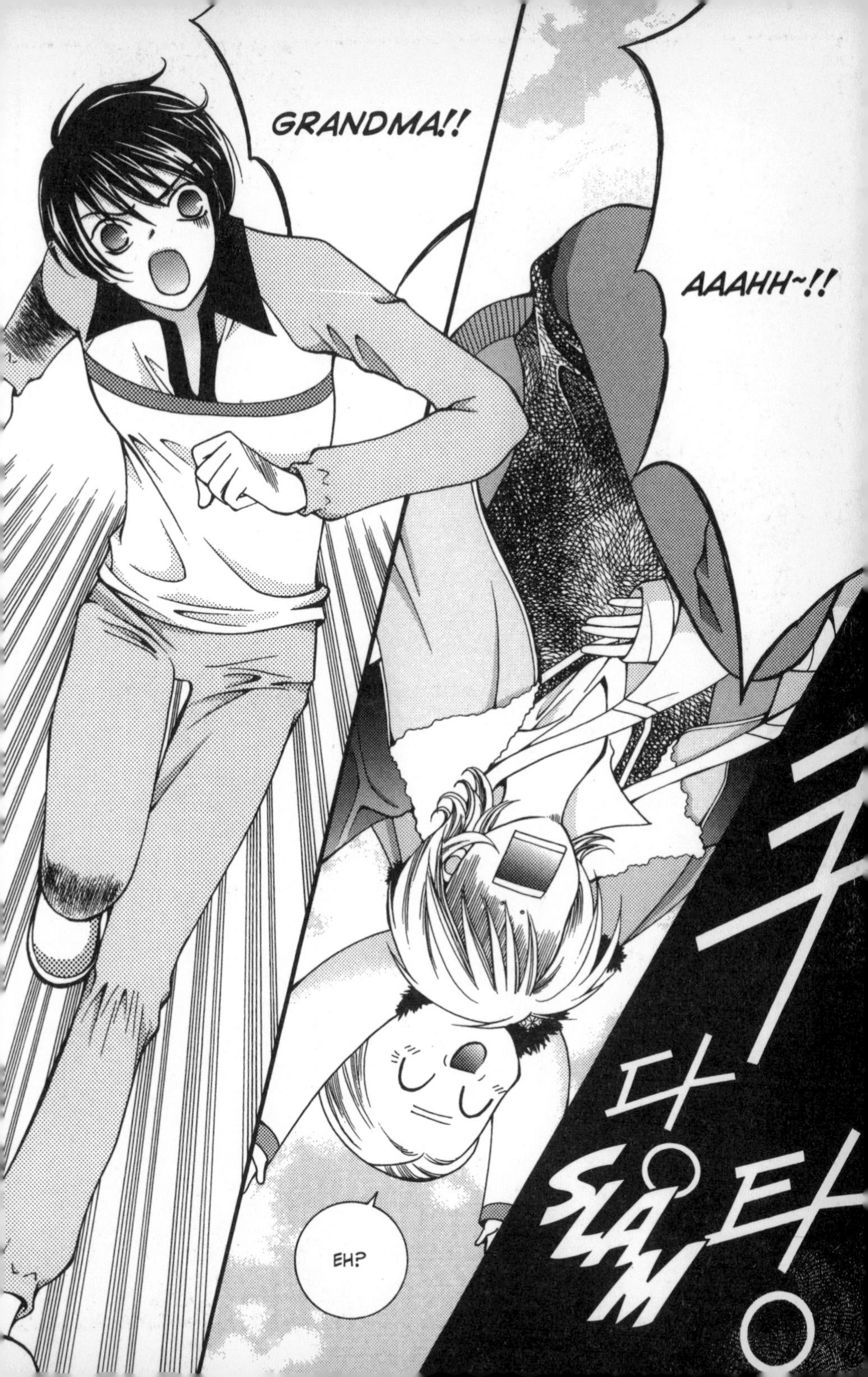
GRANDMA!!
AAAHH~!!
EH?
SLAM

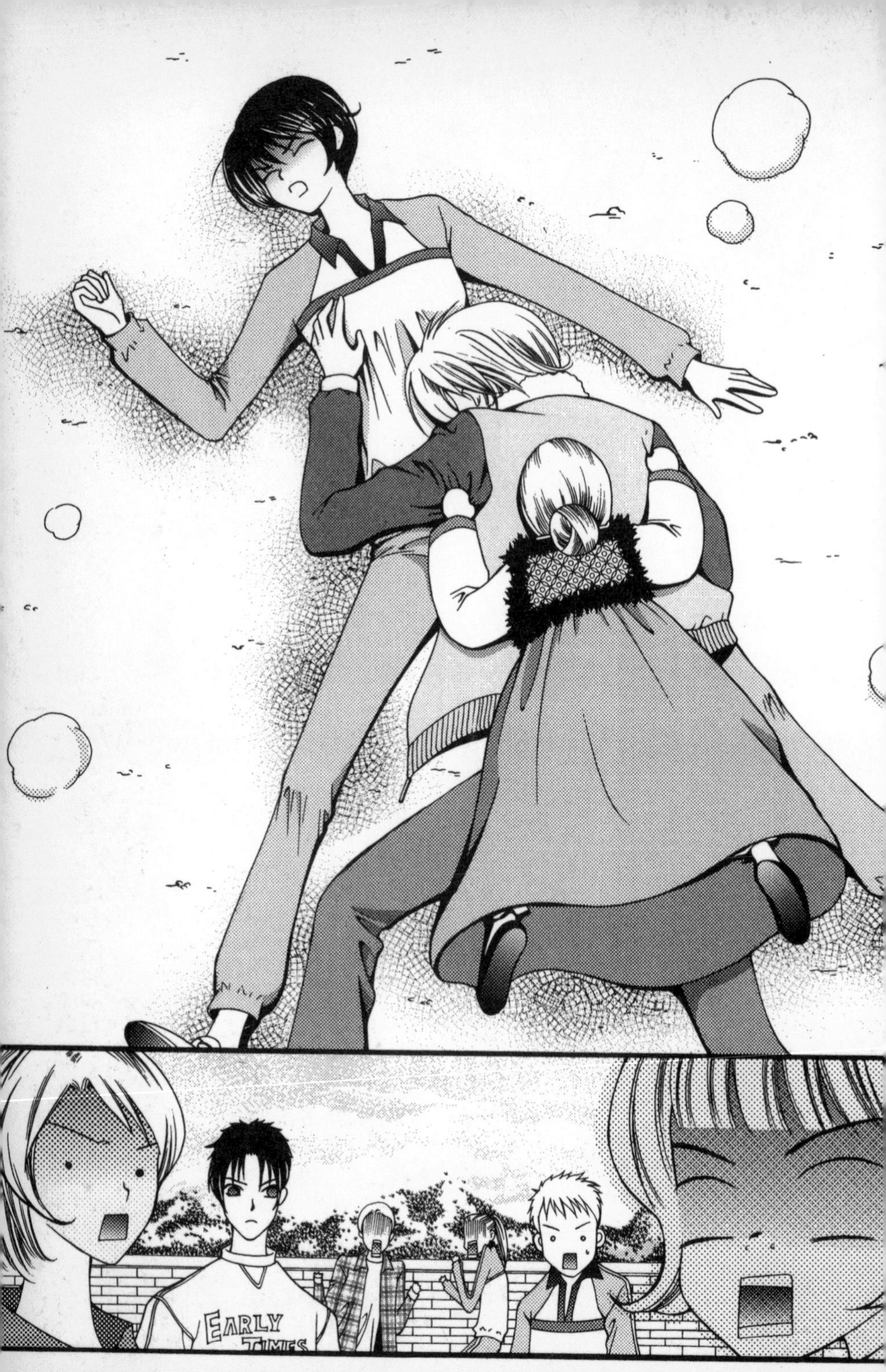
EARLY TIMES

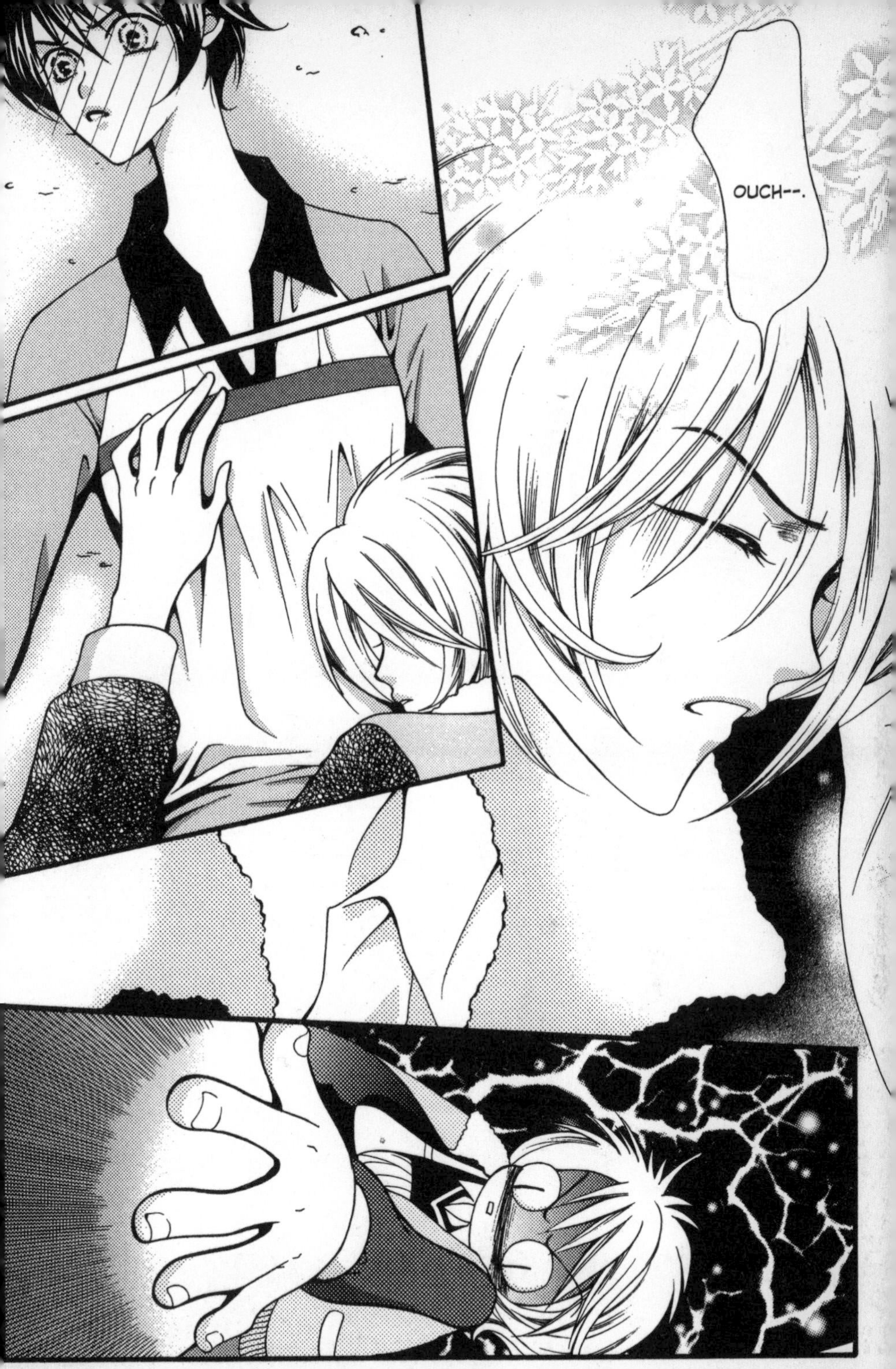
OUCH--.

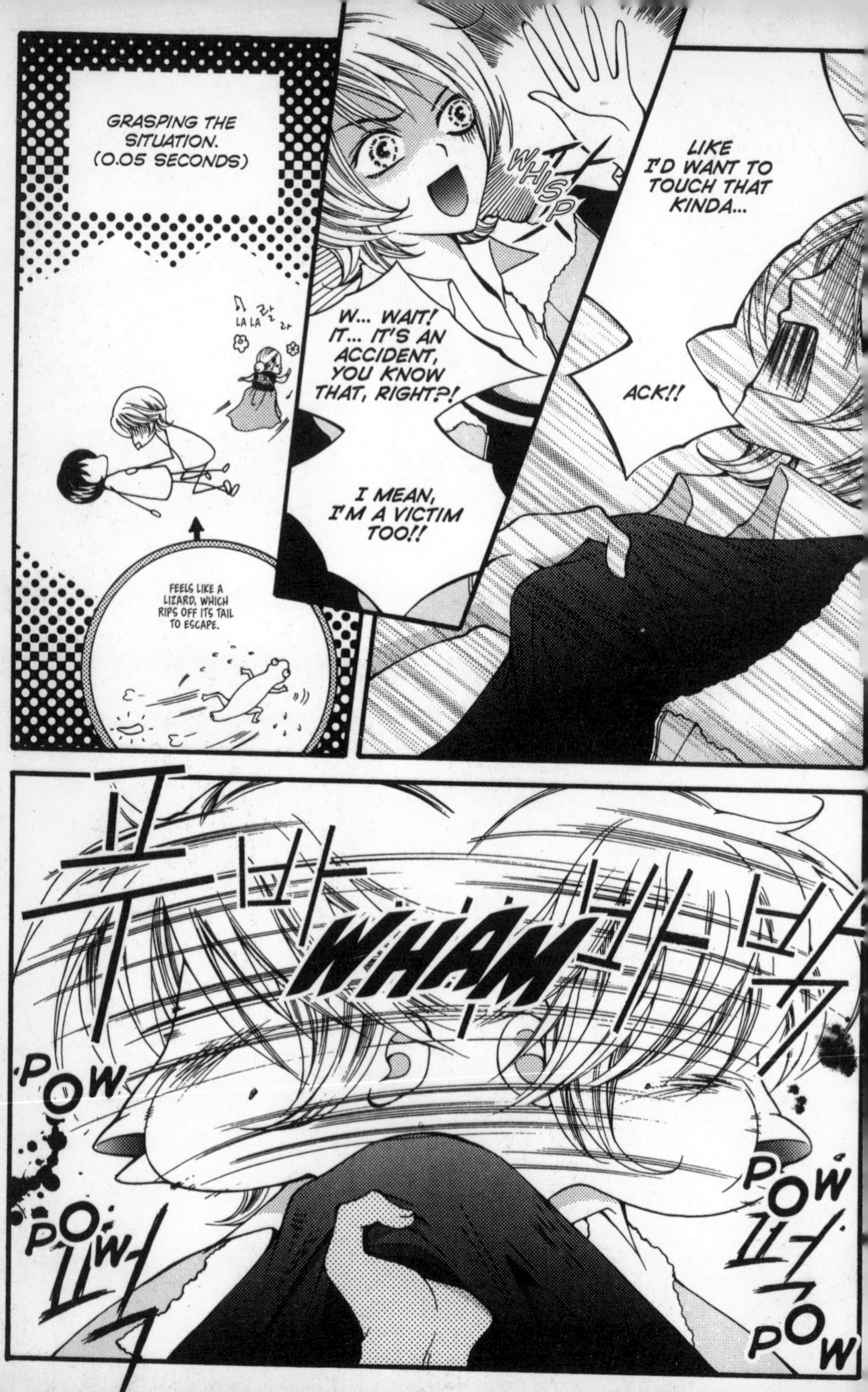
GRASPING THE SITUATION. (0.05 SECONDS)
LA LA
FEELS LIKE A LIZARD, WHICH RIPS OFF ITS TAIL TO ESCAPE.
WHISP
W... WAIT! IT... IT'S AN ACCIDENT, YOU KNOW THAT, RIGHT?!
I MEAN, I'M A VICTIM TOO!!
LIKE I'D WANT TO TOUCH THAT KINDA...
ACK!!
WHAM
POW
POW
POW
POW

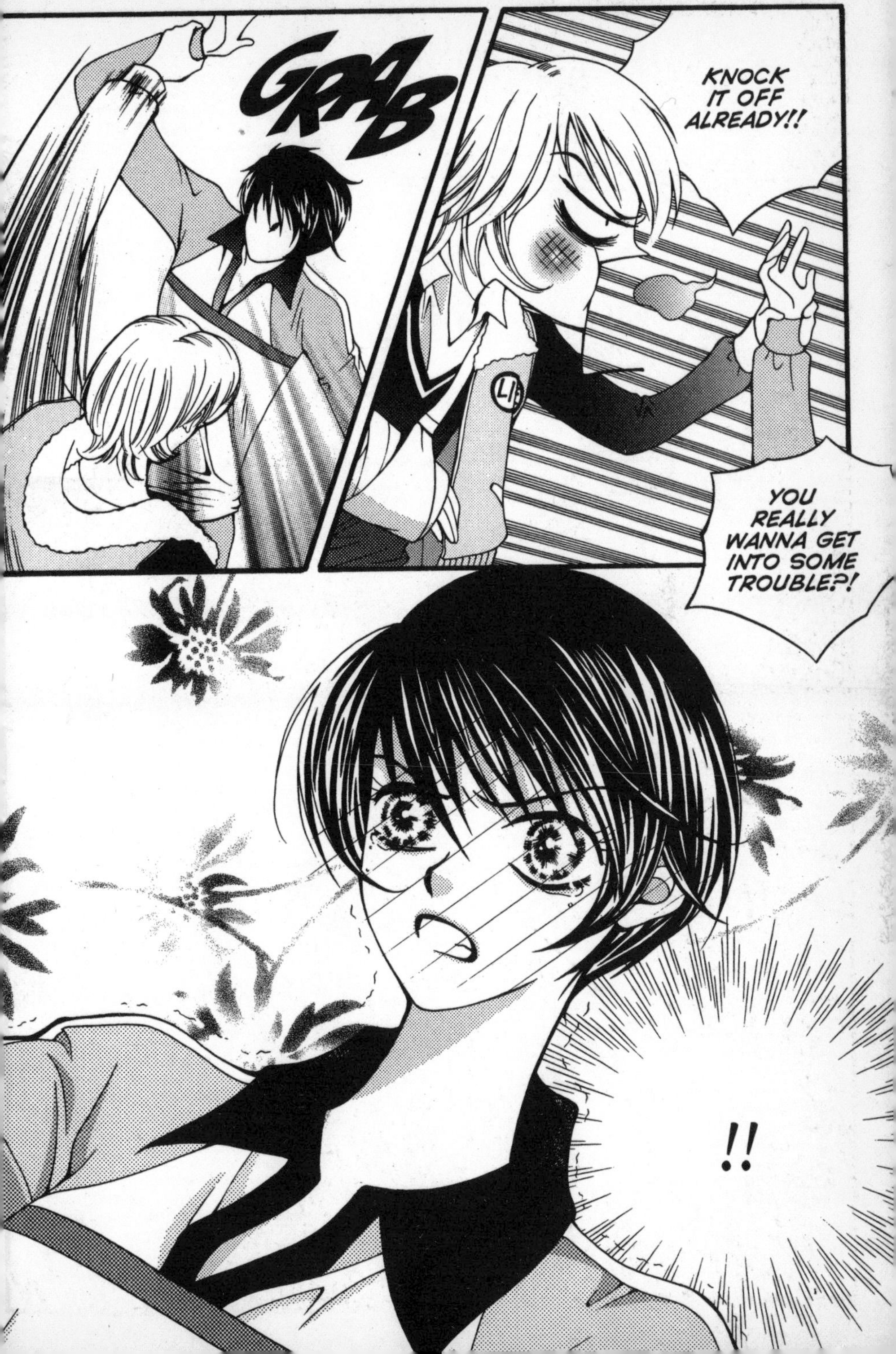
GRAB
KNOCK IT OFF ALREADY!!
YOU REALLY WANNA GET INTO SOME TROUBLE?!
!!

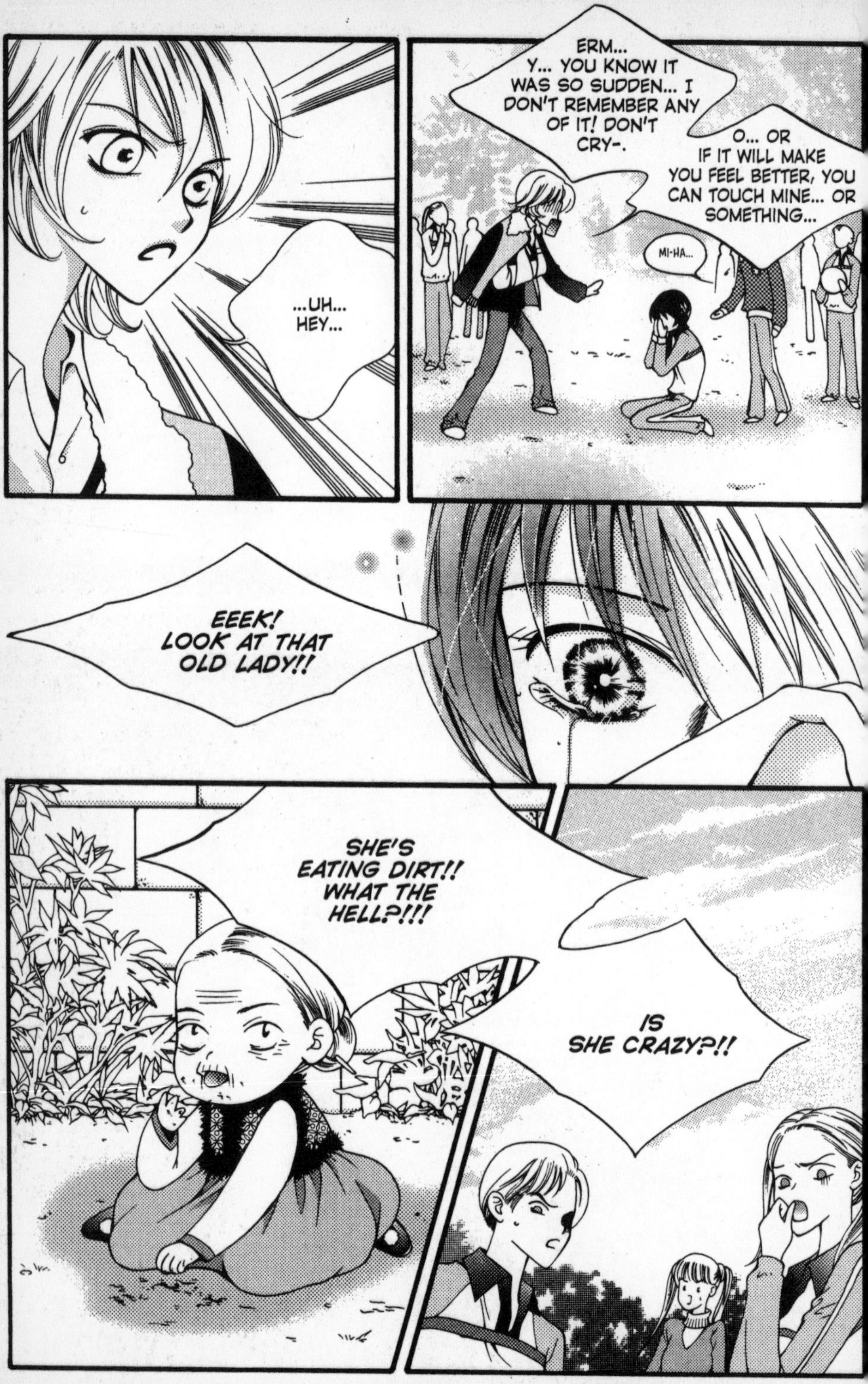
...UH... HEY...
ERM... Y... YOU KNOW IT WAS SO SUDDEN... I DON'T REMEMBER ANY OF IT! DON'T CRY-.
O... OR IF IT WILL MAKE YOU FEEL BETTER, YOU CAN TOUCH MINE... OR SOMETHING...
MI-HA...
EEEK! LOOK AT THAT OLD LADY!!
SHE'S EATING DIRT!! WHAT THE HELL?!!!
IS SHE CRAZY?!!

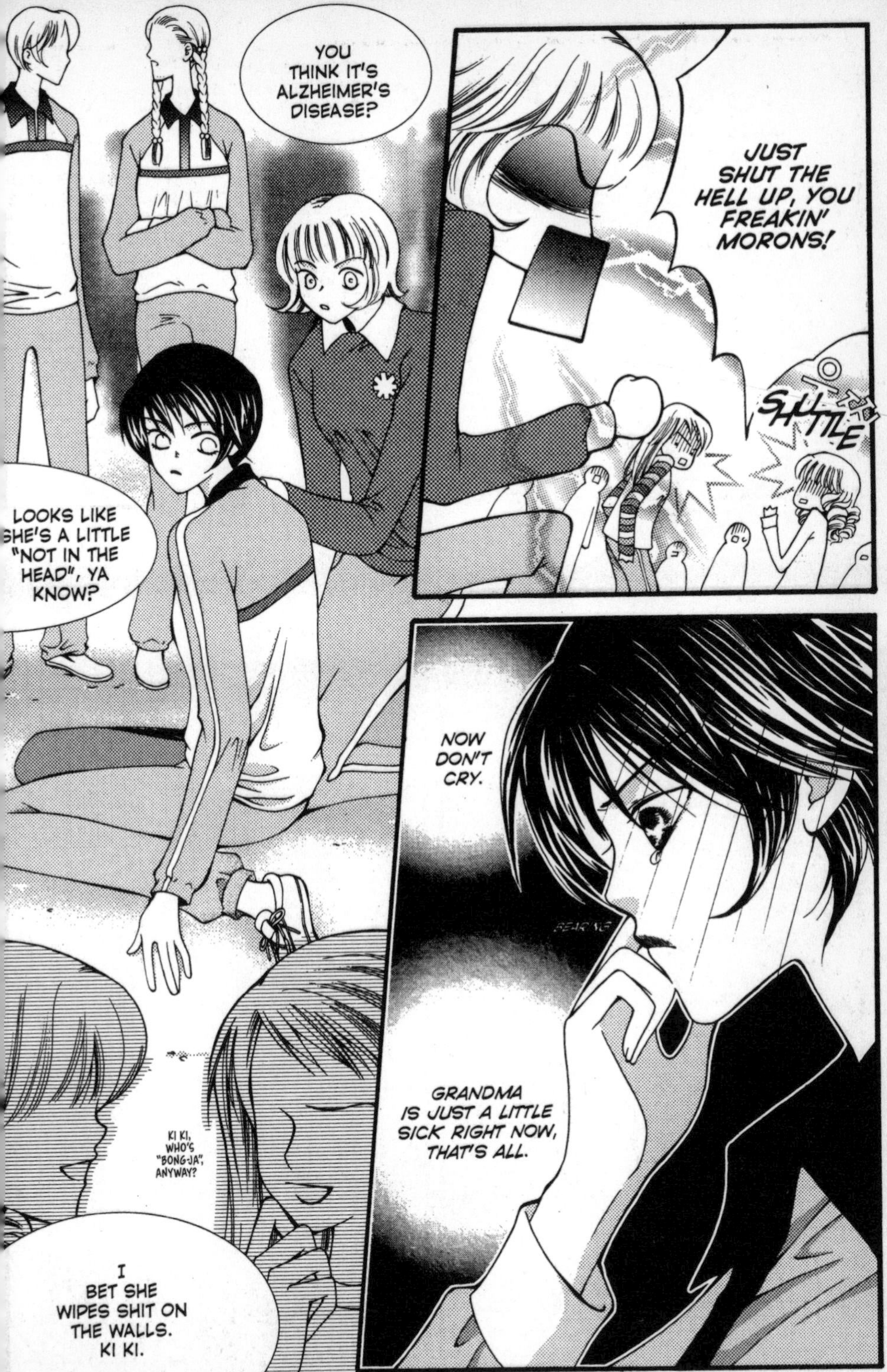
YOU THINK IT'S ALZHEIMER'S DISEASE?
LOOKS LIKE SHE'S A LITTLE "NOT IN THE HEAD", YA KNOW?
KI KI, WHO'S "BONG-JA", ANYWAY?
I BET SHE WIPES SHIT ON THE WALLS. KI KI.
JUST SHUT THE HELL UP, YOU FREAKIN' MORONS!
SHUTTLE
NOW DON'T CRY.
GRANDMA IS JUST A LITTLE SICK RIGHT NOW, THAT'S ALL.

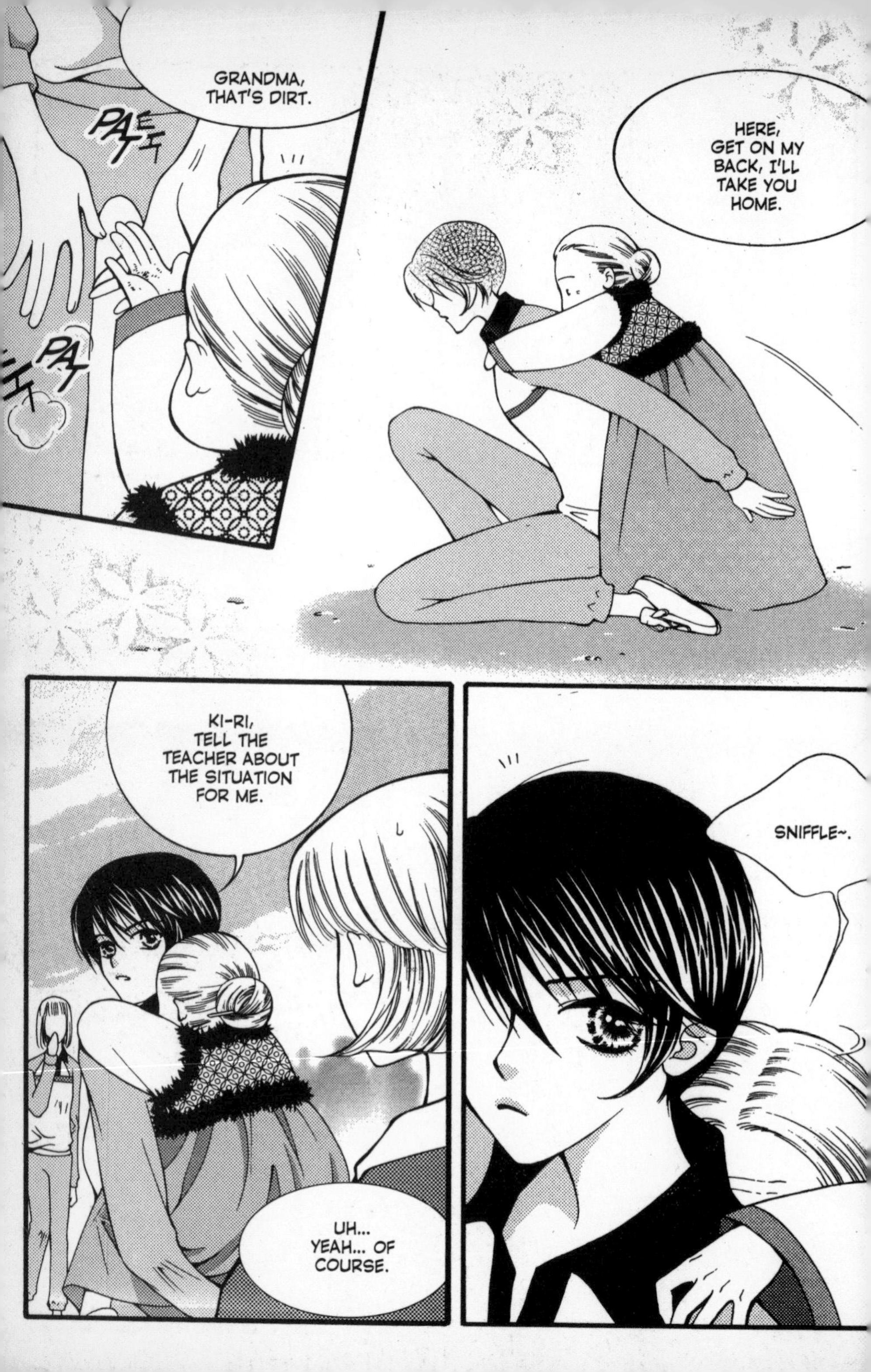

GRANDMA, THAT'S DIRT.
PAT
PAT
HERE, GET ON MY BACK, I'LL TAKE YOU HOME.
KI-RI, TELL THE TEACHER ABOUT THE SITUATION FOR ME.
UH... YEAH... OF COURSE.
SNIFFLE~.

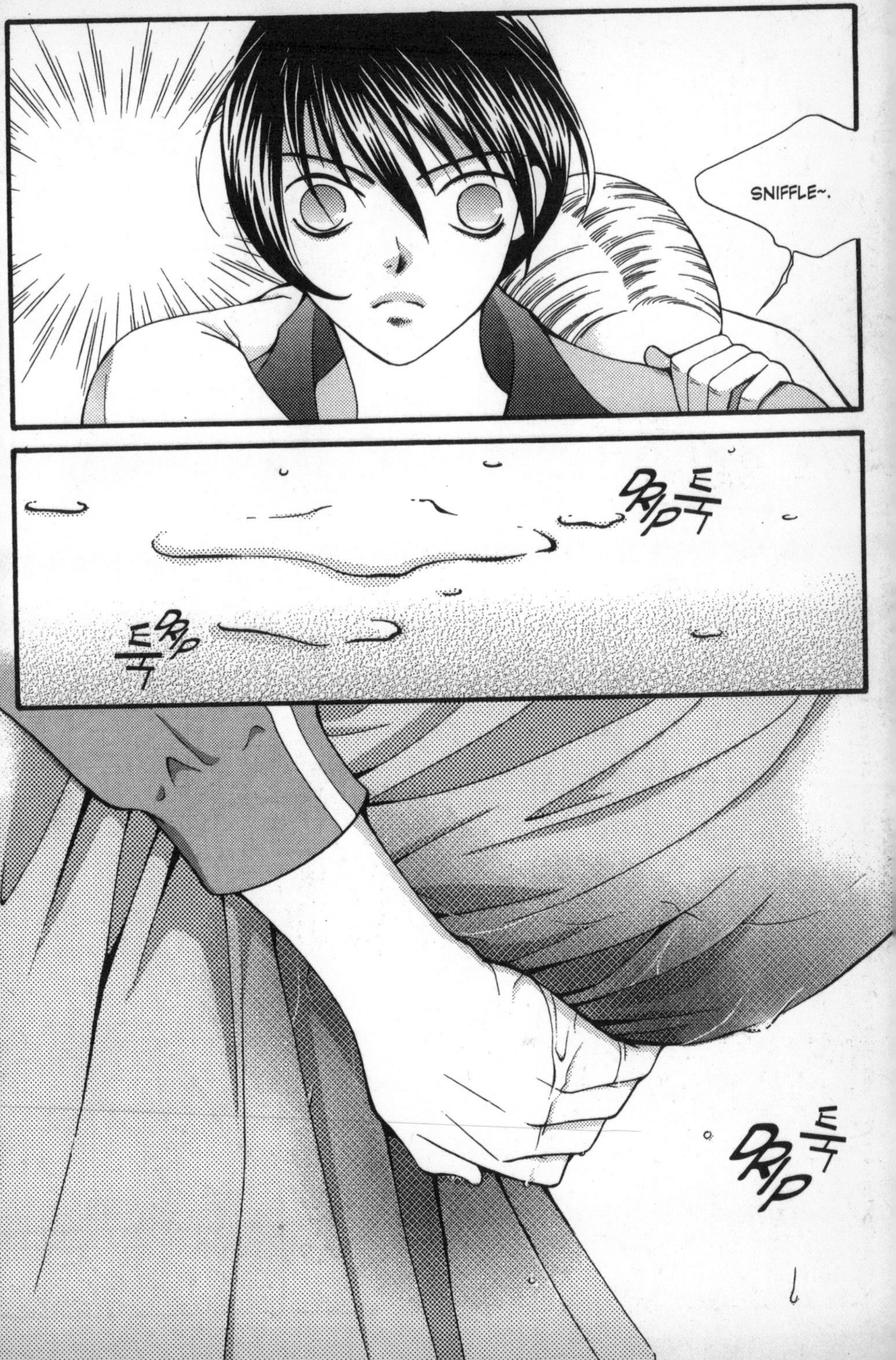
SNIFFLE~.
DRIP 툭
DRIP 툭
DRIP 툭

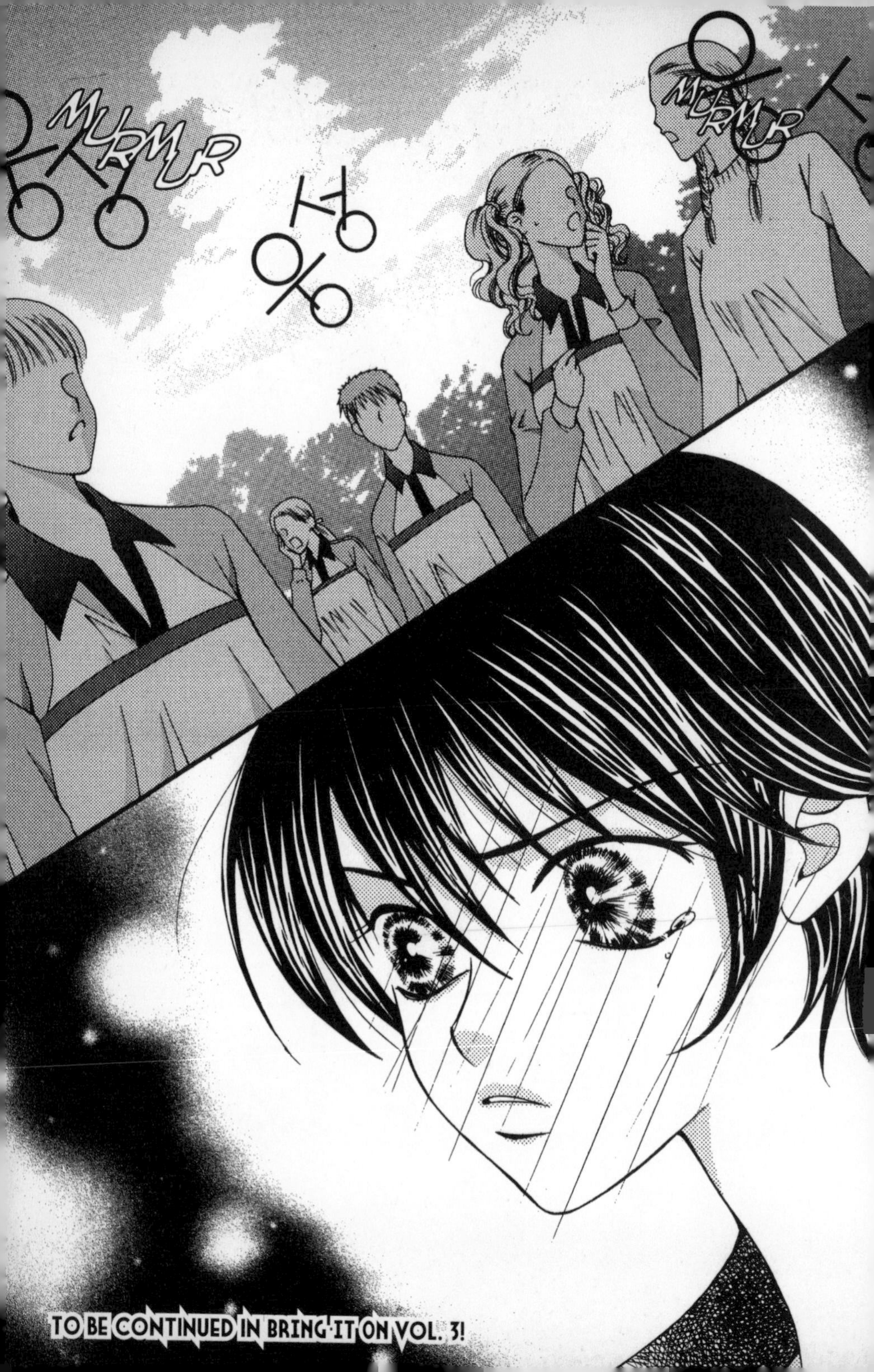
MURMUR
MURMUR
TO BE CONTINUED IN BRING·IT ON VOL. 3!

Angel Diary

vol.2

Kara · Lee YunHee

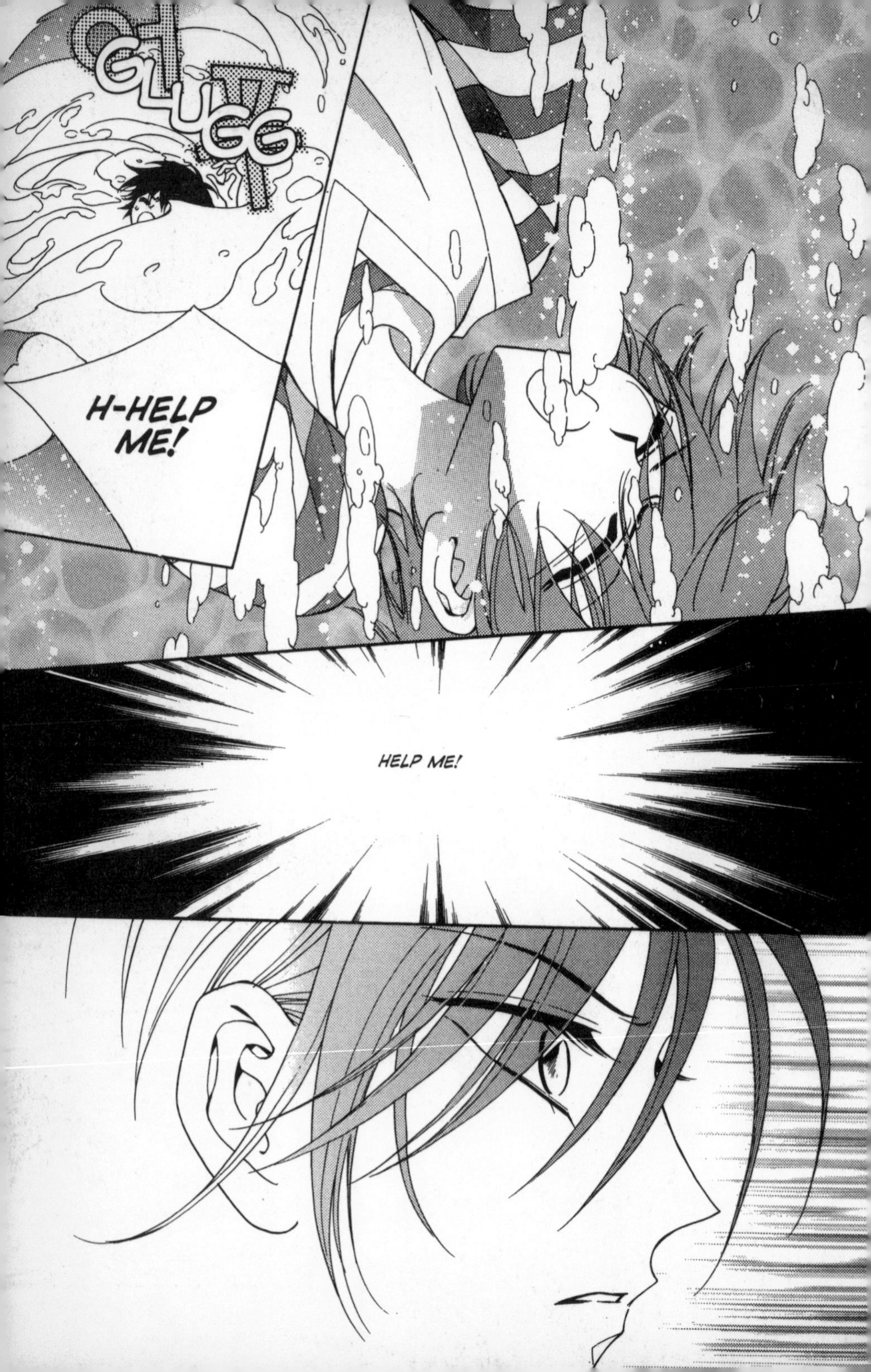
GLUGG
H-HELP ME!
HELP ME!

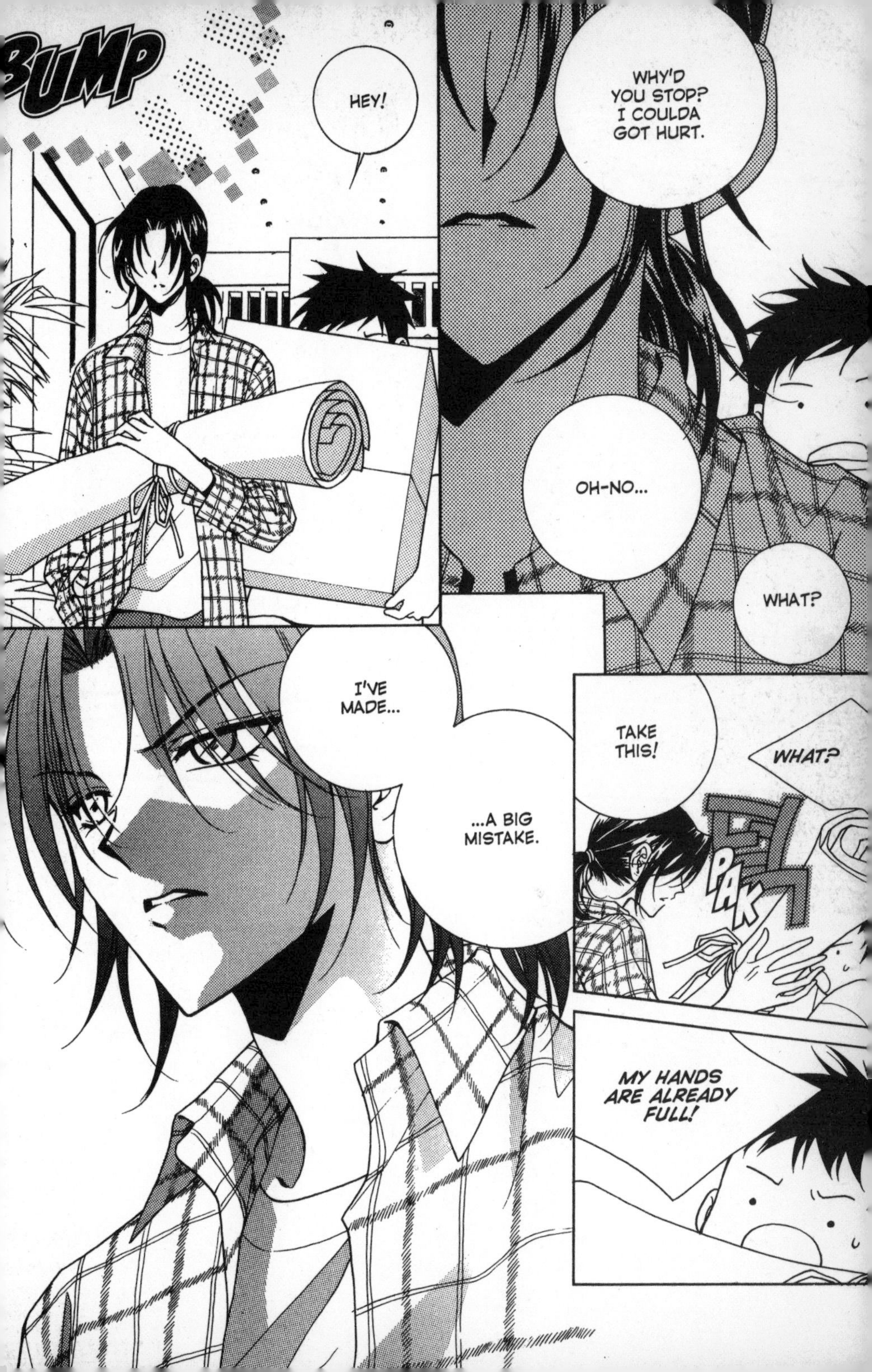
BUMP
HEY!
WHY'D YOU STOP? I COULDA GOT HURT.
OH-NO...
WHAT?
I'VE MADE...
...A BIG MISTAKE.
TAKE THIS!
WHAT?
PAK
MY HANDS ARE ALREADY FULL!

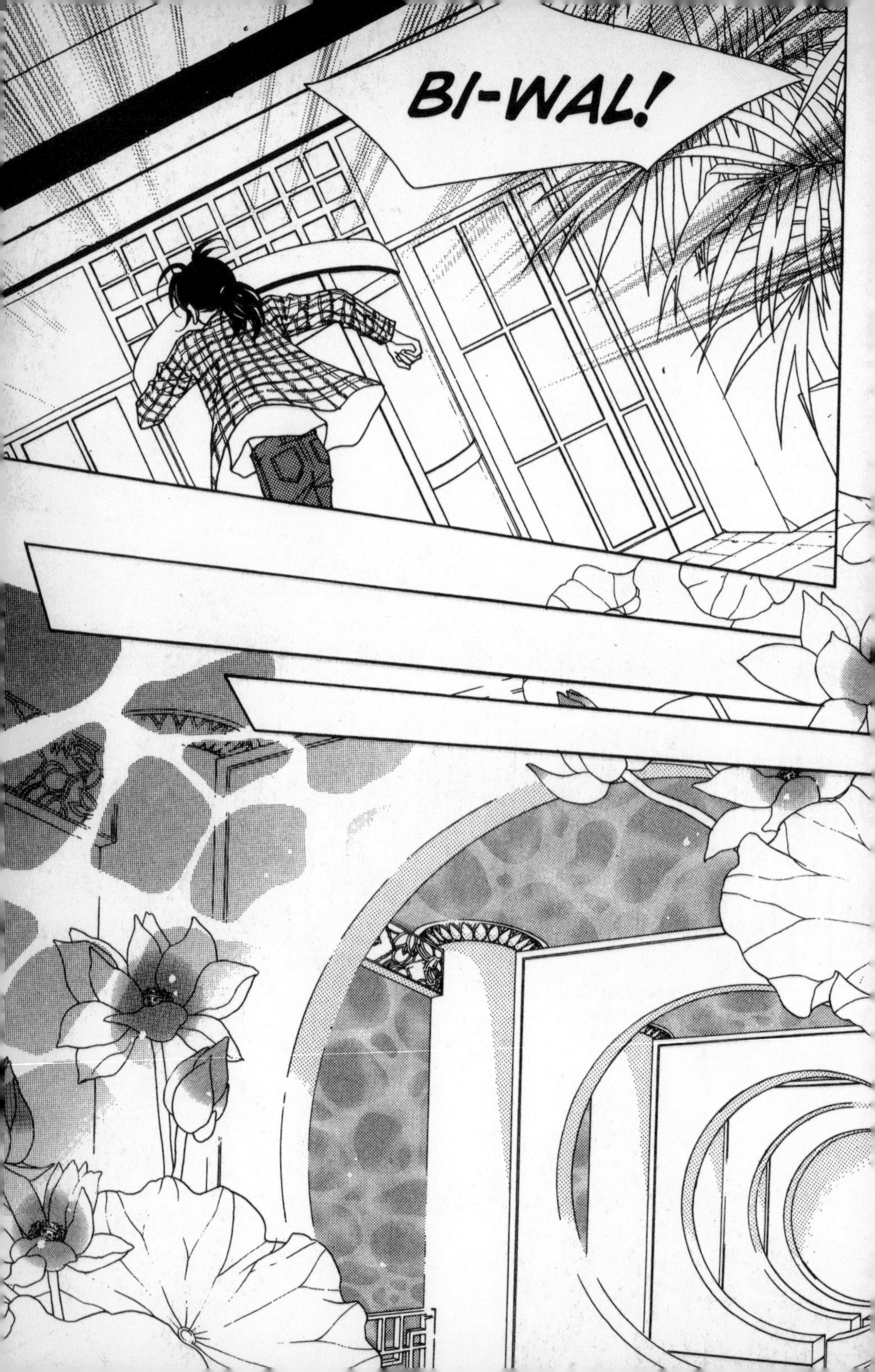
BI-WAL!

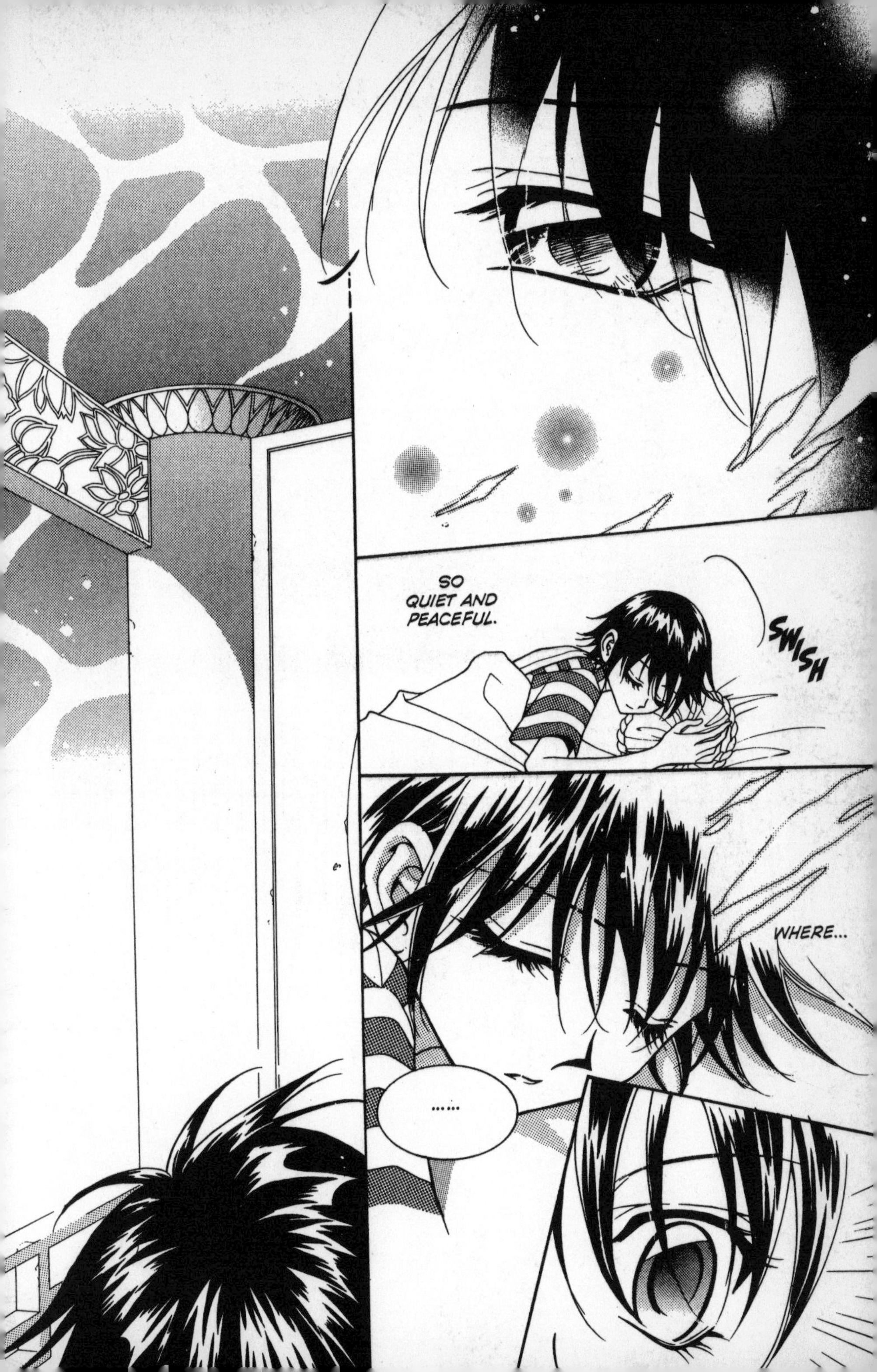
SO QUIET AND PEACEFUL.
SWISH
WHERE...
......

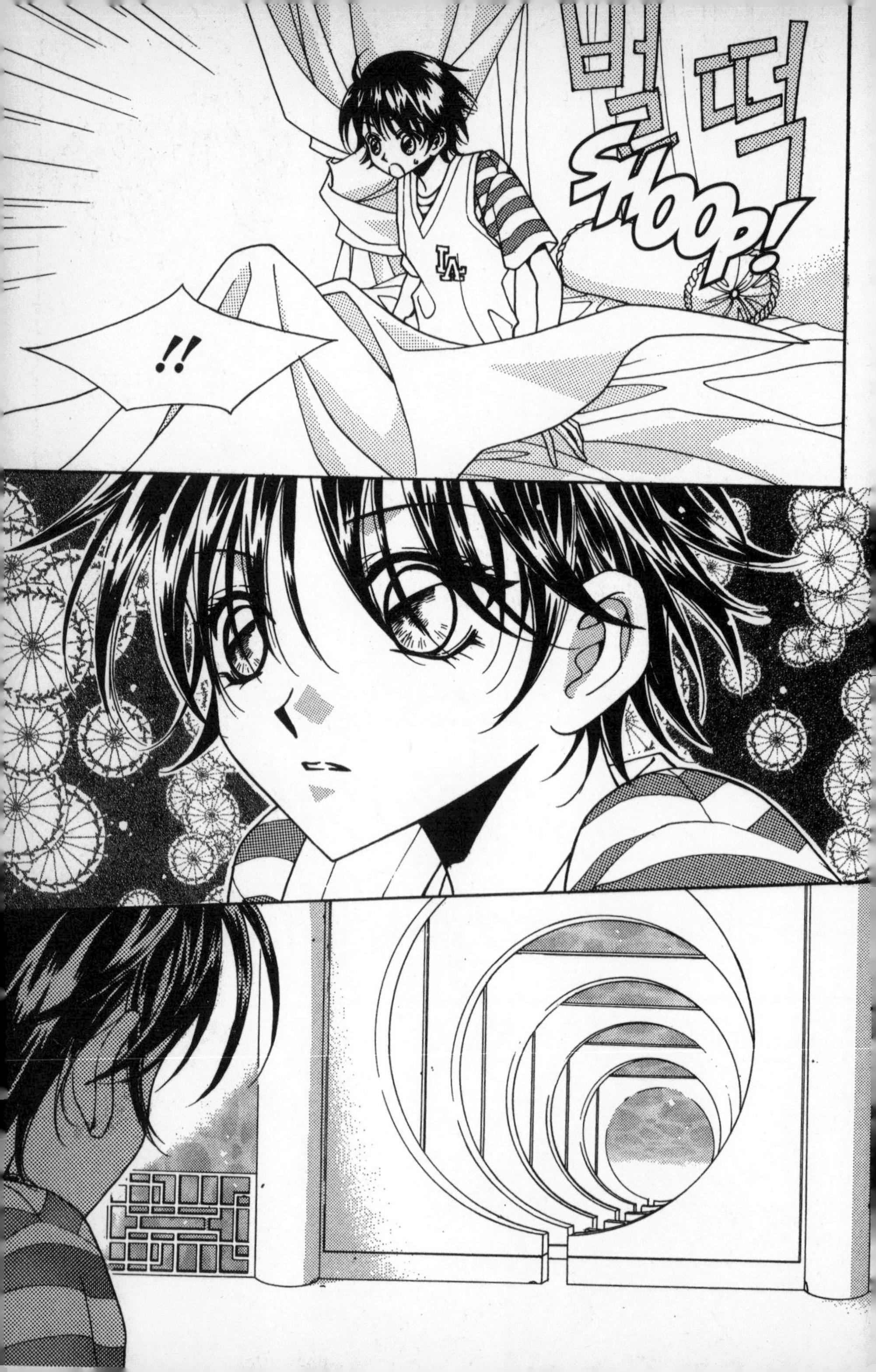
벌떡
SHOOP!
!!

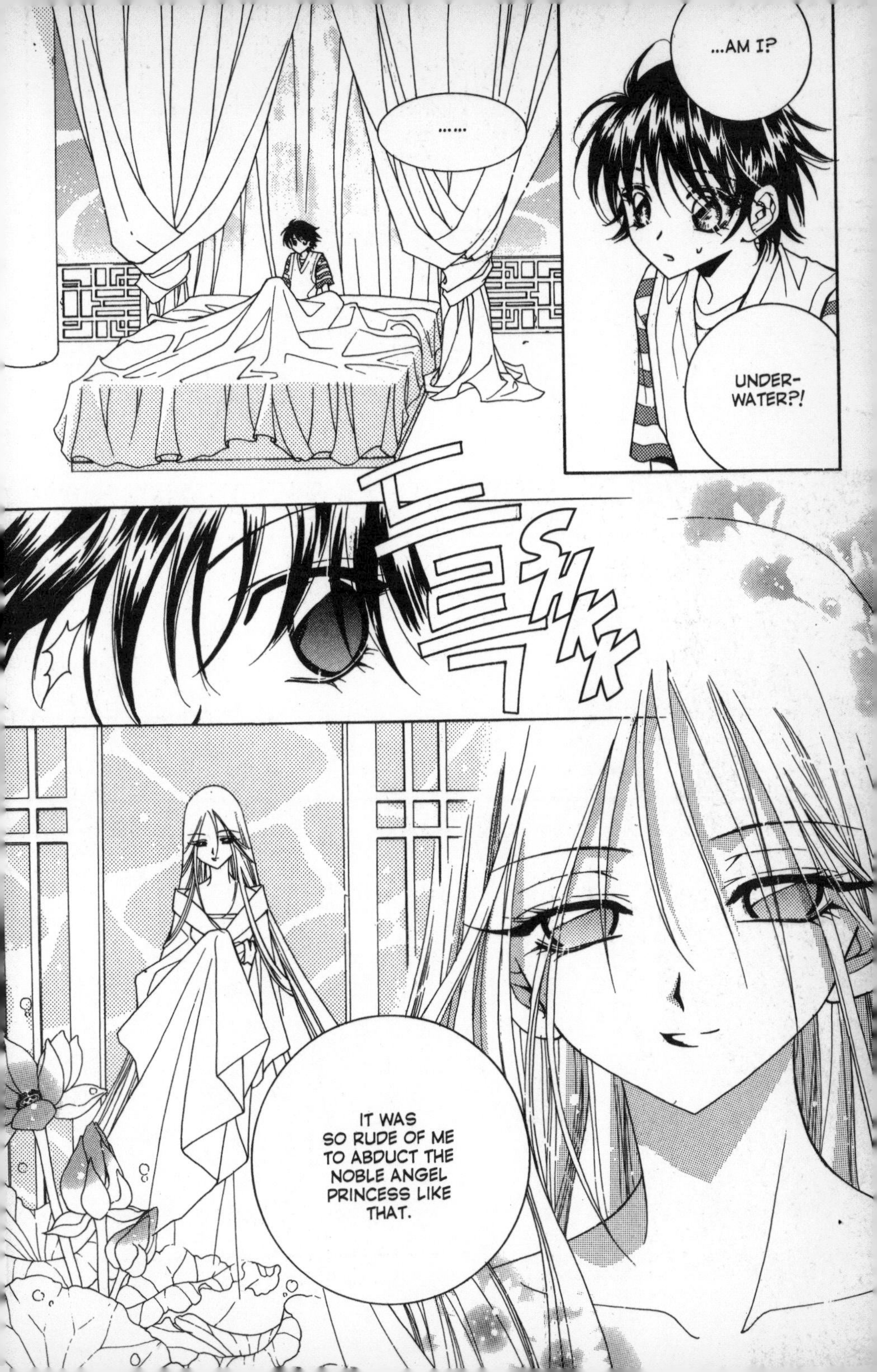

......
...AM I?
UNDER-WATER?!
SHKK
IT WAS SO RUDE OF ME TO ABDUCT THE NOBLE ANGEL PRINCESS LIKE THAT.

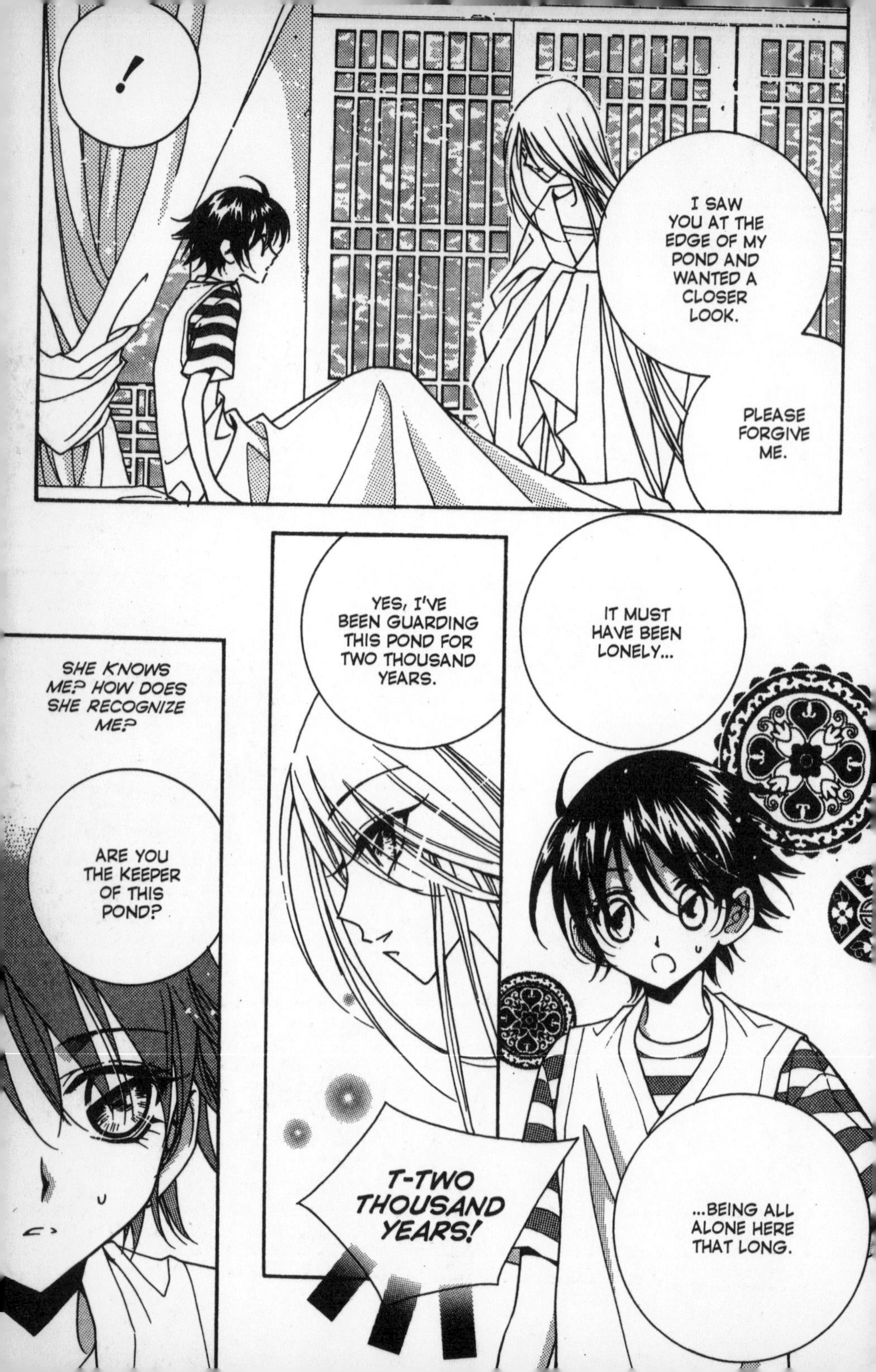

!
I SAW YOU AT THE EDGE OF MY POND AND WANTED A CLOSER LOOK.
PLEASE FORGIVE ME.
SHE KNOWS ME? HOW DOES SHE RECOGNIZE ME?
ARE YOU THE KEEPER OF THIS POND?
YES, I'VE BEEN GUARDING THIS POND FOR TWO THOUSAND YEARS.
T-TWO THOUSAND YEARS!
IT MUST HAVE BEEN LONELY...
...BEING ALL ALONE HERE THAT LONG.

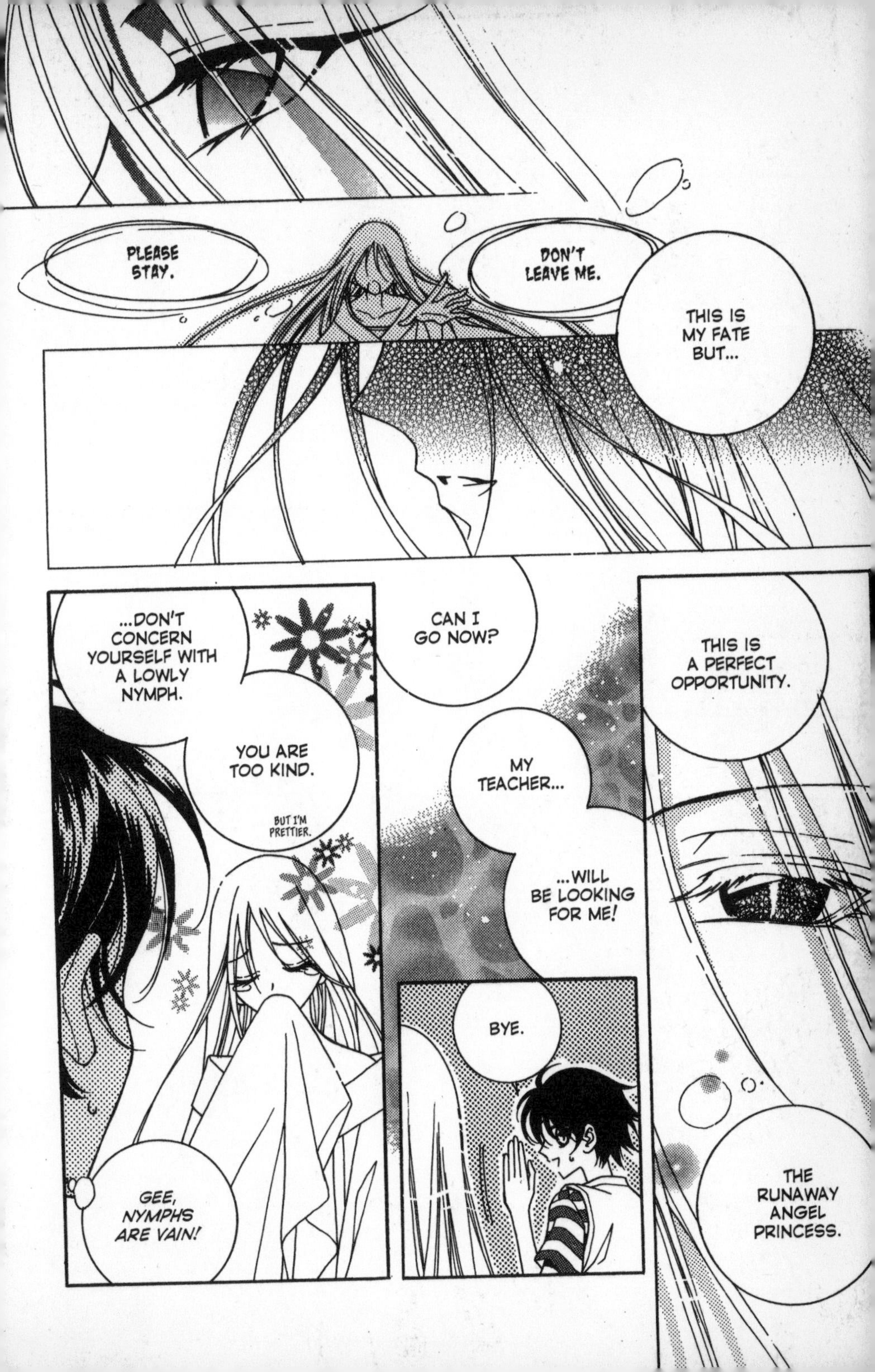
PLEASE STAY.
DON'T LEAVE ME.
THIS IS MY FATE BUT...
...DON'T CONCERN YOURSELF WITH A LOWLY NYMPH.
YOU ARE TOO KIND.
BUT I'M PRETTIER.
GEE, NYMPHS ARE VAIN!
CAN I GO NOW?
MY TEACHER...
...WILL BE LOOKING FOR ME!
BYE.
THIS IS A PERFECT OPPORTUNITY.
THE RUNAWAY ANGEL PRINCESS.

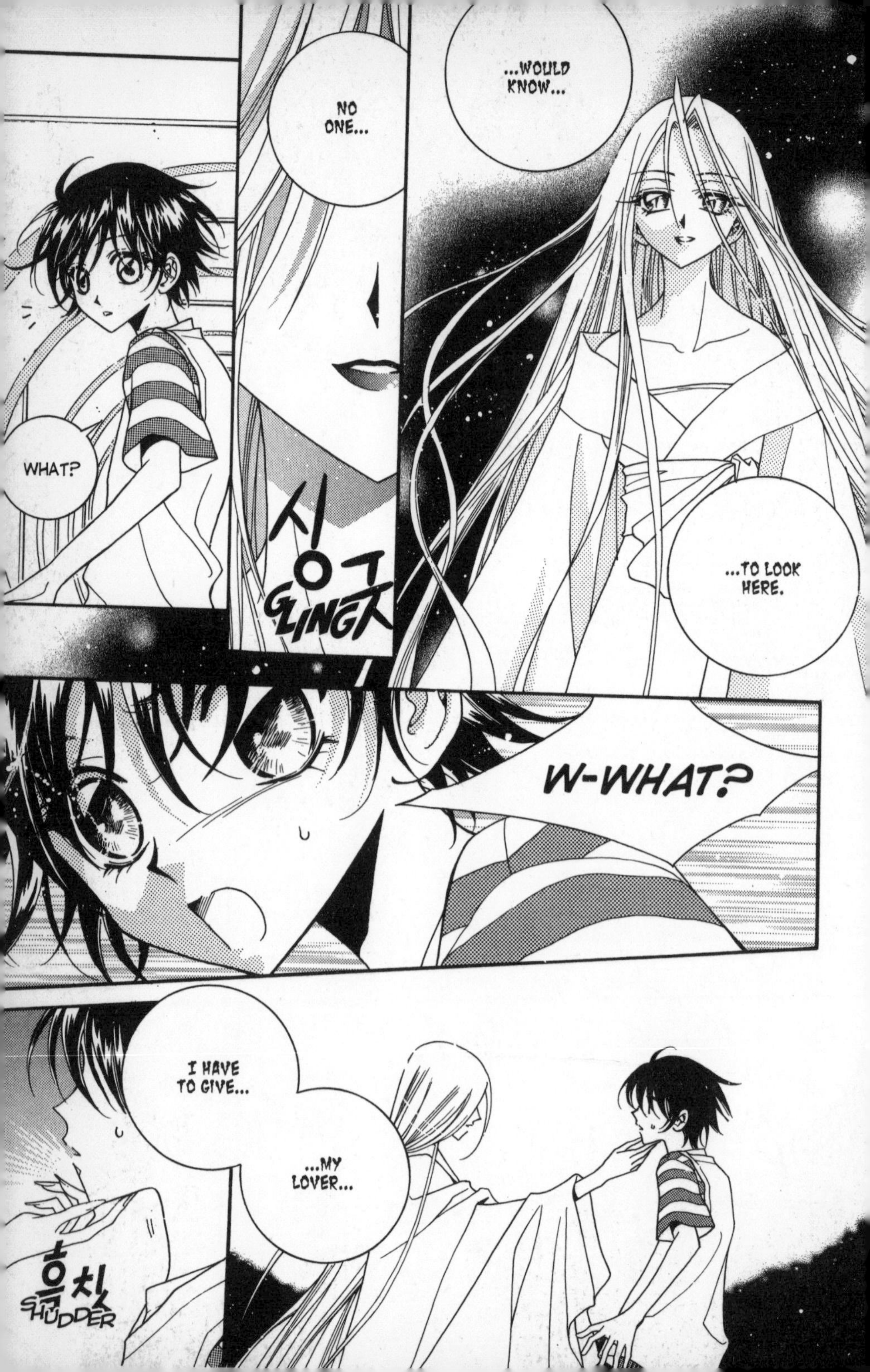
WHAT?
NO ONE...
싱긋
GLING
...WOULD KNOW...
...TO LOOK HERE.
W-WHAT?
I HAVE TO GIVE...
...MY LOVER...
흠칫
SHUDDER

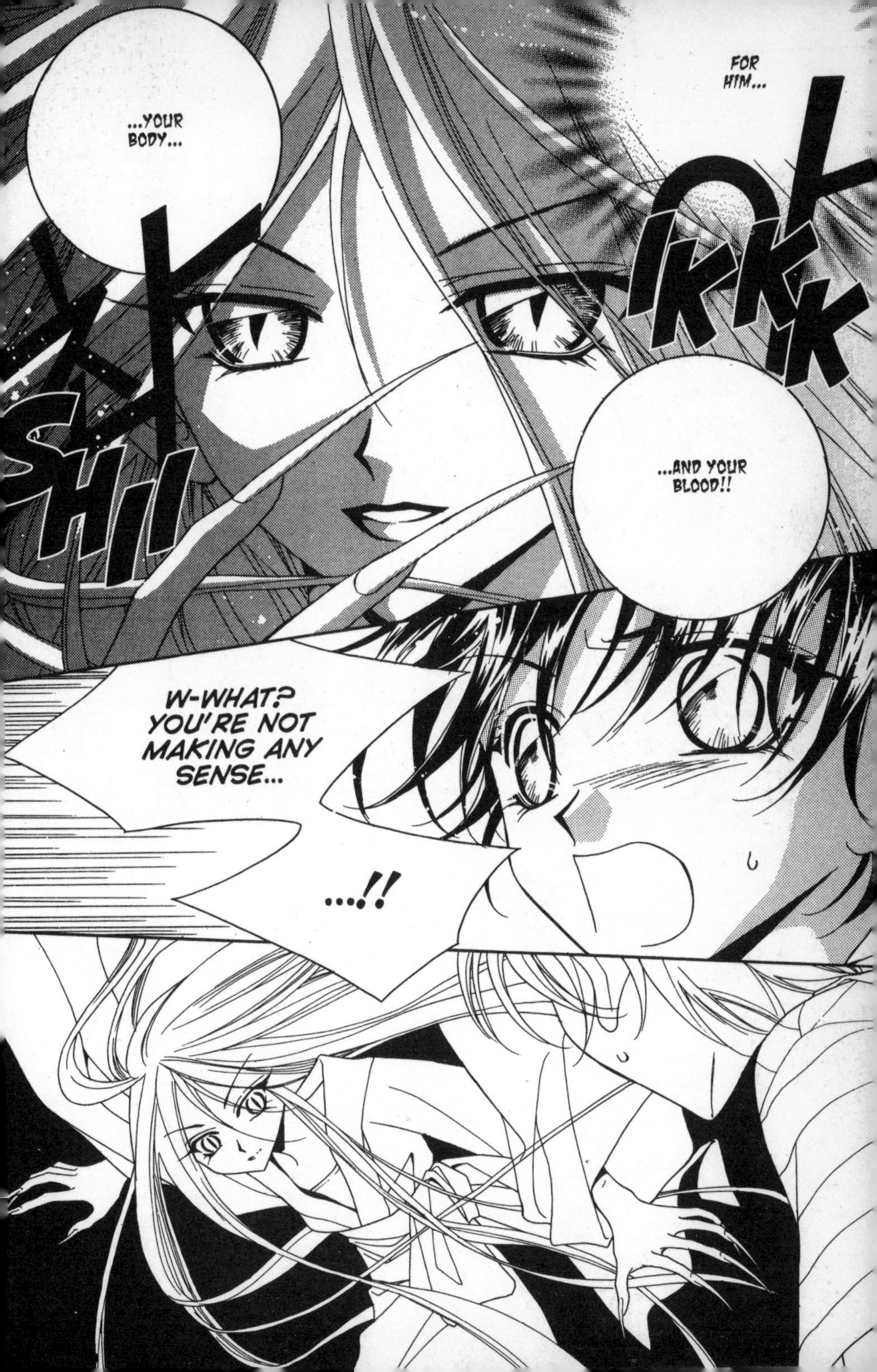
...YOUR BODY...
FOR HIM...
SHII
...AND YOUR BLOOD!!
W-WHAT? YOU'RE NOT MAKING ANY SENSE...
...!!

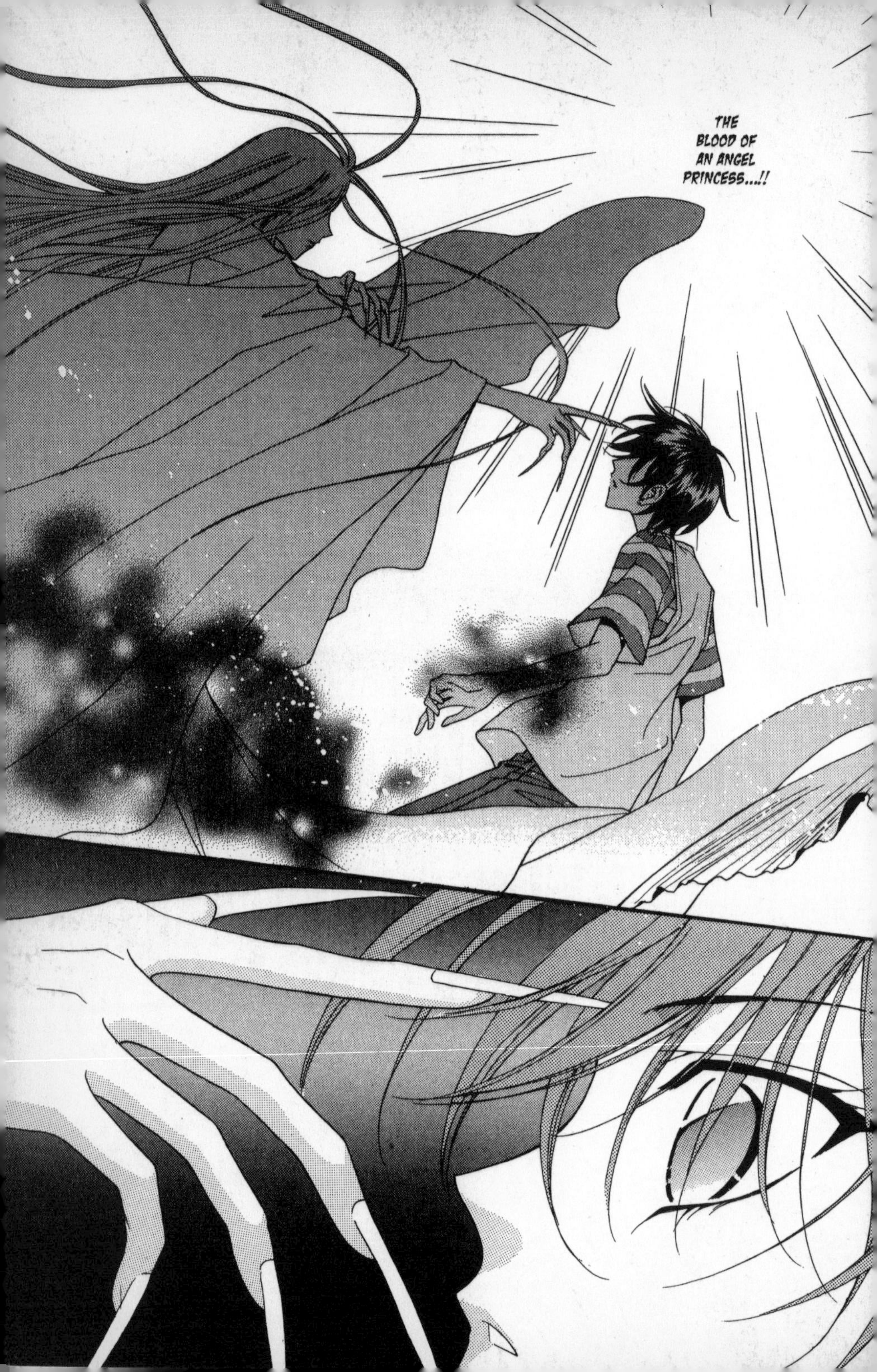
THE BLOOD OF AN ANGEL PRINCESS...!!

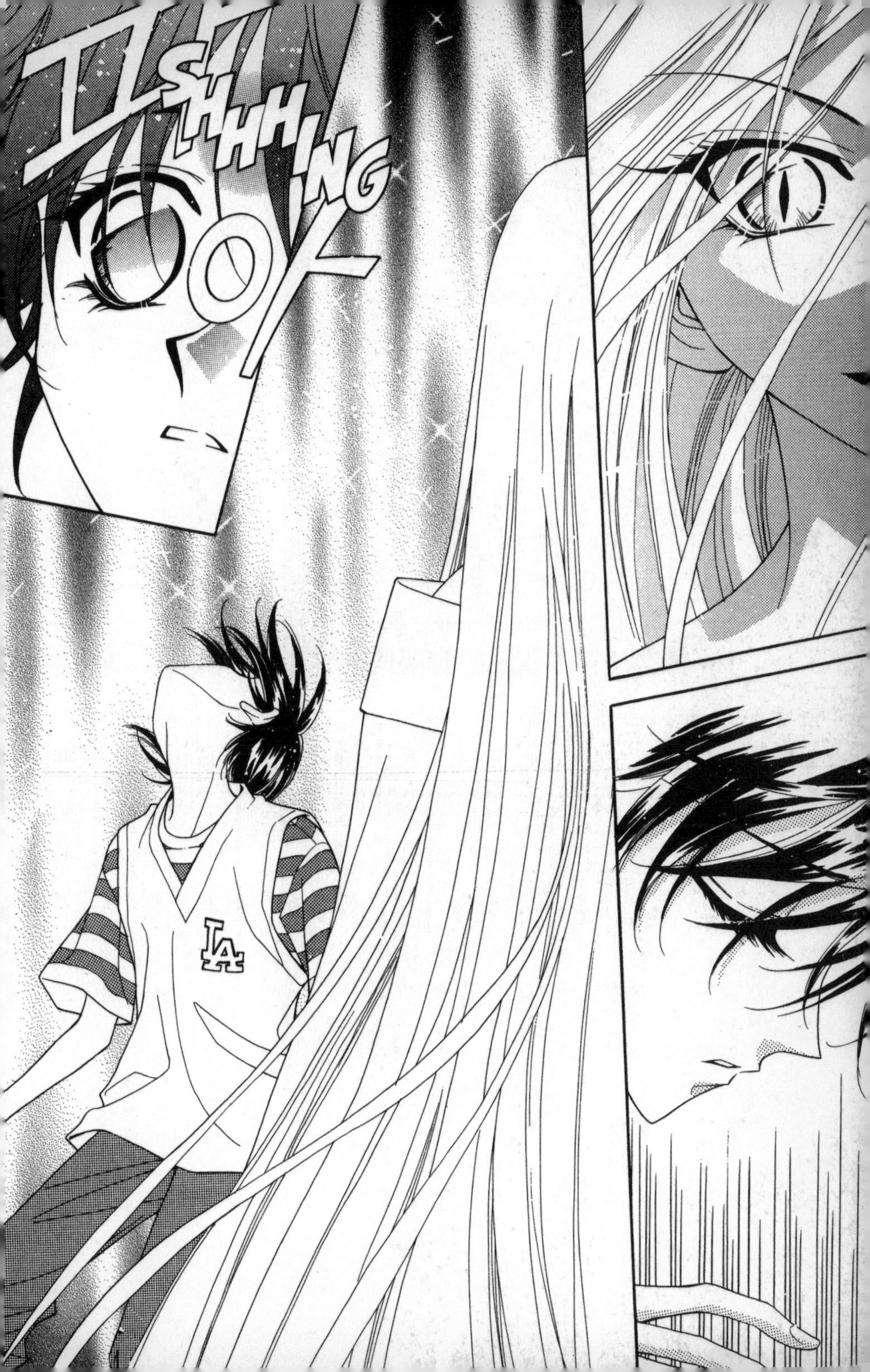
TSHHHING

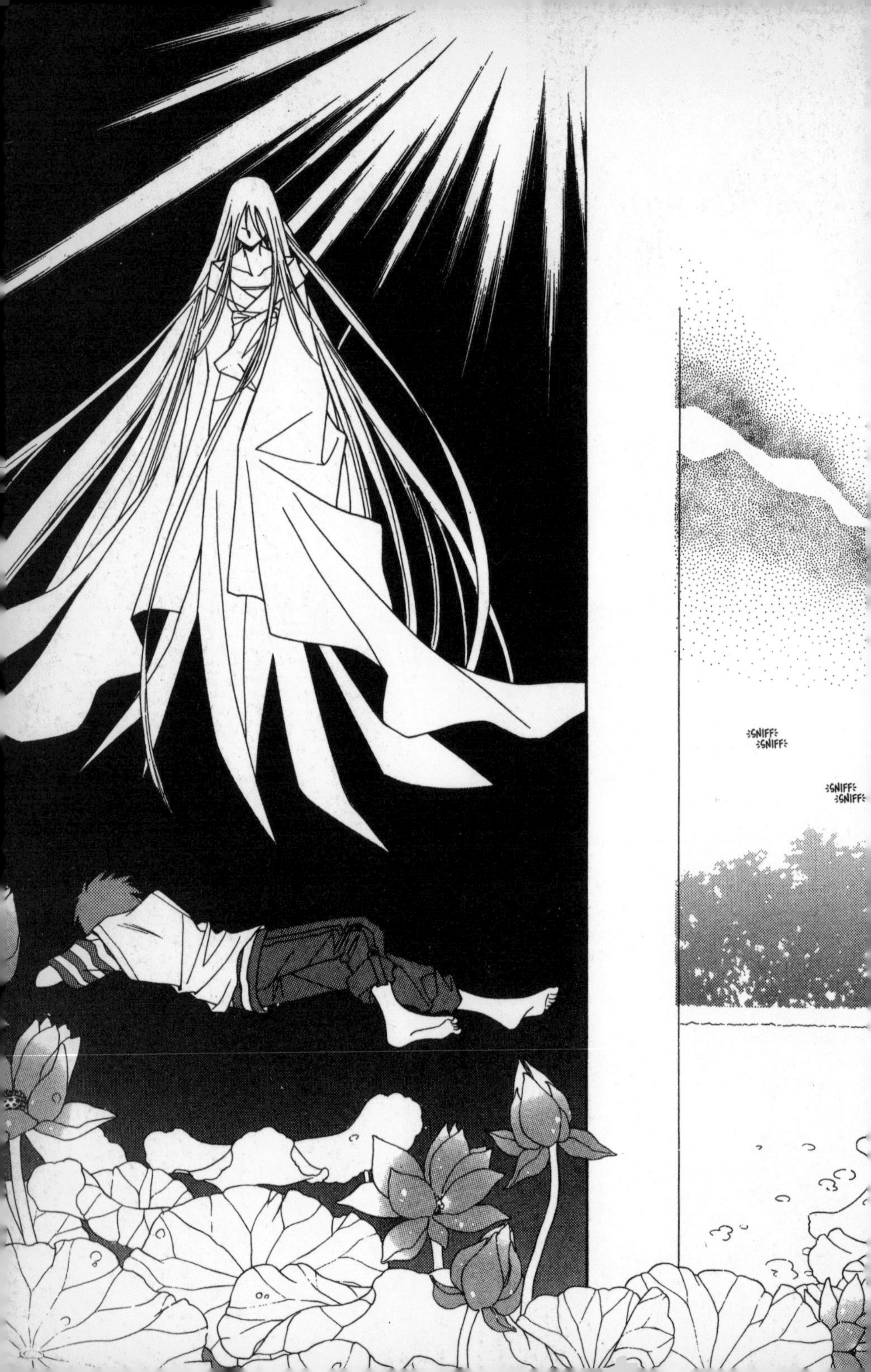
SNIFF
SNIFF
SNIFF
SNIFF

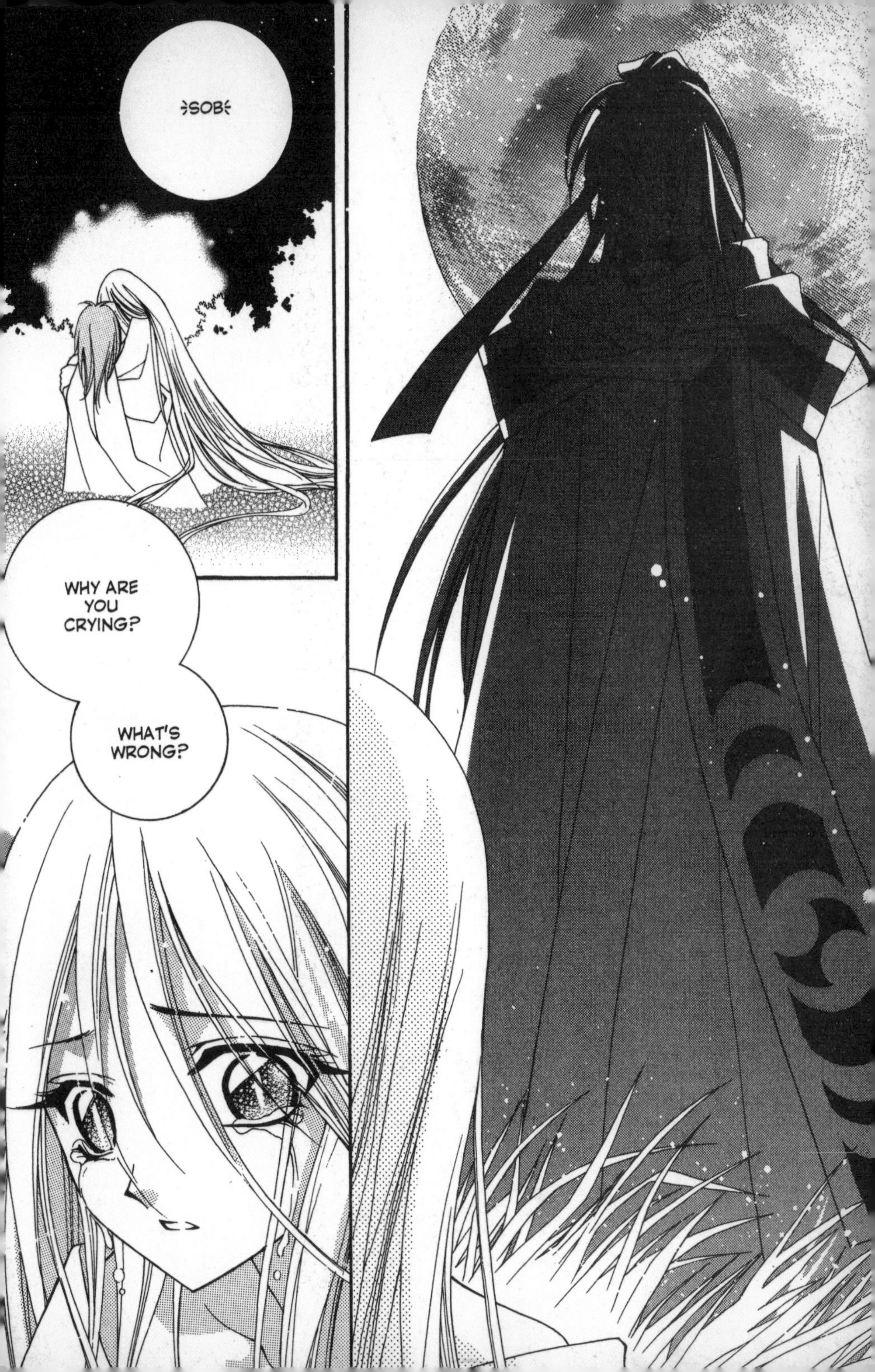
SOB
WHY ARE YOU CRYING?
WHAT'S WRONG?

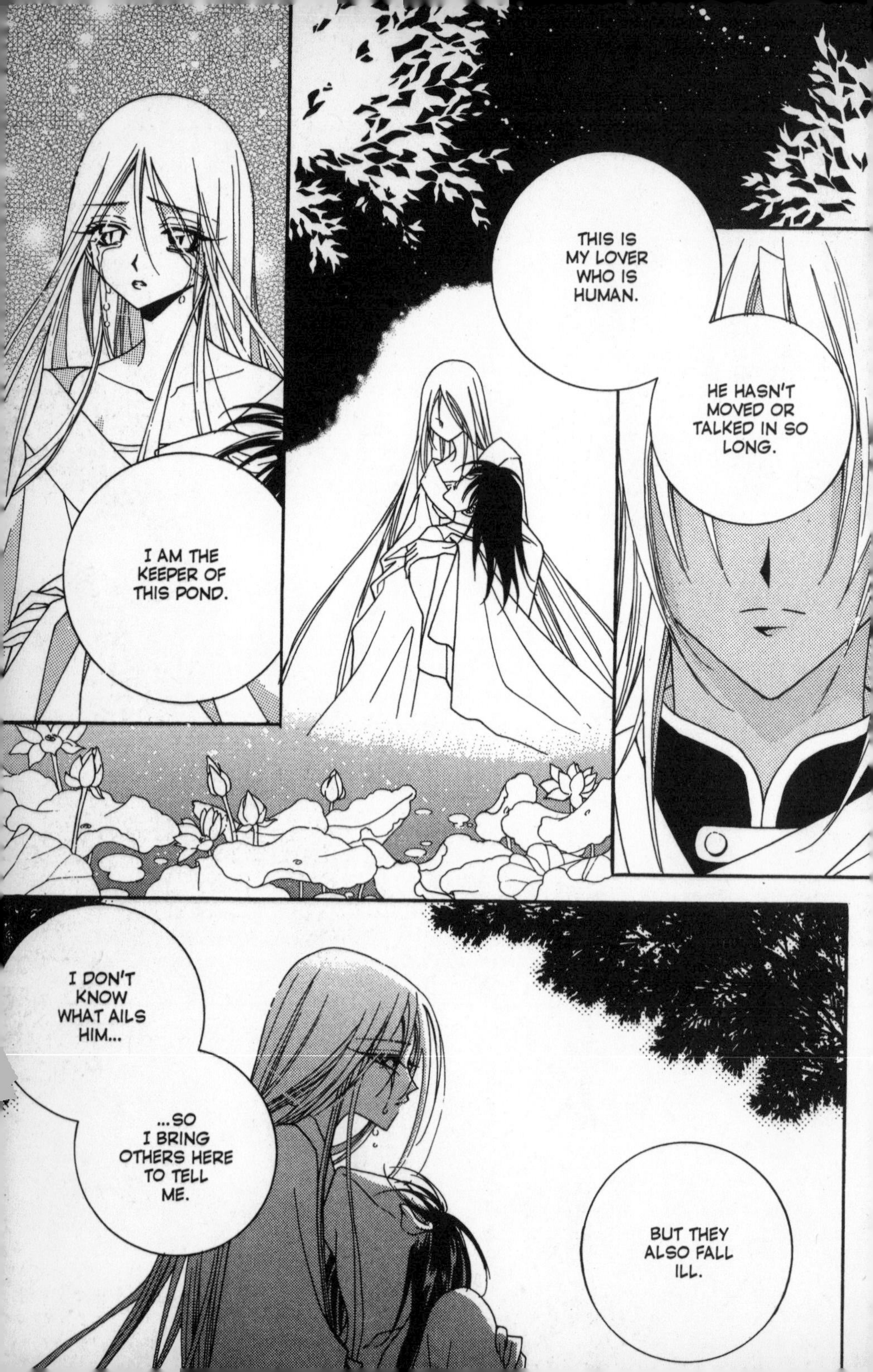
I AM THE KEEPER OF THIS POND.
THIS IS MY LOVER WHO IS HUMAN.
HE HASN'T MOVED OR TALKED IN SO LONG.
I DON'T KNOW WHAT AILS HIM...
...SO I BRING OTHERS HERE TO TELL ME.
BUT THEY ALSO FALL ILL.

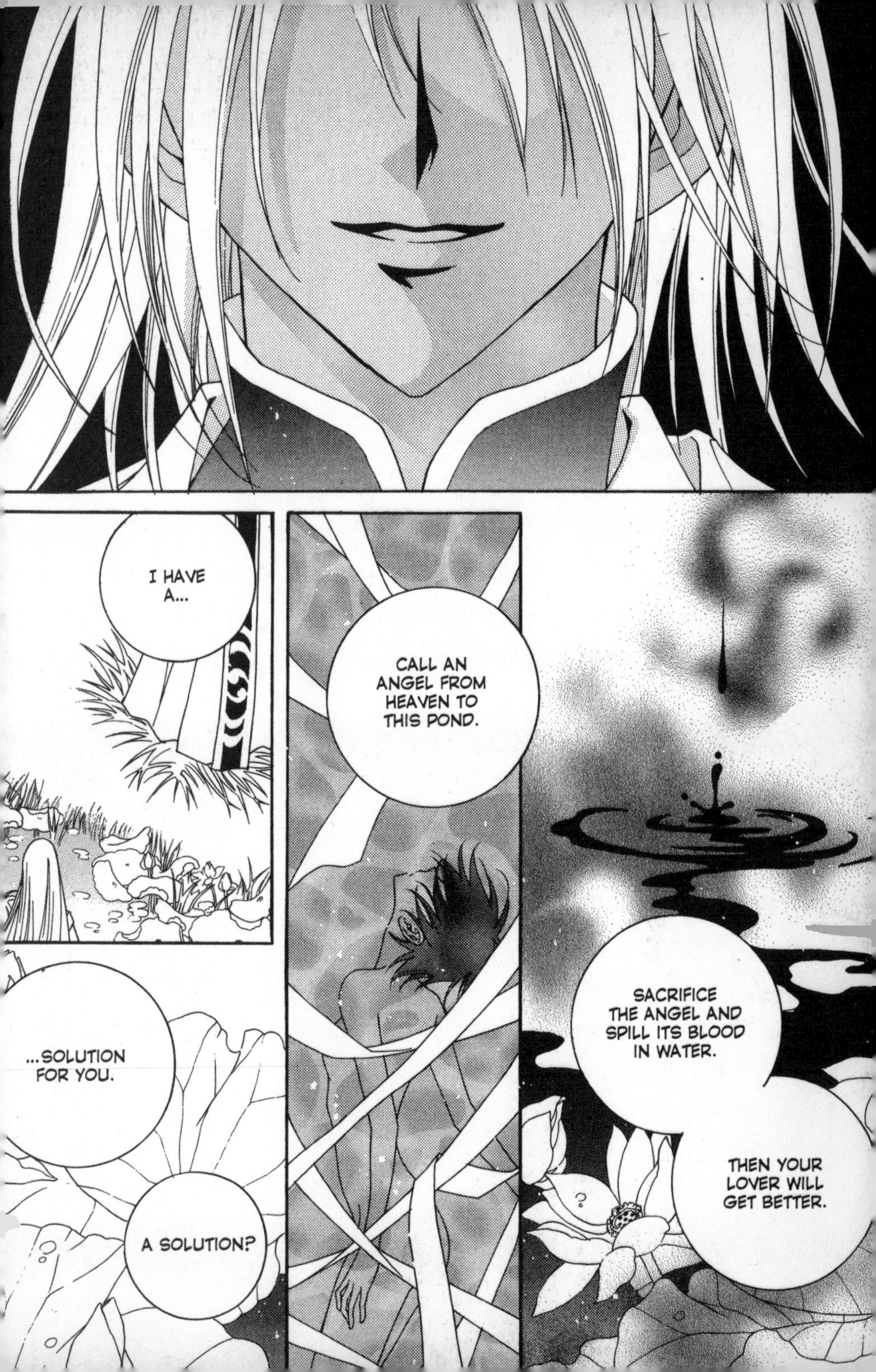
I HAVE A...
...SOLUTION FOR YOU.
A SOLUTION?
CALL AN ANGEL FROM HEAVEN TO THIS POND.
SACRIFICE THE ANGEL AND SPILL ITS BLOOD IN WATER.
THEN YOUR LOVER WILL GET BETTER.

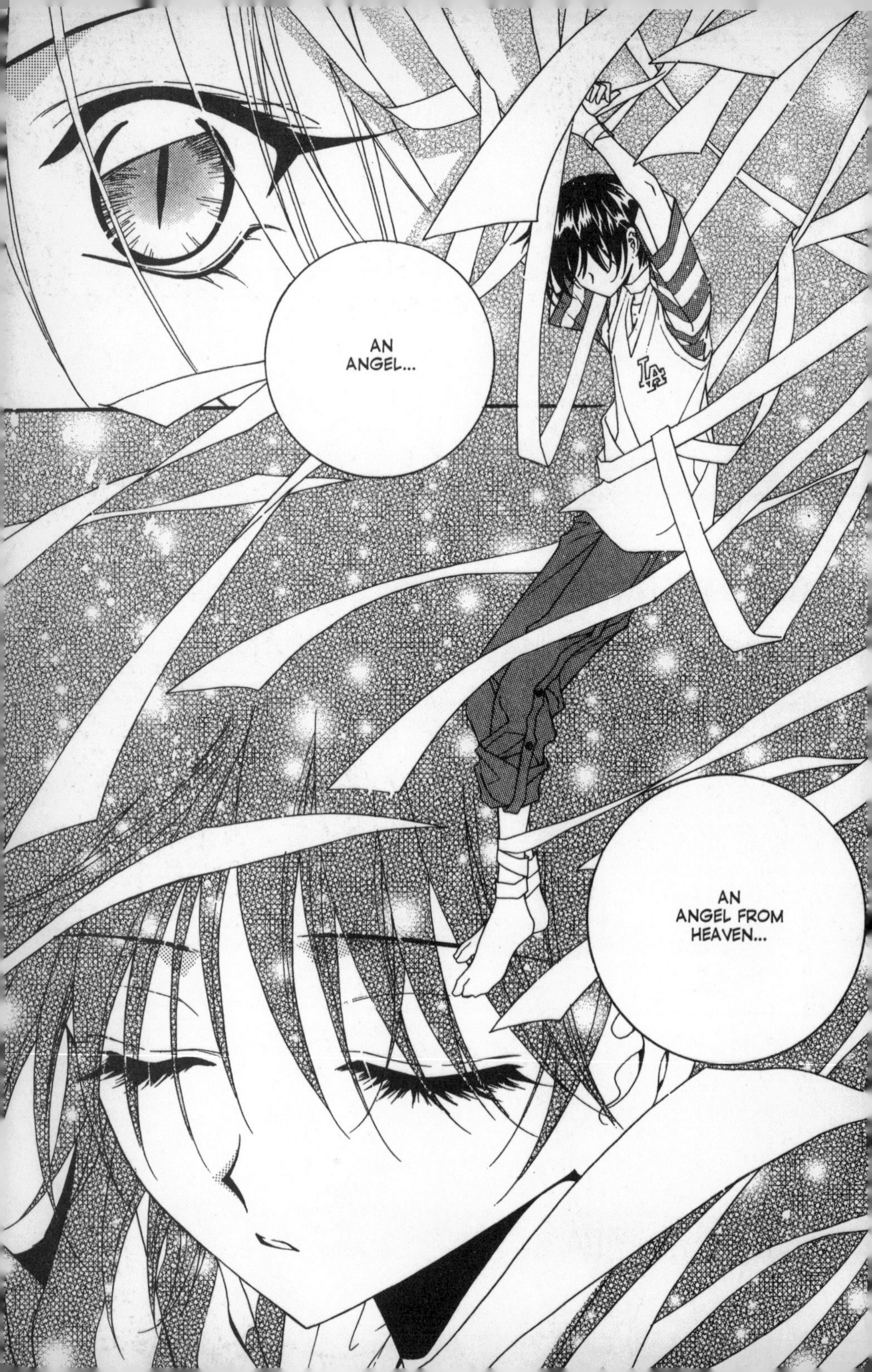
AN ANGEL...
AN ANGEL FROM HEAVEN...

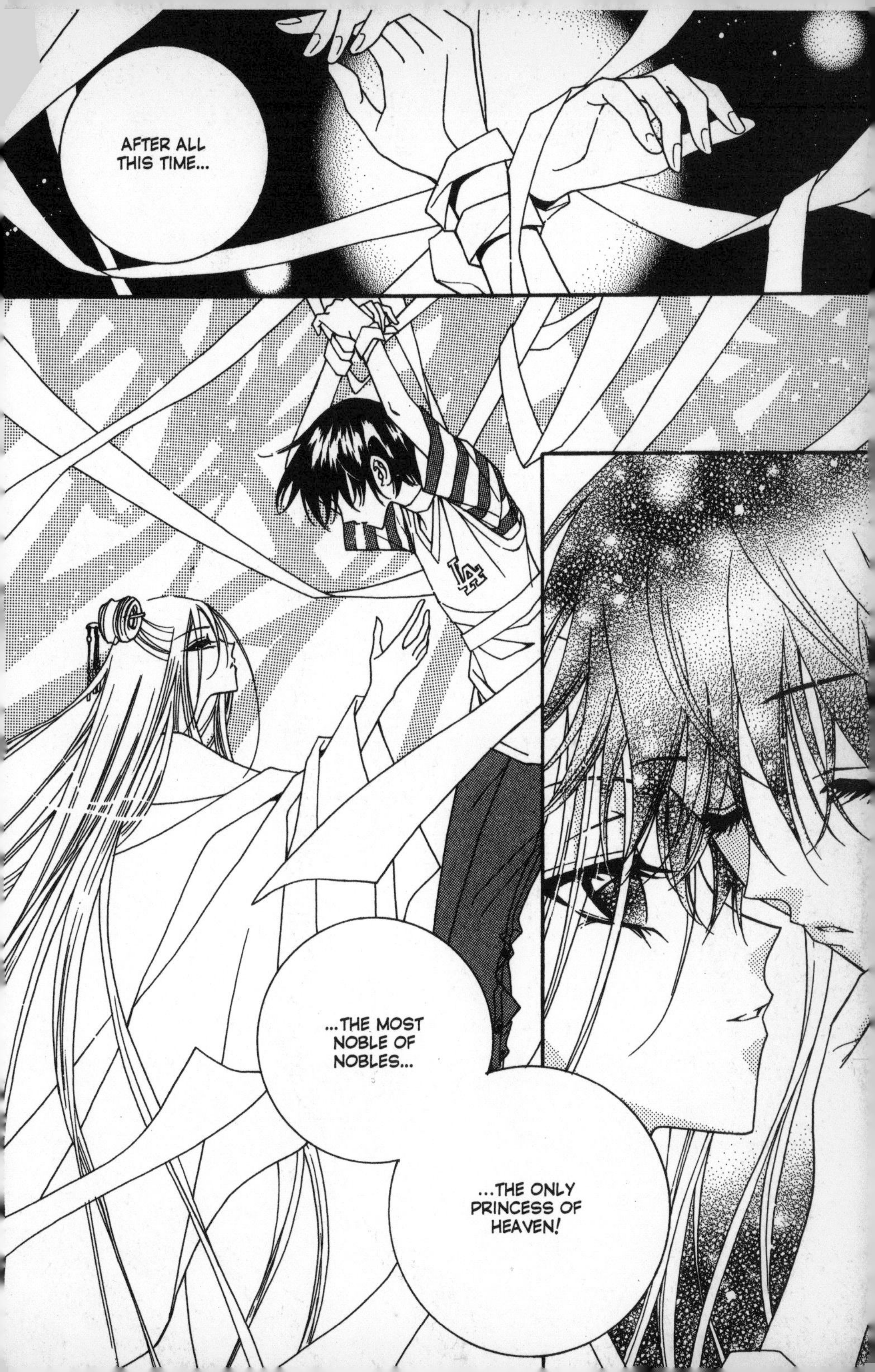
AFTER ALL THIS TIME...
...THE MOST NOBLE OF NOBLES...
...THE ONLY PRINCESS OF HEAVEN!

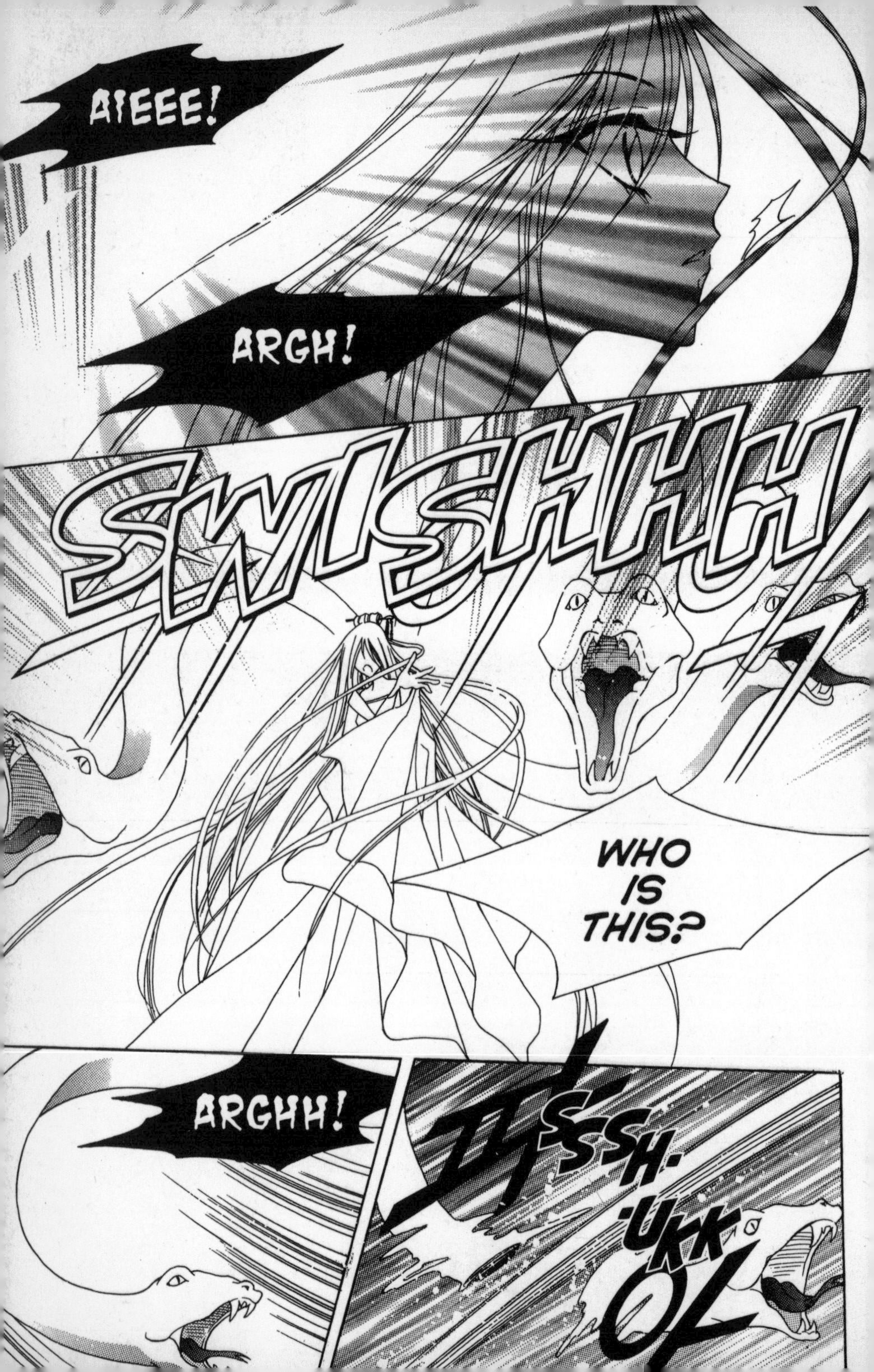
AIEEE!
ARGH!
SWISHHH
WHO IS THIS?
ARGHH!
SSH-
-UKK

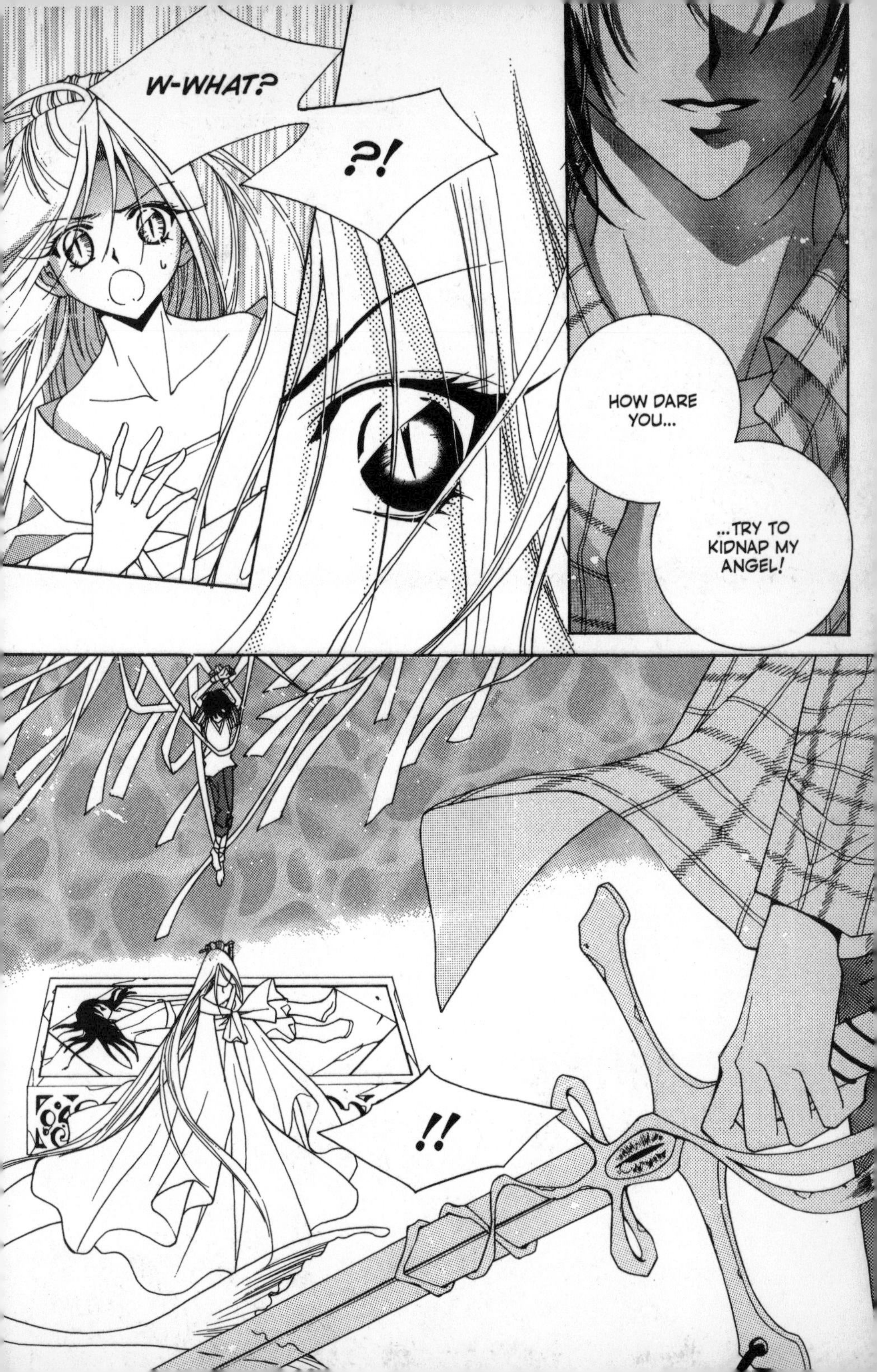
W-WHAT?
?!
HOW DARE YOU...
...TRY TO KIDNAP MY ANGEL!
!!

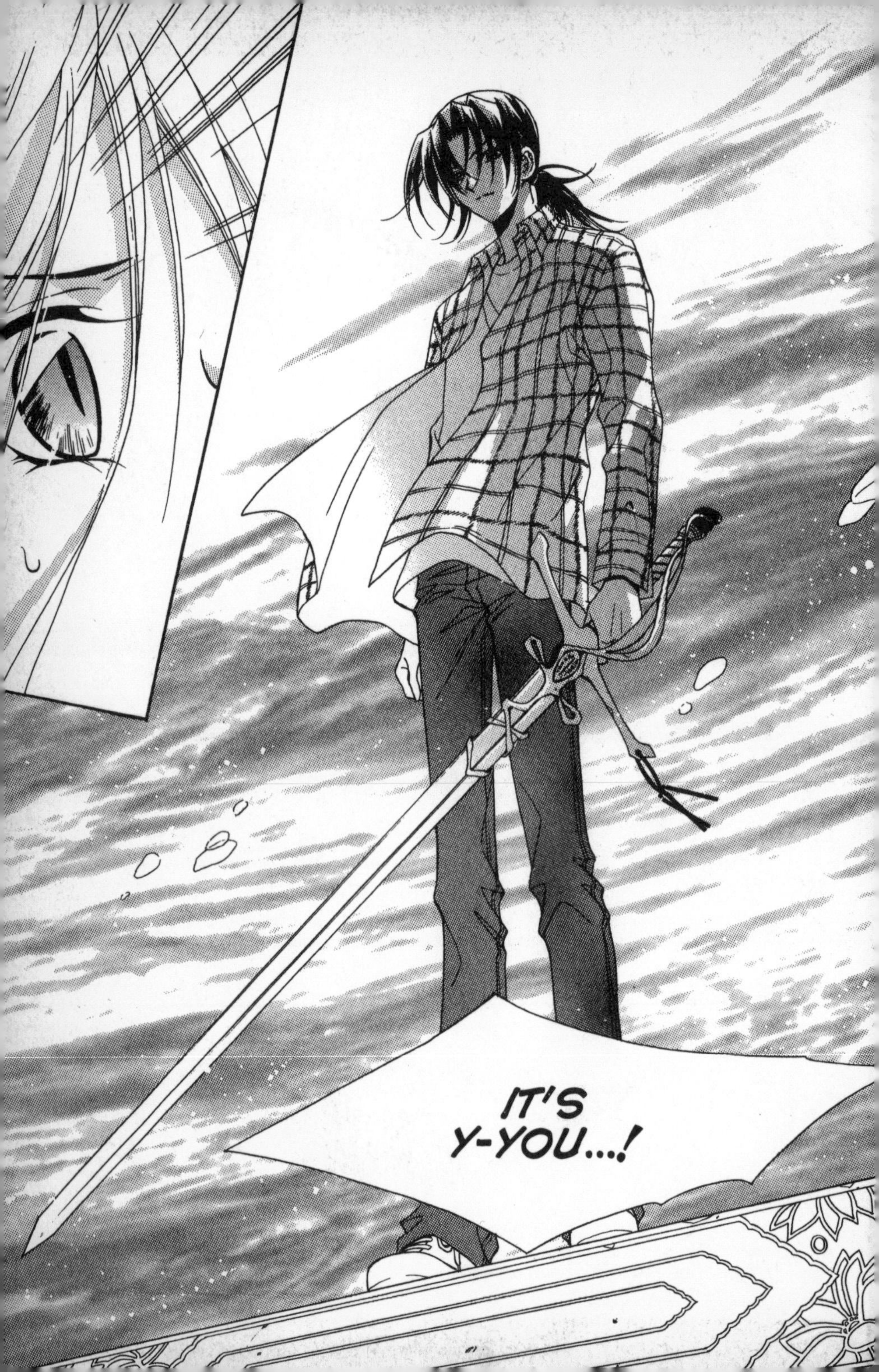
IT'S Y-YOU...!

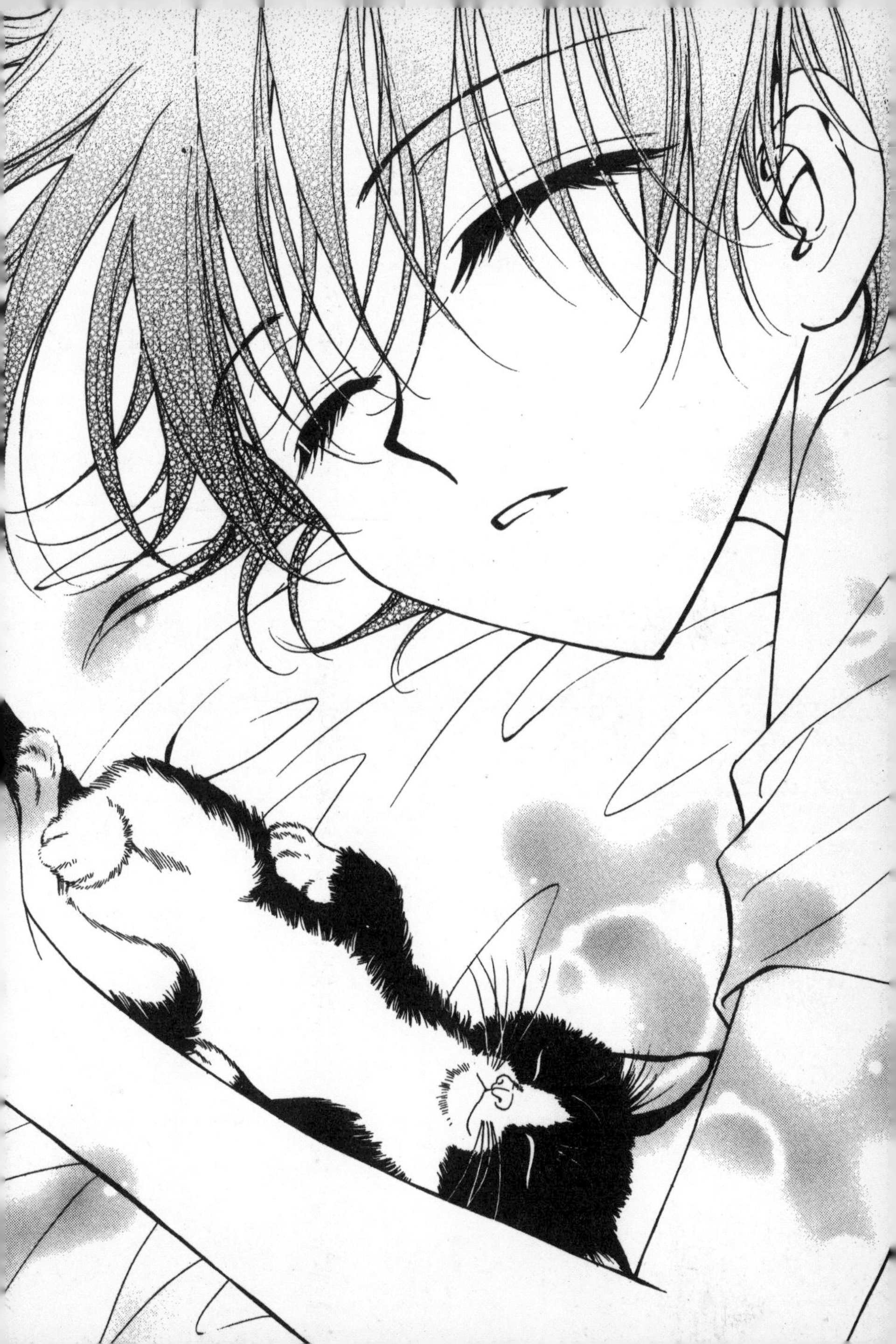

Danbi Original

Bring it on! vol.2

Story and art by HyeKyung Baek

Translation Sunny Kim
English Adaptation Jackie Oh
Touch-up and Lettering Terri Delgado · Marshall Dillon
Graphic Design EunKyung Kim
Editor JuYoun Lee

ICE Kunion

Project Manager Chan Park
Managing Editor Marshall Dillon
Marketing Manager Erik Ko
Editor in Chief Eddie Yu
Publishing Director JeongHyun Chin
Publisher and C.E.O. JaeKook Chun

Bring it on! © 2005 HyeKyung Baek
First published in Korea in 2003 by SIGONGSA Co., Ltd.
English text translation rights arranged by SIGONGSA Co., Ltd.
English text © 2005 ICE KUNION

All rights reserved. The events and characters presented in this book are entirely fictional. Any similarity to persons living or dead is purely coincidental. No portion of this book may be reproduced by any means (digital or print) without written permission from Sigongsa, except for the purposes of review.

Published by ICE Kunion.
SIGONGSA 2F Yeil Bldg. 1619-4, Seocho-dong, Seocho-gu, Seoul, 137-878, Korea

ISBN : 89-527-4471-3

First printing, January 2006
10 9 8 7 6 5 4 3 2 1
Printed in Canada

www.ICEkunion.com/www.koreanmanhwa.com